AF580673

Praise for

THE GOSPEL ACCORDING TO HOBBY LOBBY

"Michael Blanding's *The Gospel According to Hobby Lobby* documents how one family transformed a modest retail business into one of the most powerful—and insidious—forces in America. He shows how they used their growing wealth to advance a Christian nationalist agenda. A tale of extremism, carelessness, greed, and hypocrisy, Blanding's gripping narrative exposes the damage that has been wrought by a single family devoted to both God and profit."

—**Joshua Hammer**, *New York Times* bestselling author of *The Bad-Ass Librarians of Timbuktu*

"This page-turner sheds light on one family's efforts to embed Christian nationalism into the heart of our nation. Their mission is far-flung in its reach—Michael Blanding takes us from windswept Oklahoman prairies to plundered museums in Iraq to a library tucked away in an Egyptian monastery. Absorbing and fearless, *The Gospel According to Hobby Lobby* exposes a movement that is reshaping the American political landscape."

—**Kirk Wallace Johnson**, author of *The Feather Thief*

"Michael Blanding's *The Gospel According to Hobby Lobby* reads like a thriller about greed, grift, and God—yet every word is true. Blanding pairs dogged investigative reporting with a storyteller's eye for detail, to construct the riveting account of a powerful family that has remade our nation. No book has taught me more about who America is today and the forces that delivered us here."

—**Alex Marzano-Lesnevich**, author of *The Fact of a Body*

"*The Gospel According to Hobby Lobby* is a devastating exposé of the Green family, funders of Christian nationalism in the United States. This book will lift the veil from the eyes of those who have bought into the billionaire family's broken ideology."

—**Andrew L. Seidel**, author of *The Founding Myth*

"Christian nationalism is not a grassroots movement; it's a top-down movement led by billionaires and the religious activists who enjoy their patronage. As Michael Blanding shows us, the Green family of Hobby Lobby has been instrumental in spreading more than kitschy home decor—they have carried out an integrated campaign to make America Christian again. For Americans passionate about true religious liberty—including liberty from religion—this is a must-read."

—**Samuel L. Perry**, coauthor of *The Flag and the Cross*

THE GOSPEL ACCORDING TO HOBBY LOBBY

INSIDE A BILLIONAIRE FAMILY'S QUEST TO CRAFT A CHRISTIAN NATION

MICHAEL BLANDING

New York

Copyright © 2026 by Michael Blanding

Cover image © Logan Bush / Shutterstock.com

Cover copyright © 2026 by Hachette Book Group, Inc.

All rights reserved. No part of this publication may be reproduced, stored in a retrieval system, or transmitted, in any form or by any means, without the prior written permission of the publisher, including any use or reproduction for the purpose of training artificial intelligence technologies. The publisher expressly reserves this work from the text and data mining exception in accordance with Article 4(3) DSM Directive 2019/790 and any other equivalent legislation in force from time to time or elsewhere.

If you would like permission to use material from the book (other than for review purposes), please contact permissions@hbgusa.com.

PublicAffairs
Hachette Book Group
1290 Avenue of the Americas, New York, NY 10104
www.publicaffairsbooks.com

Printed in the United States of America

First Edition: July 2026

Published by PublicAffairs, an imprint of Hachette Book Group, Inc. The PublicAffairs name and logo is a registered trademark of the Hachette Book Group.

The Hachette Speakers Bureau provides a wide range of authors for speaking events. To find out more, go to hachettespeakersbureau.com or email HachetteSpeakers@hbgusa.com.

Contact your local bookseller or special.markets@hbgusa.com regarding special discounts for bulk purchases.

The publisher is not responsible for websites (or their content) that are not owned by the publisher.

Print book interior design by Sheryl Kober.

Library of Congress Control Number: 2025048141

ISBNs: 9781541703940 (hardcover), 9781541703964 (ebook)

LSC-C

Printing 1, 2026

For Mel

CONTENTS

AUTHOR'S NOTE

I met Mart Green—the oldest child of the Green family—once by accident. I was conducting research in the archives at Oral Roberts University in Tulsa, and he came in for a tour of the facility in his capacity as former chair of the university board of trustees. After introducing myself and telling him I was writing a book about his family, I asked if he'd received any of the emails I'd sent to family members requesting an interview. He said yes, and I asked if they were willing to participate in the book. He looked at me sadly and shook his head, saying with his slow Oklahoma drawl, "No, I don't think so."

A few months later, my publisher received a letter from a company lawyer who requested that all questions be sent through him in writing. I sent several dozen questions, but I never received a response. Thankfully, however, the Green family have been prolific in telling their own story through their multiple books and interviews in newspapers, videos, and podcasts—as well as, of course, the creation of their own Bible museum and multimedia campaigns to promote their faith—so I've been able to draw upon a rich number of sources in telling this story.

I've tried to be faithful to the family's point of view and fairly represent their beliefs in order to better understand and explain the impact this family of religious businesspeople has had on the politics and culture of our nation. Wherever possible, I've used their own words in expressing those beliefs, signifying a direct quote from one of their books or interviews by putting words in quotation marks or italics. In other cases, I've paraphrased their words or created composites of incidents from multiple accounts. In this way, I hope, I've remained faithful to the source material while also constructing a compelling narrative of the family members' lives and beliefs.

Prologue

J. P. Labbat pulled on his raid jacket and zipped up the front. He always felt a little nervous before an action. As a special agent with Homeland Security Investigations (HSI), Labbat had been on many raids during his twenty-five-year career, busting drug dealers and human traffickers and seizing narcotics and laundered cash.[1] Today's assignment would be different. He was planning to seize just one small object, a five-by-six-inch tablet made of baked clay, finely covered with ancient writing. On its face were two columns of cuneiform text, written with a wedge-shaped stylus and hardened in the Mesopotamian sun more than 3,500 years ago.[2]

More recently, the tablet had made its way from Iraq to London to California and finally to Washington, DC, where it now sat in a case inside the Museum of the Bible. Scholars had identified its text as a portion of *The Epic of Gilgamesh*, a narrative poem among the world's oldest works of literature, whose discovery more than a century ago changed our understanding of the Bible. The epic tells the story of a demigod king who challenges monsters, gods, and even death itself. In the passage on this tablet, Gilgamesh describes to his mother several dreams foretelling the arrival of Enkidu, a hero who will become his bosom companion. Called the Gilgamesh Dream Tablet, this item was purchased in 2014 for almost $1.7 million—making it the most expensive single object Labbat would ever seize.[3]

Now, on September 24, 2019, he climbed into a black SUV and rode with another agent to the museum, passing the white dome of the US Capitol against a blue, cloudless sky. The car pulled up outside the building's entrance, flanked by two enormous brass gates depicting the opening pages of the Gutenberg Bible. Labbat flashed his badge to the security guard, along with a federal warrant of seizure, and led fellow agents into the entry hall.[4]

Curious patrons glanced at the agents' jackets and handguns as the museum's director, Jeff Kloha, came bustling toward them. When the agents told him they'd come for the tablet, Kloha looked apprehensively at the visitors milling about the hall before leading them into a back hallway, where he examined the warrant. He was annoyed that the agents hadn't told him they were coming—or, better yet, come after hours. But he didn't protest as he led them up to the exhibit on the fourth floor. A staff member opened a display case, and Kloha lifted the tablet out and placed it gingerly in a padded case. Labbat took it and followed Kloha down a back staircase and out an inconspicuous side door onto the street.[5]

A few blocks away at the Capitol that afternoon, Speaker of the House of Representatives Nancy Pelosi would formally announce the opening of an impeachment inquiry into President Donald Trump. By then, Labbat would be contacting the owners of the tablet he'd seized: the Green family, owners of Hobby Lobby Stores.

IT'S NO ACCIDENT that Hobby Lobby, a chain of more than one thousand big-box arts and crafts stores, also possessed a valuable ancient artifact from the Holy Land. At one point, it held more than forty thousand artifacts, including cuneiform tablets, papyrus fragments, Torah scrolls, and illuminated Bibles. The owners of the company, led by chairman and CEO David Green and his son, president Steve Green, spent years tracking down these items and buying them up to stock their museum, which opened in Washington in 2017, regaling visitors with stories of the Bible's history and impact.

The exhibits on the fourth floor explain, in part, why the Green family was so determined to own these artifacts. In telling the history of the Bible from scraps of papyrus to leather-bound tomes, they stress the accuracy of the text's transmission from the earliest centuries to the modern day. That reliability is important to the Greens, who like many evangelical Christians see the Bible as divinely inspired and without error—a historically true account of the ancient world and the literal "Word of God."

The artifacts on display "stack on top of each other, like the shelves of the library of history," Steve Green has written, "offering us a mass compendium from which to learn. Each item adds a brick in the wall of evidence for the Bible."[6] He and his family believe that writers who composed the books of the Bible over the centuries wrote exactly what God intended and that it is the ultimate authority on how to live life and organize society.

The implications of that divinely inspired gift are displayed in another exhibit showing the impact of the Bible on America and the world, starting with the earliest settlers arriving in Massachusetts Bay with scripture on their minds. Everything good in American and world history—constitutional government, abolitionism, human rights, and scientific inquiry—is a result of the Bible's teachings, the exhibit argues. Anything bad, such as slavery, is merely a human misreading of the book.

Since taking up this mission to demonstrate how the Bible remained accurate and consistent from ancient times—a fact crucial to its authority—the Greens felt themselves guided by God as they built up the largest private collection of biblical antiquities in the world, spending hundreds of millions of dollars on their collection. If they pocketed hefty tax breaks into the bargain, well, that was just good business. And when it turned out that many of those items, including the Gilgamesh Dream Tablet, had been looted, stolen, or forged, they presented themselves as the naïve victims of unscrupulous black-market dealers—paying little mind to the extent to which their reckless desire to obtain items to justify their religious beliefs had led them to ignore multiple red flags in pursuit of these cultural heritage items.

THE FAMILY'S ZEAL for acquiring these items to fill their storehouse of biblical truth and goodness is by no means tangential to their larger spiritual and political goals. Over the last five decades, Hobby Lobby has grown from a self-made business selling picture frames out of the family garage into a megacorporation with more than $8 billion in annual revenue, and eighty-four-year-old patriarch David Green and his family are now among the hundred richest Americans.[7]

While others might have spent that largesse on expensive villas and yachts, the Greens have reserved nearly all of it for the Lord, living modestly while becoming the single most prolific donor to evangelical Christian causes in the country.[8] The family is best known for its crusade against the contraception mandate in the Affordable Care Act, equating certain forms of birth control with abortion. As lead defendant in the case of *Burwell v. Hobby Lobby Stores, Inc.*, the family risked their company to take their case to the Supreme Court, arguing that providing their employees with coverage for birth control violated their deeply held religious beliefs.

That case is only the most visible evidence of their religious convictions, which have held up the Bible as the authority in every area of law and culture. It's safe to say no family has done more to spread the doctrine of what's become known as Christian nationalism—a fervent belief that the United States was founded as a Christian nation and must return to its roots by enforcing biblical principles to stave off widespread calamity and decline.

In ways both visible and invisible, the Greens have devoted themselves to this goal in a passionate mission to save Americans' souls, whether they like it or not. They've propagated newspaper and TV ads to inculcate biblical values and argued for the Founders' religious intentions. They've put their vast wealth toward spreading biblical literature and almost single-handedly propped up evangelical education through donations of money and land. Behind the scenes, they've funneled millions of dollars into religious and political groups that have written the laws and fought the court cases against rights for lesbian, gay, bisexual, trans, and queer (LGBTQ) Americans and reproductive freedom, including the historic overturning of *Roe v. Wade* after nearly fifty years of nationwide legal abortion.

That's only the beginning of their fervent desire to reshape all of American life according to the teachings of their beloved book. For the Greens, "religious freedom" means the freedom to practice their Christian beliefs based on a biblical truth that they believe is incompatible with other worldviews. The museum they founded in Washington has served as something of a base camp for fundamentalist and charismatic Christians who preached "spiritual warfare" and helped foment the insurrection against the Capitol on January 6, 2021. Later, they helped put Donald Trump back into office against the odds in November 2024 as the imperfect savior for Christianity despite his godless personal life. To understand the Greens is to better understand the motivations and desires of the almost one-third of the American population that believes the country's laws should be subordinate to biblical truth—and should be brought in line with God's word in their plan for a Christian nation.[9]

CHAPTER ONE

In the Beginning

Walter Green first heard God speak to him on Sunday, May 1, 1932. The future father of Hobby Lobby founder David Green was standing by the altar of the Church of God in Emporia, Kansas, a small city on the upland prairie between Kansas City and Wichita. "I want to show you the Church," God said to him. "But if I do, you will have to give it your all in all."[1]

Tall and lanky, with brown eyes and hair, Walter had been attending services at the tiny chapel for two months but fighting its teachings. The Church of God seemed to be the "Bible church," and he wasn't interested in the Bible. "It seems as though the devil is spitting hot air in my face," he told the church's state overseer, Brother Risner. But Risner just shrugged and gave Walter passages of scripture to read, which he half-heartedly took.[2]

Now God showed Walter a vision, as he later recounted to the church's newspaper, *The White Wing Messenger*: a bouquet of roses, with one white rose higher than the others. A small card perched among the petals read, "My church, the Church of God." Shaken, Walter lingered behind to confess what he'd seen. "You are in danger," Risner told him.

"You must walk in the light." Suddenly, he heard God's voice repeating, "You must walk in the light!"[3]

Walter dropped to his knees. "Yes, Lord," he said. An unseen force led him to give Brother Risner his hand. "It is my heart's desire to become a member of the Church of God!" No sooner had Walter said the words than he felt the Holy Spirit descend upon him. He ran up and down the aisles, whirling and jumping, with tears streaming down his face. He felt like a feather floating through the air, singing in languages he didn't understand. And everywhere was Jesus Christ in a transparent white robe.[4]

"What did you see?" the pastor's daughter Marie Lark asked him when he came to his senses. Walter stammered a few words but still seemed to be speaking in an unintelligible language.[5]

Returning home, Walter kept seeing visions, including one of a little church with a solid foundation and a cornerstone engraved with the words "Jesus Christ." The rest of the church was made of people. "I got off a ways and looked to see if I could see a crack or flaw in the building of the church, but I could not," he said. "It was without spot or blemish. Christ seemed to say to me the teachings of the Church of God were the true and only doctrine of Jesus Christ."[6]

THE RELIGION WALTER encountered that night was very different from the Presbyterianism of his forebears. His grandfather James Edward Green was born in Kentucky in 1832, moved to Missouri as a young man, and bought a farm. Later known as "Uncle Jimmie" to neighbors, he appears in a grainy black-and-white photograph with a bushy beard and stovepipe hat, seated outside his farmhouse with his wife and some of their seven children in plain, homespun clothing.[7]

James's son Walter "Frank" Green is shadowed beneath a fedora and similarly shrouded in history. He drifted west to Buffalo, Wyoming, where he worked as a carpenter and ranch foreman. Along with his wife, Grace, he had eight children—including his youngest son, Walter Oliver Green, born in 1908.[8] By that time, the first rumblings of a new religious movement were rolling across the country, with reports of rural revivals where charismatic preachers performed miracles—healing the sick and "casting out devils."

After a camp meeting in the Great Smoky Mountains of North Carolina in 1902, two Baptist ministers, Richard G. Spurling and William F. Bryant, founded a new church that would dispense with creeds to focus directly on Jesus's love; it was eventually called the Church of God.[9] Theirs was one of a growing number of churches practicing "holiness" doctrine, a radical theology teaching that through prayer and devotion, Christians could be "sanctified" in the Holy Spirit and freed from sin and temptation.

Just before Walter Green's birth, in 1906, the movement erupted in revivals at Azusa Street Mission in Los Angeles, where thousands came from around the country to cram onto wooden planks, fall into trances, and speak strange languages. These adherents were "baptized" in the Holy Spirit, a more powerful experience than sanctification—demonstrated through glossolalia, or "speaking in tongues," just as the Bible says Jesus's apostles did during the Holy Feast of Pentecost. This gave the movement its name: Pentecostalism.[10]

THE MOVEMENT FOUND a receptive ear in former Quaker Bible salesman Ambrose Jessup "A. J." Tomlinson, who rose to prominence in the Church of God, now based in Cleveland, Tennessee. The southeastern United States was fertile ground for Pentecostalism, with a generation traumatized by the Civil War eager for a message of redemption. Hearing an itinerant minister preach on the power of the Holy Ghost in 1908, Tomlinson slipped off his chair in "excruciating pain and agony," seeing visions of the "awful condition" of people in South America, Africa, and Japan. Each time, God asked if he was willing to go help those people. Each time, he answered yes.[11]

The following year, the church elected Tomlinson as overseer, a position he'd hold for decades. He staged increasingly theatrical tent revivals centered on the three stages of holiness: being saved, sanctified, and finally baptized in the Holy Ghost, accompanied by speaking in tongues. Soon he was sending evangelists to preach across the South and Midwest and even overseas to Egypt, Argentina, and China.[12]

Tomlinson and other church leaders relied on the King James Version (KJV) of the Bible as the ultimate authority on both spiritual and temporal matters. "There in the lids of that Book is a system of government that must not lie hidden, unused, and unknown any longer," Tomlinson said. "We should earnestly seek to reinstate and reestablish the government under whose banner the brave apostles and their contemporaries fought, bled, and died to sustain."[13]

While the Bible may have been written by men, their hearts and minds were so moved by the Holy Spirit that "we look upon it as God's word to us," Tomlinson said. "The greatest and best law book of all books."[14] While still following the laws of the United States, the church also followed a stricter biblical law in preparation for the second coming of Jesus, which would usher in a thousand-year kingdom.[15] As "the highest voice of authority next to the Word," Tomlinson and other church elders laid down guidelines on speaking in tongues and washing of feet along with prohibitions on jewelry, tobacco, chewing gum, alcohol, coffee, and even Coca-Cola. Sexual intimacy before marriage was forbidden, as were divorce and remarriage. Members were even to avoid medicine, appealing to God to heal them by faith.[16]

Associating with nonbelievers was frowned upon, so the church became an insular community that members left only to convert others.[17] The Church of God was successful on that score, growing from around one thousand members in 1910 to more than twenty thousand by 1922.[18] Tomlinson's heavy-handed style, however, brought him into conflict with other leaders, and amid allegations of financial mismanagement, he was ousted in 1923. Undaunted, Tomlinson held up a

Bible in his last address to the general assembly and pledged that he would "once more raise the Book high up in the air and declare, this is our only rule of faith and practice."[19]

He reorganized a quarter of the members into a new Church of God—later renamed the Church of God of Prophecy—proclaiming it "God's government for His people on earth" and preaching across the country in elaborate conventions incorporating banners, brass bands, and floats.[20] Within a decade, the church had regained its previous numbers, with Tomlinson, in the words of one religious historian, the "king of the traveling pulpit."[21]

By now, Frank Green had moved his family from Wyoming to Kansas, finding work as a carpenter in Emporia. There his son Walter experienced his Holy Spirit baptism that spring night in 1932. Afterward, Walter felt a new sense of peace and confidence, proclaiming that he wouldn't give it up even if someone offered him $50,000: "My experiences with God have been more precious than gold and silver."[22]

Along with the church, Walter soon became involved with its new pastor, Marie Lark. She had arrived in Emporia the previous year with her father, Jacob Lark, and helped him set up the local Church of God in a small clapboard building with a tent revival in summer. (Many Pentecostals recognized the rights of women to preach based on a line in the Book of Joel saying that both "your sons and daughters shall prophecy.") The church immediately drew converts from a populace suffering in the Great Depression. After receiving Holy Ghost baptism, one woman who had been deaf for decades began hearing again, and a young girl bedridden from spinal meningitis began "walking around wherever she cares to go," reported Marie, who became lead pastor after her father became ill.[23]

In July 1933, Tomlinson arrived for the state convention in Kansas City, taking to the rostrum to expound on the imminent return of

Jesus. That Christ "is going to return to earth is an absolute fact according to scripture," Tomlinson taught. Only members of the rightful Church of God of Prophecy would be saved—no one else—and only when they'd made themselves perfect, "subject to" Christ "in everything."[24] That night, he officiated at the marriage of Marie Lark and Walter Green, who walked down the aisle together as "many hearts were touched by the sacredness and solemnity of the events."[25]

The new couple began to evangelize across the state, carefully avoiding any kind of entertainment deemed too worldly, including the "talkies" and baseball games, which the church viewed as wicked and corrupt. In return, Pentecostals began experiencing a backlash from mainstream society, which saw their charismatic practices of glossolalia, faith healing, and prophesying as strange and fanatical.[26] Walter and Marie read reports in the *White Wing Messenger* of church buildings burned or blown up with dynamite, services disrupted by ruffians who threw rotten fruit at preachers, and even men shooting through windows at pastors.[27]

Church members began thinking of themselves as engaged in "spiritual warfare" against the army of the devil. Anything positive that happened to them was seen as a result of their successful victory against satanic forces, while any negative consequences were often viewed as a personal failure resulting from a lack of faith or devotion to the Spirit.[28]

The world was divided into two groups, Brother Tomlinson preached—Spirit-filled believers, recognized by their ability to speak in tongues, and the disobedient, who could not.[29] After Jacob Lark died in 1935—a "soldier" fallen "in battle," wrote his daughter—Marie took up a position of leadership, preaching at state conventions and setting up a new church in a suburb of Kansas City as Walter became pastor in a nearby town.[30]

Marie stopped preaching in 1937 to have her first of six children. She had a child every year until 1942, including David Marvin Green, born in Emporia in November 1941.[31] Walter continued founding churches in Topeka and Wichita, carting his growing family with him. In 1943, Walter and Marie lamented the passing of A. J. Tomlinson, but the church continued with his son Milton, who took over as overseer for the next five decades. Under his leadership, Walter was tapped to move his family to Arizona to open a new church in Phoenix in 1946.[32]

That September, Walter traveled to the church's annual assembly in Tennessee, where more than six thousand members rode in cars and buses into the foothills of the Great Smoky Mountains to a new park the church had created called Fields of the Wood. As rain started to fall, participants climbed Prayer Mountain and marveled at a full-sized replica of Jesus's tomb. Walter marched at the head of Arizona's fourteen-member delegation and even gave a brief address in the tabernacle.[33]

Back in Arizona, more churches followed as Walter and Marie trusted in God to provide. When the bill for materials for a new church building ballooned to several hundred dollars, it outstripped the church's ability to pay. Undeterred, Walter announced a miracle at the evening service: That very day, a woman had been led by God to hand him a check for the entire amount.[34]

David Green grew up expecting such miracles, as he "met Christ" in a little Arizona church at age seven and journeyed with his family to open new churches across New Mexico, West Texas, and finally Oklahoma. A skinny kid with jug ears and glasses, David heard scripture at the dinner table and woke up at night to the sound of his parents praying. "A deep and unshakable faith in Jesus Christ flowed from my parents and filled our home," he later said.[35]

The family subsisted on Walter's meager salary, with the entire family often crammed into a two-bedroom home—David and one of his brothers sleeping in the kitchen on a rollaway. When his sisters had friends over to play, they put empty containers in the refrigerator to make it look full.[36] David helped earn money by picking cotton on weekends with a burlap potato sack on his shoulder. Most of the time, he went without shoes, building calluses on his feet so thick that he could run across a rock pile.[37]

Walter and Marie insisted on tithing 10 percent of the family's income to the church, just as the patriarch Abraham had given one-tenth of the spoils of war to the Israelite high priests. The obligation was fulfilled not by "giving directly to the poor or to individuals or good causes," the Church of God instructed, but rather by donating to the "treasury of the Church for the Lord's work."[38]

"There is a notion of urgency," said Paul Williamson, coauthor of *The Psychology of Religious Fundamentalism* and a former Church of God of Prophecy pastor. "Nobody knows when Jesus is coming, and so [they think], 'We need to spread our message around the world to save as many people as we can.' People might be hungry, but what's more important is your spiritual soul."[39]

At the same time, David's mother repeated the proverb "Honour the Lord with thy substance, and with the firstfruits of all thine increase: So shall thy barns be filled with plenty, and thy presses shall burst out with new wine." In other words, those who honored God would be rewarded with material gain. "If I heard her say it once, I heard her say it a thousand times," David said.[40]

David and his siblings learned to tithe as well, placing a dime out of every dollar they earned in the collection plate. Their parents contributed even more with "self-denial" pledges, forgoing creature comforts to support more monuments at the Fields of the Wood or church missionary work in Puerto Rico, the Philippines, Australia, and Egypt.[41] Marie spent extra time crocheting lacy doilies and selling them at church bazaars to support missionary efforts; if they didn't sell, she bought them herself.[42]

Walter was an imposing moral force, but he was reserved with his children and not openly affectionate. "He kept most of what he felt to himself," said David, who gravitated toward his mother's warmth. "Some who met her for a few moments on the street would remember her smile all their days." David seemed particularly able to draw out that smile, cheekily calling her "Mama Babe" to make her chuckle. "I was her favorite," he said. "I was able to make her laugh no matter what else was going on."[43]

She could be severe in her own way, however, with an unwavering focus on the afterlife. She hung a plaque on the wall with a line from a poem: "Only one life, 'twill soon be past / Only what's done for Christ will last." Seeing those words dozens of times a week, David was filled with a profound guilt that he wasn't doing enough for the church. "Only two things in life are eternal," she told her children. "God's Word and people's souls."[44]

In March 1956, residents of Mangum, Oklahoma, gathered at the local airfield for a revival service led by pastor Walter Green. Accompanying him were David's three sisters, Lois, Betty, and Esther, who sang hymns as the Happy Harvester Trio. Afterward, the Church of God of Prophecy's White Angel Fleet performed an air show, flying in cross-shaped formations and dropping church literature from on high.

Along with his musical sisters, both David's older brother James and younger brother Joseph had a gift for testifying in church.[45] Comparatively, David felt painfully shy and reserved, always falling short of the high standard required of a "PK" (preacher's kid).[46] He struggled in school and was forced to repeat seventh grade at Mangum Junior High. He had no friends and only felt more isolated because he washed dishes in the school cafeteria to earn a lunch pass. When it came to oral presentations, he flat-out refused, taking a failing grade instead. He was handy in other ways, however, such as helping out the electrician husband of a local teacher as a "gofer" after school. Eventually he bought his own tools and began taking on fix-it projects while hunting and fishing in his spare time.[47]

EVEN AS WALTER Green was preaching in obscurity, with rarely more than a hundred people in his congregation, the world began to discover

Pentecostalism.[48] Starting in the 1950s, Pentecostal ministers broke into the mainstream, with one of the most prominent a former dirt-poor PK from the other side of Oklahoma, Granville Oral Roberts.

Bullied as one of those strange "holy rollers," as Pentecostals were derisively called, Roberts ran away from home and disavowed church as a teenager. After collapsing from tuberculosis in 1934, however, he tried praying to Jesus and claimed to be miraculously healed. Soon after, he was baptized in the Spirit and became a pastor.[49] One day, Roberts came across a verse from the third epistle of John: "Beloved, I wish above all things that thou mayest prosper and be in health, even as thy soul prospereth." The same morning, he said, a neighbor gave him a car, and with that, he began his ministry with a new message that became known as the "prosperity gospel."[50]

Roberts insisted that God didn't want his followers to suffer in deprivation but rather to enjoy wealth and good health as rewards for their faith. He held his first revivals in Enid, Oklahoma—a few hours north of Mangum—claiming to release three hundred people from their ailments in eight weeks. Eventually he moved to Tulsa, a city burgeoning from the oil and airline industries, where he drew crowds of thousands.[51]

At the time, a rapprochement was underway between Pentecostalism and the rest of the Christian church. For decades, new fundamentalist sects based on a strict conservative interpretation of scripture had been working to find purchase within mainline Baptist and Presbyterian churches. Starting in the 1940s, some fundamentalists rebranded themselves as "evangelicals" to emphasize the importance of converting others to Christian belief.

They formed under the banner of the Reverend Billy Graham, a young six-foot-two, blond and blue-eyed Southern Baptist minister who combined conservative politics and evangelical Christianity. Graham railed at revivals about how liberal schools were poisoning America with communist teachings and urged his listeners to become "born again" in Jesus. As part of this crusade, some evangelicals reached out to Pentecostals, looking past their strange charismatic practices to find common cause in a mutual biblical worldview.

Soon Pentecostals were smoothing over their own sectarian differences, with Roberts as the face of the movement. His healing revivals became weeklong carnivals of the sick and wounded, who filed rapturously past as Roberts laid hands one by one on children with "grotesquely twisted arms and legs, hollow-eyed victims of palsy, of cancer, of rheumatic fever and polio."[52] To keep up with the throngs, Roberts came up with a novel solution: television evangelicalism, or televangelism.

Appearing in a new program, *Your Faith Is Power*, Roberts stood on a podium above an in-person audience, encouraging home viewers to place their hands on their televisions to receive healing. With his fame came criticism as newspapers began debunking his healing practices, reporting on a child who collapsed and died while waiting in line or a diabetic woman who died after throwing away her insulin. By the mid-1950s, Roberts changed his focus subtly from health to wealth. If only people would donate money as "seed faith" to his church, God would return their gifts "seven fold," he preached, even offering a money-back guarantee if they weren't repaid within a year.[53]

Borne on a sea of postwar consumerism, Roberts and other ministers preached that Pentecostals no longer had to deny themselves life's comforts—in fact, God wanted them to succeed both financially and spiritually. "We have a different message now, a positive message," said one evangelist, "and have been lifted above a life that is always 'walking on eggshells.' "[54] After decades of persecution and derision, Pentecostals could participate in the modern world. In fact, their consumerism could strike a patriotic blow against the godless communism of the Soviet Union.

While the Green family's Church of God of Prophecy stayed warily outside the coalition of other Pentecostal churches, even it loosened some of its strictures, allowing members to drink Coca-Cola, watch television, and work on Sundays.[55] As Roberts preached his gospel of prosperity, he announced the construction of a new Tulsa headquarters for his ministry, the Abundant Life Building, in 1956. Eventually it would rise seven stories, with a footprint of 100,000 square feet and a price tag of $3 million. He had even bigger plans: a "university of evangelicalism" that would open as Oral Roberts University (ORU).[56]

David Green was only vaguely aware of the burgeoning prosperity gospel when his family relocated once again, to Altus, Oklahoma, a small city of cotton farmers and cattle ranchers by the Texas border. Even at a young age, he made the connection between his mother's piety and the physical health his family enjoyed. "I never even saw one aspirin come into our house because of God's blessings," he later said. "I know that comes from the giving that she did."[57]

In the fall of 1957, Walter Green began preaching at a little brick church in the poorer part of town, a mile south of its center. Without a family car, David and his siblings walked everywhere. When he first arrived in Altus at age fifteen, David showed a rebellious streak, receiving a fine when he drove someone else's car without a license and caused a minor accident.[58] He settled down, however, when he enrolled in a vocational training program at the high school called "distributive education."

More than two dozen local businesses agreed to employ Altus High School students part-time in the afternoons, after they took math and English in the mornings. David was assigned to work as a stock boy at McLellan's Variety, a five-and-dime store on the town's main square. On a Thursday evening in November 1958, David stood solemnly on the stage in the auditorium as he received his distributive education emblem. In a candlelit ceremony, he agreed to uphold principles of community service and business ethics.[59]

David later described his time at McLellan's in reverential terms. "You could smell the fresh popcorn as soon as you came through the front doors," he said. "The wooden floors creaked as you stepped toward the candy counter to the left or the toiletries department to the right, where a smiling young clerk would say, 'Good morning!' as she waited to serve you." David took to the job instantly, even though it was far from glamorous, involving scrubbing toilets, sweeping dust off floors, and cranking out price stickers by hand.[60] But something about working with his hands and providing for people spoke to him. "I had finally found something I was good at," he said. Soon he expanded his hours to forty a week in addition to school, using his sixty-cents-an-hour wages to help buy new furniture for the family home and saving up $200 for a 1951 Ford.[61] He later waxed lyrical about arranging store displays at night "like a painter laboring over his canvas. There was beauty in it all to me."[62]

The manager, known by the felicitous nickname T. Texas Tyler, took him under his wing—at one point, even considering adopting David to give him a better life than his family could provide.[63] Perhaps Tyler saw a bit of himself in the wiry, energetic teenager. After shifts, Tyler bought David a Coke at the drug store and explained how one could mark up items to twice or even three times the price and still get people to buy them by displaying them attractively enough. "I began to see that in retail, the sky was the limit," David said. "You could always open more stores, or expand the stores you had; there was no end."[64]

At McLellan's, David's eye fell on a younger part-timer in the stationery department, Barbara Turner, and he eventually got up the courage to ask her out for Cokes. A foil to David's shyness, Barbara sang in the church choir at Altus's mammoth First Baptist Church and acted in the high school play.[65] Her family lived in a trim stone cottage just north of the square. Her father was quiet but laughed easily, while she took after her mother, who was gregarious and sometimes fiery. "Dad let her be the boss," Barbara said. "Usually, if we got reprimanded, it was with my mother."[66]

David graduated in May 1960, his yearbook photo showing a skinny face with a tall pouf of hair and an awkward smile.[67] Meanwhile, his siblings all continued to rise in the Church of God of Prophecy. His sisters Betty and Esther attended Bible training camp in Tennessee and became ministers, as did his brothers James and Joseph. His sister Lois married a pastor, making David feel like a "black sheep" as he took a position as an assistant manager at McLellan's, making $60 a week.[68]

He walked down the aisle of the Baptist Church on February 12, 1961, at age nineteen, wearing an all-white tuxedo as Barbara, seventeen and still in high school, beamed in a white polyester dress, carrying a Bible along with her orchid corsage. The couple opted for a single-ring ceremony, in which David offered Barbara a ring as a symbol of his fidelity but didn't wear one himself.[69] Before the wedding, David wrote down three goals: "to build a happy marriage, to raise healthy, well-balanced children who would serve God," and "to succeed in business."[70]

Less than seven months later, on September 2, Barbara gave birth to their first child—a healthy boy weighing seven pounds, seven ounces whom they named Mart Delyn.[71] The timing raised questions concerning their adherence to David's church's strong strictures against premarital sex.[72] It would, however, be many years before the family would become substantial supporters of figures and institutions espousing purity culture, which taught teens strict abstinence from dating and sex before marriage.

After their marriage, Barbara left her job at McLellan's to "build the family of our dreams," and soon David left too for a new position at TG&Y, a chain of department stores expanding across the region.[73] The firm had been launched in 1935 by three variety-store owners who pooled their resources to buy an Oklahoma City warehouse to store inventory. Their secret was buying goods directly from manufacturers and storing them long-term to keep costs low and profit margins high. They opened a larger store together in a defunct grocery store outside Oklahoma City and eventually opened TG&Ys across Oklahoma, Texas, and neighboring states. By the mid-1960s, the company had expanded across the country with larger Family Centers, selling a bewildering array of sporting goods, furniture, clothing, jewelry, toys, and pets and anticipating Wal-Mart's opening a few years later.[74]

In 1962, David became an assistant manager at the TG&Y in Shawnee, Oklahoma, forty minutes east of Oklahoma City.[75] While the manager groused at first about his youth—he was only twenty at the time—David won him over by cleaning and reorganizing the entire stockroom within a month. Soon, according to David, his manager was begging him to take a break. "Well, I had never taken a break and even to this day, I don't take breaks," he said.[76]

Within six months, he was manager of a store in a coveted location in Oklahoma City, overseeing six employees in a four-thousand-square-foot space and making $400 a month. He was just twenty-one years old. "From my background picking cotton, it was like a big, big thing in my life," he said.[77] Despite his swift rise, David still struggled to earn his mother's approval, as he poignantly recounted years later: "I can recall back when I was the youngest TG&Y manager going home and saying, 'Hey Mom, I'm the youngest TG&Y manager.' She said, 'Oh yeah, what are you doing for the Lord?' "[78]

It was a pattern that would continue for a decade as David became manager of a sixteen-thousand-square-foot Family Center, then an eighty-six-thousand-square foot superstore, and then multiple stores.[79] "I would be the youngest district manager and I would say, 'Hey Mom, I'm the youngest district manager, I've got 30 stores.' Whatever. 'Yeah

David, but what are you doing for the Lord?' " he said. "I could have told my mother that I'd been elected president of the United States and she would have said the same thing: 'What are you doing for the Lord?' She understood and lived by the idea that there was only one thing worth doing in this life and that was serving God."[80]

IN HER INSISTENCE on separating the spiritual and material, Marie was behind the trends of her own faith. In just two decades, Pentecostalism had gone from the backcountry cousin of evangelicals to the cooler older brother. Oral Roberts and the other televangelists continued to grow in popularity, and now other churches were adopting their strange-seeming practices. As the 1950s gave way to the 1960s, spiritual experimentation filled the air. Timothy Leary was dropping acid, beatniks were practicing Zen, and even the Beatles were dabbling in transcendental meditation at the flowing hem of Maharishi Mahesh Yogi. All of that mystical excitation rubbed off on Christianity, and Christians had only to turn on their televisions to find it.[81]

Over the airwaves, Roberts and other neo-Pentecostals were fervently preaching on their soundstages, healing the sick and promising untold wealth to those who believed—and donated. These weren't crazy "holy rollers" but respectable businessmen, with crisp haircuts and clean suits. Suddenly, glossolalia began breaking out in mainstream churches—with Baptists, Presbyterians, and Episcopalians embracing charismatic forms of worship and some becoming televangelists as well. By the late 1960s, even students on Catholic college campuses were speaking in tongues as *Time* and *Newsweek* announced a nationwide "charismatic revival."[82]

The windswept prairies of Oklahoma became the movement's headquarters after ORU opened in Tulsa in 1963 for spirit-filled Bible study. Roberts went on a fundraising binge, raising millions for the institution's endowment as ORU alumni took to the airwaves.

Soon evangelicals had a glut of ministries where they could send their money—and send they did, with televangelists pulling in a combined $1 billion annually by the end of the 1960s.[83]

Across the state in Oklahoma City, David Green would acknowledge the influence of Oral Roberts and other charismatic preachers on his own embrace of spirit-filled business. "I don't think my mother and father, being ministers, understood that we all have a calling in our lives, every single one of us," he said. "Oral Roberts understood it early on. He said to go out into your world to bring light not into *the* world—but *your* world, whether you are a nurse or a businessman or whatever."[84]

As David continued bringing his light to TG&Y, Barbara built their family, first in a rented bungalow in a suburban neighborhood on the outskirts of Oklahoma City and then in a larger home in a subdivision by the winding reservoir of Lake Hefner.[85] She gave birth to their second son, Steven Todd Green, in September 1963, and a few years later, the couple adopted a daughter, Darsee Dawn Green, born in September 1967.

Though they lived in Oklahoma City, the family paid tuition to send their children to public school in Bethany, a conservative inner suburb founded at the turn of the century by followers of the Church of the Nazarene. This church came out of the same "holiness" tradition as Pentecostalism, though it was less fundamentalist in nature.[86] There, the children attended school with other Spirit-filled believers, even as the Green family stood out for its Pentecostal beliefs. David worked long hours at the store, often not getting home before 10 pm, well after the kids were in bed.[87] Barbara became frustrated with the company's demands—including forcing him to work on Thanksgiving one year. Showing her mother's fiery spirit, she called the president of TG&Y to give him a piece of her mind, telling him Thanksgiving should be a day for family.[88]

However grueling the hours, David was getting a crash course in the retail trade. He appreciated TG&Y's central warehousing system, which allowed any store to acquire goods in just a few days. And he liked the creative sleight of hand the store used to encourage customers to spend more. In the pet department, for example, he could sell a ten-gallon fish tank below cost, and then inflate prices for the fish, gravel, and pump to go with it, making back the money. For every clever marketing ploy, however, there was also waste and inefficiency, David thought as he watched many fish and hamsters in the department die unsold.[89]

TG&Y gave discretion to individual store managers to manage their own inventory and even produce store-branded products to cater to customer preferences. David thought that this approach led to higher costs and an uneven shopping experience. The company was trying to be too many things to too many people, losing its way and squandering its potential. "All of this was showing me what could be done with specializing," he said.[90] It wasn't with pets that David decided to try out his ideas but rather with another department: crafts.

CHAPTER TWO

Be Fruitful and Multiply

One day in 1970, Hobby Lobby's oft-told origin story goes, twenty-eight-year-old David Green was sitting at a TG&Y lunch counter in Oklahoma City sharing frustrations with fellow managers Larry Pico and Jim Stoddard. As they imagined what kind of enterprise they might create on their own, Pico suggested that they manufacture clocks. "I have a better idea," David said. "Little miniature frames." A fad had emerged in home decor of hanging picture frames in clusters, each displaying a painting of a subject such as a sunflower or lighthouse. Customers kept asking for the small frames, and David had a hard time finding them.[1]

"That sounds like it could work," one of them said. The next day, they located a professional frame chopper through an equipment supplier with the steep price tag of $450. Stoddard bowed out, but David and Pico went to Penn Square Bank and signed a twelve-month loan for $600 to cover the cutter, wooden sticks, canvas, and other materials. They incorporated their venture as Greco (GREE-co), a portmanteau of Green and Pico.[2]

The $600 loan comes up repeatedly in the founding myth of Hobby Lobby—a symbol of the humble roots of the big-box behemoth.

Setting up in Pico's garage, the partners created samples and sent them out with a traveling salesman. He came back with orders for a whopping $3,500. The partners begged their supplier for more materials on credit and began furiously creating frames, ending up with $300 in profit.

As orders poured in from across Oklahoma and Texas, the partners cut at night while Barbara and the Greens' two sons, Mart and Steve—nine and seven years old—glued frames at the kitchen table by day. "What a sight!" David later rhapsodized. "I sure wish we had a picture of all of us—Barbara, little Mart and Steve, and me, with little Darsee nearby—working together around the kitchen table." They paid Mart and Steve seven cents a frame, while Barbara worked for nothing, prompting David to later joke that the business was built on "child labor and slave labor."[3]

Mart used the money to buy baseball cards, and Steve spent it on candy. Of course, they also learned to tithe, placing a tenth of their meager earnings in the collection plate on Sundays to help the church spread its faith. "I never thought about *not* tithing," Mart later said. "It is just what we did."[4]

As THE COMPANY grew, Greco returned to Penn Square for a larger loan but was turned down; thankfully, Union Bank agreed to lend them $1,000 to expand. In the summer of 1972, Greco opened its first retail store, a three-hundred-square-foot space in downtown Oklahoma City. Casting about for a snappy name, they noticed a customer in Houston calling itself "Hobby Lobby." With little thought of trademark infringement, they took the name for their own store. It had a "nice ring to it," David later remembered, "figuring our little operation in Oklahoma City was no threat to them." (By the time they expanded into Texas, the original Hobby Lobby had gone out of business.)[5]

The company's first ad ran in *The Oklahoman* on August 9, a tiny block of text wedged between notices for wool blankets and a two-bedroom house. "Grand Opening / Hobby Lobby," it read. "A complete selection of arts & crafts materials."[6] In truth, that was an overstatement. The store carried only a meager inventory of sequins, beads, and painting supplies in addition to the frames. Nor was the location ideal, situated behind the state capitol in a strip of laundromats and other shops with minimal foot traffic. But the rent was cheap, and the space had another three hundred square feet in the back behind a beaded curtain to make frames.[7]

Business was so slow the first month that Darsee, then in kindergarten, could sit on the floor for hours playing with beads, undisturbed. But traffic picked up during the Christmas season, and Greco grossed $3,200 its first year, even as David continued his day job working sixty-hour weeks as a manager at TG&Y. In search of another partner to manage the store, David approached John Seward, assistant manager of TG&Y's pet department, who worked as a watercolor artist on the side. David offered him $100 a week and 20 percent of the business to join the company.[8]

As the store thrived under Seward's eye, David was having problems with Larry Pico, who he claimed wasn't pulling his weight. In September 1973, they met at a local McDonald's, and David wrote Pico a check for $5,000 to buy out his ownership of Greco and Hobby Lobby.[9] That same month, Hobby Lobby moved into a new space a half-dozen blocks away with more than one thousand square feet. Even as the country plunged into recession in the wake of the 1973 oil crisis, the company continued to thrive. David, then thirty-one, attributed its success to an unlikely source: the flower children of the Age of Aquarius, who were eager for materials for homemade crafts. "The long-haired hippies of that era would come into our store and sit down on the carpet to string together beads of various colors," David remembered. "Thank God for them."[10]

The partners were an odd couple—David was clean-cut and reserved, with his dark hair cut respectably short for the time, while

Seward rode motorcycles and sported long hair and a bushy Jerry Garcia–type beard. Seward's outgoing personality and creative spirit complemented David's focus and attention to detail, however, and their partnership lasted the better part of twenty years.[11]

Seward drove the selection of arts and crafts materials while also taking on advertising, including hand-lettering ads himself. David focused on the merchandise, sourcing products and presenting them in attractive displays that emphasized steep discounts. Business thrived so much that they were able to open a second store on the west side of the city. In 1974, the company took in $150,000 in gross revenue, with $36,000 in profit.[12]

That was enough for David to consider quitting his job at TG&Y and working full-time for Hobby Lobby, giving up a $26,000 annual salary—even though he could pay himself only half that to start. He prayed with Barbara about the decision, with a Bible verse from Ecclesiastes as his inspiration: "Whatever your hand finds to do, do it with all your might, for in the grave, where you are going, there is neither working nor planning nor knowledge nor wisdom." Together, they decided to take the plunge. "It was a sense of providence," he said. "This was what God meant for us to do."[13]

David quit his day job in March 1975, shortly before the company relocated its second store to a derelict shopping center a few blocks away on the major thoroughfare of NW Tenth Street. The location included seven thousand square feet for inventory, a custom framing shop, and an art gallery featuring local artists and framed reproductions of old masters. Better yet, it had a huge parking lot and plenty of room to expand. The bet paid off, as the company increased its revenue by almost five times to nearly $750,000 that year.[14]

Sadly for David, his mother didn't live to see it. In April, Marie Green passed away at age seventy-one in Midland, Texas, with one of David's sisters holding her in her arms. Just before she died, Marie sat up and cried out, "Do you see them? Do you see them?" David's sister asked what she meant. "Angels," Marie said. David was happy to hear it. "At the end of my mother's life, God himself sent a company of angels to welcome her into his kingdom," he concluded.[15] David was disappointed, however, that she had never got to witness Hobby Lobby's commercial success. "I regret that she never saw it," he said, "but I do not regret she constantly urged me to do great things for God."[16]

By now, evangelicals were ascendant in Christian life. The godless '60s had radicalized many Christians who saw the toxic stew of drugs, rock 'n' roll, and shallow commercialism as a sign of the end times and vowed to reverse the demonic tide. "Street ministers" waded into the counterculture with coffee-shop ministries to convince bead-buying hippies to "get high on Jesus" instead, and self-described "Jesus freaks" combined Pentecostal worship with exuberant folk rock. Students joined Campus Crusade for Christ, an organization started by Oklahoma candy salesman–turned–seminarian Bill Bright, who sought to combat the communism infiltrating campuses with a stripped-down gospel based on accepting Jesus as your "best friend." The organization became a vibrant force, squaring off against liberal antiwar protesters and railing against a culture of "free love" and premarital sex.[17]

As the charismatic revival crested in the mid-1970s, many churches returned to more traditional forms of worship. The prosperity gospel only picked up steam, however, as Christian broadcasters multiplied like proverbial loaves and fishes, with worldwide viewership growing tenfold between 1970 and 1975—from 10 to 110 million people. The new wave of televangelists blended charismatic preaching with calls for donations as well as increasing calls to political action.[18]

Most prominent among them was Pat Robertson, a soft-spoken Southern Baptist minister who turned a failing Virginia television station into a burgeoning media empire, the Christian Broadcasting Network. His signature *The 700 Club* blended evangelical and charismatic elements in a veritable political salon, hosting guests to talk about political issues of the day.[19] Robertson helped launch Jim Bakker, a minister with Assemblies of God—the largest Pentecostal sect—and his wife, Tammy Faye, who eventually cofounded the rival Trinity Broadcasting Network with their program *The PTL Club*. Fiery Louisiana Pentecostal preacher Jimmy Swaggart started his own national program, which railed against the forces of "secular humanism" that had settled into the halls of schools and government, turning people toward false idols of sexuality and selfishness.[20]

As the women's movement arose in the 1970s, these leaders railed against feminism as a force that would destroy the American family, opposing the passage of the proposed Equal Rights Amendment. No Christian crusader espoused "family values" more than James Dobson, who created a nationwide radio network to spread conservative Christian ideals and mobilize voters. Like David Green, Dobson was the son of itinerant evangelical ministers; his father was a preacher with the Church of the Nazarene, and he even lived in the Oklahoma City suburb of Bethany with his mother while his father evangelized on the road.[21]

After studying psychology in a small Nazarene college, he went on to earn a PhD at the secular University of Southern California, where he began to fear that the riotous excesses of the '60s were getting out of control, particularly when it came to children. In 1970, he published *Dare to Discipline*, a jeremiad against the liberal parenting philosophy of Dr. Benjamin Spock. Children should be exposed to the Bible at a young age, setting a tone for the rest of their lives, he taught, and spanking and other forms of corporal punishment should be used to maintain discipline.[22]

Never strident, Dobson positioned himself as a trusted doctor to soothe beleaguered parents. As he churned out book after book, Dobson became increasingly galled by the acceptance of homosexuals, who had burst into American political life after the Stonewall riots of 1969 and were now demanding social and political acceptance. Scripture, he said, taught that "homosexual offenders" would never "inherit the kingdom of God." Dobson resigned from the American Psychological Association in 1973 over its removal of homosexuality from its list of psychological disorders. In 1977, he launched the Christian ministry Focus on the Family, with a weekly radio program broadcast on forty stations, warning with his folksy Southern drawl about a "crisis" for the American family, in which traditional gender roles were being undermined by gay and feminist propaganda.[23]

AROUND THE SAME time Dobson's espousal of "family values" was rising in popular culture, a more intellectual undercurrent of conservative Christianity was bubbling up from below the surface—one that would ultimately have a dramatic impact on American politics and be intimately wrapped up in the Green family's view of the world. Led by philosopher and theologian Rousas John "R. J." Rushdoony, Christian Reconstructionism demanded nothing less than a complete reordering of society around biblical principles. In the same way that God told Adam to "be fruitful, and multiply, and replenish the earth, and subdue it: and have dominion over" it, it was the job of every Christian to "subdue all things and all nations to Christ and His law-word," Rushdoony wrote in his landmark 1973 book, *The Institutes of Biblical Law*.[24]

Unlike some fundamentalists who believed that the Kingdom of God was yet to come with Christ's return and so were to follow secular laws in the meantime, Rushdoony taught that Christians on earth must establish the Kingdom *before* Christ would come back. To do so, they must "take dominion" over the planet in order to "reconstruct" it in the likeness of Christ.[25] The secular humanist government of the United States was to be replaced with a government based on biblical authority, organized around the Ten Commandments—from the first commandment's order to recognize no God but the God of the Bible to the fourth commandment's ban on work on Sundays to the seventh commandment's order against sex outside marriage. Punishments were to be extreme, including the death penalty for murder, adultery, incest, homosexuality, and witchcraft and even the public stoning of persistently disobedient children.[26] Nothing the Bible taught was to be ignored—leading Rushdoony to justify even slavery on biblical grounds.[27]

Such extreme positions have earned him a reputation in some circles as the "crazy uncle" of the Christian Right. Even as some Christian leaders held Rushdoony at arm's length, however, Reconstructionism and its closely related philosophy of "dominionism" exercised an enormous impact on a generation of evangelicals through Rushdoony's California think tank and his many books, which became required reading at ORU and other Christian schools.[28] "Though we hide them under the bed, we read them just the same," one activist said.[29]

Conservative leader Howard Phillips went so far as to call Rushdoony the "most influential man of the 21st century," later adding that "the whole Christian conservative political movement had its genesis in Rush." Rushdoony became a frequent guest on Robertson's *700 Club*, expounding on religious philosophy and biblical law. As Rushdoony acknowledged, Reconstruction couldn't come about all at once. It would require a gradual change in the culture led by churches, schools, and the family, with a strong father exemplifying God's authority.[30]

Another evangelist who would become tied to the Green family, Bill Gothard, set out to make that vision a reality through practical seminars on marriage and parenting that espoused a dominionist reordering of society. A graduate of biblical studies from evangelical Wheaton College, Gothard filled auditoriums and stadiums for multiday seminars on rearing religiously minded kids and teens. By 1973, he was drawing an annual attendance of 200,000 eager participants who clutched red binders full of his teachings, which eventually became known as the Institute in Basic Life Principles. At the heart of his philosophy was a biblically ordained "chain of command" in every realm of society, including the family, government, church, and business.[31]

In the family, the father ruled with unquestioned power, extending an "umbrella of protection" over his wife and children to defend them against the devil. Teenagers, Gothard taught, were like rough stones that God polished into diamonds through the abrasive pressure of parents who enforced a strict set of biblically inspired rules. Dancing and rock music, even Christian rock, were forbidden. Girls were to dress conservatively to keep from becoming "eyetraps" to wayward boys and prevented from dating entirely in favor of a "courtship" leading to marriage, overseen by the watchful eyes of their fathers.[32] Nearly forty years old, Gothard was unmarried and still living with his parents. Despite not having a family of his own, he spoke with a fervor about child-rearing that kept audiences rapt. He eventually developed a homeschooling curriculum for parents based on his biblical ideals.[33]

The principles he taught about authority were applied not only to the family but also to business, where employees were expected to be subservient to employers. "Servants, obey in all things those who are your masters," he quoted from the book of Colossians, applying the verse to a lesson in his binder about a teen clerk loafing on the job. "Do you realize that God expects you to consider that you are actually working for Jesus Christ on your job?" Gothard said. "From now on, we're going to do all of our business according to biblical principles."[34]

In negotiating contracts, for example, he taught that the biblical businessman should follow the example of King Solomon, who made his own calculations on what to pay for cedars from Lebanon rather than soliciting bids for the best offer. As one critic of Gothard wrote at the time, the problem with Gothard wasn't "that the illustrations he uses were not a practice of good business" but rather that "it is not the purpose of the Bible to give that kind of information."[35] Nevertheless, audiences ate up his presentations with their simple messages for all aspects of life. "It erased all shades of gray," said one husband after attending. "I'm convinced that God did not make gray. When it comes to moral issues, things are black or white."[36]

There are indications that Gothard's own business practices weren't always so ethically pure. When a board member in 1977 questioned why the institute had spent so much money on improving land in Michigan owned by Gothard's brother Steve, the board member was removed.[37] A few years later, Steve Gothard was accused of "sexual immorality" for having had affairs with seven women, including his personal assistant. While he was forced to resign as the institute's administrative director, he was allowed to continue running the Michigan retreat center over the protests of board members.[38]

Immensely popular in evangelical circles, Gothard was a frequent visitor to Oklahoma, drawing six thousand attendees to a downtown area in Oklahoma City in 1975 and returning often to Oklahoma City and Tulsa over the years.[39] Eventually, members of the Green family would attend his seminars and become some of his biggest financial supporters, integrating some of his lessons into their own life and work. "Through the example and teachings of Bill Gothard and the Institute in Basic Life Principles, we have benefited both as a family and in our business," David Green wrote in a blurb on Gothard's autobiography, published in 2010. "It is as we take those lessons from God's Word that Bill clearly articulates that we live the full life that God intends."[40]

David and Barbara raised their children according to conservative Christian values. As other teens were lining up to see *Jaws* and *Star Wars*, they forbade Mart and Steve from seeing movies, keeping them busy with church camps and Bible schools. Every Sunday and Wednesday, the family attended church in a small brick building in a rundown neighborhood on the south side of the city. As David worked, Barbara taught Sunday school and led the church choir. David saw a lot of his own mother in her when she got up in the middle of the night to pray, keeping track of her progress in handwritten journals.[41]

Barbara gave the kids nicknames—her firstborn, Mart, was her "lion," who "possessed the gifts of a natural leader from an early age." In 1975, Mart entered Bethany High, a school with just two hundred students. With a big mop of blond hair and oversized glasses, he was bright and popular and was elected president of student council and all-school king. He lettered in football and track, became president of the school's chapter of the Fellowship of Christian Athletes, and led "huddles" before games to celebrate Jesus as their lord and savior. In 1979, Mart graduated with highest honors, appearing in a full-page yearbook photo wearing a three-piece suit in front of a case of awards, Bible in his hand. He was "the kind of man who knows how to get things done," said David, who began to share details of his business with Mart and listen to his advice.[42]

Younger brother Steve followed two years behind, sporting a blond Mark Hamill bowl cut and shy smile. His mother called him her "lamb." Quieter and more thoughtful than Mart, he listened more than he talked and chose his words carefully. David worried about his lack of assertiveness, finding him too gentle—and perhaps seeing some of his own childhood shyness reflected in his younger son. "Frankly, I found it frustrating," he later admitted. "I came down on him rather forcefully at times." Steve tried to equal, if not outdo, his older brother's accomplishments—likewise voted all-school king, as well as vice president of his senior class and student council, and also graduating with highest honors. He lettered in basketball, track, and football, and *The Oklahoman* carried notices of the touchdown passes he snatched as a wide receiver.[43]

In 1980, David and Barbara crossed the town line into the suburb of Bethany, moving into a two-story slab home with a brick facade, peaked gables, attached garage, and enclosed swimming pool—eight thousand square feet in all.[44] In their prosperity, David continued to give back to the Church of God of Prophecy, taking out a mortgage on their new home for $116,000 and spending $120,000 to purchase a plot of land in Springfield, a tidy neighborhood of ranch-style homes in the southwest part of the city.[45] Within a week, they sold the land to the church for $100,000—essentially making a $20,000 in-kind charitable donation that they could deduct from their taxes and at the same time helping the church. The congregation broke ground on a new $1 million sanctuary and parsonage.[46] The Green children were popular in spite of their extreme religious beliefs, says one former classmate, who remembers attending a Sunday-night service at the Greens' church and hearing a fire-and-brimstone "end times" sermon by an itinerant evangelist connecting an apocalyptic vision with Middle East politics. "I remember seeing it as crazy, even from a Nazarene point of view," he says. But it helped that the family was already one of the wealthiest in town, with regular pool parties at their enormous home; at the same time, he says, Mart and Steve were always unfailingly nice and "never flashy or arrogant."[47]

David wasn't easy on the kids, insisting that they get jobs in high school. "The hardest thing for me is to not do something for you," he told them, but "God put Adam and Eve in the garden to work." Both boys worked at Hobby Lobby, painting buildings and unloading trucks along with their cousins Jeff and Randy, who lived with David's family while their father traveled as a preacher.[48] Despite a late-'70s downturn in the economy, the company continued to thrive. If anything, the arts and crafts business seemed recession-proof, as people turned to do-it-yourself hobbies and homemade gifts to save money.

The Tenth Street store began offering classes in the hot new craft of macramé—creating handwoven decor from knots and beads—as well as trendy hobbies of decoupage and tole painting.[49] The company added another seven thousand square feet to its flagship store, selling a bewildering array of needlework kits, rug yarn, tinware, and other craft supplies, as well as a new addition with plastic models, remote-controlled cars, board games, and rocket kits.[50] Barbara oversaw the selection of Christmas items that became an instant moneymaker for the store. Flush with success, Hobby Lobby opened another location downtown as well as another two hours away in Tulsa, bringing the total number to four.[51]

FROM THE BEGINNING, cheap prices were at the heart of Hobby Lobby's sales strategy, as the company bought in bulk from low-cost Asian suppliers. David began visiting overseas factories in China, the Philippines, and other countries to buy directly from the source. Early ads were full of sales to make the customer feel that they were getting a bargain: "Ready Made Frames 1/2 off!" "Cross-stitch and crochet 20% off!" "Christmas Gift Items 75% off!"[52]

Along with the low prices, David set out to have the largest selection among his competitors, with wide aisles organized for a neat and orderly shopping experience—a strategy he inherited from his McLellan's boss, T. Texas Tyler. David knew that shopping for crafts at Hobby Lobby wasn't something like grocery shopping that customers had to do, so he worked to make the experience as pleasing and enjoyable as possible for women (nearly all his customers were female).[53] As part of that environment, he subtly piped music into the stores that would be "uplifting but not harsh" to enhance "the atmosphere without dominating or distracting." Often, those songs were religious in nature, allowing Christian customers to "recognize selections they've heard in their churches or at a concert," David said.[54]

Christian values suffused everything he did at the company. Theft and sexual misconduct were automatic firing offenses, he said, and he insisted on honest dealing with suppliers, refusing kickbacks and reporting when they mistakenly delivered more product than they should.

"It's all part of our corporate commitment to follow biblical principles in everything we do," David said. "Some businesspeople think that's a noble claim but that it ties one hand behind your back. I disagree. Nothing taught in the Bible is harmful to business. Doing things God's way pays dividends—maybe not immediately, but in the long run."[55]

As David focused his energy on growing his business, evangelical Christians began focusing on a new ethical crusade that eventually became very important for the Green family: abortion. Contrary to popular perception, Christians didn't rally against abortion immediately after the Supreme Court's *Roe v. Wade* decision codified the right to it in 1973. The importance of the issue arose in the late 1970s as part of a larger alignment of religious conservatives with the Republican Party.

Though Catholics had long opposed abortion, evangelical Protestants were initially split on the issue; as late as 1968, Billy Graham's *Christianity Today* organized a roundtable of evangelical theologians who stated, "God does not regard the fetus as a soul no matter how far gestation has progressed." In support of this, the magazine cited a verse in Exodus stating that killing a woman was a capital offense, but assaulting her in a way that killed her fetus was not. "Clearly, then, in contrast to the mother, the fetus is not reckoned as a soul."[56] Other theologians pointed to Genesis 2:7, which suggests that the soul is not formed until a baby takes their first breath.[57]

When *Roe* passed, some conservative Christians decried the ruling, but others ignored it or even praised it; at their 1974 convention, Southern Baptists celebrated *Roe* as a compromise between extremes. As religious historian Randall Balmer relates, what really upset evangelicals at the time was not abortion but attempts by the Internal Revenue Service (IRS) to tax religious schools.[58]

In the wake of the civil rights movement, many white families fled public schools for private academies that liberals attacked as segregationist. When in 1975 the IRS sought to revoke the tax-exempt status of Bob Jones University in South Carolina for its racist admissions policies, evangelicals saw it as an existential threat to their ability to educate children as they saw fit. Among those who protested was forty-six-year-old Southern Baptist minister Jerry Falwell, who had founded Liberty Baptist College in Lynchburg, Virginia, and decried gays, feminists, and civil rights agitators on his *Old Time Gospel Hour* radio and TV show.[59]

As Balmer explains, a group of young conservatives saw in the battle a chance to woo religious voters to the Republican Party in the same way that liberals had used religion to foment opposition to the Vietnam War. In a 1979 meeting with Falwell in Lynchburg, libertarian activist Paul Weyrich, eventual founder of the Heritage Foundation, lamented that a "moral majority" of Christian Americans were underrepresented in society. Falwell asked him to repeat the phrase before crying out, "That's the name for this organization—the Moral Majority."[60] Founded in June 1979, the new coalition cycled through a number of issues to emphasize, including school prayer, communism, and feminism, before settling on a cause they felt could unite evangelicals with urgency and emotion: abortion.

Falwell latched on to the work of Francis Schaeffer, a Swiss-born seminarian who identified "secular humanism" as a malevolent force corrupting Western civilization. Called the "intellectual father of the antiabortion movement," Schaeffer singled out abortion for special condemnation in a 1979 book and film he coauthored with born-again pediatric surgeon C. Everett Koop. They referred to a verse in Genesis stating that God had created humans "in the image of God"—in Latin, *imago dei*—to argue that humans were unique and deserving of inherent dignity. Reverence for life had to begin in the womb, they insisted; if not, other forms of violence in society were inevitable.[61]

Antiabortion activists scoured the Bible for references to "conception" or "seed," latching on to another verse in the book of Jeremiah in which God says, "Before I formed you in the womb, I knew you."[62] Previously, it had been interpreted to mean that God has a plan for everyone, but after *Roe*, it was used specifically to refer to the notion that life begins at conception.[63]

Falwell took these scriptures and ran with them at "I Love America" rallies on the steps of state capitols around the country throughout the summer and fall of 1979. The rallies featured singers decked out in red, white, and blue, surrounded by American flags. Soft-spoken and portly, Falwell favored blue business suits and lacquered hair, looking more like a businessman in town for a sales conference than a fire-and-brimstone preacher.[64] But in the run-up to the 1980 election, he succeeded as much as anyone in tilting evangelicals toward the Republican Party.

Abortion always came first for Falwell, who called the Moral Majority "pro-life, pro-family, and pro-Bible," in that order.[65] In fact, he drew an explicit connection between abortion and promiscuity outside marriage, saying women who had abortions were necessarily "pregnant because of sin"—otherwise they'd want to keep their baby. The fight against abortion thus also became a fight against the loose morality of some single women.[66] "America needs a divine healing," he said with a Bible under his arm, "but there can be no divine healing unless there is a divine purging. Abortion must be stopped."[67] After abortion, a second target was homosexuals, who, "just like alcoholics, are people with a problem, with a need" that needed to be solved. "We're to love the sinner, but hate the sin," he insisted. But if these problems were not addressed, "the very existence of the monogamous family is in question," setting up the "disintegration of the home."[68]

In the midst of this strident political rhetoric, David Green felt inspired for the first time to put his wallet where his convictions were, showing that his business was more than just a moneymaking enterprise. In September 1979, he flew to Cleveland, Tennessee, for the Church of God of Prophecy's annual assembly, just as his father had done decades earlier, visiting the Fields of the Wood along with other participants. After decades of fundraising, the park had expanded, with twenty-nine solid concrete markers spelling out tenets of church doctrine along the steps up Prayer Mountain—sanctification, holiness, speaking in tongues, washing of feet, tithing, the second coming of Jesus, eternal punishments for the wicked, and other points of faith.

Across the parking lot, another mountain had been cleared of trees and covered in huge concrete blocks spelling out the Ten Commandments in the language of the King James Bible. Each letter was five feet tall, and together they stretched for a hundred yards across the mountainside with the words that Moses had supposedly brought down from Mount Sinai. At the top, a gigantic Bible looked out over the valley.

Lost between the two mountains was a small monument with lines from the Gospel of Matthew 28:19: "Go ye therefore, and teach all nations, baptizing them in the name of the Father, and of the Son, and of the Holy Ghost." Known as the Great Commission, the words are seen as the last words of Jesus to his apostles after he rose from the dead, an admonition to carry his teachings across the globe and an inspiration to the church's missionary work.

The next day, David filed with other congregants into the church's brutalist concrete tabernacle to listen to speaker after speaker extol the virtues of Christ and detail the coming battle of Armageddon, when the Antichrist would fight Jesus for control of his kingdom. The church leader in charge of translating and distributing biblical literature around the world made an impassioned call for funds, likening the texts to life-giving rain. "Our Church dollars are producing more souls in the far away places that are so dry and thirsty and hungry for the living waters," he said.[69]

David shifted in his seat, thinking of the doilies his mother had sold at the church bazaar to support missionaries overseas. Until now,

David had always made his tithes of 10 percent to the church. What more could he give? Surely he couldn't risk any of the money he needed to expand Hobby Lobby. *Maybe later*, he told himself. *I need to use every dollar now to grow this business.* The following morning, after leading a pledge of allegiance to the Bible, overseer M. A. Tomlinson announced a new crusade focused on upholding family values as the heart of the church—echoing the broader message of evangelicals such as Dobson, Gothard, and Falwell. "We are all aware of the attack Satan is making on the entire family structure," he said. "Our concern requires that we arise and launch a counter-attack." Everyone in the audience, he said, must work to spread God's word, "not just when everything is pleasant, not just when we have no opposition—we must work while it is day, while we have the opportunity!"[70]

David thought about the message later as he gazed out the airplane window on this way home. At that moment, he heard a quiet voice inside say, *You need to give $30,000 for Bible literature.* He recognized it as God, but he pushed it away. *That's impossible*, he prayed. *God, I don't have $30,000.* But the voice insisted. *You're serious about this, aren't you?* he thought. Maybe there was a way. If he broke the amount into four payments of $7,500, he could pay one a month through the rest of the year. When he got home, he prayed with Barbara, and they agreed it could work, so they dropped four postdated checks in the mail to Tennessee.

A few days later, David got a call from a church official who told him that four missionaries in Africa had held a prayer meeting for literature funds on the same day the Greens had sent the checks. "Looks like God answered their prayer!" he said. When David heard that, "something clicked inside me." All of his lingering guilt about not living up to his mother's plea "to do something for the Lord" disappeared, and for the first time, David felt at peace. "It settled permanently inside of me that God had a purpose for a businessman," he said. "He had called me. He had blessed me. There must be a role for people like me in the work of the Kingdom of God."[71]

From then on, Hobby Lobby would be a "company that gives," David vowed. "Since I believe there's a real heaven and a real hell, I want to direct as many people toward heaven and away from hell as I can."[72] That gift was more precious—and more generous—than any other purpose he could think of, potentially affecting the world for thousands of years in the future. "Giving like we do is exciting," David said. "It's an adventure."[73]

In the coming years, David and his family would devote more and more of their money and time to that adventure, working to ensure that Jesus's message of salvation reached around the globe. But first, David would experience his own crisis of faith.

CHAPTER THREE

Thy Kingdom Come

One day in 1982, David found himself outside an oil company facility in Oklahoma City, praying. He walked around the plant, beseeching God to stop taking Hobby Lobby's employees away.[1] For months, Hobby Lobby had been losing its best people, as Oklahoma was in the midst of an unprecedented oil and gas boom. It had started in the Anadarko Basin in West Oklahoma, where prospectors had discovered new natural gas deposits by digging ultradeep wells. By the early '80s, they were investing billions in new leases as newly rich oilmen took helicopters to Dallas and private jets to Europe. For the first time, Oklahoma had a per capita income on par with the rest of the country.

Hobby Lobby initially capitalized on this good fortune, opening several new stores and a giant warehouse alongside the Oklahoma River, allowing the company to buy in even larger quantities. Each time another store moved out of the Tenth Street shopping center, Hobby Lobby gobbled up the space, now occupying a full fifty thousand square feet.[2] The company began selling more expensive items to appeal to newly rich Oklahomans, including Samsonite luggage, grandfather clocks, and exotic foods such as "bird's nest soup."[3] Seward oversaw a fine art department with numbered lithographs selling for more than $1,000 each. Still, the parking lot filled early every morning, the overflow spilling into a neighboring field. "Christmas shoppers are elbow-to-elbow in the five stores owned by Greene and Seward," read an article in *The Oklahoman* during the 1980 holiday season, spelling David's name wrong in the company's first major newspaper feature.[4]

The pair were so confident that they didn't even consider opening a store in one of the indoor shopping malls that were fast becoming the center of American social life. "We don't feel we need the built-in traffic," Seward said. "We'll create our own."[5] Real estate agents began advertising homes as "close to Hobby Lobby" as church groups and homemaker associations planned social outings to stores. ("We oohed and aahed over everything they had," said one satisfied Okmulgee housewife.")[6] Hobby Lobby ended 1980 with two hundred employees and sales of $10 million.[7] Even then, David had loftier ambitions—"Thirty stores, each of them doing $2.5 million a year in sales volume," he said. "Wouldn't that be great?"[8]

As DAVID AND Hobby Lobby prospered, the next generation of Greens was thriving as well. After Mart graduated from high school, he took classes at Bethany Nazarene College and a semester at the church's Tomlinson Bible College in Tennessee, but he felt that he'd rather be working. He called his father to remind him about a conversation they'd had about opening a new store selling Bibles and other religious books. "You're really going to do it?" Mart asked. David turned it back on him: "Well, you wanna do it? If you come home I'll help you get a loan."[9]

Mart returned to Oklahoma City, and David helped him locate space in a shopping center near their home, suggesting that he sell office supplies in addition to books.[10] In the summer of 1981, at age nineteen, Mart opened Mardel Office & Christian Supply (named for a combination of his first and middle name, Mart Delyn), promising a "vast range of office supplies" along with "Oklahoma's largest selection of religious books."[11] By now, Christian publishing was a phenomenon, with multiple books by James Dobson and Billy Graham topping the charts along with the apocalyptic fiction of Hal Lindsey and Schaeffer and Koop's antiabortion book.[12] The store grossed $8,000 in sales its first month, $34,000 its second, and soared to $91,000 a month by Christmas.[13]

When Steve graduated from high school in 1981, he thought about college but decided "I'd be further ahead if I were to just go ahead and start working." He joined Hobby Lobby full-time as store operations manager, his father's liaison between branches and corporate headquarters.[14]

Meanwhile, the new church building David had funded was going up fast, with a majestic triangular brick facade and soaring white steeple. In one of its first ceremonies, Mart walked down the aisle on a Friday night in January 1982 to marry Diane Kay Maddox, a longtime Bethany resident with a shy smile and blunt-cut bangs who had been a cheerleader as well as a fellow member of math club and student council.[15]

By now, David was setting aside money every year for the church's missionary work, feeling like God was personally blessing him with the continued success of the company. Hobby Lobby opened a new location focused specifically on fashion, stocking calico fabrics so homemakers could sew the flounced skirts of the "prairie style" then in vogue across the country, while Mart opened a Mardel next door.[16] By Hobby Lobby's tenth anniversary, the company had seven stores with annual sales of $18 million—double the amount of just two years earlier.[17]

The only problem was that the raging economy from the oil boom threatened to decimate Hobby Lobby's workforce. As civic boosters predicted a hundred-year spike of prosperity, the gas companies were able to offer wages David just couldn't match. In desperation, he drove out to the oil plant to pray for God to stop taking employees away. To his delight, God listened, personally rewarding his faith. "From that day on, we stopped losing our best people," he said. "God cares about our problems. He cares about employee retention."[18]

A more secular explanation for the reversal can be found in the events of Fourth of July weekend 1982, when Oklahoma City's Penn Square Bank suddenly collapsed. Initially founded in a shopping mall, the bank had grown flush on increasingly risky loans to wildcatters, ultimately lending $2 billion on some $500 million in assets and selling shares to other banks as well. When the price of oil dropped from $40 to $28 a barrel due to supply increases, Penn Square watched its borrowers default on loan after loan, spurring a Bailey Bros. Building & Loan–style run on Friday, July 2. Bank employees brought ice water to depositors who lined up outside its headquarters in 90-degree heat. By Monday, the bank was insolvent—the country's largest-ever banking collapse.[19]

At the time, David took pleasure in the comeuppance of Penn Square, which had denied Hobby Lobby a loan when the company was first starting out. "If Penn Square had only been willing to take a $1,000 risk on us, they would have had at least one good loan to show the auditors!"[20] he joked. But eventually, the bank's demise would ripple out to take down the entire Oklahoma economy, and Hobby Lobby with it, bringing the company to the brink of disaster.

EVEN AS THAT time bomb was ticking, David and his family could celebrate the fact that the country was waking up to Jesus at last. In April 1980, a half-million evangelicals poured onto the National Mall under overcast skies for the Washington for Jesus rally, marking the arrival of the religious right as a political force. Organized by broadcaster Pat Robertson and Campus Crusade's Bill Bright, the event featured fasting, speeches, and lobbying with a clear message: the nation had sunk into a pit of immorality due to drug use, homosexuality, and abortion and had to be saved. "We have enough votes to run the country," Robertson thundered. "And when the people say, 'We've had enough,' we are going to take over."[21]

There was no question whom those votes would go toward—the California actor–turned–presidential candidate Ronald Reagan. While born-again Baptist Jimmy Carter had been a huge disappointment to evangelicals, Reagan represented the muscular platform they craved, with his support for school prayer, the teaching of creationism, and a constitutional amendment to protect "the right of life for unborn children."[22] In August, Reagan made an appearance with a who's who of evangelical leaders, including Robertson, Bright, Falwell, and Tim LaHaye—a Christian author and political operative who had been influenced by Rushdoony and argued that America was a Christian nation that must be governed by biblical authority in family, church, and government.[23] Reagan touted his love of the Bible. "All the complex answers facing us at home and abroad," he said, "have their answer in that single book."[24]

A few weeks later, he won the presidency in a landslide due in no small part to white evangelicals, who voted for him by a two-thirds margin.[25] Soon Rushdoony himself came knocking at the White House with a delegation of religious conservatives seeking to restore tax-exempt status for religious schools that had engaged in racial segregation. But Reagan shocked them by opposing the move. "He expects loyalty while giving none," Rushdoony fumed.[26] Reagan at least stayed tough against communism, calling the Soviet Union an "evil empire" in a speech to the National Association of Evangelicals in March 1983. In the same speech, he told the group that belief in separation of church and state had been confused, and the Founders had "never intended to construct a wall of hostility between government and the concept of religious belief."[27] At Bright's suggestion, he declared 1983 the Year of the Bible.[28]

Beyond such symbolism, however, Reagan's tenure proved frustrating to evangelicals on culture issues, as the amendment to support school prayer failed by eleven votes in the Senate and an amendment to overturn *Roe* failed by eighteen. Adding insult to injury, Reagan appointed Sandra Day O'Connor, a judge with known proabortion views, to the Supreme Court.[29]

In fact, polls showed wide support for *Roe*, with more than 75 percent of Americans approving of abortion in some or all cases. That didn't stop evangelicals from continuing to push on the issue. In 1981, Francis Schaeffer issued a new rallying call in *A Christian Manifesto*, singling out abortion as antithetical to the beliefs of the Founders and urging opponents to picket abortion clinics and bring lawsuits to prohibit taxpayer funds from going toward the procedure.

That legal strategy was picked up by his son, Franky Schaeffer, an admirer of Rushdoony, who helped launch a legal advocacy organization called the Rutherford Institute with the elder Reconstructionist. Warning of a "religious apartheid" suppressing the views of Christians, the organization pursued a new strategy of taking on cases in court to defend state laws on abortion as well as Christian homeschooling and school prayer, setting a pattern for other legal groups to follow.[30]

Falwell included *A Christian Manifesto* in a "God Bless America Survival Kit" that he mailed to thousands of supporters. In his own manifesto, *Listen, America!*, Falwell presented the most comprehensive fundamentalist vision for America, echoing Rushdoony and LaHaye to contend that America had been founded as a Christian nation; "Only by godly leadership," he concluded, "can America be put back on a divine course."[31]

That meant fighting against both the USSR abroad and feminists and homosexuals at home to return America to a biblical worldview. "A thorough study of the Bible will show that it is indeed the inerrant Word of the living God," Falwell wrote, adding that the "Bible clearly states that life begins at conception" and abortion was "murder according to the Word of God."[32]

By the time the elder Schaeffer died in 1984, his ideas were ensconced among evangelicals, if not yet among mainstream Republicans. Despite their disappointments, evangelicals had little choice but to support Reagan for reelection against liberal Democrat Walter Mondale. Falwell openly campaigned for the incumbent, calling Democrats the party of "homosexuals, militant feminists, socialists, freezeniks, and others of the ilk." In the end, 80 percent of evangelicals voted for Reagan, who breezed to reelection on the strength of a booming economy bolstered by military spending.[33]

DESPITE THE PROBLEMS brewing in Oklahoma, the decade of materialism was now in full swing as Wall Street corporate raiders minted money through leveraged buyouts and hostile takeovers. Everything in the culture celebrated excess: Robin Leach wishing his viewers "champagne wishes and caviar dreams" while touring celebrity homes and brash playboy Donald Trump slapping his name on New York skyscrapers and Atlantic City casinos. Even among less wealthy Americans, chunky jewelry, designer handbags, and other signs of conspicuous consumption were legion.[34]

While some evangelicals decried such displays, the most prominent among them indulged them. The early '80s were a new Jerusalem for televangelism, symbolized by Jim Bakker's bright suits and gold chains and Tammy Faye's caked-on eyeshadow and platinum-blond bouffant. The husband-and-wife preachers touted their wealth in an array of consumption, including million-dollar mansions, twin Mercedes sedans, and a sprawling Christian theme park. They became masters of the fundraising appeal, weeping, rejoicing, and persuading viewers with close-up camera shots to send in money for promises of untold riches in return.[35]

They were not the only ones vying for the bank accounts of the faithful, as televangelist preachers turned the prosperity gospel into high art. Traditional Pentecostals may have looked askance at the charismatic televangelists siphoning off the savings of born-again believers all over Middle America, but devotees were more than happy to send in seed checks of $50, $100, or $500 in hopes that a piece of the wealth paraded in the media would return to them.[36]

The creator of it all, Oral Roberts, now commanded an annual budget of $125 million between his TV show, public revivals, and namesake university. His metastasizing Tulsa-based empire added a law school, a business school, and—most shockingly for the onetime faith healer—a fully accredited medical school in a three-tower complex he called the City of Faith. When funds for construction lagged, he said a nine-hundred-foot-tall Jesus appeared to him and lifted the entire complex off its foundation. A half-million people responded with $5 million in a month.[37]

David's own prosperity seemed like a reward for his unshakable faith as God continued to rain down blessings upon him. Even after the Penn Square collapse, the recession-proof Hobby Lobby seemed only to benefit as people once again turned to hobbies, and banks were only too eager to lend to a solid investment in a sea of red ink. David snapped up loans to add two or three stores every year, including Hobby Lobby's first stores outside Oklahoma in Wichita, Kansas, and Little Rock, Arkansas, in 1984.[38]

Even with the growing distance, David stuck to TG&Y's strategy of using a single warehouse to stock the stores, moving his corporate headquarters into a new 86,500-square-foot warehouse and office complex on SW Thirty-Sixth Street, facing the airport. Construction cost $1.2 million, a mere fraction of the $30 million in annual sales brought in by the company's stores.[39]

Mart followed in his father's wake with new locations of Mardel, taking advantage of the booming trade in Christian books—with James Dobson's child-rearing books as perennial bestsellers alongside books on relationships by Tim LaHaye and his wife, Beverly, and books by and about Ronald Reagan.[40] As Mart expanded his reach, Steve continued to rise through the ranks at Hobby Lobby, with stints in purchasing, legal, and accounting, in hopes of learning the business well enough to take over for his father one day.[41]

Despite Steve's work ethic, David remained disappointed by his soft-spoken son's gentle style of management. He added Steve to his prayers, begging God to give him a stronger backbone. Behind his introverted persona, however, Steve had a penchant for risk-taking, including a lead foot behind the wheel. In 1983, the nineteen-year-old played a game of chicken with his seventeen-year-old girlfriend, Jackie Denise Chartier, a Pentecostal from the Tulsa suburb of Coweta whom he'd met at a summer camp.[42] As they careened toward each other, "no one turned off," as Steve later recalled, and they crashed head-on, totaling both cars.[43]

A year later, Steve married Jackie at the Coweta Church of God of Prophecy, sporting a mustache and all-white tuxedo with a baby-pink bow tie and cummerbund to match Jackie's white dress and pink bouquet. Officiating the ceremony was a pastor from the mother church in Cleveland who was head of the church's world literature department, which Hobby Lobby had continued to fund.[44] Two months later, Steve attended Bill Gothard's Basic Seminar and applied biblical principles to their marriage and parenting as the couple began having children. Later, they took a weeklong vacation together to Fort Worth, Texas, to attend Gothard's Advanced Seminar.[45]

As the boys were distinguishing themselves at work, their sister, Darsee, was still attending high school. She lacked the academic drive of her older brothers, earning a solid B average in classes, but made up for it in spunk as an enthusiastic member of the pep club and cheerleading squad.[46] Barbara called her their "monkey," and David favored her as "vivacious, creative, and a fount of happiness." Chosen as homecoming queen her senior year, Darsee also won awards for speech and creative writing and acted in the school play. After graduating in 1985, she worked part-time as a receptionist at Hobby Lobby while studying for a year at Southern Nazarene and grew close to a tall Bethany High grad named Robert Stanley Lett who excelled at both academics and basketball. Soon the two were engaged.[47]

EVEN AS HOBBY Lobby managed a dozen stores by 1985, a disaster was looming. Following the Penn Square collapse, a steady beat of bank closings finally trickled down to Main Street as manufacturing and service jobs disappeared. At the time, Steve was teaching a new Bible class for young married couples at the insistence of his youth pastor, reading the entire book over three and a half years.[48] One day over lunch, he told his father he was worried about Bible passages that frowned on taking on debt.

"We're up to our eyeballs," Steve said. "What if the market doesn't respond the way we think it will?"[49] Steve had reason to be concerned, as he had just bought Mart's former home as an investment and was paying two mortgages at once, but David shook off the warning. Meanwhile, the price of oil continued to fall, dipping into the $20s by mid-1985 and then below $10 as Saudi Arabia increased production, just in time for Hobby Lobby's busy Christmas season. Grandfather clocks and art prints now seemed like frivolous luxuries and even craft supplies unessential as the stream of customers dried up with the flow of oil in the derricks.[50]

David begged creditors for leniency as he struggled to make loan payments, but they refused. He began dodging calls as he fought to pay water and electricity bills. When the company completed inventory, he found that despite $25 million in sales, Hobby Lobby had lost nearly $1 million in 1985, an amount greater than the last two years of profit. The central-warehouse strategy that had kept costs down now came back to bite them as hundreds of thousands of dollars' worth of unused inventory sat dormant. The company reduced truck trips, leading to even less product at stores. David canceled raises and slashed hours, cut down on advertising, and sold off property, but nothing helped. He stopped sleeping, captive to the endless march of numbers through his head.[51]

That spring, David began praying under the heavy mahogany desk inside Hobby Lobby's new headquarters. Crawling under there was the only way he could talk to God without feeling the ever-present shame of failure. *What would you have us do differently?* he begged. While he'd heard instructions from God in the past, now he heard only mockery: *If you're so big, I'm going to let you have it by yourself.* God was punishing him, David concluded. He'd gotten proud from all his years of success, and now God had removed his blessing, just as he had from the Old Testament kings who'd turned their backs on Jehovah.[52]

David took to wandering at night in Bethany's Eldon Lyon Park, literally crying out to God for help. He couldn't get around the gnawing worry that he'd ruined his family through his arrogance and greed. His three children were all employed by the company, as were Darsee's fiancé and his two nephews. If it went under, they'd all be out of work. While Barbara also prayed nonstop, she seemed somehow stronger than he. "It's God's business," she assured him. "If he takes it away, we'll do something else."[53]

David wasn't the only one who was stressed. As Steve and Jackie struggled to keep up with their mortgage payments, Jackie started working part-time at Hobby Lobby as a buyer's assistant, even as she was pregnant with their first child.[54]

One day in April 1986, David called the family to his Bethany home to tell them they were in "serious trouble," fighting back tears as he described his fears of losing the company. "Dad, it's okay," twenty-four-year-old Mart told him. "Our faith is not in you—it's in God. If we lose the businesses, we'll still be okay." The words struck David like a lightning bolt—a "humbling and powerful moment in my life that I will never forget," he later said. Steve chimed in, "Whatever happens, Dad, we love you." It was like the air being let out of a balloon. The family talked soberly about the missteps the company had made in getting away from the core arts-and-crafts business to sell high-priced luxury items; if it was going to survive, they would need to get back to their roots.[55]

THE FAMILY CAME together a month later to celebrate Darsee and Stan's wedding at the Springfield church.[56] Meanwhile, David continued to rob Peter to pay Paul, taking out a loan of $200,000 from First National Bank of Oklahoma City, which insisted that he keep $40,000 of it in a certificate of deposit account even though he'd be paying interest on the whole amount. *They know I'm desperate, and they think they can do anything to me*, David seethed.[57] In June, he took out another loan for $1.3 million from Union Bank but was already behind on payments by November.[58]

The bank sent a letter demanding "immediate and full payment" or it would sue.[59] It was a standard demand letter for nonpayment, but David felt unfairly persecuted, as if the bank were coming after him only because he had some cash flow, unlike the oil companies that were deep in the red. "I shuddered," he said. "They were threatening to foreclose on everything we owned." He found a new lender in the Bank of Oklahoma, which was willing to pay off the loan. Afterward, he had the demand letter framed and hung up at headquarters "as a reminder of what we had survived."[60]

Slowly, the company sold off its high-end products as it returned to its original mission of low-priced goods. By the end of 1986, Hobby Lobby was again showing a profit of $1.2 million.[61] David cautiously celebrated the turnaround, daring to hope that his company—and his family—had weathered the storm. As traumatic as the experience was, difficulties during a downturn are not uncommon for young companies. He could have learned lessons about the risks of taking on too much leverage or diluting his brand with superfluous product lines.[62] But David drew a different conclusion, one that would have a dramatic impact on the way he lived his life ever after—choosing to follow God in all things.

While he had always said his company "belonged to God," the trauma of nearly losing it redoubled his conviction to always consult God as a silent partner. "Whenever I consider taking a risk in business, I dare not leave him out of the equation," he told himself. "What he thinks is what I desperately need to know. Otherwise, I can get in huge trouble."[63]

From that moment on, everything in life seemed a personal message to him from God—and everything depended on how he responded.

IF DAVID NEEDED another object lesson in the Proverb "Pride goeth… before a fall," he had only to look at the spectacular demise of televangelism beginning in 1986, when Pentecostal Jimmy Swaggart openly accused fellow Assemblies of God preacher Marvin Gorman of adultery.[64] Gorman admitted to one act of "attempted intercourse" as his ministry went bankrupt. But Swaggart was far from done, as he also investigated another rival for holy dollars, PTL's Jim Bakker. He publicly accused Bakker of a "tryst" with church secretary Jessica Hahn, who later said Bakker had raped her in a Florida hotel room before then paying her nearly $300,000 in hush money. (Bakker claimed they'd had consensual sex.)

Bakker's ally Oral Roberts accused Swaggart of "sowing discord among the brethren." But Roberts had his own problems; after his City of Faith lost money as soon as it opened, he told his followers that God had instructed him to raise $8 million or God would "call Oral Roberts home" to heaven. Swaggart said he was embarrassed for his fellow Pentecostal, "telling people that if they don't send money, that God's going to kill him." Meanwhile, allegations mounted against Bakker of sexual encounters with both men and women as well as fraudulent fundraising practices that eventually sent him to prison.

A few months later, Gorman got payback when an investigator he hired took a photo of Swaggart entering a New Orleans motel with a prostitute. Swaggart tearfully confessed his sin, and the media had a field day exposing the hypocrisy of men of God who preached family values they couldn't live up to. Televangelist viewership fell from fifteen million to ten million as the flashy preachers became symbols of the decade's greed. Jerry Falwell took over PTL from Bakker but eventually shuttered the network, and even his Moral Majority foundered. Roberts's City of Faith closed in 1989, and the Moral Majority disbanded the same year as Falwell lamely declared, "Our mission is accomplished."[65]

Nothing could have been further from the truth. Reagan's second term was as much a letdown to evangelicals as his first, with the abortion amendment a dead letter as soon as Democrats took over Congress in 1986. Some began taking up Franky Schaeffer's call for civil disobedience, including used-car salesman and part-time pastor Randall Terry, who founded Operation Rescue in 1987 to picket abortion clinics with grotesque pictures of aborted fetuses and encourage followers to risk arrest by locking arms to prevent entry.

Frustrated that the president had given conservative Christians visibility but few accomplishments, Pat Robertson decided to run for president himself, counting on the white evangelical vote to propel him to victory. The taint of the televangelist scandals, as well as publicity about some of his more extreme comments on the *700 Club*, however, wounded his candidacy. In 1986, he frightened potential voters with comments that "God's plan... is for his people to take dominion" over government, a reference to the Reconstructionist dogma of Christians such as Rushdoony.[66] Billy Graham's *Christianity Today* ran a series of articles condemning dominionism, declaring it out of step with American democracy.

Rushdoony did himself no favors when he appeared in a PBS interview saying he really believed that, according to the Bible, homosexuals, unchaste women, and disobedient children should be executed. "Some of it rubs me the wrong way," he said. "But I'm simply saying this is what God requires."[67] Robertson failed to win majority support even among evangelicals, as Republicans threw their weight behind Reagan's vice president and eventual winner George H. W. Bush, who practiced a quieter form of Christian faith. By that time, the media and academia were writing the obituary for evangelical politics.[68]

THE TELEVANGELISM SCANDALS of the late 1980s had no effect on the Green family's faith. After Hobby Lobby's near-death experience, David and his children turned even more strongly to the Bible as their guide. On his first overseas business trip to China in 1988, Steve stared out the train window at farmers in mile after mile of rice fields, contrasting the lack of industry under communism with the free-market wealth of the United States, which he attributed to the Bible's influence, based on the eighth commandment, "Thou shalt not steal."[69]

While Victorian utopianists and Latin American liberation theologists have found support for socialism in Jesus's defense of the poor, conservative white evangelicals saw the Bible as unrepentantly capitalist. The view is spelled out most clearly by Rushdoony's son-in-law, Gary North, who took up Rushdoony's mantle in the 1980s with a ten-part series on biblical economics. He argued that socialism by its very nature seeks to replace faith in God with faith in mankind, amounting to a "government takeover" of the functions God delegated to the individual, the family, and the church.

In her book *Building God's Kingdom*, religious studies scholar Julie Ingersoll argues that the influence of the Reconstructionist worldview on right-wing economic policies is vastly underrated. "God 'owns' everything," she writes, explaining the philosophy, "and insofar as humans have ownership they do so only by virtue of God's grace and under God's authority and primarily in the context of families and for the purpose of dominion."[70] David adopted that view in the wake of the oil crisis, when he gave "ownership" of Hobby Lobby to God to fulfill his purposes.

He primed his family for the task, beginning by smoothing over his frustrations with Steve's introverted leadership style. "Steve, I'm sorry," he told him. "I need to find out who you really are, and then work with that."[71] It turned out that Steve had a gift for real estate, and he oversaw Hobby Lobby's continued expansion. David found a place for Darsee, too, as creative director, overseeing advertising and store design. Mart needed no correction, as he was already doing well as head of Mardel, which continued to thrive on the ever-growing catalog of Christian books.

David latched on to the writings of popular Christian author Randy Alcorn, whose new book, *Money, Possessions, Eternity*, spelled out biblical economics in a user-friendly way. In a book replete with Bible verses, Alcorn argues in dominionist fashion that the Bible gives men and women "authority over all his creation" at the same time that it "repeatedly emphasizes God's ownership of everything."[72] In the wake of the televangelist scandals, he insisted that people were just stewards of their possessions, with God ultimately sitting in judgment on how well they used them. Alcorn put his own principles into practice when he was arrested several times for blocking abortion clinics and ordered to pay $8 million in damages. Refusing to pay money "to people who would use it to kill babies," he put all of his possessions into his wife's name and established a religious nonprofit, Eternal Perspective Ministries, to receive the royalties from his books.[73]

David took these teachings to heart as Hobby Lobby continued its turnaround, slowly paying off its debts and ending the decade with $75 million in annual sales. The company now had thirty-four stores, with trucks traveling as far as Albuquerque in the West, Omaha in the North, and Memphis in the East, and was breaking ground on a new $10 million, 800,000-square-foot warehouse complex.[74] David had reached the goal he'd set for himself a decade earlier: thirty stores, each doing $2.5 million in sales. At this rate, he figured the company would be pulling in over $200 million annually in five years. *What more could I do with that money?* he asked.[75]

IF ANYTHING, BUSH's moderate conservatism was even more of a disappointment to the faithful, as he reached out to gay activists and appointed prochoice David Souter to the Supreme Court. Only on foreign policy did he earn their support. After the fall of the Berlin Wall weakened communism in 1989, conservative hawks found a new enemy in Iraqi dictator Saddam Hussein, who invaded oil-rich Kuwait in the summer of 1990, drawing the United States into war on the doorstep of the Holy Land.[76]

Apocalyptic predictions exploded as doomsayers irresistibly associated Iraq with ancient Babylon and televangelists trotted out maps of the Middle East in their appeals for cash.[77] Hobby Lobby stores sold out of yellow ribbon in support of American troops. When US and British forces did invade, they routed Saddam in a one-hundred-hour war that showcased the might of America's reinvigorated war machine.

Meanwhile, Robertson organized his campaign mailing list into a new group, the Christian Coalition, which avoided Falwell's divisive tactics with the help of Ralph Reed, a baby-faced political operative. Rather than make controversial public pronouncements, he quietly mobilized conservative voters to win state and local races. "I do guerrilla warfare," he said. "You don't know it's over until you're in a body bag."[78]

As Bush faced political headwinds against liberal Arkansas governor Bill Clinton and right-wing populist Pat Buchanan in the 1992 election, he made a belated appeal to the Christian Coalition for support. In return, he veered to the right on social issues, with a platform that Reed championed as "the most conservative and most pro-family platform in the history of the party."[79] It advocated banning abortion, opposing civil rights protections for gay individuals, and returning prayer to schools. Though Bush lost, the new alliance held as Republicans and evangelical Christians became increasingly indistinguishable.[80]

To them, the new president Clinton represented the worst excesses of the 1960s: a liberal who had smoked marijuana and opposed the Vietnam War, supported gay rights and abortion, and—if allegations could be believed—repeatedly cheated on his wife. If anything, *she* was worse, a career woman who'd chosen a life in law and politics rather than staying home to raise her daughter. When Clinton enacted "don't ask, don't tell" to allow closeted gays to serve in the military, evangelicals' fears seemed to be realized.[81]

By the midterm elections, the Christian Coalition had dropped its "guerrilla" tactics to openly campaign for conservative politicians, ushering in Republican control of Congress under speaker Newt Gingrich's Contract with America. When that plan emphasized tax cuts, health care, and crime but not cultural issues, some evangelicals felt that Reed had been duped—or worse, was complicit.[82]

The biggest criticism came from James Dobson, the avuncular founder of Focus on the Family, who had created a political arm, the Family Research Council (FRC), which now mobilized Colorado voters to pass a measure amending the state constitution to prevent civil rights protections for homosexuals.[83] Dobson railed against Clinton, abortion, and secular humanism, declaring Christians under attack. He peppered his books with purported scientific evidence, using authoritative statements such as "most studies show" or "the weight of evidence proves."[84]

When in doubt, he fell back on the ultimate authority: the Bible, which couldn't be any clearer that homosexuality was a sin, for example, saying in Leviticus 18:22, "Thou shalt not lie with mankind, as with womankind; it is abomination" and in 20:13, "They shall surely be put to death." The apostle Paul, he said, had also called out "men who have sex with men" in a list of wicked people who will not "inherit the Kingdom of God."[85] Liberal theologians pushed back against that handful of Bible verses mentioning homosexuality. The prohibitions in Leviticus, they said, were part of purity laws including not eating shellfish that had been done away with by Christians, and Paul was referring to gay sex based on lust, not all gay relationships—but Dobson remained steadfast in his beliefs, influencing a generation of Christians.[86]

He now turned to the courts in the wake of Rushdoony and Schaeffer's Rutherford Institute with his own legal organization, the Alliance Defense Fund (ADF), created with Bill Bright and Florida megachurch pastor D. James Kennedy, whose book *Reconstruction: Biblical Guidelines for a Nation in Peril* was based in part on Rushdoony's ideas. The organization would raise money to train lawyers to support those ideas in religious freedom cases across the country.[87]

In a bipartisan compromise, Bill Clinton signed a new bill, the Religious Freedom Restoration Act, on the South Lawn of the White House on a sunny November day in 1993. Known as RFRA ("RIF-ra"), the law declared that the federal government should not "substantially burden a person's exercise of religion." If there was "compelling governmental interest" contradicting that exercise, the government must use "the least restrictive means" to further it. The law was passed nearly unanimously by Congress, supported by evangelical Christians, Muslims, Mormons, and the American Civil Liberties Union (ACLU) alike.[88] Over time, however, RFRA grew into something far different—a giant cudgel that those seeking to enshrine Christian ideals in society had at their disposal.

HOBBY LOBBY CONTINUED its expansion spree, doubling in two years to seventy stores with nearly $200 million in annual revenue by 1993, three years ahead of David's prediction.[89] David still relied on analog processes for distribution, eschewing the use of barcodes as he swore that it was quicker to ship products from overseas without waiting to tag them and that cashiers at stores got to know products better if forced to type in SKUs with every transaction.[90]

Though Hobby Lobby had long held off from expansion into Texas in deference to Dallas-based rival Michaels Stores, it was now expanding aggressively into the state with dozens of stores from El Paso to

Houston. "There's the drive to go out and conquer," Steve said. Michaels had many more stores and trounced Hobby Lobby sales with $1.2 billion annually, but Hobby Lobby's stores were larger, averaging more than fifty thousand square feet compared to less than twenty thousand for Michaels. The biggest difference between the two chains, however, was that Michaels was publicly traded, allowing it to leverage its stock to rapidly expand the company.[91]

That was unthinkable to David, who retained private control to keep freely giving company profits to his church's mission work. For years, the company also donated to arts organizations under the direction of Seward. In 1994, Seward decided to leave the company to focus on his own art practice, and David bought out his share, setting up a new family trust to assume ownership of Hobby Lobby.[92] Overwhelmingly, the Greens' donations were directed toward efforts to get people around the world to read the Bible. "We don't mind supporting good things in our community, but this kind of giving is not the central reason we exist," David said. "Since I believe there's a real heaven and a real hell, I want to direct as many people toward heaven and away from hell as I can."[93]

He may have offered Hobby Lobby to God to conquer his pride, but now a different kind of pride motivated him as he predicted the family's efforts could send millions of people to heaven: "I want to know that I have affected people for eternity," he said. "I matter 10 billion years from now."[94] Around the time Seward left the company, Mart approached his father, saying he'd been thinking the same thing. While the missionary work they supported was harvesting souls for Jesus, surely there was more they could be doing with the vast profits Hobby Lobby and Mardel were reaping. David agreed, thinking about a phrase common in evangelical circles: "You can't out-give God"—a favorite of prosperity gospel preachers who argued that no matter how much one gave to religious causes, God always gave back more. Suddenly he heard God's voice in reply: *Well, you haven't really tried, have you?*[95]

CHAPTER FOUR

Teach All Nations

On Christmas 1994, David Green had a revelation.[1] The whole family had been over the previous night, grandchildren filling the house with excitement: Mart now had three boys—Brent, Tyler, and Scott—and a daughter, Amy, spaced between ages ten and four. Steve had the mirror image: one boy, Derek, and three girls—Lauren, Lindy, and Danielle—between eight and one. Now David and Barbara quietly ate their breakfast on Christmas morning as David picked up *The Sunday Oklahoman*.[2]

Turning its pages, he became troubled, "bombarded by all the advertisements featuring reindeer, snowmen, Christmas trees, and, of course, Santa Claus." What he didn't see was Jesus Christ. *Why in the December 25th issue did this whole newspaper have nothing to say—not a single paragraph—about the birth of Jesus?* he thought. *Wasn't the arrival of the baby in Bethlehem the whole origin of Christmas?* "There wasn't even a 'Merry Christmas' to be found in the entire paper," he later recalled. "Lots of 'Seasons Greetings,' and 'Happy Holidays,' but that was all."[3]

David presents this story as a seminal moment in his decision to advocate for his faith on a more public stage. Yet it seems that he was seeing what he wanted to see. In fact, the paper that day contained dozens of mentions of Christmas, starting with a large front-page photo of a live nativity scene with baby Jesus in the manger. An accompanying story, "Christmas Unites Christians," discussed various beliefs around the truth of Jesus's birth. Other stories included an editorial about Christian charity, an opinion piece about the three wise men, and a wire story about pilgrims journeying to Bethlehem. The paper even ran a Christmas message from First Lady Hillary Clinton in which she wished the country a "Merry Christmas"—one of twenty instances of the phrase in the paper, compared to fourteen "Happy Holidays" and just four "Season's Greetings."[4]

Perhaps it isn't surprising that David called out an attack on Christmas, given that conservatives had been decrying the "political correctness" that urged more inclusive holiday greetings as yet another example of secular humanism replacing Christian belief. (A decade later, Fox News host Bill O'Reilly would declare a full-blown "War on Christmas.") At any rate, David now vowed to do something about it, so he approached Barbara and the kids. Hobby Lobby was no stranger to placing ads—why not make one to market Jesus? Barbara enthusiastically embraced her husband's plan to let people know where the family stood "regarding the Lord."[5]

Next Christmas, Hobby Lobby placed a small ad in *The Oklahoman* proclaiming, "Merry Christmas!" in bold letters along with the hope that readers might find "the greatest gift ever given" this Christmas, the "gift of eternal life." It was signed "Hobby Lobby Stores, Inc." Beneath it was a larger, half-page ad for Hobby Lobby featuring half off Christmas trees, garlands, stockings, and candy.[6] The ad marked Hobby Lobby's first foray into a more public proselytizing—rather than just quietly funding missionary work, it would now loudly proclaim that it was a company based on faith.

The evangelizing was risky, potentially turning off some customers. But as far as David was concerned, God had interceded to save his company, and now it was time to give back. "I knew, of course, that some people would say a 'secular business' should not get involved in such a thing. But I've never been real fond of the word *secular*," he said. Among other definitions in the dictionary, he found, it meant *without God*. "Was that what I wanted Hobby Lobby to be? Not at all."[7]

As David was planning to take a public stand for Christ, a shocking tragedy befell Hobby Lobby's hometown. A blast ripped through the center of Oklahoma City at 9:02 am on April 19, 1995, turning the Alfred P. Murrah Federal Building into a smoking heap of twisted metal and rubble. Immediately, media suspected an attack by Middle Eastern terrorists. The real culprit was Timothy McVeigh, a twenty-six-year-old ex-army soldier. He had acted in retribution for the 1993 FBI raid on the Branch Davidian compound in Waco, Texas (the group was led by David Koresh, who preached apocalyptic prophecies based on the biblical book of Revelation), leading to a firestorm that killed eighty-six people. The Oklahoma City bombing killed more than twice that—168 people, including nineteen children.[8]

The bombing took place just ten miles from the Green family home, close enough to feel the ground shake.[9] Afterward, the city was wracked by an outpouring of grief, and Hobby Lobby stores sold out of red, white, and blue ribbons to drape over buildings. Along with donations from other corporations, the company donated $150,000 for a memorial on the site, now a grassy park with 168 bronze-and-glass chairs.[10] Most of Hobby Lobby's donations, however, continued to be directed toward a more eternal purpose—getting the Bible into the hands of people around the world.

Once David and Mart decided to increase the pace of their giving, they challenged each other to double their donations every six months. As ambitious as that seemed, the Lord continued to provide. In 1995, Hobby Lobby opened its one hundredth store in Gladstone, Missouri, and sales reached more than $350 million. "We've been doubling our sales every two years in this decade," Steve told *The Oklahoman*, predicting sales of $1 billion by the end of the century.[11]

The family launched a new company, WorldWood, to manufacture wood products, and Darsee explored her own line of candles and potpourri, called Darsee and David's. The newly completed headquarters building stretched a half mile, a "continuous span of red-tile roof among cow pastures west of the airport," a reporter noted. Despite the warehouse totaling one million square feet of space, the company was already planning another 700,000-square-foot location across the street.[12]

Mardel had meanwhile become the second-largest Christian bookstore chain in the country, with eleven stores; its Tulsa location alone sold up to 250 Bibles in a day.[13] Christian books were more popular than ever with the publication in 1995 of the first of the apocalyptic Left Behind novels, cowritten by right-wing politico Tim LaHaye and Larry Jenkins, in which those who aren't taken by Jesus in the rapture are "left behind" to fight the Antichrist. Loosely based on the biblical books of Daniel and Revelation, the books were instant bestsellers at Mardel and other Christian booksellers—a fever dream of right-wing politics, with the Antichrist consolidating his hold over the United Nations and starting World War III as a plucky band of freedom fighters led by a steel-jawed airline pilot and a bad-boy journalist take on the forces of darkness. Female characters are relegated to being objects of desire, saintly housewives, or caviling shrews.[14]

David continued to pour money into Church of God of Prophecy missionary projects, including a church in Bulgaria, built after the fall of its communist regime, and a church and medical clinic in Zaire. He dedicated file folders to each project, filling them with documents and photographs and tucking them into a file drawer behind his desk. By 1997, he had twenty projects and justified the expense to a reporter as an essential part of the company's bottom line: "You really want it to be something more eternal than, 'You came, you bought a yacht and a jet, and that's it.' "[15]

DESPITE THE SUCCESS of these projects, David and Mart itched to go bigger. One morning at Mardel, a publisher's representative came in pitching a coffee-table book about Wycliffe Bible Translators, full of photos of smiling white missionaries aboard turboprop planes and dugout canoes or poring over texts with brown- and black-skinned people.[16] Named after the translator of the first English Bible, John Wycliffe, the organization had been founded by William Cameron Townsend, the son of California citrus farmers, who sold Bibles in Guatemala.[17]

"Uncle Cam," as he was known, was troubled by a verse in Revelation that describes a vision of a multitude from "every nation, tribe, people and language" appearing before Christ after the second coming. Some evangelicals interpreted this to mean Jesus wouldn't return until people of every language could read the Bible, and Townsend planned to fix that.[18] Only "2,000 tongues to go," he gamely declared, creating a worldwide movement funded by donors including a fundamentalist California oil baron and the heir to the Quaker Oats fortune. Even as he sent translators forth, the task grew as linguists updated the number of worldwide languages to six thousand, including four thousand without an adequate Bible translation.[19]

The pretty photos Mart viewed that day bely the troubled history of the organization. While Wycliffe proselytized about harvesting souls, a sister organization, the Summer Institute for Linguistics (SIL), based at the University of Oklahoma (OU), handled in-country logistics for the organization. In its zeal to reach off-the-grid tribes, the SIL was accused throughout the twentieth century of making deals with repressive governments to exploit natural resources and working with the CIA to root out communist revolutionaries in the jungles. Whatever the truth, the network of airstrips and outposts built by Wycliffe and the SIL necessarily opened up remote areas to mining and oil industries, which displaced native populations in the name of "progress."[20] Mart saw none of this as he flipped through pages detailing the courage and sacrifice of the missionaries. At his Oklahoma store that afternoon, he passed a bulletin board with a notice for a coming Wycliffe banquet at a nearby restaurant, and he took it for a sign. He was inspired to donate and challenged his parents and siblings to give as well.[21]

David found his own new cause in Bob Hoskins, a former child evangelist turned missionary who in 1987 had created a book of scriptures for schoolchildren at the request of the education minister of El Salvador.[22] He later created an English version called *The Book of Hope*, a "harmonization" of the Gospels that told the life of Jesus chronologically, smoothing out the contradictions between different books of the New Testament. By 1997, his Florida-based organization OneHope had distributed them to some thirty-five million children worldwide, "most of them right in the public-school classrooms, by government invitation," the organization declared.[23] One Sunday, David and his family saw a presentation on the group at their church. Afterward, David invited Hoskins to meet him in Oklahoma City, where he agreed to donate $2 million.[24]

Barbara got in on the charity act as well. After a pastor at their church began volunteering for a homeless shelter called City Rescue Mission, Barbara stepped in to help raise more than $2 million—with $600,000 donated by the Greens themselves. Of course, the goal was more than just providing shelter; at the church's annual convention in Tennessee, the pastor announced that the project had also led to the salvation of more than three hundred souls the previous year.[25]

Meanwhile, Hobby Lobby's holiday ads became bolder. For Christmas 1997, the company took out a full-page ad[26] in newspapers across the country, showing a misty tableau of disembodied hands reaching upward while a large hand surrounded by white light reached down. "When man reaches for God, we call it religion," the text read. "When God reaches for man, we call it Christmas." Smaller text assured the reader that God "knew you before you were born"—a reference to the antiabortion verse in Isaiah—before asking, "How will you respond?"[27]

Evangelicals across the country were answering that question by redoubling their effort to remove the morally bankrupt occupant of the White House and replace him with a God-fearing Christian. In 1995, James Dobson warned GOP aspirants that they "will not be able to double-talk, sidestep, obfuscate, and ignore the concerns" of evangelicals anymore. When he met with Gingrich, however, the speaker told him flat-out, "We don't have the votes to end abortion," agreeing only to push for incremental change on culture issues, such as laws making it easier to sue abortion clinics and prohibit adoption by gay couples.[28]

The Republican nominee for president in 1996, Bob Dole, did little to excite evangelicals, with a moderate stance on social issues even as he kept a hard line on taxes. While Ralph Reed and the Christian Coalition supported Dole, Dobson withheld his endorsement. That spring, Clinton confirmed evangelicals' worst fears by vetoing a bill banning late-term abortions occurring in the third trimester, which conservatives branded "partial birth abortion."[29] (The procedure is very rare and usually done only when the life of the mother is at risk.)

At the same time, Dobson and other religious conservatives were alarmed by rulings in Hawaii suggesting that same-sex couples might be allowed to marry there. At their urging, Congress introduced the Defense of Marriage Act (DOMA), which would allow states to deny the legitimacy of gay marriages performed in other states. At the time, less than 30 percent of Americans supported gay marriage. As Clinton quietly signed the bill into law, it was celebrated by conservative commentator Bill O'Reilly, who headed a new network, Fox News, that had been launched to target white Christian conservatives.[30]

In the end, Clinton easily beat Dole, who was still supported by a majority of evangelicals, but in lower numbers than four years earlier. Reed resigned from the Christian Coalition, and the organization imploded, leaving Dobson's Focus on the Family as the primary political voice for white evangelicals. Dobson flexed his power by threatening to leave the Republican Party if it didn't move right on social issues. "If I go," he said, "I'll take as many people with me as possible."[31] GOP politicians begged Dobson to stay, proposing a new direct forum for evangelical leaders to meet with congresspeople. Over the next few years, the House introduced bills to ban late-term abortion, reinstitute school prayer, and prevent gay adoption, only to see all of them die.

Even as Focus was pushing family values, a new emphasis on sexual purity was sweeping churches and Christian youth groups. In many ways, the purity movement was a mainstreaming of the "courtship" principles Bill Gothard had preached for decades through his Institute in Basic Life Principles (IBLP). It was further spurred by the 1984 book *Passion & Purity* by celebrated missionary Elisabeth Elliot. Her husband, Jim, had been killed in Ecuador in 1956 along with four other missionaries when a tribe they were trying to convert, the Waodoni, turned violent. A feature in *Life* magazine and wall-to-wall newspaper coverage made the men martyrs to Americans back home. Surprisingly, Elliot later went to live with the Waodoni along with the sister of one of the other missionaries, Rachel Saint—a shocking example of Christian forgiveness in action.

Elliot wrote a book about the incident, *Through Gates of Splendor*, which inspired a generation of missionaries. Decades later, she wrote *Passion & Purity* as an idealized version of her courtship with Jim, contending that it was a woman's responsibility to repel men's advances and resist the temptations of premarital sex, which she called "impure."[32] The themes were picked up by a middle-aged Christian author, Josh McDowell, who toured the country with hard-rock group Petra, promising young men "mind-blowing" marital sex if they could resist fornication.[33] By the mid-1990s, purity culture had taken off with True Love Waits, which distributed pledge cards to teens promising to wait until marriage, and Silver Ring Thing, which encouraged girls to wear silver purity rings as an outward sign of chastity.[34]

In the 1990s, Elliot endorsed a new program launched by Gothard's group to teach young women strict gender roles called Excellence in Character Educational Leadership (EXCEL).[35] By age sixty, Gothard—who was still living with his mother—had grown his organization into a $30 million empire with a homeschooling curriculum that recruited girls to an EXCEL training center in Dallas, one of dozens of IBLP facilities around the country. There, in what one newspaper called "Virgin Academy," girls in long navy skirts and high-necked blouses learned to develop a "meek and quiet spirit," remaining chaste and subservient as they dreamed of serving their future husbands.[36]

Young men channeled their energy into emergency response, auto mechanics, and construction through the Air Land Emergency Rescue Team (ALERT) program, based in rural Michigan. The program employed a quasi-military structure that broke down recruits before teaching them absolute obedience. Gothard opened other institutes, including a Character Training Institute in an old Holiday Inn in Oklahoma City, purchased by local businessman Garman Kimmell, who leased the building to Gothard for $1 a year.[37] An executive with Kimmell's company, Tom Hill, created a secularized version of Gothard's program called Character First!, removing references to Jesus and the Bible.[38]

Within a few years, Character First! was offered at two hundred public schools across the country as well as police departments, and corporations.[39] Hobby Lobby adopted it for twelve thousand employees nationwide as David promoted it in an early IBLP video, saying, "Obviously in our culture, you've seen a lot of deterioration of character, so it should be obvious to just about any businessman that this is a great need."[40] Some parents pushed back against its use in schools, and even some evangelical leaders criticized Gothard's ministry for perverting the ideas in the Bible. His justification for submission to authority, argued one Christian minister, actually came from a verse that compared rebellion to witchcraft and in no way supported the overarching "umbrella of protection" upon which Gothard based his ministry.[41]

The criticism didn't bother the Greens, who saw in Gothard's institute another exciting way to inculcate biblical values by lending it financial support. In 1997, Hill alerted Steve Green there was a dilapidated former Veterans Administration hospital in downtown Little Rock that was being sold for well under market value.[42] Hobby Lobby purchased it for $299,000 and a year later donated it to Gothard for a new ALERT Academy. "I have been very impressed with the ministry," Steve said at the time. "It has affected my life and my family's life for the better."[43] The following year, the company made a grander gesture, buying the hotel housing the Character Training Institute from Kimmell for $2.3 million and donating that to Gothard's organization as well.[44]

Alongside the purity movement, a men's movement called the Promise Keepers was experimenting with new forms of masculinity based on a commitment to marriage and protection of the women in their lives. In 1997, more than half a million men descended on the National Mall to pray and sing hymns. To feminist critics, it was the same patriarchy in new packaging—condemning abortion, feminism, premarital sex, and homosexuality, which founder Bill McCartney called "an abomination against almighty God."[45]

The organization inspired men to read a raft of Christian self-help books, all advertised heavily at Mardel, which sold tickets to Promise Keeper rallies in Tulsa and Oklahoma City.[46] Mart also supported so-called crisis pregnancy centers to actively dissuade women from considering abortion. Mardel sponsored annual citywide "baby showers" in Oklahoma City and Tulsa to collect baby gear and maternity clothes for new mothers and distributed them in a celebration along with balloons released with "prayers for the unborn children."[47]

With the new emphasis on sexual purity, conservative Christians were especially galled when news leaked that President Clinton had had an affair with intern Monica Lewinsky while in office and then seemed to lie about it under oath. As House Republicans launched an impeachment, Dobson penned a letter, scolding, "Character does matter. You can't run a family, let alone a country, without it."[48] To critics' chagrin, Clinton's approval only went up during the ensuing trial, which failed to remove him from office.

Among the many letters Hobby Lobby received in response to its religious ads, one stood out—a message from Dick Eastman, a minister based in Colorado Springs who commended the company for "perhaps the finest Christmas communication introducing the reality of Christ I can recall seeing."[49] In the 1970s, Eastman had started a "prayer corps" of young people in California, carrying on prayers twenty-four hours a day. He subsequently marshaled his prayer warriors against communism, attributing the 1986 meltdown of the Chernobyl nuclear power plant in the Soviet Union, the fall of communism in Eastern Europe, and even the toppling of the Berlin Wall to specific acts of prayer.[50]

More recently, Eastman had spoken in militaristic terms about the need for Christian missionaries to "penetrate the darkness" of "demonically controlled regions" of the world that were "headquarters" of "non-Christian religions such as Islam, Hinduism, and Buddhism."[51] His weapon was a gospel booklet distributed door-to-door through his organization Every Home for Christ, which he told the Greens had reached 900 million households in over 180 countries and received some 22 million decision cards from those who'd turned to Christ.[52] Suitably impressed, David prayed before adding Every Home for Christ to the list of charities through which Hobby Lobby was working to spread the Bible around the world.

By the end of 1997, Hobby Lobby numbered more than 160 stores in 17 states, with $540 million in sales, as David received increasing recognition, including an award for National Entrepreneur of the Year for the retail industry from Ernst & Young.[53] Still, he heard his mother's voice echoing in his ears: "What have you done for the Lord?" He started thinking about the fourth commandment: "Remember the Sabbath Day to keep it holy." Hobby Lobby saw its biggest sales on Sundays, with weekend hobbyists spending $100 million on that day annually. However, David began to worry that he was keeping employees from a day of church and family.[54]

Atlanta-based fast-food chain Chick-fil-A had recently closed its stores on Sundays, and now Hobby Lobby followed suit with a pilot program at its new locations in Nebraska.[55] If it didn't work, David figured it wouldn't hurt the company's core business. The company put a sign in the windows announcing that the stores were "Closed Sundays to Allow Employees Time for Family & Worship" and watched as sales immediately took a dive. Within weeks, however, they rebounded and were soon above preclosure levels. Some customers intentionally chose to shop at Hobby Lobby, and the company received letters in favor of the switch by ten to one.[56]

In a newspaper report, Hobby Lobby advertising director Bill Hane declared Hobby Lobby "Christian without apology," saying it was rolling out the new hours in other stores. Still, he mused, "you wonder if you're shooting yourself in the foot by dropping one of your prime sales days."[57] Reading that, David heard God's mocking voice in his ear: *So if you're blessed, you're going to be obedient? But if the numbers don't work for you, maybe not?* David told Hane that if any other reporters asked, "tell them we're closing all the stores on Sunday, period." Over the next two years, Hobby Lobby implemented the hours companywide.[58]

According to the company, the change helped it recruit higher-quality employees. Being Christian was never a requirement of employment at Hobby Lobby, said Steve, though recruiters did look for honesty, responsibility, and other qualities inherent in the scriptures.[59] The Sunday closure "attracted better employees, because they like the idea that they're going to be able to get off on Sundays to worship and be with their families."[60]

In addition to the secular recognition, David was now honored for his religious commitments with the presentation of the Ten Commandments Leadership Award by the National Clergy Council, an evangelical group founded by Rob Schenck, a Jewish man from Long Island who had converted to become a Pentecostal pastor. Schenck had been a prominent leader of the militant antiabortion group Operation Rescue and had recently moved to Washington.[61]

The Ten Commandments award was given "to those who use their resources and stations in life to promote principles consistent with the Commandments"; David received the award at a ceremony on Capitol Hill in January 2000 for "recognizing a day for worship is more valuable than additional sales," giving him newfound prominence as a Christian leader.[62]

MEANWHILE, MART CONTINUED to donate to Wycliffe, paying to print new editions of Bibles in several languages after literally decades of work by translators. After he'd funded several printings, a Wycliffe representative invited him to a dedication ceremony for a new New Testament in Guatemala. Now thirty-six, Mart sported a tuft of spiky brown hair that, along with his heavy black-framed glasses, made him look vaguely owllike. At some point, he had adopted the habit of exclusively wearing green shirts—a nod to his last name—which soon became his calling card. As he flew over the Gulf of Mexico, Mart read a handwritten sheet that Wycliffe had prepared. Two American translators had first come to Guatemala in 1958 to work with the Eastern Jacaltec people, who spoke an offshoot of Mayan understood by thirty thousand people.[63]

You've got to be kidding me, thought Mart. *This couple has been down here my entire life.* What's more, Mart read, only eight thousand of the Eastern Jacaltec people could read, and of those, only four hundred were Christians. Mart considered the return on investment. *We spent $21,000 to pay for the printing of this Bible*, he thought. *This is the last time I'm going to do this.* Arriving in Guatemala City, he boarded a bus for the eight-hour trip to a city on a plateau overlooking the jungle on the Mexican border. He settled into a $1 tin-roofed hotel; after a restless night, all he could think about was going home and telling his family about the misadventure.[64]

As the ceremony commenced, he watched a Mayan named Gaspar who had helped with the translation walk up to receive his copy and burst into tears, covering his face in a handkerchief. Mart was amazed. He'd sold thousands of Bibles but had never seen anyone cry to receive one. In that moment, the Holy Spirit planted a wicked thought in his head: *Why don't you tell Gaspar he's not a good return on investment?* The moment changed his life, he later said. "At that exact moment, it went from 'Why would anyone spend their life to do this?' to 'How am I going to make sure everybody on earth has God's word?' "[65]

Mart lay awake that night listening to cats run around the roof. In the early hours of the morning, he realized that he sold thousands of copies of the Bible but rarely read it himself. Suddenly another thought popped into his head: *What kind of return on investment is Mart Green?* He had just seen a man cry over finally receiving a Bible in his own language, and here he took it for granted he could read it in English. From then on, he vowed, he would not only read the Bible himself every morning but also do everything he could to make sure others could read it.[66]

BACK IN OKLAHOMA, Mart worked to make good on that promise, wrangling an invitation through Bill Hane to a conference for the North American Forum of Bible Agencies. During one session, participants lamented that no matter how many Bibles they distributed, it didn't matter if people didn't read it. They wondered if they could put together a marketing campaign. "You guys are onto something," Mart blurted out. "Do it!"[67]

That night, Mart had a hazy vision of a giant campaign to spread the Bible around the globe, along with a world-class museum complete with an IMAX theater. *The price is going to be so big that all the donors are going to have to come together*, he thought, recording the vision in his journal. Among the conference attendees was Rob Hoskins, the son of Bob Hoskins, who'd distributed *The Book of Hope* to children around the world. Together, they discussed a TV advertising campaign along the lines of the successful "Got Milk?" ads by dairy producers—only selling the Bible instead.[68]

Along with Hoskins and his wife, Diana, Mart incorporated Bearing Fruit Communications as a nonprofit media company, with Hobby Lobby general counsel Peter Dobelbower as registered agent and Hobby Lobby headquarters listed as the address.[69] The lines between Hobby Lobby, Mardel, and Bearing Fruit were porous, with Hane, Dobelbower, and other employees working for all three.

After some brainstorming, they settled on a tagline: "This Book Is Alive!" Soon they were producing thirty-second commercials with the help of a Tulsa-based film producer, Tom Newman. Mardel and Hobby Lobby together paid $40,000 for the first month of broadcasting on Oklahoma City stations and solicited other Christian companies to donate as well.[70]

In considering other subjects for commercials, Mart thought back to a meeting he and Diana had attended at Wycliffe's Pennsylvania headquarters, where they'd seen a presentation by Steve Saint, son of missionary Nate Saint, one of the missionaries killed in Ecuador; Nate's sister Rachel had gone to live with the Waodoni along with Elisabeth Elliot. Appearing with Saint was Mincaye, one of the tribesmen who had killed the missionaries and later converted to Christianity.

Mart now grabbed a tape recording of the talk and played it in his car, listening as Mincaye spoke about how he'd converted to Christianity based on "God's carvings"—the Bible. "We acted badly, 'til they brought us God's carvings," he said. "Now we walk his trail." Mart pulled over into a Wal-Mart parking lot and began to cry. *This is a "This book is alive" story if I ever heard it!* he thought. *The most violent society now lives in peace, and the answer is God's Word transformed their life.*[71]

Though he felt strongly that someday there should be a movie based on the story, the project went on the back burner as Bearing Fruit took over the production of Hobby Lobby's annual holiday ads. For Christmas 1998, the company created a full-color design depicting a blond baby Jesus with Botticelli-like curls playing on the floor of his adoptive father Joseph's carpentry shop with a long nail that threw the shadow of a cross. Hobby Lobby ran the ad everywhere it had a store, from the *Galveston Daily News* to the *Kansas City Star*, along with a hotline number to call to learn more about Jesus.[72]

Hobby Lobby received dozens of letters in response to the ads, the majority of them "overwhelmingly positive," according to the company. But some took issue with the company so aggressively advocating for its faith. One reader called one of the ads "about the silliest—and sickest—ad I've ever read," while another complained that Hobby Lobby was "mixing religion with business" and "flexing your corporate clout" to proselytize. "Are you a business or a church?" another demanded.[73]

The attacks only confirmed to the Greens that they were on the right course, following in the footsteps of missionaries and martyrs throughout history. David estimated that thirty million people had seen the ads in just the first five years and that hundreds, if not thousands, must have found Jesus. If a few were offended or felt that the ads weren't "politically correct," then that was a small price to pay. "There is no getting around the fact that Jesus offends some people," David said. "Nevertheless, he is too important in my life for me to cower in fear of mentioning his name."[74]

By now, David had a new problem: He was making more money than he knew how to spend. By January 2000, Hobby Lobby had over two hundred stores, with sales of more than $800 million.[75] Not fifteen years before, he'd been afraid he would lose the company; now, at fifty-eight, he was losing sleep over what it might become. The estate planners he and Barbara had hired recommended that they sign the company over to their children, who would pass it along to theirs. But would later generations squander the wealth he'd made? "The immense profits we were enjoying had become a source of worry to me," said David, who "knew that wealth has to be handled wisely to keep it from being destructive."[76]

One night, praying in his backyard, he once again heard God speak to him, saying, *I wonder if the Jones family owns this business you got?* David answered, "Well, I couldn't be giving it to my kids if the Jones family owns it." As the import started to dawn on him, he heard God command, *This company belongs to me. Don't touch it. It's mine.* The words sent a chill down his spine as he looked up at the Oklahoma sky. He thought of his namesake, King David, who in his moment of triumph brought the Ark of the Covenant containing the Ten Commandments into Jerusalem. One of the handlers who was helping transport the ark reached out to steady it, and God smote him dead. *Don't touch it. It's mine.*[77]

David went back into the house and solemnly wrote on a piece of paper, "I own Hobby Lobby. Signed, God." Though he'd given credit to God since the oil crisis, "now God's ownership of the company had come to me in searing revelation." Didn't Psalms say, "The earth is the Lord's and everything in it, the world, and all who live in it"?[78] He wasn't an owner of the company; he was a mere steward of God's design. Neither he nor his family was entitled to the wealth God had created.

Nor was the government. After the successful donation of the Little Rock hospital and the Oklahoma City hotel to IBLP, Hobby Lobby began buying other distressed properties to donate to Gothard and other ministries. Hobby Lobby could deduct donations to religious charities from its taxes—not at the price it had paid but at the fair market value at the time of the donation. Given a 20 percent corporate tax rate, a property paid for itself at five times the purchase price.

"Our goal is not necessarily to get tax breaks," said general counsel Dobelbower. "Our goal is to get tax breaks so we can give more money away."[79] In early 2000, the company swooped in to buy a 2,200-acre wooded college campus in Big Sandy, Texas, paying $9 million for the property, which included dorms, classrooms, an airstrip, a nine-hole golf course, and a radio station. The company then donated it to IBLP for an orphanage for two hundred children and a new ALERT Academy for three hundred students, the largest property the organization had ever received. "It's a win-win for both of us," said Steve, who brought Gothard out to look at the campus before donating it.[80] "He's able to get on the property without putting out the cash. We're out the cash but are able to recoup it through a donation and subsequent tax write-off."[81]

David began praying all the time to ascertain the Lord's will, "giving God the vote" as if he were another shareholder. When he felt that the warehouse was disorganized and costing him money, he prayed to God for two weeks. At the end, God revealed ways he could economize—for example, by charging full price for some items the company was selling for 40 percent off. "We took in extra sales because we listened to the Lord," he said.[82]

In another case, he was looking to acquire a company but not sure it was a good deal. He thought of the Old Testament story of Gideon, who had an army of thirty-two thousand but attacked with only three hundred in order to prove God's might. David made a lowball offer he knew wouldn't be accepted unless God willed it—and was turned down. "God voted no, and I trust that he had reasons for his choice that I know nothing about (and may never know until heaven)."[83] As a business strategy, it made no sense—but it gave David peace of mind to know he was following God's will. With all the profits the company was taking in, David could afford to pass up an acquisition if it didn't feel right. Still, he was filled with anxiety about exactly what God had meant when he'd said the company was his—and how David and his children could best use it to glorify God's name.

Ultimately, the answer came from Mart. As the various family members each donated to religious causes—David spreading biblical literature around the world, Steve acquiring land to donate to Bible-believing ministries, and Mart funding Bible translation and advertising efforts—it seemed that they were all circling around the same theme. At a family meeting one day, Mart made it explicit. His grandmother Marie had always said only two things were eternal: God's word and man's soul. "What is the one word our family is going to be known for 50 years from now?" he asked. "What would it be 50 years from now that people will say, 'Oh yeah! The Greens were known for . . .' " He supplied the answer himself: "Bible."[84]

CHAPTER FIVE

Good Book

To truly understand the Green family, it's essential to understand the cause to which they've devoted themselves—the Bible. The book is at the center of their lives, a source of solace and inspiration, a manual to guide their actions, and a narrative for them to share with the world. Despite its name—derived from *biblos*, the Greek word for book—it's not one book but many, a compendium of history, laws, stories, polemics, and songs. Scholars and religious leaders disagree about who wrote it and when, and even about what belongs in it and what doesn't. As influential as the book is, only one-fifth of Americans have read it cover to cover; over half have read none of it at all.[1] Most people engage with it in bite-sized chunks from the vantage of a church pew, with its overall scope obscured. The way the book has been interpreted over the centuries, however, has been crucial in determining the society that evangelicals hope to create.

Tradition holds that the Bible's first books were written by Moses, the ancient lawgiver who brought the Ten Commandments down from Mount Sinai and led the Israelites to the Promised Land of Canaan around 1250 BCE. Almost no religious scholar believes that now—if indeed they even believe Moses existed.[2] In general, conservative scholars argue for an older date of authorship, while liberals believe in more recent dates of composition. Most agree, however, that the Bible's first scraps were committed to text by Israelite scribes sometime around 800 BCE.[3]

Its authors were not in a good place. After arriving in Canaan, the Israelites thrived for only a couple hundred years before they broke into two kingdoms—Israel in the north, with Samaria as its capital, and the smaller Judah in the south, centered on Jerusalem. They were in a precarious location at the fulcrum of the so-called fertile crescent between two powerful neighbors, Egypt and Assyria. Eventually Assyria invaded, wiping out the northern kingdom in 722 BCE and scattering its populace. Judah survived a while longer, becoming a vassal state of Assyria's successor, Babylonia. But ultimately the people of Judah revolted, and the mighty king Nebuchadnezzar sent armies to conquer Jerusalem in 586 BCE. He took the city's elite, including its priests, into captivity in Babylon.[4]

The traumatized priests did their best to hold their people together and resist assimilation by keeping alive the oral and written traditions they'd brought with them. Taking stories from both kingdoms about the creation of the world and the patriarchs of their people, they presented a coherent narrative that would give the people a common identity.[5] The Bible's compilers, most scholars believe, also wove in a distinctive strain of narrative known as "deuteronomistic" (after the book of Deuteronomy, "second law" in Greek). This narrative was preoccupied with a single theme: obedience to the one true God, Yahweh, and the need to stamp out worship of any competing deity or pay the consequences.[6]

When the Persian king Cyrus conquered Babylonia in 539 BCE, he allowed the Israelites to return from their generation in exile.[7] They rebuilt their temple in Jerusalem, and according to tradition, the scribe Ezra presented the five scrolls known as the Torah or the Pentateuch—Genesis, Exodus, Leviticus, Numbers, and Deuteronomy—in the city square. The scrolls begin with the creation of the world, with God forming the earth and its first humans in seven days out of a formless void. Soon evil enters when Adam and Eve are tempted by the serpent to disobey God and are exiled from paradise as punishment. Later generations descend so far into wickedness that Yahweh wipes them out, preserving only Noah, his family, and a floating zoo of animal life to repopulate the earth.

From there, the story introduces the patriarch Abraham, who tradition holds was born in the Mesopotamian city of Ur around 2100 BCE. As part of a new covenant, God promises the fertile land of Canaan to him and his descendants. That covenant passes to Abraham's son Isaac and Isaac's son Jacob, to whom God gives a new name, Israel, and who fathers twelve children through four women, whose descendants will become the twelve tribes of Israel. From the beginning, there is strife: The ten oldest brothers are jealous of Joseph, his father's favorite, and sell him into slavery in Egypt. Nevertheless, he thrives in the pharaoh's court and becomes his most trusted adviser. When famine drives the rest of the Israelites to Egypt, Joseph reveals himself, and they are reconciled.

The tribes live in harmony until the pharaoh eventually enslaves them. It's then up to Moses to lead the Israelites to freedom, safely passing through the "sea of reeds" while the pharaoh's army is drowned by God's intercession. Yahweh delivers the Ten Commandments on Mount Sinai, and the Israelites then wander for forty years in the wilderness before crossing into Canaan. Moses himself never makes it. He's punished after Yahweh instructs him to strike his staff against a rock to bring forth water, and he strikes it twice instead, demonstrating an apparent lack of faith in God's power. He's condemned to die on the banks of the River Jordan in sight of the Promised Land. With that, the Torah comes to an end.

Moses's successor, the warrior Joshua, leads the conquest of Canaan with a vengeance, laying waste to its cities. He starts with the strategic hub of Jericho, the walls of which God sends tumbling down. Scholars believe the book of Joshua was written around the same time as the Torah as a continuation of the deuteronomistic narrative describing the covenant between Yahweh and his chosen people. The book of Judges follows, chronicling a gory period of tribal warlords. The next book, Samuel, describes the rise of the first king, Saul, who unites the various Israelite tribes into one kingdom as he battles the Philistines. His protégé David, a shepherd boy from Judah, rises to prominence after slaying the Philistine hero Goliath and takes over as king after Saul is killed in battle.[8] A short Golden Age follows, in which David establishes the capital at Jerusalem.

Finally, the book of Kings closes out the deuteronomistic narrative as David's son and successor, Solomon, builds the first temple on Mount Zion. Unfortunately, it's not to last, as Israel and Judah fracture into separate kingdoms and weaken under a string of kings who often stray in their obedience to God, leading to the eventual conquest by the Mesopotamian empires.

Coming into the Bible cold, it is almost incomprehensible to believe it could be the basis for morality. With the exception of Joseph, its protagonists are unerringly *bad*—lying, cheating, stealing, killing, and treating their women terribly. Extramarital sex and polygamy run rampant. Abraham sleeps with his wife's maidservant, who gives birth to another son, Ishmael, whom he abandons in the wilderness. Jacob takes two wives, Rachel and Leah, and still sleeps with their maidservants to father his twelve children. His son Judah sleeps with a prostitute who turns out to be the former wife of his own dead son.

The later Israelite kings are no better. Saul becomes jealous of David and tries repeatedly to murder him. David not only seduces the beautiful Bathsheba but also arranges to have her husband killed in battle. Solomon ruthlessly assassinates his half-brother and any other rival claimant to the throne. That's to say nothing of Judah's king Manasseh, who worships idols and burns his son as a sacrifice. God's judgment is applied inconsistently, even capriciously, to these wicked rulers. Sometimes he comes down hard on them, and sometimes he lets them slide—Manasseh has the longest reign of all—as he continues despite everything to honor his covenant with Abraham.

Indeed, Yahweh's punishments of the Israelites pale in comparison to his bloodthirsty rampage against everyone else. In the invasion of Canaan, he orders wholesale genocide of the tribes currently living there, telling the Israelites, "Do not leave alive anything that breathes. Completely destroy them."[9] At Jericho, the Israelites "destroyed with the sword every living thing in it—men and women, young and old, cattle, sheep and donkeys."[10]

Beyond these unsettling passages, readers of the Bible in its entirety are apt to leave with another impression: Much of it is depressingly dull. Despite the thrilling exodus from Egypt and famous stories of David versus Goliath or Samson and Delilah, much of the early chapters is taken up with long, tedious recountings of genealogy, exhaustive enumerations of laws, and repetitive lists of the purposes for animal sacrifices, with little relevance for modern readers.

Of course, whether the history described in the Bible is *true* is another question. The earliest passages describe events that happened more than a thousand years before they were apparently written down. Some scholars believe the story is largely accurate, passed down through oral tradition for centuries. Others see it as a complete fabrication, created after the fact to provide justification for the conquest of Canaan or as a post hoc explanation for the later misfortune of the Israelites.[11] Most scholars fall somewhere in the middle—dubious of the early stories of the origin of Israel and its early kings but generally confident in the depiction of events after about the eighth or ninth century BCE, when the kingdoms divided and histories were preserved in writing.[12]

Even on its own terms, the Bible contradicts itself constantly. Throughout Genesis, two strains are woven together, sometimes with competing details.[13] There are four accounts of Moses receiving the Ten Commandments, each with slightly different enumerations of the commandments inscribed on the stone tablets.[14] The book of Chronicles retells the deuteronomistic history with different facts, whitewashing details such as David's affair and Solomon's fratricide. Whether the authors intentionally rewrote history or relied on different sources is up for debate.[15]

Over the centuries, religious authorities have provided many explanations for the Bible's more problematic elements. Some have argued, for example, that the shocking details about polygamy and genocide must be understood in the context of their time, when ancient tribes were fighting for survival. The morally ambiguous heroes make for a more compelling narrative, showing how God works through imperfect people. The stories of God's judgment and mercy show how he punishes the disobedient but rewards the faithful, even if none can ever fully live up to his laws. And then there are those who have argued that the Bible was never meant to be taken literally at all.

Despite all of these questions and contradictions, the Bible was unique in the ancient world as a collection of writings held apart as sacred, serving as the basis for the religion now known as Judaism.[16] To the Torah, priests added a group of writings known as Prophets, or Nevi'im, including the books of Isaiah, Jeremiah, Ezekiel, and twelve others sent by God to warn the Israelites against straying from the worship of Yahweh. These books are even more opaque to the modern reader, with collections of pithy sayings loosely arranged by chronology or theme that have been widely open to interpretation by later generations.[17]

Some offer up words of hope, including passages in Isaiah about a baby to be born to the king of Judah who will be a "great light" known as Immanuel (literally "God is with us"). Some scholars believe the book refers to an actual king, Hezekiah, who ushered in a brief period of prosperity around 715 BCE.[18] Others, however, have interpreted this as a king yet to come. Similarly, Ezekiel describes a future descendant of the house of David who will reunite the kingdoms as an "anointed one," using the Hebrew word *mashiah*—or, as we know it today, messiah.

Starting around the sixth century BCE, the Hebrew Bible grew with texts collectively called the Writings, or Kethuvim. They include Psalms, poetic prayers of worship—many attributed to David—as well as three books attributed to Solomon: Proverbs, a collection of aphorisms; Ecclesiastes, an existential meditation on the nature of life; and Song of Songs, a blatantly erotic love poem. They also include some narratives: The short book of Ruth tells of a virtuous foreign woman who marries an Israelite, becoming an ancestor of David. Esther, by contrast, is about a Jewish woman who marries a king of Persia and is able to prevent a genocide of the Jews. The book of Daniel tells the story of a prophet during the time of the Babylonian captivity who is persecuted by the Babylonian king Nebuchadnezzar.

Most scholars treat these books as fiction, imaginative "tall tales" that often seem to be as much about the times in which they were written as about the times they describe. Daniel, for example, dates to the second century BCE, after Israel had been conquered yet again by Alexander the Great, ultimately becoming part of the Greek-speaking Seleucid Empire. The story can be read as an allegory of the times, with Daniel's persecution by the Babylonians representing the Jews' persecution at the hands of the Seleucids. In a vision, Daniel sees four rampaging beasts with features representing the four empires that had conquered Israel by that time: the Babylonians, the Persians, the Greeks, and the Seleucids. The last beast is destroyed by a messiah-like savior called the "son of man," who some scholars believe represents the Maccabees, a Jewish sect that led a successful revolt against the Greek rulers in 167 BCE and established an independent state that lasted for a hundred years. As with the messianic figures in Isaiah and Ezekiel, however, this figure would later be interpreted as a savior yet to come.[19]

Despite clashes with Greek rulers, the Jewish religion was heavily influenced by Greek culture. In the third century BCE, the Greek king of Egypt, Ptolemy II, asked the high priest in Jerusalem to send seventy-two elders to translate Hebrew scripture, producing the Greek-language Septuagint (after the Greek word for seventy). The translation led to a wider circulation of the scripture, opening it up to new interpretations. The Greek-speaking Jewish philosopher Philo tried to bring order to the unruly text of the Hebrew Bible by applying the teachings of Plato, who saw the visible world as an allegory of divine ideals. In his own writings, Philo transformed the otherwise obscure Hebrew Bible into a series of allegories. Disregarding its literal meaning as history, he used a complicated system of names and numbers to find hidden truths in the books. Adam and Eve symbolized the body and the senses, respectively; Cain's murder of Abel represented the love of self overcoming the love of God; and Abraham's wanderings represented the soul's quest for a spiritual home. In addition to those specific associations, Philo established a tradition of reading the Bible as an allegory for higher concepts and ideas beyond the literal meaning of the text that would later be taken up by other thinkers.[20]

The new Greek translation also exposed the text to the potential for misinterpretation. In Isaiah's prophecy about the royal baby, for instance, the Hebrew text refers to a "young woman," which the Septuagint translates as a "virgin"—a slip that would take on significance years later as prophesying a miraculous virgin birth.[21] Ultimately, the dynasty founded by the Maccabees turned out to be just as cruel and corrupt as the leaders they'd overthrown, spurring a new wave of prophets calling down God's judgment. Those calls only increased after the Romans conquered Judah, now Judea, in 63 BCE. Some predicted a coming messiah who would liberate the region, creating a new heaven on earth; some found that savior in the life and death of Jesus of Nazareth.

OUTSIDE THE BIBLE, there's little independent information about Jesus. The first-century Jewish historian Josephus makes passing mention of "Jesus, the so-called messiah," and "Jesus, a wise man" who was condemned to death and later appeared alive to his disciples. The Roman historian Tacitus mentions a "Christus" who "was put to death by Pontius Pilate" and whose followers were called Christians.[22] Apart from that, almost everything we know about Jesus comes from the Bible itself, in a collection of scriptures known as the New Testament. It tells of a healer and teacher, born in Bethlehem and raised in Nazareth, who preached poverty, nonviolence, and love. At the same time, he commanded his followers to prepare for the coming Kingdom of God, who would reward the virtuous and condemn the wicked.

For years after the Roman conquest, Judea was nominally ruled by the half-Jewish puppet king Herod the Great, who at least provided a semblance of autonomy. After his death in 4 BCE, Rome split the land between Herod's sons and imposed more direct rule under the prefect Pontius Pilate, increasing Jewish unrest among the various sects. The Pharisees advocated a strict observance of ritual purity, the Essenes preached the coming of the Messiah, and the Zealots fomented open rebellion. Amid this tension, Jesus was branded an agitator, and he was executed by crucifixion around the early 30s CE. After his death, some disciples insisted that he had risen from the dead and appeared to them. His followers spread across the Mediterranean. Paul, the most prominent among them, was a former Pharisee who wrote letters in Greek to congregations in nearby locales, including the Galatians, Romans, and Corinthians. Those letters later became the earliest books of the

New Testament. Jesus, Paul proclaimed, was the messiah—in Greek, *christos*—who had "died for our sins according to the scriptures."[23]

Unlike Judaism, the Christian religion was open to everyone, Paul asserted. By dying on the cross, Jesus had undone the disobedience of Adam, humankind's common ancestor, and extended God's covenant with Abraham for anyone to be saved.[24] Paul reinterpreted many stories of the Hebrew Bible in allegorical fashion as actually being about Jesus and found prophecies of his coming in Isaiah, Ezekiel, and Daniel. A letter to the Hebrews by an anonymous author went even further, arguing that Christ had sacrificed himself for humanity, just as the priests had sacrificed animals in the temple, and therefore Jesus's law now superseded Moses's.

Above all, Paul insisted that the world was about to end—and soon—and people had one last chance to accept Jesus as God before he returned to establish a new kingdom on earth. As this radical eschatology was taking root, a new tragedy befell the Jews. In 66 CE, the Zealots rose up against the Romans, holding Jerusalem for several years before the emperor Vespasian and his son Titus brutally put down the revolt in 70 CE, burning the second temple to the ground. The loss was incalculably traumatic for the Jewish people, and some followers of Jesus saw in the destruction a sign that end times were near.

INTO THIS MOMENT of high anxiety emerged several new biographies of Jesus known as the Gospels. Dating them is one of the trickiest endeavors in biblical studies, akin to "a line of drunks, propping each other up, with no fixed wall to lean on," as one twentieth-century scholar said.[25] Consensus dates Mark from the 70s, Matthew and Luke from the 80s or 90s, and John last, around the dawn of the second century, a chronology that means even the earliest gospel was written some forty years after Jesus was crucified.[26]

Tradition holds that Matthew and John were among the twelve disciples of Jesus, while Mark and Luke were companions of Paul, but most scholars believe the Gospels were written by later Christians and attributed to these followers only after the fact. After all, Jesus's disciples would have been quite old by the time the Gospels were written and unlikely to have written in polished Greek. Based on oral stories and perhaps earlier writings, each Gospel has its own ordering of events, adding and subtracting details to suit its narrative. Details of Jesus's birth, his parables and sayings, and his trials and execution differ among them, and they often contradict each other. While this may seem odd for sacred scripture, the texts are often seen as presentations of spiritual and political truths rather than a journalistic rendering of events.

The first three (Mark, Matthew, and Luke) share much of the same material, expounding on Jesus's life and teachings in a narrative style. Mark wastes little energy on Jesus's moral or ethical teachings. Writing around the time of the Roman sack of Jerusalem, he paints Jesus as a militant messiah who constantly references the razing of the temple as a symbol of the destruction of the Jewish religion and start of something new. Mark stresses the imminent arrival of Jesus and the need to embrace him to enter the kingdom of God.

Matthew and Luke seem based on Mark as well as a lost source scholars dub Q (from the German word for source, *Quelle*). They tell many of the same stories with a different tone that emphasizes Jesus's moral teachings. Perhaps as the years went by and the return of Jesus wasn't imminent, they realized that Christians would need to learn to live in the world. By this time, the Jewish religion was also showing a surprising resurgence. The leader of the Pharisees had managed to escape Jerusalem's fall and was rallying other rabbis around him to create a new liturgy without the temple. In response to this challenge, Matthew and Luke emphasize Christian supremacy over the Hebrew Bible, with every prophecy for a coming savior or king, including Daniel's "son of man" and Isaiah's royal child Immanuel, interpreted as a reference to Jesus. They mine the Septuagint for material, finding coded messages among the patriarchs, prophets, and Psalms that prefigure Jesus's biography.[27]

While Mark has no nativity story, both Matthew and Luke detail Jesus's birth in great detail to demonstrate how it fulfills the prophecies, down to the Greek mistranslation from Isaiah that the messiah would be born to a virgin mother, which finds its incarnation in the immaculate conception of Jesus's mother, Mary. To fulfill the prophet Micah's prediction that the messiah would come from Bethlehem, David's city, Matthew details a census ordered by Caesar Augustus that requires every Roman citizen to return to the town of his ancestry, even though no historical record of such a census exists and the scale of it would have been mind-boggling. Luke merely says Mary and Joseph lived in Bethlehem before moving to Nazareth. A cynic might say the authors deliberately added these details to retroactively prove Jesus's messianic status. For centuries, however, they have been taken as powerful proof of Jesus's divinity.[28]

Matthew and Luke also make the Jewish scribes and Pharisees the villains of their Gospels, taking pains to exonerate the Romans—perhaps to protect Christians against charges of rebelliousness, as the Romans had now begun persecuting the followers of this upstart faith.[29] In Matthew, Pontius Pilate even washes his hands of the execution, blaming it on the Jewish leaders—lines that would be used centuries later as justification for anti-Semitism.

The last gospel, John, is written with an approach very different from that of the other three. It focuses less on the events of Jesus's life than on long intellectual sermons on the deeper meanings of his teachings and represents Jesus as God's word made flesh, sent as a sacrificial lamb to take away the sins of the world. It leans into Jesus's divine status, giving him new powers beyond healing the sick; he turns water into wine and raises the dead. Scholars believe this Gospel was written for a persecuted sect of Christians in Asia Minor who had a particularly us-versus-them mentality. As such, the animosity against Jews reaches new heights in this Gospel, which incessantly criticizes the Pharisees and depicts Jewish crowds calling out for Jesus's crucifixion.

To a lesser extent, themes of persecution run through one of the last books to be written for the New Testament, Acts. It focuses on the deeds of Paul and the other apostles as they attempt to spread Christianity around the Mediterranean world under the guidance of the Holy Spirit and describes their miraculous ability to "speak in other tongues" and heal the sick "in the name of Jesus."[30] It also tells of Christianity's first martyrs at the hands of Jewish and Roman authorities, ending with Paul sitting in a cell, presumably on the verge of execution himself.

John is also sometimes credited with the New Testament's strangest book, Revelation, which depicts an epic battle at the end of the world between the forces of light and darkness, led by Christ on one side and a beast known as the Antichrist on the other. Eventually Christ wins, throwing the beast into a pit of fire until God inexplicably releases Satan from prison, spurring more battles and destruction before the final establishment of a New Jerusalem.[31] The book's vivid apocalyptic imagery and inscrutable symbolism have made it irresistible for generations of doomsayers feverishly predicting the end of the world.

THE CHRISTIAN BIBLE as we know it today was more or less completely written by 100 CE, though it would take several more centuries before its books were solidified into a canon. Both before and after that time, it would continue to undergo new interpretations for new audiences and worshippers. As Christians continued to face persecution from both Romans and Jews, they worked hard to defend their nascent religion with rational apologiae, written commentaries that presented the story of the Bible as one of the disobedience of the Jewish people—from Adam's fall to the moral backsliding of the patriarchs and kings—who were saved for the benefit of all humankind by the coming of Jesus.

They also worked to universalize the religion to make it more palatable to Roman society. Picking up on Philo's allegorical reading of the Bible, the second-century apologist Justin claimed that Jesus was an incarnation of the divine *logos* (law) that had spoken through saints and philosophers from Moses to Plato. Later generations of Christians doubled down on the allegorical method of Bible study, with the third-century sage Origen arguing that all Hebrew scripture could be interpreted only through Jesus. Moses parting the sea of reeds was a prefiguration of baptism, and the food laws of the Torah—such as the prohibition on eating shellfish or mixing meat and dairy—were only allegories for purity that didn't need to be followed literally.[32]

Persecution of Christians abruptly ended at the dawn of the fourth century with the conversion of the Roman emperor Constantine. As Latin became the official language of the church, the scholar Jerome was commissioned by the pope to translate the book to create the Latin Vulgate (from *editio vulgata*, or "common version")—the book Christians would read, and monks would painstakingly copy, for the next millennium. At the same time, Jewish scholars reinterpreted the Bible through commentaries known as the Talmud, a well-digested reading of the Hebrew Bible that—along with the Torah—has become the basis for the Jewish religion today.

As the ancient world gave way to the Middle Ages, Catholic priests interpreted the Bible through church liturgy, presenting it as a profound mystery focused on the drama of Jesus's death and resurrection.[33] Ordinary people could earn their way to heaven by attending mass and observing the sacraments. Knights and soldiers earned spiritual benefits by participating in crusades against the Muslims who had taken over the Holy Land, and rich people could literally buy their way into heaven by purchasing "indulgences" as forgiveness from sin.

Even as the allegorical and symbolic readings of the Bible reached their height, some scholars insisted on returning to the text itself. The most influential scholar of the Middle Ages, Thomas Aquinas, made a breakthrough in biblical analysis with the idea that God was in fact the "author" of the Bible, who used humans as his instruments to spread his word. While God sometimes used allegory to make a point, Aquinas argued, there was nothing allegorical in the Bible that wasn't presented literally elsewhere; with enough study, anyone could divine God's true spiritual intent.[34] As Johannes Gutenberg's first printed copies of the Vulgate rolled off his printing press in Germany, that idea would take hold like wildfire.

WHEN THEOLOGY PROFESSOR Martin Luther posted his ninety-five theses on the door of Wittenberg church in 1517, his main issue with the church was its emphasis on doing "good works" to achieve absolution from sin—especially taking issue with the purchase of indulgences by rich people. While humans would always fall short of God's laws, he argued, absolute faith in Jesus was enough to be saved. That salvation was available from the scripture alone (*sola scriptura*); that is, the Bible was to be read not by priests as a source for allegorical fables but by anyone as a practical guide for life. Mostly that meant showing how humans were irredeemably flawed and could be redeemed only by surrendering to Christ. That idea launched the Protestant Reformation, pitting the authority of the church against that of scripture and emphasizing the need for all believers to read the Bible on their own.[35]

Reading the Bible necessarily depended on understanding it, and a push for translations began.[36] Even before Luther posted his theses, Dutch scholar Desiderius Erasmus published a new version of the New Testament in Greek—relying on several different Greek manuscripts that were not necessarily the best or most accurate versions. Nevertheless, his version became the basis for nearly all translations that followed, including Luther's new translation into German. In England, John Wycliffe had translated the Vulgate in the fourteenth century. Now William Tyndale translated Erasmus's Greek New Testament as well as much of the Old Testament from Hebrew by 1535. Though he was executed as a heretic, his translation was eventually licensed by Henry VIII after the king's own split from the Catholic church. Several more English editions followed before King James I commissioned a new official version, bringing together fifty scholars to labor over English, Greek, Hebrew, and Latin texts to create the King James Version (KJV) in 1611. This version serves as the basis for most English-language Protestant Bibles today.

As more people read the Bible, however, not everyone saw it the way the Protestant reformers did. New scientific discoveries challenged biblical truth, over time spawning the Enlightenment, a new movement that prized rationality over faith. The Amsterdam-based Sephardic Jew Benedict de Spinoza was one of the first to call the Bible's authenticity into question, proposing that the Pentateuch was written not by Moses but thousands of years later by multiple authors around the time of the Babylonian captivity—a view similar to that held by scholars today. More than just calling the Bible's composition into question, however, Spinoza also questioned its teachings, rejecting the Old Testament depiction of a jealous, vindictive God. Rather than explain it away as allegory, he simply declared the Bible to be mistaken and not worth following as a moral example.[37]

That radical—if obvious—notion opened the floodgates of skepticism across Europe, as Enlightenment thinkers openly criticized the Bible for its irrational, even childish view of the divine. Many identified as deists; they believed the only rational way to understand good and evil in the world was to see God as a cosmic clockmaker who set the universe in motion and left humankind to figure out the rest. As for salvation by faith, the question was faith in *what*. The deists contended that the Bible was true only because it said it was—or, as Enlightenment philosopher Matthew Tindal wrote in the 1730 "deist's Bible," "It's an odd jumble, to prove the truth of a book by the truth of the doctrines it contains, and at the same time conclude those doctrines to be true, because contain'd in that book."[38]

By the nineteenth century, moral philosophers felt free to pick and choose which parts of the Bible to accept. New geological finds, such as dinosaur fossils, poked more holes in the biblical account as scientists declared the earth to be at least hundreds of millions of years old, contradicting the biblical timeline of only about six thousand years. In 1859, biologist Charles Darwin's *On the Origin of Species* argued that all species, including humans, evolved over time rather than being the instantaneous work of a creationist God. A new "higher criticism," beginning in Germany, treated the Bible itself as an object of scientific inquiry, picking apart its narrative strands to understand how and why it had been written.[39] Liberal Christians adapted to these new realities, continuing to believe Jesus was divine, even if many of the Bible's stories were embellished or imagined. Conservatives, however, saw the danger in that idea: If you reject part of the Bible as untrue, what was to keep you from jettisoning all of it? They pushed back against these heretical notions, not just in Europe but increasingly in the United States.

America's first settlers arrived with Bibles in hand. The Puritans who came to New England invoked the stories of the Old Testament to see themselves as new Israelites, blessed by God to serve as an example to the rest of the world. They set up a government according to Mosaic law, with biblical punishments meted out for sin. Heretics were hung on Boston Common, and hostile Native American tribes, like the Philistines, were destroyed.[40]

As Massachusetts became an increasingly important commercial hub, that biblical mission was watered down by new settlers who didn't share that vision.[41] Other colonies, such as Rhode Island and Pennsylvania, pursued a more tolerant course toward other faiths from the beginning—the start of an ebb and flow of biblical authority in America over the next four hundred years. In the 1740s, a revival known as the Great Awakening spurred new religious devotion among worshippers who bypassed church hierarchy to advocate a personal relationship with God. Worshippers particularly held up the KJV as the ultimate authority on God's word.

As deism crossed the Atlantic, the Bible's influence faded once more as it became more a tool for argument than an unquestioned sacred text.[42] Leading up to the American Revolution, Thomas Paine argued in *Common Sense* that God himself was opposed to monarchy, since the ancient Israelites had no king. Loyalists countered that monarchy runs through the Old Testament.[43] Paine's argument carried the day. After the war, however, Paine turned away from the Bible, arguing in *The Age of Reason* that "the obscene stories, the voluptuous debaucheries" were more like "the word of a demon than the word of God."

The backlash against Paine's work was so total that it singlehandedly ushered in a new age of religious fervor known as the Second Great Awakening. Both mainstream churches and burgeoning sects of Baptists and Methodists turned to the KJV as "a single textual authority of extraordinary unifying force," according to religious historian Mark Noll. The American Bible Society printed thousands of copies, and missionary societies set out overseas to fulfill the "Great Commission" to Jesus's followers to take his teachings to all peoples.[44]

As the young country barreled toward civil war in the latter half of the nineteenth century, both sides again marshaled the Bible to their cause. Slaveholders justified slavery with multiple passages from the Old Testament, such as the verses in Leviticus stating, "The heathen that are round about you; of them shall ye buy bondmen and bondmaids" and pass them to children "to inherit them for possession."[45] Others pointed to passages in the New Testament in which Paul implored servants to obey their masters. The Africans they enslaved, meanwhile, saw themselves in the Bible's stories of captivity and liberation, such as Moses's exodus from Egypt, which they memorialized in hymns sung in the cotton fields of the Deep South.

Abolitionists appealed to Jesus's "Golden Rule" to treat others as we ourselves would be treated or cited a Mosaic pronouncement against "man-stealing" to argue against slavery. Even some abolitionists were forced to admit, however, that it was necessary to "torture the Scriptures" to find support for their cause, and the most prominent, William Lloyd Garrison, eventually discounted the Bible altogether.[46] When war broke out, the Bible was the "first casualty" of the conflict, says Noll, "shattered amid the intellectual debris of debates over slavery and the material rubble created by two great armies both convinced that God was on their side."[47]

Long before Darwinism and higher criticism crossed the Atlantic to challenge biblical truth, the centrality of the Bible faded from American life as it became more of a storehouse of stories and quotes rather than an all-authoritative text. Its influence further diminished with an influx of Catholic and Jewish immigrants in the late nineteenth and early twentieth centuries, eroding Protestant orthodoxy.

While mainstream churches adapted to these changes, some Christians redoubled their efforts to assert the Bible's authority. In 1886, Chicago-based preacher Dwight Lyman Moody founded the Moody Bible Institute to restore the early colonial belief in scripture as a guiding light in society, which had strayed into war and chaos by abandoning it.[48] He pushed back against Darwinism and German higher criticism as fanciful "theories." Instead, he educated a corps of followers that God's truth was a coherent doctrine, knowable by anyone through a commonsense reading of the Bible.[49]

They were joined by conservative religious scholars at Princeton Theological Seminary who taught a new concept of "biblical inerrancy" that went far beyond the *sola scriptura* of the Reformation, contending that the Bible was absolutely reliable and never wrong. Mistakes in the book, argued theologian Charles Hodge, were no more than specks of sandstone in the marble blocks of the Parthenon.[50] Admittedly, they had to come up with some creative ways to make the Bible's literal words make sense. When the Moody Bible Institute's James Brookes counted only 490 years in the Bible between the Babylonian captivity and the second coming of Christ, he surmised that 483 of them had already passed, followed by a massive "parenthesis" of some two thousand years before a final seven years of tribulation described in Revelation. Brookes's protégé C. I. Scofield popularized such notions in the Scofield Reference Bible, a dense tome full of marginal notes that sold twelve million copies and influenced A. J. Tomlinson, who incorporated aspects of its theology into the Church of God of Prophecy.

Conservative Christians coalesced around *The Fundamentals*, a twelve-volume set spearheaded by the Moody Bible Institute that created the basis for fundamentalist Christianity in the twentieth century. It spelled out five main pillars of belief: biblical inerrancy, the virgin birth of Mary, the miracles performed by Jesus, his death as atonement for humankind's sins, and his resurrection. Of these, the most important was inerrancy, seen as the basis for all others. Though the Bible was written by many different people over many years, fundamentalists argued that they were all mere stenographers of the divine, making scripture an "absolute transcript" of God's mind.[51] The burgeoning movement gained traction after World War I, when the destruction in Europe followed by the rise of modernism and communism seemed to some like the end times. Fundamentalists eventually joined the battle against the concept of evolution—the very symbol of the materialist view of the world. At their urging, several states passed laws against the teaching of evolution in schools starting in the early 1920s. When a young biology teacher named John Scopes defied Tennessee's statute, William Jennings Bryan, former secretary of state and failed presidential candidate who championed rural America, joined the battle on behalf of the school district. Against him, the ACLU hired an urbane agnostic, Clarence Darrow.

The ensuing court battle took place in a hot Appalachian courtroom thirty miles north of the Church of God's headquarters in eastern Tennessee. Journalists such as H. L. Mencken framed it as a "clash of two worlds," with backwoods fundamentalism on one side and sophisticated modern science on the other. Darrow humiliated Bryan, asking question after question betraying the absurdity of a literal interpretation of the Bible: How could Eve be created from Adam's rib? How did a great fish swallow Jonah? What happened to the earth's rotation when the sun stopped in the book of Joshua?

Bryan was forced to admit he didn't know, saying, "I do not think about the things I don't think about." Darrow pounced: "Do you think about things you do think about?" Ultimately, Scopes lost the case, but the true losers were the fundamentalists, whom Mencken savagely mocked as "uneducated *homo boobiens*."[52] Fundamentalism retreated from the public forum while continuing to take root in small churches, mission organizations, and Bible colleges. It reemerged in the 1940s as evangelicalism. The fight over how to read the Bible, however, never really ended.

Debates raged at seminaries and universities throughout the next few decades, with even some "new evangelical" scholars finding the concept of biblical inerrancy to be out of step with contemporary historical research. By the 1970s, however, the doctrine of inerrancy had come out on top both in scholarly circles and in popular books such as Harold Lindsell's *The Battle for the Bible*, which declared in full-throated fury that the Bible "does not contain error of any kind," being an entirely accurate account both historically and scientifically.[53]

In 1972, biblical apologist Josh McDowell published his first edition of *Evidence That Demands a Verdict*, a rational defense of the Bible in which he argued that even though it was written by more than forty authors over a 1,500-year span, it nevertheless demonstrates a "unity which binds the whole together" that could be inspired only by God. One of the primary spokespeople for Campus Crusade for Christ and a later advocate for the purity movement, McDowell purported to prove the truth of the Bible through rational argument, deriving proofs from history, archaeology, and literature, sometimes selectively applied.

He claimed that the Gospels, for example, were all written soon after Jesus's death by people close to him and clearly indicate that Jesus referred to himself as the messiah. If he wasn't, then he was either a "liar" or a "lunatic," both of which seemed "out of character" with his "moral teachings."[54] That left only one explanation: Jesus really was who he said he was—the son of God. McDowell doesn't spend much time considering the possibility that Jesus's words and actions might have been distorted—intentionally or not—by later generations of followers, and he too easily dispenses with the internal contradictions in the Gospels. "Much more remarkable, it seems to me, are the agreements, and the subtle harmonies that pervade them," he said. "I believe one can hold the Scriptures in his hand and say, 'The Bible is trustworthy and historically reliable.'"[55]

McDowell's books were immensely popular among Christians eager for a rational defense of biblical inerrancy, including David Green and his children, who saw in them confirmation of the truths of the Bible taught by their own church. Steve later remembered reading McDowell's book over a cup of coffee during high school and finding that it deepened his faith, and Mart sold later editions of it at Mardel.[56] It and similar books bolstered the Greens' belief that the Bible was the true word of God, and it was incumbent upon believers to share it with the world.

CHAPTER SIX

Peace Be with You

You need to make that movie." It was May 1999, and OneHope's Rob Hoskins was on the phone to Mart, urging him to tell the story of the missionaries killed in Ecuador. Only Mart had the resources to make it happen, Hoskins told him—and it fit the goal of their company Bearing Fruit to spread Christ-consciousness. "I've never even been in a movie theater," Mart reminded him. "How in the world would I get the rights to do a film?" After praying about it, however, he decided spreading the word of God outweighed his reservations about worldly entertainment and agreed to pursue the project.[1]

Though Mart had no experience in the movie business, he had confidence that he would succeed in it, just as he'd succeeded in everything else so far in his life. If God wanted the movie made, he'd make sure it happened. Mart contacted Tom Newman, who came aboard as producer, and together, they reached out to Steve Saint, son of slain missionary Nate Saint. After his aunt Rachel had died in 1994, Saint had moved his family to Ecuador for a year to live with the Waodoni, establishing a nonprofit to aid the tribe. "I can't speak for the Waodoni," Saint told him, "but I can introduce you to them."[2] Four months later, Mart was in Ecuador, traveling by bus, plane, and finally a small boat into Waodoni territory. He spent several days meeting the tribesmen, including Mincaye and others who had killed the missionaries. The Waodoni were wary; for years, they'd dealt with tourists coming to see the famous tribe that had killed the Christians. This would be different, Mart promised—a story from the tribe's perspective that could warn powerfully against violence.[3]

At some point, the conversation turned to the shooting at Columbine High School in Littleton, Colorado, where twelve students and a teacher had recently been killed by two classmates. "That's just the way we used to act, killing for no reason," the Waodoni said, according to Mart. "If our story can help others in North America then we want to tell our story." They worked out a deal for the rights, with half the proceeds going to Saint's missionary project. To direct, Mart turned to Jim Hanon, a commercial director who had worked on Bearing Fruit's Jesus campaign. Though Hanon had never made a full-length film before, Mart wasn't worried. "Everybody told me not to use a first-time director, that it's not smart. But I didn't go by that. I went by faith," he said. "By fact he's not [qualified]; by faith he is." Together, they decided that instead of leaping into a feature, they'd make a documentary first, both to familiarize themselves with the story and to generate excitement for the eventual feature.[4]

For more expertise, the team added seasoned producer Bill Ewing, whose credits included *The Patriot*, *Men in Black II*, and *Spiderman*. A born-again Christian, Ewing had stepped away from a senior VP position at Sony/Columbia, as he was "in the process of discovering God's plan."[5] He now became president of their new company, Every Tribe Entertainment, named after the verse in Revelation about people "from every nation, tribe, people and language" appearing before Christ.[6]

To set up the financials, Mart hired a new adviser, Bill High, who had recently left a career as a lawyer to work with wealthy Christians on philanthropic endeavors. Mart and the family put up almost the entire $2 million budget for the documentary, which included interviews with all five of the missionaries' widows and seventeen days in Ecuador interviewing tribe members. They aimed to tell the story of how the tribe had given up violence with the help of the two courageous women who had brought them to the Bible.[7]

By 2002, the documentary was complete. As the team screened it at a Christian film festival in Indianapolis, Saint beamed, calling it "the Waodoni's story as much as it is the story of the five missionaries." The film, however, strangely buries the tribe's point of view. Titled *Beyond the Gates of Splendor* in reference to Elisabeth Elliot's book, it begins with a shocking reenactment of the Waodoni chanting and killing one another, lamenting that "blood feuds and vendettas had created a cycle of killing" that "threatened the very existence of the tribe."[8]

A husband-and-wife anthropologist team then suggest that there is something inherent in the Waodoni that caused their extreme violence—a hyperfixation on independence and autonomy, such that if anything threatens those things, "you kill." That simplistic depiction is at odds with most scholarship about the Waodoni, which attributes their violence at least in part to centuries of conflicts with European settlers—including Jesuit missionaries who converted them and rubber companies that hunted and enslaved them.[9]

Regardless, the documentary contrasts the Waodoni's savagery with a Norman Rockwell–esque depiction of the smiling young missionaries. Footage of the meeting with the tribespeople on the beach, filmed by the missionaries themselves, would be mesmerizing if not for an overbearing orchestral score. Following the tribe's attack, a full third of the ninety-minute film chronicles the aftermath from the missionaries' perspective, including a three-minute depiction of the recovery of Nate Saint's body set to dirgeful piano music.

The film includes little analysis of the causes for the encounter, which was due in part to the hubris of the missionaries. A member of the SIL, Rachel Saint had come to Ecuador feeling destined to make first contact with the Waodoni. That spurred a competition with her brother Nate and the other men, who rashly headed into the jungle in secret, barely learning any Waodoni words.[10] The film omits that backstory even as it harps on the missionaries' nonviolence, saying they refused to fight when slaughtered. It repeats a claim that one Waodoni man was struck accidentally by a bullet fired into the air; several anthropologists who interviewed the Waodoni, however, were told that a missionary intentionally shot the man during the attack—a report that appears nowhere in the film.[11]

Beyond the Gates also spends little time on attempts by Rachel Saint and Elisabeth Elliot to Christianize the tribe, glossing over an ongoing conflict between the two women as Saint jealously herded the tribe into a missionary settlement under her supervision, accepting payments from Texaco-Gulf in exchange for keeping the tribe contained. Elliot became disillusioned, eventually leaving Ecuador and writing a new book, *The Savage My Kinsman*, in which she questioned the notion that the Waodoni were more violent than other people; she had observed modesty, selflessness, and generosity among them that she said put many so-called Christians to shame.[12]

While Saint did establish schools and medical clinics, by the 1990s, her settlement was a "shanty town" of "tin-roofed shacks" where residents were "visibly less healthy than those who lived in more traditional ways," according to *New Yorker* writer Joe Kane.[13] By then, few Waodoni even "described themselves as *cristianos*, and the local church built by the missionaries decades before had fallen into disrepair," says anthropologist Casey High.[14] None of this complexity is reflected in the documentary, which presents a simple story of Bible over savagery, as if reading the book alone had reversed centuries of violence. Meanwhile, the documentary lingers on a trip through America by Mincaye, who is amazed by shower faucets and grocery stores. At one point, he watches a black-and-white World War II movie, stunned by the violence of planes bombing people they don't even know.

IRONICALLY, AT THE same time that Mart was creating his film about nonviolence and Christian forgiveness, the US was in the midst of the largest mobilization of military might in decades—one wholeheartedly supported by Bible-believing evangelicals. In the wake of the Clinton intern sex scandal, conservatives found a moral savior in Texas governor George W. Bush, a born-again Christian who touted so-called compassionate conservatism, taking a hard line on culture issues while promoting church-based organizations as providers of social services.[15]

With Republicans in the presidency and both houses of Congress, evangelicals were newly welcomed into the halls of power. Prolife news conferences and Bible studies took place within the congressional complex. "I had virtually unlimited access to the US Capitol," recalled National Clergy Council head Rob Schenck. "We held the keys to the kingdom."[16] Dobson and other evangelical leaders were frequent visitors to the White House as evangelical attorney general John Ashcroft enforced a new executive order to prevent agencies from discriminating against religious groups.

Before evangelicals could use that power, however, America was thrown into turmoil by the attacks on the World Trade Center by radical Islamic terrorists on September 11, 2001. Bush quoted Psalm 23 as he swore revenge, vowing that the country would "go forward to defend freedom and all that is good and just in the world."[17] Other evangelical leaders declared the attacks a punishment from God for America's sins. Appearing on Robertson's *700 Club*, Falwell included feminists, gays and lesbians, and "abortionists" among those who "helped this happen."[18]

Even as some evangelicals distanced themselves from those extreme remarks, they geared up for an epic battle between Christianity and Islam. "We will rid the world of evil-doers," Bush declared. "This is our calling." Not since the Cold War had America had such a clear enemy, as *Christianity Today* declared that "religious terrorism is the communism of the 21st century."[19] Bush unleashed a massive bombing campaign and ground assault in Afghanistan to uproot terrorist leader Osama bin Laden and next proposed to invade Iraq, claiming that Iraqi president Saddam Hussein had stockpiled chemical and nuclear "weapons of mass destruction" that could be deployed against the US.

Conservative Christians supported the invasion in numbers far ahead of the general public. After all, Saddam Hussein ruled over land that had once been ancient Babylon, which biblical prophets had long associated with evil, and Revelation taught that the temple would need to be rebuilt in Jerusalem before Jesus would return. As if prophesying the moment, the Left Behind series, now on its tenth book, told of the Antichrist building a glittering New Babylon from which he waged war on Christians and Jews throughout the Middle East.

When the US invaded in March 2003, Iraqi forces put up little resistance against the barrage of bombs followed by a tank column barreling its way to Baghdad. Soon American troops were toppling a twenty-foot-tall statue of Saddam in the capital as newly liberated Iraqis looted shops and ransacked the exhibit halls of the Iraqi Museum. "Stuff happens," Secretary of Defense Donald Rumsfeld said, shrugging in response to the destruction.

Back home, Hobby Lobby celebrated its three hundredth store, opened in an Oklahoma City suburb in June 2003. By now, the company had stores stretching from Florida to Wyoming with annual sales of $1.3 billion, buoyed by a surge in sales for the new fad of scrapbooking.[20] Mardel had expanded at a steady but slower rate, now featuring eighteen stores, even as Mart stepped down from day-to-day operations to focus on filmmaking. Christian retail was big business, with the Left Behind novels outstripping all other book sales and Christian rock outselling classical and jazz as the fifth most popular music genre in the country.[21]

The year brought another milestone for David, who appeared for the first time on the Forbes 400 list of wealthiest Americans at number 224. Now sixty-two, David had a full head of white hair above his black-rimmed glasses but showed no sign of retiring anytime soon. In an interview in his Oklahoma City headquarters, David came across as shy and soft-spoken, sitting in a black upholstered chair and expressing annoyance about the recognition of his wealth. "That's not what we're about. We're about serving God," he insisted, laying his hand on a stack of gospel pamphlets. "Hobby Lobby is only the means to an end."[22]

The family occasionally ventured into funding more worldly causes—for example, contributing to a civic project to put a new dome on the Oklahoma state capitol. Such donations were a rarity for the company, however. It spent the majority of its largesse donating to three charities—Wycliffe Bible Translators, OneHope, and Every Home for Christ—along with a select group of smaller ministries. The Greens were also buying up properties on a massive scale to donate to religious groups—some $100 million worth between 2000 and 2002.[23] David, Barbara, Mart, Steve, and the rest of the family met every few months to decide where to contribute, often based on their own personal relationships or word of mouth and frequently taking the recipients by surprise. In Oklahoma, they purchased a former nursing home for a Christian boarding school for troubled teens run by Steve's former youth minister.[24] In Branson, Missouri, they bought up a 2,672-seat theater for a megachurch associated with the Assemblies of God. "Obviously it's a tax write-off, but we do it for the ministry, that's our motivation," said David.[25]

One transaction outside Chicago shows just how lucrative such deals could be for Hobby Lobby. In 2002, the family paid $9 million for an eighty-acre campus that had been headquarters of the Safety-Kleen Corporation, offering it to Jerry Falwell for a satellite campus for his Liberty University. The offer came just a few months after Falwell's controversial comments blaming gays and abortionists for the 9/11 terrorist attacks, which didn't seem to faze the Greens. Falwell turned down the property, saying it was too far from his main campus in Virginia, and Hobby Lobby donated it to an evangelical megachurch instead. The pastor estimated its worth at $53 million.[26] If the Greens were able to deduct that from their taxes, then at a 20 percent corporate rate, the sale would have more than paid for itself.

Falwell pointed the Greens toward a former industrial site in Lynchburg. The family snatched it up in 2003 for $10.3 million and donated it to Falwell for a new home for his Thomas Road Baptist Church and Liberty University Law School to train the next generation of Christian lawyers.[27] David, who described Falwell as a personal hero, said that Falwell had told him that the donation put his plans to expand the campus five years ahead of schedule. Meanwhile, the Greens claimed a $29 million tax deduction for the property in 2004—nearly three times what they'd paid for it a year before and about half of the annual profits of $60 to $70 million that Hobby Lobby had generated for the family trust that owned the company.[28]

The Greens weren't the only businesspeople mixing God and work. A slew of executives were suddenly using the workplace to bear witness to their love of Christ, speaking of the office as their "mission field."[29] Based on Title VII of the Civil Rights Act, businesses could hold prayer meetings and promote religion in the workplace so long as it was "non-coercive" and hiring and promotion didn't depend upon participation.[30] Groups such as the Marketplace Network held gatherings to teach Christian businessmen how to avoid running afoul of labor laws, counseling them to place "conversation starters" such as Bibles or books such as *God Is My CEO* on their desks.[31]

Tom Phillips, CEO of Raytheon—the world's second-largest weapons maker, which provided hundreds of millions in bombs and missiles for Operation Iraqi Freedom—held a weekly Bible study called the Tuesday Club for high-powered Christian executives in Boston. In a departure from the prosperity gospel, the new wave of Christian executives de-emphasized the material rewards of faith in favor of a "servant leadership" model, forming a "covenantal relationship" with employees. They were still unabashedly capitalist. Alaska Airlines CEO Bruce Kennedy implemented the placement of Bible verses on meal trays but also presided over a two-month work stoppage over poor work conditions. Employees picketed his church and placed a cross on his lawn reading, "Would Jesus Do This?"[32]

No company was more overt about its faith than Chick-fil-A, whose official statement of purpose was "to glorify God by being a faithful steward of all that is entrusted to us." CEO Truett Cathy held church services at company headquarters and offered Christian marriage counseling through groups using materials from Dobson's Focus on the Family. The company donated hundreds of millions to other Christian organizations, including scholarship funds at Christian colleges, Christian foster homes, and character-building programs such as Gothard's Character First! in schools.[33]

Hobby Lobby ministered to employees with two chaplains at headquarters and another two who traveled the country. "But there's never any way that we try to push anything on anybody," David said. "We are not trying to proselytize."[34] Nevertheless, in delivering Christmas bonuses every year, Steve made sure that employees received a card from the company reminding them that Jesus "offers eternal life to whoever believes in him" and urging them to contact a "Bible-believing church in your area."[35] Steve started a church for employees from Hobby Lobby's Oklahoma City campus, holding services on Sunday nights and showing religious movies.

David was unapologetic—even provocative—about the company's approach to faith. "This is something that other people might not consider politically correct—nor do we intend to be," David said.[36] In his books and interviews, he revels in stories about employees accepting Christ through company intervention. When general counsel Peter Dobelbower raised legal concerns about David offering a "gospel invitation" at a comanagers meeting, David brushed them aside.[37]

"Fifteen people gave their lives to Christ today," he told the attorney. "You tell me—what is the cost of a soul?" According to David, "Peter teared up and silently walked out of my office." The company now starts every comanager meeting with a prayer, handing out cards for people to accept Christ as their savior. David said 80 percent of people do. In Hobby Lobby's world, people are ripe to accept Jesus—and therefore the promise of eternal life—with just a little push. The possibility that you might offend someone with a different set of beliefs, or even a different vision of eternity, seems a small price to pay. "While obedience often carries risk," David said, "listening to the Holy Spirit's prompting always pays off."[38]

In 2002, the Greens provided employees with a new book encouraging people to incorporate evangelical Christian principles into everything they did: *The Purpose-Driven Life* by Rick Warren, a Southern Baptist pastor of a California megachurch. Warren was not a typical pastor; with short, spiked hair and Hawaiian shirts that strained at the belly, he preached an empathetic evangelicalism. "We never use the pulpit for politics," he said. "We believe in loving people into the kingdom."[39] When it came to his theological principles, he was staunchly conservative, believing in a literal and inerrant Bible and opposing abortion, homosexuality, and women as preachers.

Warren's Southern California church boasted over sixteen thousand members organized around small groups with common interests coming together for Bible study and tracking the trends of evangelicalism in the '80s and '90s that drifted from traditional denominations toward more informal parachurch networks.[40] His book simultaneously tells people they are special—"God *longs* for you to discover the life he created you to live—here on earth, and forever in eternity"—and that they can discover their purpose only by reading God's "Owner's Manual": the Bible.[41]

In the shock and disruption of the 9/11 terrorism attacks, Warren's book offered answers to a nation looking for meaning; it sold ten million copies in just over a year, becoming one of the best-selling books of all time. What truly made the book a success, however, was its marketing strategy, with thousands of churches reading one of the book's forty chapters per day in a "forty days of purpose" project and businesses such as Hobby Lobby buying it in bulk to give to employees. As *Christianity Today* put Warren on its cover as "America's most influential pastor," the book's publisher could rightly say that the book "is more than a bestseller, it's become a movement."[42]

As COPIES FLEW off the shelf at Mardel, Mart continued to find his own purpose in filmmaking. While the nonprofit Bearing Fruit sought distribution for *Beyond the Gates*, for-profit Every Tribe Entertainment ramped up preproduction for a feature film on the missionaries, *The End of the Spear*. Once again, Bill Ewing oversaw production and new filmmaker Jim Hanon directed. For the role of Mincayani, a composite character representing the tribesmen who had killed the missionaries, the production cast Dominican American actor Louie Leonardo. For the crucial role of Nate Saint, they considered Chad Allen, a twenty-nine-year-old former teen heartthrob who'd appeared on the Western TV drama *Dr. Quinn, Medicine Woman* and seemed to offer the perfect combination of bravado and sensitivity. There was just one problem, they discovered: He was gay.

Growing up in a strict Catholic family in California, Allen had starred in sitcoms as a child and appeared in teen magazines before landing the role of Matthew Cooper, Dr. Quinn's ne'er-do-well son. Off-screen, he pursued a wild life of drugs and partying at clubs. When a tabloid photographer snapped a picture of him kissing another man, his publicist concocted a nonsensical story that the man was a prostitute whom Allen had kissed by accident. Nevertheless, letters came pouring in from gay men about how much it meant to see him represent them. He came out in a cover story in *The Advocate* in 2001 and began speaking out publicly while getting sober and joining a gay-friendly church in Pasadena.[43]

According to Mart, the Every Tribe team had no idea about Allen's sexuality before they offered him the part. Allen remembers things differently, saying that he was clear that he was gay before he was cast. "What came back to me was unequivocal—that they felt God had called me to do this role, and they weren't going to back down from that," he says now. Mart apologized to Saint for casting a homosexual in the part of his martyred father but said the company could run afoul of California's labor laws if it backed out now. Besides, recasting the role would throw off the whole shooting schedule. Saint later said God had revealed to him in a dream that he wanted Allen for the role.[44]

Three days before filming, Allen appeared on the talk show *Larry King Live* to defend the rights of gay people to marry. The producers were mortified. Allen sat down with Saint, telling him he would back out if the filmmakers weren't comfortable—even if that meant breaching the contract he'd signed. According to Allen, Saint seemed honestly conflicted, but suggested they fly in his airplane together and leave it up to God, saying "if we come down safely, then we've got our answer." As they touched back down to ground, he says Saint told him that he "was committed to walking through with me whatever came."[45]

The next several months were brutal as actors and crew filmed in Panama, battling spiders and mosquitoes and hacking through the jungle with machetes to reach locations. For Allen, it was a different ordeal, as he faced constant pressure on set to "repent" his gay lifestyle, repeatedly invited to Bible study and prayer vigils. While Saint and Hanon stood by him, Allen says, "it became very clear to me that about half the people there wanted me to serve their idea of God's will, which was admitting my sexuality, my love, was sinful and destructive. I was feeling constantly torn, and very lonely." Mart was distant from Allen on set, as he struggled to produce the movie, praying hard for a miracle to allow filming to finish. Once again, he and his family financed almost the whole film as the budget ballooned to some $17 million.[46] As they took the footage back to Oklahoma to edit the film, they could only wonder how it would be received.

EVEN AS THE film was in production, gay marriage was becoming the talk of the nation. In Massachusetts, seven same-sex couples had sued to marry based on the state constitution. As the country awaited the verdict, Dobson said a win for the plaintiffs would mean the end of "the family as we have known it," and "with its demise will come chaos such as the world has never seen."[47] Dobson had become increasingly involved in politics since a case in Alabama in which Judge Roy Moore had placed a monument to the Ten Commandments outside the courthouse in 2003. After courts demanded that it be removed, Dobson lashed out at judges, saying that in case after case, an "unelected, unaccountable, arrogant, imperious judiciary appointed for life" ruled against Christians, "determined to make all of us dance to their music."[48]

Unfortunately for him, the trend continued in Massachusetts, where the state's highest court legalized same-sex marriage, ruling 4–3 for the plaintiffs. As couples celebrated, Dobson and other conservatives demanded a vote on a Federal Marriage Amendment (FMA) to the Constitution that would officially enshrine marriage as a "union of a man and a woman."[49] In a new book, *Marriage Under Fire*, he insisted that only heterosexual marriage could satisfy women's "deep longings" for romance, self-esteem, and contentment and men's need to be respected and have their dreams supported, citing "more than ten thousand studies" that supposedly showed that children thrived in families with a mother and father. Many social scientists disagreed with his conclusions, saying he'd "cherry-picked" his research, and some scholars even pleaded that he "cease and desist" misrepresenting theirs.[50]

As the 2004 election pitted George W. Bush against Democrat John Kerry, Bush signed new laws to end late-term abortion and support funding for abstinence-only education. On gay rights, however, Bush frustrated evangelicals by supporting civil unions and openly appointing gay officials. Finally in 2004, Dobson gave Bush an ultimatum: Support the FMA or the Christian Right would abandon his campaign. Bush conceded, coming out in support of the measure, but when the bill came up for a vote, it fell short of the sixty needed in the Senate. Nevertheless, Dobson endorsed Bush, and pastors took to pulpits across the country to implore parishioners to vote, including Rick Warren, who sent out a letter saying opposing same-sex marriage was "non-negotiable." Their efforts brought out evangelicals in vast numbers, helping Bush retain the White House and spurring hope that he would take a stronger stand. In the words of longtime conservative activist Richard Viguerie, "If you don't implement a conservative agenda now, when do you?"[51]

THREE DAYS LATER, Mart's documentary *Beyond the Gates of Splendor* premiered in theaters. Mart took a page from Rick Warren's marketing, inviting members of more than a thousand churches to a special screening. With the phenomenal box-office success of Mel Gibson's

The Passion of the Christ, a gory retelling of Jesus's crucifixion, and the continued success of the Left Behind series, Christian media seemed to be having a moment, and Mart intended to be a part of it. "Story tellers are shaping our culture," Mart told *The Oklahoman*. "I decided to stop complaining and start creating."[52] Despite the marketing push, the documentary flopped in theaters, with limited distribution outside Oklahoma and Texas, grossing under $40,000 in its theatrical run.[53] The lackluster showing only made Mart redouble his efforts to break through with the feature film.

Nowhere was conservative media more successful than in the rise of the cable network Fox News, which surpassed CNN to become the most watched cable network in 2004. That December, Fox News host Bill O'Reilly aired a segment called "Christmas Under Siege," arguing that all over the country, "Christmas is taking flak." It felt like the culmination of the Christmas ads that Hobby Lobby had launched a decade earlier, which were still running in 250 papers nationwide to the tune of $5 million a year. Now the ADF, the Christian legal organization cofounded by Dobson, launched its own campaign to defend Christmas, sending letters to public schools advocating for religious symbols to be included among the Santas and reindeer. "It's a sad day in America when you have to retain a lawyer to wish someone a Merry Christmas," said ADF lawyer Mike Johnson.[54]

It wasn't just Christmas under assault; egged on by Fox's coverage, Christians felt held hostage by the despotism of unaccountable judges. Increasingly, the Christian Right looked to control of the Supreme Court as its highest goal.[55] Just two years after Alabama judge Roy Moore had been ordered to remove the Ten Commandments monument from his courthouse, the Supreme Court ruled in 2005 on another display of the Ten Commandments, this time on the grounds of the Texas state capitol. For decades, courts had relied on a three-pronged test for whether an action violates the separation of church and state. Known as the "Lemon test" after the 1971 case *Lemon v.*

Kurtzan, it required that an action have a secular purpose, neither promote nor hinder religion, and not unduly "entangle" government with religion.[56]

In a 5–4 ruling, however, the Court set aside the Lemon test to rule instead that the monument was "part of an unbroken history of official acknowledgment by all three branches of government of the role of religion in American life," in the words of Chief Justice William Rehnquist. Set among other monuments on the Texas capitol grounds, he said, the monument was part of the state's history, not advocacy of particular religious principles.[57] Even as conservative Christians celebrated the case as the first in decades to rule on behalf of church over state, they suffered defeat the very same day, as the Court also ruled 5–4 that a display of the Ten Commandments inside a Kentucky courthouse did violate the Constitution.

If nothing else, the cases showed how important a single justice could be when it came to issues of religion. When two seats opened in 2005 with the death of William Rehnquist and retirement of Sandra Day O'Connor, conservatives swung into action with a campaign to secure the court spearheaded by Leonard Leo, a conservative Catholic lawyer with the Federalist Society. For Rehnquist's seat, Bush delighted conservative Christians by nominating John Roberts, a Catholic who'd once signed a brief in a case arguing that *Roe* should be overturned.[58] For O'Connor's, however, he put forward White House counsel Harriet Miers, who had given a speech advocating choice a decade earlier. Conservative leaders organized their constituents to flood the White House with calls, and Miers withdrew her nomination.[59]

Eager to shore up his conservative base, Bush took Leo's suggestion to nominate Samuel Alito, a Catholic former member of Reagan's Justice Department who in a 1985 memo had urged the administration to pursue an incremental approach to ending *Roe v. Wade*, with the eventual goal of banning abortion outright. When asked about it during his confirmation hearings, however, Alito said he would keep "an open mind."[60]

MEANWHILE, HOBBY LOBBY continued to expand into Florida and Virginia as it brought its total number of stores to 370 by the end of 2005, tallying $1.5 billion in total sales.[61] David rose to number 133 on the Forbes list of richest Americans, with $2 billion in estimated net worth.[62] The year also saw a new milestone in the company as Steve, forty-one, became Hobby Lobby president even while David continued to oversee the company as CEO.[63] David also continued to direct charitable donations, including donating a 180,000-square-foot former hospital in Pompano Beach, Florida, worth $4.5 million to OneHope. The property would be a supercenter for missionary organizations, with plans to add a pool, tennis courts, dormitory, and conference center named for David's mother, Marie Green.[64]

The feature film *The End of the Spear*, with Chad Allen in the role of Nate Saint, premiered in January 2006. It closely followed the storyline of the documentary, beginning with a similar montage of tribesmen killing each other in the rain and darkness, even spearing babies and children, to the strains of melodramatic music. As the missionaries arrive, Allen and a towheaded child actor playing young Steve Saint stand on a dirt landing strip beside a yellow prop plane. "If the Waodoni attack, will you defend yourselves?" the boy asks. "Son, we can't shoot the Waodoni," says Nate, handsome in a white T-shirt and a 1950s haircut. "They're not ready for heaven. We are."

When he and the other missionaries confront the Waodoni, one spears Allen in the chest as he turns in slow motion. He clutches the shaft as he falls to his knees, blood spreading over his white T-shirt as he watches his fellow missionary Jim Elliot shoot his gun into the air. A mournful soundtrack swells, and the sky bursts open with rain, lightning flashing on the Waodoni's faces as they survey the horror.

The film does a better job than the documentary in presenting the Waodoni's perspective, spending considerable time with Mincayani and the other tribesmen to explain the tragic misunderstanding that caused the killings. On the other hand, it follows the same general themes, presenting the Waodoni as ruthless savages and the Christians as nonviolent martyrs. The tribe is overcome with regret as they invite the two white women—Rachel Saint and Elisabeth Elliot, both in immaculate gingham skirts—to join them.

In the film's climax, the grown-up Steve Saint, again played by Allen, takes a trip down the river with Mincayani to the beach where the missionaries were speared. Overcome with grief, Mincayani demands that Saint kill him in revenge for his crime. Saint chooses mercy, and the two embrace while in flashback, Mincayani shares his memory of the day, including a detail he'd never told anyone: As the Waodoni look up, they see angels descending in a bright light from heaven to take away the souls of the missionaries. "My father lost his life at the end of the spear, and it was at the end of the spear that Mincayani and I found ours," Saint says as he flies a plane into the sunset.

MART HAD HIGH hopes for the film, envisioning it as a box-office smash that could break through to mainstream audiences. On top of the $17 million budget, Every Tribe pledged $12 million in marketing, including banners hung in churches and "Spear Gear" swag such as hats, T-shirts, jewelry, and home decor.[65] The company invited congregations to some three hundred select screenings in advance of the nationwide release.[66] "It's a story of reconciliation," said Saint, who authored a companion book. "Everyone has relationships that they would like to be reconciled. Maybe this will give them hope that they can be."[67]

Initial reviews panned the movie for its heavy-handed plot and manipulative soundtrack. *The New York Times* called it a "film of few words and no developed characters" with "an inescapable air of

Kiplingesque smugness."[68] The *New York Daily News* said, "The story feels as whitewashed and disingenuous as an episode of 'Lassie.' "[69] Perhaps the most cutting "review" of all was by a Waodoni activist group that issued a "formal denouncement" against their depiction in the film by foreign actors.[70] The only saving grace was a positive assessment of the performances of Louie Leonardo as Mincayani and Allen as both Nate and Steve Saint.

A week before the official release of the film, however, that asset became a liability as evangelical Colorado pastor Jason Janz posted an open letter decrying the movie's decision to cast an openly gay actor as a revered missionary martyr. "We must realize that the Christian message and the messenger are intricately related," he said, comparing the choice to pop star "Madonna playing the Virgin Mary." The letter sparked a movement among Christians to boycott the film.[71]

Allen didn't back down, appearing again on CNN's *Larry King*, this time along with Albert Mohler, president of the Southern Baptist Theological Seminary, to debate gay marriage. After the appearance, Mohler published an editorial criticizing the "very reckless decision" to cast Allen in the film, saying Every Tribe had "chosen an actor—perhaps even *the* actor—least likely to be able to make us forget him and see Nate Saint."[72]

The filmmakers said in a prepared statement that the only message of the film was to promote "what it can mean to live what the Bible says is true" and that "we cannot single out the personal choices of one of the cast for scrutiny."[73] In a conversation with Randy Alcorn of Eternal Perspective Ministries, Mart went further, saying he wouldn't have made the offer to Allen if he had known he was gay, but "I learned that God loved Chad more than I did and that He wanted Chad on this project."[74] Alcorn assured his followers that both Mart and Saint had been "devastated" when they'd found out about Allen's homosexuality, and at least in part, their desire to work with him was in hopes he would "come to know Jesus," which "would of course require repentance" for his gay lifestyle.[75]

Despite their attempts to follow God's plan, apparently it wasn't his will for the film to do well, as it opened to a disappointing $4.2 million weekend. Condemnations continued to pour in. One of the harshest was from the son-in-law of one of the slain missionaries, Dan Kachikis, who accused the filmmakers of deliberately keeping Allen's sexuality a secret from the families, prioritizing pragmatism over Christian morals. Had they known, he said, family members wouldn't have given their life rights to the film. "They would have lost time, missed deadlines and opening dates, they would have lost money," he said. "Practically speaking, the easier decision was pray, have a dream and say 'yes' to Chad."[76]

Every Tribe went into damage control, dropping Allen from publicity for the movie and hiring a Dallas-based PR firm that tried a new pitch: The filmmakers had hired Allen on purpose to "demonstrate the love of Christ and to be consistent with the message of the film, which is about forgiveness."[77] Without evangelical support, however, the film faltered, grossing only $11.7 million for a year, less than half of the $27 million spent on production and publicity. In a memoir published a year later, Saint condemned homosexuality, calling it "unnatural" and "a perversion" that "threatens the historic fabric of our country," though he did add that after making the film with Allen, "I no longer find homosexuals disgusting."[78]

A few years later, Mart reflected on the incident, saying, "The issues get more complicated when you get to know people—the people involved in these issues. And you realize it's not so black and white all the time."[79] The key, he said, was love: "If we can learn to love each other and respect each other, we can have differences. I don't have to change my convictions, but yeah, I think love can make a difference." As open-minded as that view might seem, it's hard to escape the conclusion that the Greens were suffering the consequences of their own actions. After all the years they'd spent supporting people and organizations who denounced LGBTQ people, they were now bearing the brunt of those attacks—or, to put it in biblical terms, "For they have sown the wind, and they shall reap the whirlwind."[80]

For Allen, the experience was a turning point in his life. Soon after, he joined a gay-friendly church in Pasadena. He left acting to study psychology, writing his thesis on the experience of shame in gay men—particularly shame from religious trauma. "I couldn't shake this feeling, that a lot of people were saying that I didn't repent, and therefore Satan won," says Allen, now a therapist practicing in Vermont and Massachusetts. "I could see these people doing what they believed was good, what they believed was God's will, even though their actions felt so painful and hurtful to me. In my opinion, they just had a limited view of what goodness looked and sounded and acted like."[81]

No matter how Mart's words suggest a more inclusive embrace of other points of view, his brother was about to show just how inflexible evangelical views of religion could be when it comes to advocating for a singular view of truth based on a particular reading of the Bible.

CHAPTER SEVEN

One Nation Under God

Evangelical author David Barton stands in front of Philadelphia's Independence Hall on a chilly spring day. "Does America really have a godly heritage?" he asks before answering his own question: "Indeed it does. Abundant documentary evidence to that fact is available in tens of thousands of historic documents."[1] The scene is from the 2005 film *America's Godly Heritage*, one of dozens of films and books Barton has made to demonstrate the influence of Christianity on the Founding Fathers.

Barton is tall and lanky, wearing a long leather jacket over a ribbed baby-blue T-shirt and tight black jeans, looking decidedly hip for a historian—never mind a Christian historian. Moving inside, he stands in the room where the Constitutional Congress met and expresses all of the ways the delegates referenced the Bible during their deliberations. "Few today know that virtually every one of the fifty-five Founding Fathers who framed the US Constitution were members of orthodox Christian churches, and many were outspoken evangelical Christians," he claims.[2]

In fact, Congress issued more than a dozen proclamations calling for national days of prayer and fasting, Barton continues, picking up pamphlet after yellowed pamphlet from a table lined with candlesticks and inkpots. Most notable, he says, is a 1782 Bible printed by Robert Aitken—the first English-language Bible produced in America—that Congress recommended "to the inhabitants of the United States," including schoolchildren. "Indeed!" Barton concludes. "Congress itself was America's first Bible society."[3]

Watching Barton's film in church, David Green nodded first in satisfaction and then in outrage. *Why didn't more Americans know of this godly heritage? And why had it been hidden so long?* he thought. As voice actors playing the Founding Fathers delivered quote after quote referencing the Bible, accompanied by jaunty colonial-style music and Barton's never-ending supply of historical documents, he resolved to do something about it. "I remember getting really upset when I heard about how people were trying to change our history books so they wouldn't include the faith of our Founding Fathers," David said.[4]

Just as with the Christmas ads, it seems that David was seeing what he wanted to see. It's hard to find evidence of any concerted effort to remove religion from textbooks. In fact, the opposite was occurring in neighboring Texas, where conservative activists—including Barton—were arguing before the state board of education for *more* explicit references to the Bible and Christianity to be put *into* textbooks.[5] David was determined to join Hobby Lobby's resources to the fight. With Mart preoccupied with his film, he turned to his other son, assigning Steve the task. After Steve spoke with Barton by phone, the historian came to Hobby Lobby headquarters armed with stacks of rare books to show David and Steve how the faith of the Founders had been whitewashed.[6]

On July 2, 2006, Hobby Lobby ran its first Fourth of July ad under the heading "In God We Trust," stylized in calligraphy to look like a historical document. Beneath was a selection of quotes from presidents, congresspeople, Supreme Court justices, and others attesting to their religious beliefs. "It is the duty of all nations to acknowledge the providence of Almighty God, to obey His will, to be grateful for His benefits, and to humbly implore His protection and favor," George Washington says. "Before any man can be considered a member of civil society, he must be considered a subject of the Governor of the Universe," chimes in James Madison.[7] "It is the duty as well as the privilege and interest of our Christian nation, to select and prefer Christians for our rulers," adds first chief justice John Jay. That quote was a favorite of Barton's, who used it to argue that America had been founded as a Christian nation, to be ruled according to Christian principles. At the bottom, the ad included the same 800 number used in the holiday ads to encourage people to accept Jesus as their savior, along with Hobby Lobby's address and website.[8]

BARTON BEGAN QUESTIONING the conventional story about the Founding Fathers—that they were Bible-doubting deists—in the mid-1980s when rummaging through boxes of Supreme Court decisions in a Fort Worth law library. "I saw a whole different view of government," he said. "Saw a whole different view of faith and religion and morality in public policy." Barton had no formal training as a historian. He'd grown up in Texas, west of Fort Worth, where his parents had founded their own church and Bible school, before attending ORU. After his revelation about the Founders, he created a nonprofit in 1988 called WallBuilders after a verse in Nehemiah decrying the state of Jerusalem following the Babylonian exile: " 'You see the trouble we are in: Jerusalem lies in ruins, and its gates have been burned with fire. Come, let us rebuild the wall.' "[9]

The following year, Barton self-published *The Myth of Separation*, arguing that the Supreme Court had gotten it wrong when it had mandated a strict separation between church and state in 1947, leading it to forbid school prayer in 1962 and the teaching of the Bible in 1963. The phrase "a wall of separation between Church and State," used by

Thomas Jefferson in an 1802 letter, was never meant to take religion out of public life, Barton argues; quite the opposite, it was supposed to insulate religion from government interference, a "one-directional wall protecting the church from the government." Similarly, the amendment stating that "Congress shall make no law respecting an establishment of religion, or prohibiting the free exercise thereof," takes for granted that Americans were Christians, he says, and was trying only to prevent any one form of Christianity from becoming dominant. "As long as someone was pursuing some form of orthodox Christianity, he was protected in the freedom of worship and conscience," Barton writes.[10]

He is equally clear about the disastrous consequences of separating the Bible from public life, showing in pages of graphs how crime, divorce, and abortions all rose precipitously when prayer was removed from schools.[11] "Is it simply coincidence" that those statistics rose "after the nation's leaders repudiated God and his principles?" he asks in another book, *America, to Pray or Not to Pray?*[12] Barton hit the road, outfitting a van with a loft bed and lecturing at churches while his wife homeschooled their three children. Along the way, he frequented antiquarian bookstores to acquire more than seventy thousand books and documents supporting his beliefs, which he stored at his Fort Worth headquarters.[13]

Eventually Barton entered politics, launching a lobbying firm in 1998 and becoming vice chair of the Texas Republican Party. His ideas rapidly took root. In 2004, the state party affirmed that "the United States of America is a Christian Nation, and the public acknowledgment of God is undeniable in our history." As fellow Texan Tom DeLay became House majority leader, Barton increasingly traveled to Washington, where he gave tours of the US Capitol and briefed conservative legislators and their families.[14] *Time* featured him as one of its twenty-five most influential evangelicals in America, noting that his "relentless stream of publications, court amicus briefs and books" had "made him a hero to millions."[15]

Barton has mainstreamed the idea that government should be run according to Christian principles, providing a patriotic underpinning for positions that Reconstructionists had pushed for decades. He's spoken of a "providential history" in which God has chosen America as a special nation and found in the Bible justification for conservative ideals of limited government and taxation. He's said the Founders intended to prohibit abortion when they wrote in the Declaration of Independence about the "unalienable" right to "life" and that homosexuality is an "aberration" against the "law of nature and nature's God" professed by the Founders, agreeing with Falwell that AIDS was God's punishment for homosexual behavior.[16]

As Barton's ideas gained prominence, both mainstream and evangelical historians pushed back against his sloppy approach to history. In 1995, scholar Robert Alley first took him to task for quoting James Madison on the need to "sustain ourselves according to the Ten Commandments," which seemed antithetical to the Founder's beliefs. In fact, the quote came from a secondary source that misquoted Madison. "Barton's claims have no relationship to the truth," Alley wrote in disgust, "but can be floated easily to support political agendas." In response, Barton published a retraction of a dozen "unconfirmed quotations," stopping short of calling them false.[17]

In addition to citing misattributions, historians have criticized Barton's habit of hanging on to any reference to God by the Founders to support his idea that the United States was founded on biblical principles. "This approach to history writing—one hesitates to call it scholarship—elevates the significance of isolated statements over context, rhetorical usage, or a lifetime of work," writes historian Stephen K.

Green (no relation to Steve).[18] In the *America's Godly Heritage* video, Barton touts a 1984 study showing that the Bible was the most frequently quoted source in writings of the founding era of the late eighteenth century. That fact is less impressive, however, when considering that most of the writings analyzed were printed religious sermons. Considering only political writings, "the Bible's prominence disappears," wrote the study's author Donald Lutz, with just 9 references out of 528.[19]

While some colonial laws were based on the Bible, most historians argue that its influence had ebbed by the time of the Constitutional Convention. The Founders' debates are full of references to English common law, the Magna Carta, and especially Enlightenment political philosophers John Locke and Baron de Montesquieu, while the Bible is mentioned only once, by Benjamin Franklin, one of the least religious of the Founders. That's not to say many of the Founders were not themselves religious. Few were outright deists; most subscribed to an Enlightenment understanding of religion as consisting of rational natural laws, using terms such as "Nature's God" interchangeably with the "Law of Nature" in a concept of the divine that wasn't necessarily based on the Bible—though not opposed to it either.[20]

The Declaration of Independence includes four references to a higher power: stating that all men are "endowed by their *Creator* with unalienable rights" and that "the Laws of Nature and of *Nature's God* entitle" Americans to independence and ending with an appeal to the "*Supreme Judge* of the world" and the "protection of *divine Providence*." While Barton argues that those phrases prove that the delegates recognized "transcendent biblical natural law," most historians argue that the language fits better into an Enlightenment view of an impersonal higher power. More telling is what's *not* included: any reference to Yahweh, Jehovah, or Jesus Christ—or, for that matter, sin and redemption or the coming of God's kingdom.[21]

The Constitution includes no reference to religion except for one clause explicitly prohibiting the use of religious tests for candidates for federal office, which reversed requirements in some state constitutions.[22] Barton goes on to argue somewhat tortuously that the "principles," if not the words, in the Constitution are derived from the Bible despite clear evidence from the records of the Constitutional Convention that they come from Enlightenment philosophers.[23]

After the Constitution was ratified, early American leaders were careful not to inject religion too heavily into public life. The first law signed by President George Washington established a secular oath of office, taking out references to "Almighty God."[24] When a Jewish congregation expressed concern that they'd be treated as less than full citizens, Washington wrote that the United States "gives to bigotry no sanction, to persecution no assistance."[25] When negotiating a treaty with the Barbary Coast pirates, his administration assured them, "The government of the United States is not in any sense founded on the Christian Religion."[26]

When Washington did refer to a higher power during his presidency, it was in public prayer requests and Thanksgiving proclamations, including the quote in Hobby Lobby's Fourth of July ad. Pulitzer prize–winning historian Jon Meacham makes the distinction between the kind of "public religion" the Founders engaged in as a part of official ceremonies and the private practices they engaged in as part of a specific Christian sect. "History will afford frequent opportunities of showing the necessity of a public religion, from its usefulness to the public; the advantages of a religious character among private persons," said Benjamin Franklin, even while he expressed "some doubts" about the "divinity of Jesus." When one of the more religious Founders, Benjamin Rush, publicly stated that the "hand of God was employed" in the writing of the Constitution, he was criticized by other Founders.[27]

On the other hand, Thomas Jefferson explicitly sounded the alarm in a statute for religious freedom in Virigina in which he called out the "impious presumption of legislators and rulers . . . who being themselves but fallible and uninspired men, have assumed domination over the faith of others, setting up their own opinions and modes of thinking as the only true and infallible." His colleague in crafting the Bill of Rights, James Madison, took it further, saying he "regarded the practical distinction between religion and civil government as essential to the purity of both" and warning that "the danger cannot be too carefully guarded against." As for the Aitken Bible, while Congress endorsed its printing in the midst of a wartime shortage, it never funded the enterprise, ruling against it in two separate votes. In the end, Aitken produced his Bible independently.[28]

It wasn't until the Second Great Awakening in the nineteenth century that historians of the time began looking back at the founding in religious terms, seeing in it the "providential hand" of God. Over the decades, that idea took on a life of its own so that by the early twentieth century, President Woodrow Wilson could say that "America was born a Christian nation" and decades later, President Harry Truman could declare that "the fundamental basis for all government is in this Bible right here, and it started with Moses on the Mount." By the time the Christian Right came to prominence, Falwell was saying, "Our Founding Fathers established America's laws and precepts on the principles recorded in the laws of God, including the Ten Commandments," while James Dobson simply stated, "We have been, from the beginning, a people of faith whose government is built wholly on a Judeo-Christian foundation."[29]

When Hobby Lobby published its first Fourth of July ad in 2006, the Greens received an immediate and unexpected backlash. Dozens of angry letters came pouring into headquarters. Steve was perplexed, spending hours poring over them. "How can this be a Christian nation if not everyone is a Christian?" one demanded. "I guess you were trying to make a difference, but you left a lot of people out." A Christian mother said she would stop shopping at Hobby Lobby, scolding, "You must realize that all your profitmaking is due to the multicultural and open nature of American society. Why promote this divisiveness?" Others seemed hostile to the very idea of religion.[30]

Steve felt frustrated. According to his fundamentalist beliefs, the appeal to coexistence—or worse, atheism—was incompatible with the Bible's teaching that there was one absolute truth found in God. "I could already see the folly in the attitude that we should just all get along and coexist with one another," he later said. "The problem with coexisting is that two opposing truth claims cannot both be true."[31] The question was, what worldview should we live by?

Steve had always been quieter and more unassuming than his brother—or his father, for that matter—speaking in a thoughtful drawl and keeping his hair clipped short in an almost military haircut. He'd long had a more philosophical relationship to the Bible, having made a meticulous study of the book when teaching Bible study classes as a younger man. Now he set out to answer this new question by consulting conservative Christians whom he considered experts in the field, eventually recording his findings in a book titled *Faith in America*.

He started by flying out to Fort Worth to visit Barton, heading west of the city to the small town of Aledo and up a gravel road to WallBuilders headquarters. Barton opened a heavy steel door to show Steve his library, with shelf after shelf of rare books and file cabinets filled with letters and proclamations. Display cases held other ephemera, including Revolution-era rifles and uniforms, a button from George Washington's military uniform, and several locks of Washington's hair that he had given to Alexander Hamilton.[32] Acquired over decades, the contents of the vault, all personally owned by Barton, had risen in value into the millions.

After the tour, Barton sat Steve down in the conference room to explain how he looked at America's Christian heritage. The words

"Christian nation," he said, didn't mean that all citizens had to be Christian or even adhere to Christian theology. But just as the quotes in Hobby Lobby's ads proclaimed, it did mean that "a Christian nation is a nation founded upon Christian and biblical principles, whose society and institutions are shaped by those principles." That Christian worldview, he continued, was crucial to America's exceptional place in the world and should be taught in schools and celebrated in government. The critics who accused him of taking quotes out of context, he assured Steve, were mistaken.[33]

"David, this time together has been incredibly informative," Steve said by the end, excited by the confirmation that it wasn't pluralism or atheism that had inspired the values of the United States. "It was the Christian worldview that 'has so strongly shaped and molded' America's founding," Steve later wrote. "America's foundation on biblical principles is the primary element that led to our great success as a nation."[34]

As Bush's second term came to an end, however, the nation as a whole seemed reluctant to agree. In 2007, a resolution to recognize the "rich spiritual and religious history of our Nation's founding and subsequent history" failed to pass. At the same time, new scandals rocked conservatives. First, House majority leader Tom DeLay, who had played a key role in connecting Christians with lawmakers, resigned after he was indicted for money-laundering campaign contributions. (His conviction was later overturned on appeal.)

Even more damning was a scandal involving Ted Haggard, a megachurch pastor from Colorado Springs. A male sex worker identified Haggard as a frequent customer, saying the pastor had often bought crystal meth from him to enhance their sex. Haggard resigned from the church and the organization, admitting that he'd bought drugs from the man but claiming he hadn't taken them and saying he'd only received massages, though he also confessed to "sexual immorality."[35] Not since the televangelist scandals of the 1980s had evangelicals suffered such a crisis of faith. Liberal activists and the media alike decried the hypocrisy of a movement dictating sexual morality whose leaders couldn't adhere to their own standards.

EVEN AS THE evangelical world struggled, Hobby Lobby continued its unstoppable growth, with one newspaper calling it the "everlasting Gobstopper" of Oklahoma City real estate. By the end of 2007, Hobby Lobby counted nearly four hundred stores, stretching as far as Montana and West Virginia, with annual sales of $1.8 billion.[36] The profits flowed into the family's pockets; David maintained his place on the Forbes list of richest Americans, with estimated wealth of $1.8 billion as well.[37] He and his family continued to buy properties large and small to donate to churches, steadily earning tax breaks for Hobby Lobby—the latest an eighteen-acre campus north of Boston bought for $3.5 million and donated to Zion Bible College.[38]

To some, it seemed that the Greens were almost single-handedly propping up religious higher education, which was struggling across the country. Falwell's Liberty University was buried in more than $100 million in debt.[39] The school's crisis deepened in May 2007, when Falwell collapsed in his campus office and died of heart failure, bringing an end to one of the most influential figures in the history of the Christian Right. His forty-four-year-old son, Jerry Falwell Jr., became chancellor of the university, while his younger brother Jonathan became chief pastor of Thomas Road Baptist Church.[40] The difficulties Liberty was facing, however, were nothing compared to the crisis that broke around Tulsa's ORU.

In 2007, two professors filed suit against the school, exposing the lavish lifestyle of President Richard Roberts and his family—including a $39,000 clothes shopping spree by his wife, Lindsay; a $29,000 trip to the Bahamas aboard the university's private jet for their daughter; and stables full of horses, all charged to the Oral Roberts Evangelistic Association ministry.[41] Roberts, Oral's son, denied the allegations, saying it was mere "intimidation, blackmail, and extortion."[42] Even so, he took a leave of absence and eventually resigned as his father came out of retirement to help run the school, telling students in a chapel service, "The devil is not going to steal ORU."[43]

The scandal seemed yet another example of evangelical Christian leaders not living up to their own beliefs, consuming the university at a time when it was already $52 million in debt. Reading about it, David worried about what might happen if the institution fell apart and asked family members whether they might step in to help.[44] "This is God's college," Mart told his family over Thanksgiving weekend in a moment of clarity after coming off a forty-day fast of nothing but juice.[45] As their profits had piled up, the Greens had been looking for a new ministry to support—what if this was it?

Ultimately, the family agreed it would give $8 million immediately, with another $62 million after a ninety-day review of ORU's finances, so long as changes were made to properly manage funds, including separating the university from the ministry. Mart became the family's public face of the endeavor as newspaper and TV reports hailed him as a "Good Samaritan," a "white knight," and the "Angel of ORU."[46] As part of the plan, the university dissolved its board of regents and created a new board of thirteen trustees, with Mart as the chair and the other members chosen by the Green family; Oral Roberts would stay on as a lifetime trustee, while Richard became president emeritus.[47]

Such a replacement of the entire governing body of a school was unprecedented, said Doug Lederman, editor of *Inside Higher Education* at the time.[48] Mart justified the extreme measures as necessary to save such an important bulwark of Christian education. "If ORU goes down, it affects all the Christian colleges," he said. For the board, Mart and his family chose many of their close friends and associates, including OneHope's Rob Hoskins and SIL director Frederick Boswell.[49]

The gift put the Green family on *The Chronicle of Philanthropy*'s list of Americans who'd donated the most in 2007. They had a lot to be proud of—rescuing a bastion of conservative religious education from its own poor choices while at the same time consolidating their own power and influence within religious circles. Still, David couldn't shake the lingering sensation, inherited from his mother, that he wasn't doing enough for God. After the donation, Mart asked him, "Dad, have we outgiven Grandma yet?" David reminded him of Jesus's parable of the widow who put her last two coins in the collection. "No, son, we still have not outgiven Grandma," he said. "She gave out of what she had; we've always given out of our excess."[50]

WHILE MART WAS raising his public profile, Steve was pursuing a more private mission. As they were celebrating Jackie's thirty-ninth birthday over a hibachi dinner, one of their daughters piped up, "Mom, we think we need to adopt a baby from China!" Jackie and Steve looked at each other, skeptical. With the arrival of Grace in 2000, they now had five children—and Jackie was busy homeschooling the youngest and driving her two oldest to a Christian high school. "Our quiver is full," she told the children, a reference to the Quiverfull movement, a new evangelical push for large families in order to better spread the word of God. It became popular with the 2008 debut of the TLC show *17 Kids and Counting*, featuring Jim Bob and Michelle Duggar, followers of Bill Gothard's Institute in Basic Life Principles, including its strict rules on parental authority and sexual purity. At the children's insistence, Jackie and Steve prayed and ultimately decided to grow their own family by adopting their sixth child from China.[51]

Meanwhile, Steve continued his evangelical walkabout to define a Christian worldview. After meeting with Barton, he traveled next to the Cincinnati suburbs, just over the Ohio River in northern Kentucky. Driving in a light rain, Steve followed the highway exit through a rock wall topped with two large metal stegosauruses announcing his arrival at the Creation Museum. More dinosaurs greeted him at the main building along with Ken Ham, a cheery Australian with an Abe Lincoln–style neck beard who had opened the museum in 2007. "Dinosaurs always get the kids interested," Ham told Steve affably as he led him past a riparian tableau of animatronic Stone Age children cavorting near dinosaurs that swiveled their heads and munched fake leaves.[52]

The scene was set not hundreds of millions of years ago but just a few thousand, according to Ham. As one of the prime adherents of "young earth creationism," he taught that the earth, along with all of its creatures, was literally created in six twenty-four-hour days only six thousand years ago. "We can say, 100 percent, absolutely for sure, that humans lived with dinosaurs!"[53] reads *Dinosaurs of Eden*, a children's picture book he wrote. Now he guided Steve through the museum exhibits, designed to prove that "the account of origins presented in Genesis is a simple but factual presentation of events."[54] The only reason dinosaurs aren't mentioned in the Bible, Ham says, is that the word for "dinosaur" wasn't coined until the nineteenth century; the KJV does mention "dragons" in several places, however, and Ham believes they were actually dinosaurs that gradually went extinct.[55]

Even some fundamentalists of the early twentieth century read the seven days of Genesis metaphorically. "I do not think they were twenty-four hour days," William Jennings Bryan said on the stand at the Scopes trial, admitting that he couldn't say exactly how old the earth was. After the trial, many evangelicals accommodated mainstream science, but some saw the answer in greater literalism. The idea took hold in the 1960s with a book cowritten by theologian John Whitcomb and hydraulic engineer Henry Morris, *The Genesis Flood*, which argued that what seemed like millions of years of fossils had actually been laid down in just a year of flood and that the animals had been created by God more or less as we see them rather than through gradual evolution. Morris went on to found a college in California to put scientific methods in the service of scriptural literalism.[56]

Ken Ham came across Morris's ideas while working as a biology teacher in Australia, where he struggled to square textbooks with the fundamentalist beliefs of his family. He resigned in 1979 to become a "full time creationist" before coming to the US in 1987. That same year, the US Supreme Court ruled against teaching creationism in schools. Undaunted, Ham began lecturing nonstop, creating his own organization, Answers in Genesis (AiG) in 1994 to bring the idea to a more mainstream audience. In 2004, Liberty University gave Ham an honorary degree, with Falwell describing his work as "one of the most important Christian ministries in the world."[57]

Ham's organization is in the vanguard against Darwinism, which has always been fundamentalism's enemy number one. By 1999, Kentucky had quietly deleted the word *evolution* from its curriculum, replacing it with "change over time."[58] Kansas decided to remove the teaching of evolution altogether, only to reinstate it two years later. In 2005, President George W. Bush publicly advocated for "intelligent design" in schools, teaching creationism without naming a creator—but the Supreme Court shot it down. All the while, Ham worked on his plans for a creationism museum, fighting critics who derided his vision as the "Fred and Wilma Flintstone Museum."[59]

The effort started scrappily, with exhibits bought at auction from a defunct Baltimore science center and dinosaur sculptures built by a taxidermist who moonlighted as a folk singer. Ultimately, however, Ham raised $27 million for the project and hired an evangelical designer who had previously worked on attractions at Universal Studios in Florida to create a sophisticated multimedia experience.[60] In a theater off the main atrium, seats rumble as dinosaurs tramp, and water sprays the audience as floodwaters roll.[61] "With its wide-open spaces and interactive exhibits, the place feels like a slick museum of natural history, updated for the Hollywood age," *The New York Times* said when it opened.[62] Less charitably, *The Atlantic*'s Jeffrey Goldberg called it "not a museum so much as it is a 3-D hellfire sermon with a food court."[63]

MUCH MORE THAN just a showcase for creationism, the museum is a defense of biblical literalism writ large. The first exhibit room that Ham led Steve into off the atrium told visitors they have to choose between two viewpoints: "God's word" or "Human Reason" (described as an "arbitrary philosophy"), as the "starting point for evaluating everything around them." A dark, claustrophobic hallway spelled out the consequences of the second choice. Newspaper articles stuck to the walls described a society in chaos, with stories about school shootings and Islamic terrorism interspersed with articles about gay marriage, euthanasia, and abortion. At the end was a wrecking ball labeled "Millions of Years"—that is, the length of time scientists believed the earth had existed—that had crashed through the foundations of a church, with cracks extending to a suburban family home.[64]

Looking voyeuristically through peepholes, Steve could see a boy playing violent video games while his brother looked at pornography on a computer, a teenage girl talking to her friend about having an abortion, a mom gossiping in the kitchen while her husband checked out in front of the television—a complete family breakdown as a result of embracing the theory of Darwinian evolution.[65] Steve posed a question to Ham: "What would you say to a young high school or college student who gets regular and routine bombardments concerning evolution as the truth and creation as a lie?"[66]

The answer was contained in the rest of the exhibits, which depicted a timeline of the world if the Bible is taken literally, starting with a life-sized diorama of the Garden of Eden. A buff Adam is offered the fruit of the tree of knowledge by a supermodel version of Eve, surrounded by dinosaurs and other animals. After Adam's fall, visitors descend through a dark mélange juxtaposing Cain's murder of

Abel with a violent T-Rex, nuclear war, and drug abuse before passing through a forty-foot-tall replica of Noah's Ark.

According to Ham, the flood occurred in 2248 BC, when the entire earth was covered in water. To explain how Noah fit all the animals on the ark, he supposes that Noah had to save only one thousand pairs of animals representing different "kinds" of creatures—such as cow, horse, and dog—which could engender other species through natural selection. That was different than "molecules-to-man evolution," Ham assured Steve, while failing to explain how one thousand pairs of animals could create two million species in just four thousand years, an average of one new species a day.[67]

Ham sees the scientific method as mere "speculation" when applied to anything in the distant past that a person didn't observe themselves, whereas the Bible provides reliable truth. "Every word is 'inspired' (God-breathed)," the museum says in its statement of faith. If we "mistakenly" think we see a contradiction, we must look more closely to clear up our error: "If the Bible says something happened, we are to believe it, up front, right away, without hesitation."[68] Ham's explanations are a master class in posing a question and then coming up with a way to justify an already drawn conclusion. To explain how fossils are arranged in distinct layers, with simple sea creatures on the bottom, followed by dinosaurs and then mammals, for example, he imagines that they died in that order during the flood, with humans clinging to rafts as long as possible to die last.[69]

Ham's philosophy doesn't even hold up on its own terms, University of Dayton professors Susan and William Trollinger point out in a book-length critique of the museum. Throughout the museum, for example, the earth is presented as a spherical globe in space despite the description of it in multiple biblical passages as a disc of land topped by a heavenly dome of stars. Some arguments are particularly eyebrow-raising. A placard labeled "Where Did Cain Get His Wife?" explains that the first humans must have married brothers and sisters, but incest was allowed then since there "would have been very few mutations in the human genome" that could cause birth defects—just so long as it was within the bounds of marriage between "one man and one woman." In another exhibit on slavery, the museum contends that slavery in the Bible was nothing like the "harsh slavery" found in the United States. While acknowledging that "various distortions of Bible passages were used to try to justify slavery" in the US, the museum suggests that the real culprit was Darwinism, even though slavery had existed long before Darwin's *Origin of Species* was published in 1861—only four years before the Emancipation.[70]

Despite these sometimes bizarre exhibits, the combination of Jesus and dinosaurs made the museum an instant hit with homeschooling parents and other evangelicals yearning for scientific backing for the young earth described in the Bible. In its first year, the museum defied projections of 250,000 visitors to welcome more than 400,000; within three years, a million peopled had trodden its pathways from Eden to Christ, including Steve, who told Ham that "all of this information has been so helpful" as he made his way back to the rental car.[71]

On the flight home, he looked out the window of the airplane, lost in thought, just as David had been decades earlier on his way back from Tennessee. In his conversation with Ham and others, Steve had become more and more convinced that the biblical worldview "really is absolute and absolutely from God." On the other hand, one thought still nagged him—the entire biblical worldview, from a belief in a young earth to the Christian basis for America, depended on the Bible being true. *Why should we trust that the Bible is God's Word?* Steve thought as he looked out over the clouds. Answering that question would send him on a new life-changing journey.[72]

CHAPTER EIGHT

And You Shall Find

A few months after meeting Ken Ham in Kentucky, Steve was on another plane, heading to a far more exotic location. Along with him were two companions: Johnny Shipman, a stocky Texas oil-man turned rare-book seller, and Scott Carroll, an archaeologist with a full head of prematurely white hair and an ever-present grin. They had shown Steve a video of a rare artifact—a manuscript copy of the Gospel of John on purple-dyed vellum, lettered in gold, and asked if he would like to buy it from a family in Turkey that was "motivated to sell it." They added, "While we are overseas, we can arrange to meet with other contacts we have as well." Arriving in Istanbul in November 2009, Steve was disappointed to find that the family had decided not to sell the manuscript. Nevertheless, Shipman and Carroll took him on a whirlwind tour of museums and dealers' shops, exciting him about their pet project: creating a museum of biblical artifacts.[1]

The museum, they told him, could demonstrate how the Bible had remained unchanged throughout history, an idea that appealed to Steve as he sought to bolster the case for the Bible as the true and inerrant word of God. He got more excited as they took him down crowded alleys in Jerusalem to antique shops where dealers laid out thickly wrapped scrolls and delicate pieces of papyrus, all covered in strange scripts that Carroll read with ease. Steve came back with passion excited "like a spark beneath dry wood," he later wrote. For years, he'd watched his brother, Mart, take the lead on ambitious projects—translating Bibles, making a film, rescuing a university. Here was his chance to expose thousands, perhaps millions, to the Bible's message of salvation, embarking "upon an adventure that would prove to have meaning for us as a family, for our nation, and for the world."[2]

Shipman had first met Mart Green through *The End of the Spear.* The flamboyant Texan couldn't be more different than the understated Greens, favoring pinstripe suits with silk pocket squares and downing several pink martinis with lunch. The son of a Baptist minister, he'd worked in the oil business before branching into private equity and jewelry. By 2000, he'd opened Shipman Rare Books and conceived of a National Bible Museum to share his treasures with the world.[3]

Carroll, by contrast, had grown up Catholic in Toledo but had never been religious; at one point, he was expelled from school for "setting fire to a church." While attending West Virgina University on a wrestling and football scholarship, however, he began talking to fellow athletes about Jesus and embraced evangelicalism with all the fervor of a convert. In 1980, he transferred to Tennessee Temple University to study ancient languages, history, and religion, graduating a year after the film *Raiders of the Lost Ark* swung into theaters, depicting the dashing archaeologist Indiana Jones on a quest to locate the ark containing the Ten Commandments. Carroll seemed to model his career after that of the hero—mild-mannered academic during the semester and swashbuckling explorer on breaks.[4]

While studying with evangelical historian Edwin Yamauchi at Miami University, he participated in archaeological digs of Christian monasteries in Egypt. He taught for six years at an evangelical college in Massachusetts before returning to the Midwest in 1993 to work for Robert Van Kampen, a Chicago multimillionaire who'd assembled one of the world's largest collections of early Bibles and Christian manuscripts in the belief that if enough versions of the Bible were collected, they could help recover the "uncorrupted" original text.[5]

Carroll helped Van Kampen create an archival library called the Scriptorium, convincing him to hire his former classmate Jerry Pattengale and former mentor Yamauchi to run it, at the same time using Van Kampen's money to fund more digs in Egypt.[6] When the billionaire died in 1999, his family moved the Scriptorium to Orlando, Florida, where it became the centerpiece of the Holy Land Experience, a biblical theme park featuring daily reenactments of the crucifixion with a bloodied actor in a loincloth raised on a cross. It included a one-hour multimedia walk-through of the collection detailing the transmission of the Bible over the centuries, featuring an animatronic John Wycliffe and display cases with Van Kampen's most prized books.[7]

Through rare-book circles, Carroll met Johnny Shipman, who took over funding his ventures, including a quixotic quest to find Christopher Columbus's sunken ships off the Dominican Republic.[8] By now, Carroll had landed a new position at Cornerstone University in Michigan, where he guided students in creating replicas of biblical scrolls using pressed cowhide donated by a local upholsterer and quills plucked from roadkill.[9] When Shipman enlisted him to help gather artifacts for a National Bible Museum in Dallas, Carroll signed on enthusiastically. However, he realized they'd need to find wealthy patrons with much deeper pockets to make the vision a reality.[10]

For centuries, believers had been trying to prove the authenticity of the Bible through historical artifacts, with mixed results. During the nineteenth century, British and French archaeologists raced each other to map the Holy Land in an attempt to identify the remains of sites mentioned in the Bible.[11] French consular official Charles Clermont-Ganneau made the first significant discovery in the region in 1868: an inscription on a large black basalt standing stone known as the Mesha stele. It referred to conquests by the Israelite king Omri and the subsequent defeat of Omri's grandson by the Moabite king Mesha, corresponding to a passage in the book of Kings and providing one of the first independent corroborations of an event in the Hebrew Bible.[12]

Thirty years later, British archaeologist Sir William Matthew Flinders Petrie made an even more significant discovery at the Egyptian site of Thebes, when he uncovered a stele referring to the conquests of the pharaoh Merneptah in 1207 BCE. Among the list of the defeated is a description of "Israel laid waste—his seed is no more," the only contemporary reference to Israel outside the Bible. It not only confirms that Israel existed but also implies that the exodus could have occurred before 1250 BCE, the consensus date arrived at by scholars. Petrie revolutionized archaeology when he excavated the Holy Land's many "tells," huge mounds that hide the remains of ancient cities. He rightly surmised that the ruins were stratified by layers, which could be accurately dated by identifying coins or pottery shards among the artifacts.[13]

After the British claimed Palestine following World War I, archaeology in the region was dominated by American archaeologist William Foxwell Albright, who was animated by a fundamentalist belief that the Bible was historically true and could be proven by archaeological research.[14] He gathered more evidence for the exodus by showing that certain tells indicated destruction by sudden fire around 1230 BCE, corresponding to Joshua's conquest, followed by rougher pottery that Albright identified as having belonged to Israelite settlers.[15] Around the same time, other American archaeologists identified a gate and stables at the site of Meggido corresponding to those supposedly built by King Solomon in Israel's golden age.[16]

American evangelicals latched on to these finds and others as powerful evidence of the biblical narrative. In early editions of *Evidence That Demands a Verdict*—the book that influenced Steve Green as a teenager in the 1970s—Josh McDowell quotes Albright as saying,

"There can be no doubt that archaeology has confirmed the substantial historicity" of the Old Testament, and "discovery after discovery has established the accuracy of innumerable details." He even quotes Jewish archaeologist Nelson Glueck, who supposedly discovered King Solomon's silver mines in 1934, as saying, "No archaeological discovery has ever controverted a biblical reference."[17]

By the time McDowell was writing, however, that wasn't true. After World War II, British archaeologist Kathleen Kenyon pioneered a more meticulous method of digging by dividing sites into five-meter squares to create more accurate findings; her method is still used today. She excavated some of the most important biblical sites, including Jericho, which the Bible says Joshua conquered after God sent the walls tumbling down. Contradicting earlier archaeologists, Kenyon showed that the walls had actually fallen around 2400 BCE, a thousand years before the exodus supposedly occurred, and the city had been abandoned by 1550 BCE, calling into question the very idea of the conquest of the city—and by extension the entire exodus.[18]

In the 1970s and 1980s, a new generation of Israeli archaeologists threw biblical accounts into even more doubt by showing that aside from a few cities such as Meggido and Hazor, there was no evidence of *any* destruction in the thirteenth century BCE, the time of the supposed Israelite conquest—and most cities hadn't even been fortified. In fact, there was little distinction between Canaanite and Israelite settlements. Based on detailed surveys of the region, archaeologist Israel Finkelstein has argued that Israelites were not invaders from outside after all but nomadic people who lived in hill towns and gradually took over Canaanite cities after they had diminished on their own or been sacked by sea peoples from the Mediterranean or incursions from Egypt.[19] "The emergence of early Israel was an outcome of the collapse of the Canaanite culture, not its cause," Finkelstein and coauthor Neil Asher Silberman write in their 2001 landmark book, *The Bible Unearthed*. "And most of the Israelites did not come from outside Canaan—they emerged from within it."[20]

Within just a few decades, this new theory caught hold, quickly becoming the scholarly consensus and contradicting one of the most iconic stories of the Hebrew Bible: the exodus and the invasion of Canaan. Other archaeologists found evidence contradicting the history of David, Solomon, and other kings presented in the Bible as well. And if those weren't true, what did that say about Moses and the Ten Commandments—or, for that matter, Adam and the creation? In the newest edition of *Evidence That Demands a Verdict*, McDowell downplays findings of archaeologists such as Kenyon and Finkelstein, proposing alternative theories of Joshua's conquest and other biblical episodes contradicted by modern research and focusing instead on evidence that bolsters the biblical account, including the Mesha and Israel steles.[21]

More than anything, he and other biblical apologists rely on a separate form of evidence, based not on stones and inscriptions but on the text of the Bible itself. One of the prime arguments for biblical truth, McDowell argues, is the sheer number of biblical manuscripts, going back more than a thousand years. If those texts could be shown to be consistent reaching back to antiquity, it could prove that biblical history has been faithfully recorded over the centuries, making it more likely to be true.

THAT'S THE PROJECT Shipman and Carroll were pursuing with their Bible Museum. As they did, Shipman thought of Mart Green as someone with a deep interest in the Bible as well as the money to spend on building a museum. The two headed to Oklahoma City in 2005 to pitch the Green family on the idea, telling them it would be an unprecedented way to expose more people to the greatest book ever written. Additionally, the project could be beneficial to the Greens. By buying up biblical artifacts and engaging scholars to study them, they could increase the value of the artifacts by not just three or five but ten or even fifty times, reaping a healthy tax break when the time came to donate them to the museum.[22]

The family politely turned down the offer, but Steve invited Carroll to speak at his church in Bethany the following spring. Carroll presented on "Battle for Truth: *The Da Vinci Code* and the Armor of God," a response to the popular thriller by Dan Brown that had sold sixty million copies based on the idea of a global conspiracy to hide the fact that early Christians didn't believe Jesus was the son of God.[23] Although the book was fiction, many readers had become intrigued by the thought that the church had intentionally suppressed scripture that contradicted its teachings.

Carroll tried to show that this wasn't true. "Some people think Bibles float down from heaven and land in hotel room drawers," he told his audience to appreciative laughter.[24] The truth was much more complicated—a line of transmission stretching for thousands of years. For his talk, Carroll spread out a fifty-foot-long display of books and manuscripts obtained through his work with the Scriptorium, from cuneiform tablets dating from the time of Abraham to Tyndale, Wycliffe, and Luther editions of the Bible and a first-edition KJV. Taking into account all surviving copies of the Old and New Testaments, he said, there were over forty thousand separate pieces of scripture. "When they are all compared, they are about 98 percent accurate, which is absolutely astounding by any measure," he said.[25] That was powerful evidence, he said, that the Bible of today is reliable and without error. His talk went over so well that he returned to Bethany that fall for a seven-week program.[26]

For all the distress *The Da Vinci Code* caused among evangelicals, however, a more serious attack was brewing. In 2006, Bart Ehrman, a New Testament scholar, published a new book, *Misquoting Jesus*, that called the idea of biblical inerrancy into question. Ehrman had been born again in high school and later attended the fundamentalist Moody Bible Institute, where he became passionate about the Bible, repeating the mantra "The Bible is the inerrant word of God. It contains no mistakes. It is inspired completely." His doubts grew, however, at the evangelical Wheaton College, where he studied Hebrew and Greek and started seeing contradictions between early translations. No matter how soon after Jesus's death the Gospels had been written, the earliest complete copies of them date from hundreds of years later—by which time they could have undergone any number of changes.[27]

Moving on to Princeton Theological Seminary, Ehrman was struggling to explain an esoteric point in Mark when his professor told him gently, "Maybe Mark just made a mistake." That opened the floodgates, as Ehrman suddenly began finding mistakes and contradictions everywhere. In Mark, Jesus was crucified the day before Passover, while in John, he was crucified the day after; Acts says Paul went to Jerusalem after his conversion, but his own letters say he didn't; Luke says Joseph and Mary went to Bethlehem a month after Jesus's birth, while Matthew says they fled into Egypt. The issue wasn't just the inherent contradictions between books of the Bible but also the thousands of differences between early manuscripts, which were much more significant than conservative scholars let on.

"How does it help us to say that the Bible is the inerrant word of God if in fact we don't have the words that God inerrantly inspired, but only the words copied by the scribes—sometimes correctly but sometimes (many times!) incorrectly?"[28] Ehrman writes. For instance, the story of the woman taken in adultery (in which Jesus tells a crowd, "Let he without sin throw the first stone") is one of the best-known stories of the Gospels. Yet it's missing in the earliest texts of the Gospel of John, leading scholars to believe it was a later addition.[29] Even more consequentially, one of the oldest copies of the Bible, found at Egypt's Saint Catherine's Monastery, is missing a passage crucial to the Pentecostal faith.

SAINT CATHERINE'S SITS within one of the most rugged and unforgiving landscapes in the world, the rock desert of Egypt's Sinai Peninsula.

Every day, tourists and pilgrims pass by its walls of yellow brick in the early morning on their way to climb the 7,500-foot peak Jabal Mousa—Mount Moses. Christians know it better as Mount Sinai, the legendary mountain where the biblical patriarch received the Ten Commandments. Built by Justinian monks in 530 CE, Saint Catherine's, clinging to the mountain's foothills, is the oldest continuously operating Christian monastery in the world. Inside, a bramble shrub hanging over one of the interior walls is supposedly the "burning bush" through which Yahweh first spoke to Moses, telling him to lead his people out of Egypt. Bedouins sell small cuttings to tourists in search of a relic to bring home to Dallas or Cincinnati.

Surprisingly, Saint Catherine's is also home to one of the world's largest libraries of ancient manuscripts. As tourists departed following their climb one morning, a Bedouin porter opened a heavy door into the building, where a Greek Orthodox priest named Father Justin was waiting. "Hope you don't mind if I prepare bread while we talk," he said, climbing a narrow stairway to a cramped kitchen with simple wooden furniture and religious icons on the walls. Originally from El Paso, Texas, Justin spoke with an American accent, belying his long white beard and black robes. He'd earned a degree in Greek and Byzantine history from the University of Texas, starting a long journey to become the monastery's head librarian.[30]

Saint Catherine's isolation and dry climate protected its treasures over the centuries, he said, leading the way up into a bright, modern library lined with cases of books and manuscripts. From one, he pulled out a water-stained leaf of parchment covered with four columns of faded Greek lettering, part of the Codex Sinaiticus, one of the oldest and most complete texts of the Christian Bible, dating back to the fourth century CE.[31] The entire document was in the Saint Catherine's library until 1844, when a German adventurer named Constantin von Tischendorf came in search of ancient manuscripts, hoping to prove that the Bible had been reliably copied for centuries. Von Tischendorf convinced the monks to let him take the manuscript to Saint Petersburg, Russia, promising to return it. The czar, however, reneged on the promise. Eventually the document was sold to Great Britain, where it remains one of the jewels of the British Library today.

The monastery wasn't completely bereft, however; in 1975, a monk discovered a few remaining leaves that had been hidden in a sealed-off room. In 2003, Saint Catherine's collaborated to create a beautiful new facsimile version.[32] Justin now cracked open one of the volumes, flipping to the last page of the Gospel of Mark. "This ends at verse 8," he pointed out with his finger, describing how after Jesus's death, the women who followed him found his tomb empty. Later versions of Mark, however, continue with another twelve verses describing how Jesus reappeared to his disciples after being raised from the dead, exhorting them to go out and spread his teachings, similar to the Great Commission in Matthew. "So people are saying, was this the original ending? Why are the following verses not there?" said Justin. "There is a huge controversy about this."[33]

Some scholars believe the verses about the resurrection were added centuries later, while others believe they were just left out of this copy. "Liberal scholars read into it and conservative scholars read into it in an opposite direction, and that to me is fascinating," Justin said. To some, however, figuring out which verses were in the Bible and which weren't is a far-from-academic argument. The missing verses of Mark are the ones that describe how followers of Jesus will be known by their abilities to speak in tongues and heal the sick—one of the bases for Pentecostal beliefs in glossolalia and faith healing as signs of the Holy Spirit baptism. The suggestion of their absence raises the stark question: How can we live by God's word when we are not sure exactly what it is?[34]

EHRMAN PRAYED ON this question but eventually came to an inescapable conclusion: The views of the Bible "as the inerrant revelation from

God were flat-out wrong."[35] Even as scribes were conserving scripture, they were changing it, he concluded, making any biblical manuscript unreliable.[36] In the wake of the *Da Vinci* mania, his book broke through to mainstream audiences, reaching number five on the *New York Times* bestseller list and earning Ehrman profiles in *The Washington Post* and *The Dallas Morning News*, which called him a "new breed of biblical scholar."[37]

And yet Shipman and Carroll continued to pursue their dream of creating a museum that would show a more coherent view of how the Bible had been formed. Working together, they acquired some $2 million worth of artifacts by early 2008.[38] Once a year, Carroll traveled to Oklahoma to talk to the Greens about funding the museum—each time, "they listened, but showed me the door."[39] The family was deep in the midst of other projects such as Mart's films and was reluctant to get involved with the high-priced antiquities market.

With his experience in real estate, Steve eventually told Carroll that if they could find a property for the museum at a reasonable price, the family would put up the money. That spring, Carroll and Shipman came close to acquiring Dallas's former NBA stadium, a 900,000-square-foot property where Carroll envisioned creating a veritable "Smithsonian of biblical antiquities."[40] When the site fell through, he and Shipman explored other properties in vain.

If evangelicals needed a more urgent reason to bring the Bible back into public life, they found it in the 2008 election. Republicans fielded John McCain, a war hero who showed little interest in culture issues. The Democrat seemed a million times worse: A one-term Illinois senator and former community organizer, Barack Obama was the son of a Black man and a white woman; his mother had worked as an anthropologist in Indonesia, where Obama had been exposed to Islam as a child. Although he was Christian, he embraced a pluralistic worldview that accepted a multiplicity of faiths. "Whatever we once were, we are no longer just a Christian nation; we are also a Jewish nation, a Muslim nation, a Buddhist nation, a Hindu nation, and a nation of nonbelievers," he said.[41]

Despite such appeals to unity, Dobson relentlessly attacked Obama's "fruitcake interpretation of the Constitution." On social media, darker allegations spread that Obama was a "secret Muslim" or even the Antichrist foretold by biblical prophecy.[42] As McCain's campaign foundered, he attempted to appeal to religious conservatives by choosing as his running mate Alaska governor Sarah Palin, a "hockey mom" who had been raised Pentecostal and openly touted her faith, decrying abortion and same-sex marriage and advocating for creationism in schools.[43] In the end, only 74 percent of white evangelicals voted for McCain, while 24 percent voted for Obama, the highest percentage for a Democrat in decades. That was enough to ensure his victory as liberals celebrated a return of hope and conservatives decried the election of the "first Marxist president."[44]

Obama invited Rick Warren to give the prayer at his inauguration, angering those on both sides. "Help us, O God, to remember that we are Americans, united not by race, or religion, or blood, but to our commitment to freedom and justice for all," Warren prayed.[45] Obama's victory highlighted a larger issue within the electorate—Americans were becoming less religious and had been for years. A 2008 survey found that the number of Americans who identified as Christians had fallen from 86 to 76 percent over the previous two decades, while the "nones," that is, people with no identified religion, had risen from 8 to 15 percent of Americans, while 34 percent called themselves "born-again" or "evangelical."[46]

The Greens were doing their part to reverse those trends, now pushing the Hobby Lobby holiday ads out in 290 newspapers that reached an estimated audience of forty-four million people.[47] After the bottom fell out of the US economy in a financial crisis brought on by risky housing loans, Hobby Lobby weathered the worst recession since the Great Depression unscathed. In fact, it actually increased sales 10 percent and added 25 new stores in 2009 to bring its total to nearly 450 stores in 34 states.[48]

For all of the money the Greens donated to charity, David realized he'd been neglecting the needy closer to home. "It hit me with sledgehammer force," he said, "I also had to do everything in my power to care for our employees."[49] The company raised the minimum wage for all full-time employees to $10 an hour—far above the national minimum wage of $6.55.[50] The increase didn't include part-time workers, who were more than 60 percent of the total, but it elated full-time workers. While undoubtedly generous, the move wasn't completely altruistic, as David estimated that savings from higher productivity and lower turnover more than paid for it. "The truth is that it has cost absolutely nothing to give these raises," he said.[51]

The family continued to plow its money into real estate deals to benefit Christian ministries, by 2009 reaching a total of forty-three properties, including hospitals, colleges, theaters, and abandoned grocery stores, valued at more than $200 million in all.[52] Steve continued to support the IBLP, giving a talk at its ALERT center in Big Sandy alongside Bill Gothard and Jim Bob Duggar.[53] Mart continued to serve as chair of ORU's board, and the family invested another $10 million in the college.[54] By the end of the year, the college's debts had been slashed to zero. A frail ninety-one-year-old Oral Roberts inaugurated a new president, Mark Rutland, a former missionary and president of a Christian college in Florida, who thanked the family, saying, "The Greens are kingdom givers."[55] In December, Roberts—who as much as anyone had launched evangelical Christianity, Pentecostalism, and the prosperity gospel onto the public stage—died, secure in the knowledge that his vision had outlived him.[56]

Even as they publicized this charitable work, the Greens were donating millions more in secret through vehicles called donor-advised funds (DAFs). A growing trend in philanthropy, they allowed a donor to put money into a fund sponsored by a nonprofit organization, reaping immediate tax benefits, and then advise the organization later regarding which charities to support. While the sponsoring organization wasn't legally obligated to spend the funds in accordance with a donor's wishes, in practice, it almost always did. Since those organizations provided information to the IRS only in aggregate, the particular donations by donors were obscured, allowing the Greens to hide the specific recipients of their largesse.[57]

The Greens set up their funds with the help of Bill High, the Christian financial adviser Mart had met while making his films. High ran a charitable organization called the Servant Foundation, which was an affiliate of the much larger National Christian Foundation (NCF), a DAF sponsor for high-worth Christian clients like the Greens.[58] Within a few years, the Greens would report that they made 90 percent of their contributions through DAFs set up at the NCF.[59] A reporter later obtained the NCF's confidential tax form for 2009, which showed that Hobby Lobby and its related companies had donated $65 million that year to the NCF—the largest source of its $384 million in revenue.[60]

Among recipients of the NCF's millions that year were many of Hobby Lobby's favorite charities, including Every Home for Christ, OneHope, and Mart's film company. More controversially, the NCF also donated millions to organizations involved in antiabortion, anti-LGBTQ, and religious liberty causes, including Campus Crusade for Christ, the FRC, and the ADF. Led by Alan Sears, a former Reagan-era prosecutor and outspoken critic of the "homosexual agenda," the ADF had lent legal assistance to lawsuits against buffer zones for protesters of abortion clinics and to ban gay leaders in the Boy Scouts.[61]

As the economy struggled, the family finally took an interest in Shipman and Carroll's Bible museum. The worldwide antiquities market plummeted, and collectors were willing to sell at discount prices. Thus, Steve found himself on that plane to Istanbul in the fall of 2009 in search of the rare Gospel of John. He came back prepared to jump into the project with both feet and agreed to fund the two collectors on trips around the world.

Carroll and Shipman quickly alerted Steve to a coup—an English translation of Psalms dating from around 1340, set for auction at Sotheby's in London. Predating Wycliffe's translation by forty years, the so-called Rosebery Rolle was expected to sell for upward of £60,000 ($93,000). With Steve's authorization, Shipman kept raising his paddle as the bidding rose past £100,000 pounds until the hammer fell at £180,000 ($290,000). "We were elated" to own such an important piece of biblical history, Steve said.[62]

They soon discovered an even more significant manuscript for sale. An unlikely duo of Bible hunters, Scottish twin sisters Agnes and Margaret Smith, were lovers of antiquity whose parents had left them a fortune. They set out in 1892 at age forty-nine to visit Saint Catherine's, the monastery at the foot of Mount Sinai. They returned several times over the next few decades in search of new manuscripts.[63]

On one of their trips, they found a page from a palimpsest, a manuscript in which one script was written over another. The bottom writing, they realized with a thrill, was a copy of the Gospels written in Palestinian Aramaic, a language close to what Jesus and his disciplines would have spoken, dating before the sixth century CE. Over the next few years, Agnes pieced together the entire manuscript, which she named the Codex Climaci Rescriptus, publishing it in 1909. After the twins died in the 1920s, the manuscript sat at Westminster College in Cambridge until, falling on hard times during the global recession, the college decided to sell it at auction at Sotheby's in July 2009, listing it with an estimated price of £400,000–600,000.[64]

While the document had most likely been translated from Greek, Sotheby's dangled the prospect that it may have relied on an oral tradition in Aramaic as well, potentially reflecting the actual words spoken by Jesus and his followers.[65] Despite that claim, it failed to find a buyer at auction. Now, Carroll and Shipman came knocking, negotiating a price of £395,000 ($650,000) for Steve to acquire one of the most significant biblical manuscripts in private hands. "We couldn't believe our luck," Steve later enthused. "In the biblical artifact world, this was like acquiring a Monet."[66]

Seeing and touching these items that dated back more than a millennium gave Steve and Jackie a new appreciation for the Bible. "The adventure of it all had sucked us in," they wrote. "Very quickly the world of biblical manuscript collecting was impacting our own faith."[67] That manuscript could just as well have shaken Steve's faith, as it included a completely original story about Jesus converting a Roman soldier found in no other copies of the Gospels—again calling into question the faithfulness of transmission over time.

A few months later, the family exponentially increased its holdings with the acquisition of the entire collection of the Christian Heritage Museum, a Maryland institution that owned twenty thousand religious books and artifacts. The collection included a rare first printing of the KJV, known as the "he" Bible for a typo that used the wrong pronoun in the book of Ruth; a page from a 1454 Gutenberg Bible; and a 1685 edition of the so-called Indian Bible, printed in the Wampanoag language by missionary John Eliot. The item Steve was most excited to acquire was a copy of the Aitken Bible, the one endorsed by Congress in 1782 that David Barton held up as evidence that America had been founded as a Christian nation.[68] It took on new relevance as Barton joined a burgeoning conservative political movement that was thrusting the Founders' biblical views into the mainstream.

THOUSANDS OF PROTESTERS poured onto the National Mall dressed in tricorn hats and revolutionary garb. It was April 15, 2009—tax day—and these disgruntled conservatives were decrying a $787 billion stimulus bill President Obama had championed to jump-start the economy, bailing out some of the financial institutions that had caused the mess. They styled themselves the Tea Party, throwing tea bags over the White House fence to protest taxes and government spending as compatriots rallied around the country.

While ostensibly libertarian, the protests appealed to evangelical Christians fighting against government impingement on religious liberties. In a Boston rally, one speaker railed against Obama's statement that America wasn't a Christian nation. "Every founding document of this country has cited our creator," he said. "That is the foundation of our liberties and God-given freedoms."[69] If that sounds like talking points from a David Barton video, it's no accident. Barton had become a virtual spokesperson for the movement, tying together biblical values and limited government.

He appeared as a regular guest of Fox News's popular host Glenn Beck, who yoked the Tea Party to religious nationalism. "Something huge is happening in America. I believe it's the Third Great Awakening," Beck said, placing the Tea Party on "the right side of a cosmic contest between good and evil."[70] He often spoke of Barton as a spiritual lieutenant in that battle, calling him "the most important man in America right now." Barton tied together the libertarian and Christian wings of the Tea Party movement, saying Jesus himself would condemn the capital gains tax, minimum wage, and estate tax on inherited wealth.[71]

As Hobby Lobby produced a new July Fourth ad with quotes from the Founders, polls showed that born-again or evangelical Christians accounted for about half of Tea Party members, with an overwhelming number opposed to abortion and same-sex marriage.[72] Nothing stoked their furor more, however, than Obama's attempt to reform the country's health-care system. When Obama signed the Patient Protection and Affordable Care Act, he hailed it as a major step forward for society, guaranteeing universal health care through government subsidies and ensuring coverage of preexisting conditions; at the same time, it required every American to obtain insurance or pay a fee to opt out. Deriding it as "Obamacare," Republicans condemned it as a massive expansion of government power, forcing hardworking Americans to subsidize medical care for the lazy.

The majority of white evangelicals opposed it as socialism and for providing funds to organizations such as Planned Parenthood that performed abortions. Buoyed by groups such as Focus on the Family, which spent millions targeting prolife Democrats who had voted for the bill, Republicans trounced Democrats in the 2010 election, taking over the House and nearly taking the Senate.[73] Among the freshmen in the House was Jim Lankford, a Baptist pastor from Oklahoma who derided Obamacare as unconstitutional and vowed to sponsor legislation to repeal the new law.[74] Steve and Jackie each contributed $2,400 to his campaign. David and Barbara, meanwhile, contributed $2,500 to Scott Pruitt, the new state attorney general, who vowed to challenge Obamacare in court.[75]

MEANWHILE, STEVE CONTINUED to focus on his growing collection of biblical antiquities. There was one type of item that he and his partners were most eager to attain—fragments of the Dead Sea Scrolls, whose discovery in Israel in 1947 had eclipsed the most optimistic dreams of manuscript hunters. As the story goes, a trio of Bedouin goatherds threw a rock into a cave one evening at Qumran near the Dead Sea and heard pottery smash. They ultimately discovered ten jars stuffed with scrolls of animal hide covered in Hebrew text and took the stash to a Bethlehem cobbler known as Kando, who sold antiquities out of the back of his shop.

The largest scroll turned out to be a near-complete copy of the book of Isaiah, dating from Roman times—a thousand years earlier than surviving Hebrew texts from the Middle Ages. As Bedouins and Israeli archaeologists continued excavating, they found a dozen caves full of texts, apparently belonging to an ascetic Jewish sect called the Essenes. Estimates number the scrolls from 20,000 to 100,000 fragments, including every book of the Bible except Esther, written in Hebrew, Greek, and Aramaic.[76] Conservative scholars such as Josh McDowell point to the remarkable similarity of the Great Isaiah Scroll to early Hebrew texts as evidence of the Bible's continuity.[77]

At the same time, there is ample variety in the texts, ranging from thousands of small differences to two separate "editions" of some books, including a completely rewritten version of Genesis. One scroll adds a whole paragraph to the book of Samuel. Elsewhere, the height of David's antagonist Goliath is given as only six foot nine rather than the nine foot nine in the Bible—making him a formidable warrior but hardly a giant.[78]

The Israeli government acquired most of the scrolls, carefully guarding their contents until the 1990s. Some fragments, however, were transported into Europe and the United States, including one hundred now owned by Norwegian businessman Martin Schøyen. In the early 2000s, Kando's son William began selling new fragments he said his father had stored for years in a vault in Zurich. Most were no bigger than a quarter, with scratchy Hebrew characters on shriveled brown animal skin.[79]

The chance to own one of them proved irresistible to collectors—including Steve, who met with William Kando in Jerusalem and was shown pictures of a large fragment that included a passage from Genesis.[80] Steve balked at the price—$40 million.[81] Shipman assured him that Kando was living in "a dream world" if he expected that kind of money.[82] The team opted instead for more affordable fragments sold out of a museum located inside a Hampton Inn in Arizona, the unlikely headquarters of one of the world's largest dealers in rare Bibles. It was co-owned by Jonathan Byrd, a millionaire former Indy

500 race-car team owner, and Craig Lampe, a biblical scholar who had bought fragments from William Kando.[83] Steve purchased four of them, including snippets from Exodus and Psalms, for $314,000 in total.[84] Carroll went to fetch them in December 2009, just after resigning from his academic post to become executive director of the nascent museum and a full-time Bible hunter.[85]

CARROLL NOW SET out on an around-the-world adventure as an emissary of the Bible museum, waxing poetic on a flight from Qatar to London about eating breakfast over the ancient city of Ur, "where the biblical Patriarch Abraham lived," and lunch over Erfurt, Germany, "where Martin Luther joined the monastery." Landing in London, he "evaluated antiquities for several hrs. and then went to see *Phantom*. Awesome!"

Carroll negotiated for items by the thousands with Steve's checkbook, vacuuming up "stacks of medieval manuscripts," bronze bowls, gold plaques, Roman coins, Egyptian textiles, and hundreds of Torah scrolls.[86] The latter are controversial for collectors; according to Jewish law, damaged or deteriorated scrolls are supposed to be buried or restored for reuse.[87] Within months, however, the Greens had amassed more than two thousand—the largest collection in the world. Torah scrolls also provided one of the greatest opportunities for tax write-offs. They were in high demand among American collectors, so the Greens could acquire them overseas for as little as $5,000 each and then could have them valued at between $50,000 and $250,000 back in the US.[88]

In Zurich, Carroll dined on venison and celery soup with members of Kando's family before getting a glimpse of fragments—including the large fragment from Genesis—in the vault.[89] In the end, Kando agreed to sell seven Dead Sea Scroll fragments for $1.5 million as Steve came to Zurich personally to transact the sale.[90] Among them was a fragment of Jeremiah that predicted the coming of a messiah and one from Daniel in which he is literally touched by an angel. Kando sold the prized Genesis fragment to California rare-book dealer Michael Sharpe.[91] He then agreed to sell it to Steve for $425,000.[92]

Carroll sent the objects to Oklahoma City, where the family stored them in a section of their vast warehouse complex. Steve tapped his twenty-one-year-old daughter Lauren to curate the collection, promoting her from an assistant position in Hobby Lobby's craft department. Shortly afterward, she graduated from OU, where she'd majored in history, literature, and philosophy with a minor in religious studies.[93]

David first mentioned the collection in a business publication interview in March 2010—just four months after Steve started collecting. The family now had "probably one of the largest if not the largest private collection of Bibles in the world," he casually disclosed. "God opens up the doors," he continued. "This kind of just happened, and so we know we're supposed to do this."[94] By June, the collection was in the weekend section of *The New York Times*, featuring a color photo of Steve and Scott Carroll holding up a heavy Bible in ancient Ethiopic. "Our goal is to inspire people with the story of the Bible and its history," Steve told the reporter over sandwiches at Hobby Lobby's offices. By now, estimates of the collection's value ranged from $20 to $40 million, according to experts who were stunned by the pace of acquisitions.[95]

"No one in recent memory has spent so much so quickly on Bibles," said one university curator. In fact, the family was buying up so much material that they seemed to be driving up prices. At the same time, some experts derided the collection as superficial; it included too many mediocre items rather than true biblical treasures. "Book dealers are bibliophiles, but these men are coming at it with a strong belief that the Bible is the word of God and they want to show that," sniffed a rare-book dealer from Switzerland.[96]

God continued to open doors for Hobby Lobby as the company expanded to stretch from coast to coast, from California to New

England. Hobby Lobby raised its minimum wage again, to $11 for full-time employees as well as an increase for part-time workers to $8 an hour.[97] By now, three hundred entities a year, including churches and nonprofits, were appealing to the family for donations, and David, Barbara, and their children met once a month to decide how much to contribute to each, saying no to the vast majority.[98] In 2010, the company bought a large ranch in California from the ailing ministry of a televangelist and donated it to Rick Warren's Saddleback Church for an overnight retreat center.[99] The same year, Forbes named the Green family the top lifetime giver to religious charities, estimating its donations so far at $500 million.[100]

"From the track record of corporate earnings that is now building year by year," David said, "it seems to me that God is smiling on this philosophy of giving."[101] He was not alone in connecting faith and business success. Across the country, businesspeople continued to promote Jesus in the workplace, reading new books such as *Jesus: CEO* and *Moses on Management*.[102] More surprisingly, after losing face during the televangelist scandals of the 1980s, the prosperity gospel came roaring back. Its poster child was Joel Osteen, pastor of a Houston, Texas, megachurch with forty thousand members, who gave people hope for economic recovery with a bright smile and endless optimism. "This year will be a year of your unprecedented favor, that we will see promotions, bonuses, that you will open up doors that no man can shut," he promised.[103]

Fresh off the Dead Sea Scrolls acquisition, Steve made an even more dramatic purchase. In July 2010, he flew with Carroll to Dubai in the United Arab Emirates, a major center for trading due mainly to one Iranian dealer, Hassan Fazeli Trading Company. Dealers around the Middle East shipped Fazeli their treasures to broker with wealthy foreigners, and Carroll and Steve were there to view a huge collection of cuneiform tablets and other objects dating back thousands of years.[104]

Originating in ancient city-states of Mesopotamia, cuneiform consists of marks pressed into clay with a wedge-shaped reed stylus. Some tablets date back four thousand years to the purported time of Abraham and the other patriarchs and corroborate accounts of biblical figures and events, such as the Babylonian king Nebuchadnezzar and the Assyrian siege of Jerusalem. In 2007, researchers discovered the name of a minor Babylonian official mentioned in Jeremiah on a tablet at the British Library, which some took as proof of the book's accuracy.[105]

Arriving at Fazeli's apartment, Carroll and Steve walked into a chaotic scene, with tablets strewn across the flat. More than a thousand sat in stacks on the coffee table, spilled out of cardboard boxes and cookie tins, and even filled the bathtub. With them were several hundred larger cuneiform bricks as well as thousands of rounded clay seals known as bullae and tiny stone cylinder seals, which were rolled in wet clay in ancient times to personalize correspondence.[106]

Fazeli was joined by representatives of two Israeli dealers, Abraham Antiquities and Khader Baidun and Sons, who had helped arrange the sale. Steve took in the scene in wonder as Carroll examined the tablets. Afterward, Carroll took Steve to a restaurant, where, Carroll later claimed, he expressed reservations. Something about it didn't feel right. Why was the meeting conducted at Fazeli's flat rather than his gallery? Why were the items in such disarray? The deal could be risky, he said he told Steve. Steve assured him, "My family is not averse to risk."[107]

On the way home, US Customs officers stopped Steve at the airport and discovered that he was transporting a Bible worth over $1 million that he'd purchased while abroad. They told him he wasn't required to pay duty on religious items but did need to declare them. Steve decided that if he was going to be collecting rare antiques, he'd better consult an expert on the law. A week later, Hobby Lobby's counsel Dobelbower contacted Patty Gerstenblith, a professor at DePaul University and a lawyer specializing in cultural heritage law, who agreed to meet.[108]

But first, the Green family cut ties with Johnny Shipman. Though Shipman had initially created the Bible museum, he had been increasingly sidelined as Steve dealt with Carroll directly. Carroll had been getting frustrated with Shipman for a while, accusing him of disappearing for weeks on end and failing to pay his fees.[109] Now Hobby Lobby sent out a terse email to associates: "Mr. Johnny Shipman no longer represents the Green Collection." Reached in London by a reporter, Carroll said that the decision had been made by "mutual agreement."[110] Years later, Steve would only say the family wanted to "take more ownership of the project."[111] (Shipman continued trying to raise money for his National Bible Museum until his death in 2013.) Carroll stayed on with the organization as a new member came on board—Cary Summers, the head of a Nazareth theme park in Israel, who was currently helping build a replica of Noah's Ark for Ken Ham's Creation Museum.[112]

In early August, Professor Gerstenblith arrived at Hobby Lobby's headquarters, where Carroll showed her the collection before leading her into a conference room to deliver a presentation on antiquities law.[113] An archaeologist by training, Gerstenblith now lectured on the topic at least once a week. The importation of antiquities had increased along with the growth of the international art market following World War II, she told them. In response, the United Nations cultural agency, UNESCO, had agreed to a convention in 1970 that made importing or exporting artifacts of countries' "cultural property" without permission illegal for countries that ratified it. The US had done so in 1983, eventually inking bilateral agreements to enforce the convention with thirty countries, from Afghanistan to Yemen.[114]

After her presentation, Dobelbower asked Gerstenblith to send a report with this information, including laws related to importing artifacts from various countries—among them Iraq. Along with Syria, Iraq was known as the main source for cuneiform. That set off alarm bells for Gerstenblith, given the looting in the region during the Iraq

War. "Anybody who knows anything about the field, certainly legally speaking, has known that at least since 2003, you can't import anything from Iraq," she later said.[115] She underscored the fact in her report, noting that importing "any artifact likely from Iraq" would be "carrying considerable risk."[116]

Nevertheless, Carroll continued to negotiate the cuneiform sale, meeting with Abraham and Baidun in Israel only to discover that the artifacts belonged to the family of another Israeli dealer, Barakat and Sons. They were asking $2 million for the collection of about 5,500 objects, but Carroll told Steve he could negotiate the price down—and that the items could later be appraised for almost $12 million. Abraham sent Hobby Lobby a statement that Barakat had acquired the items locally in the 1960s, before the UNESCO convention had gone into effect, and that they had been stored in the United States in the 1970s before being transported to Dubai for the sale.[117]

In December, Steve signed a purchase agreement for $1.6 million. Following the instructions from Fazeli, Hobby Lobby wired the money to five different names under seven separate bank accounts. When Hobby Lobby's customs broker expressed concern about the possible seizure of packages from the Middle East, the company decided not to use its usual shipping processes for overseas deliveries. Instead, the dealers would send packages directly by FedEx. The company provided multiple addresses for these shipments, including locations for Hobby Lobby, Mardel, and other affiliated companies.[118] "That has proven to be an effective method of shipping the items" in the past, Lauren assured Hobby Lobby's executive assistant. "We have the proper paperwork specifying that the items have been in private family ownership before the UNESCO laws were put in place."[119] Very soon, however, that assertion would be called into question.

CHAPTER NINE

Out of Egypt

Several times the size of a shoebox, a package arrived at the FedEx processing facility in Memphis just after New Year's 2011. It was flagged immediately. Addressed to Steve Green at Mardel headquarters in Oklahoma City, the package bore a shipping label identifying its contents as "hand made clay tiles (sample)" with the country of origin listed as Turkey. Customs officers were immediately suspicious when they saw the sender: Hassan Fazeli. They'd been told by the Customs and Border Protection's National Targeting Center to look out for anything sent by Fazeli. Now, opening the package, they found fifty cuneiform tablets, with traces of dirt as if they'd recently been dug out of the ground, a sign they might be illicit.[1]

When Special Agent Brent Easter took up the case, he could see that this was the tip of the iceberg. Any package valued at more than $2,000 had to be declared in a formal entry to customs, a process that required added inspection and fees. However, the invoice inside falsely listed "hand made miniature clay tiles," valued at $5 each, for a total of $250, avoiding that scrutiny. Over the next two weeks, agents detained four similar packages; altogether, there were hundreds of cuneiform artifacts. A search through FedEx's records found that at least ten more packages from Fazeli had already made it through to the Greens, yet none of them had been formally declared. On January 19, 2011, Easter ordered the packages seized and sent to a climate-controlled warehouse in Queens.[2]

As an agent with Homeland Security Investigations (HSI), Easter had been targeting Fazeli for more than two years in a probe called Operation Lost Treasure. In August 2008, agents had seized a package sent by Fazeli to New York containing a limestone head representing the Assyrian king Sargon II, which had been broken off the statue of a winged bull near Mosul, Iraq. The investigation uncovered a broad international conspiracy to loot and sell artifacts to museums and galleries, resulting in the recovery of items from Libya, Egypt, and Afghanistan.[3]

Growing up in Connecticut in the 1980s, Easter had worn the same Halloween costume year after year: Indiana Jones, complete with leather jacket, wide-brimmed fedora, and bullwhip. After studying archaeology at Brandeis, he joined HSI in 2006 to live out his childhood fantasy, rescuing cultural objects from criminal organizations from India to South America. Now thirty-two, he'd traded his fedora for a Red Sox cap but retained Indy's sly grin and dogged pursuit of artifacts, creating dossiers on traffickers around the world. "These criminal prosecutions are very, very hard to make," he told CNN. "You have to oftentimes prove knowledge in these cases—that somebody *knew* that a piece was stolen." Archaeology, he added, "is not about finding truth, it's about finding facts."[4]

Customs sent notice to Hobby Lobby that the items had been seized. Hobby Lobby responded that the items had been lawfully purchased, attaching the provenance statement declaring that the items had been legally removed from Israel and stored in the US before 1970. It had sent so many different payments because the tablets were owned by different Israeli dealers, including Barkat, Baidun, and Abraham, the company said.[5] None of it made any sense to Easter. If the collection had been in the United States for many years, how could it belong to Israelis? And why would someone transport thousands of ancient objects from the US to the Middle East just to ship them back again?

Laws and ethics about collecting foreign artifacts have been shifting for centuries. In 1799, the Scottish noble Thomas Bruce, seventh earl of Elgin, oversaw the transport of marble panels from the Parthenon in Athens to England. "The Greeks of today do not deserve such wonderful works of antiquity," he said. "Indeed, it is my divine calling to preserve these treasures unto all ages!" The so-called Elgin Marbles ended up in the British Museum in London, and the Greek government has demanded their return ever since. They have even opened a shining new museum to house them, while ironically, the British galleries have fallen into disarray, with a persistent leaky roof when it rains.[6]

The British Museum is full of artifacts of dubious provenance, some seized in moments of colonial conquest, such as the so-called Benin Bronzes—more than nine hundred brass, ivory, and wooden objects looted during the British takeover of the kingdom of Benin in 1897. Others fall into a gray area, such as the famed Rosetta Stone, a basalt block from Egypt that the British took from French forces as a spoil of war. The French have their own share of Egyptian treasures, carted away by Napoleon before Egypt's Ottoman rulers banned exports of antiquities in 1835. Even then, laws were not always successful at stemming the flow of artifacts. Cairo souvenir stands are full of images of Egypt's most famous sculpture, an eighteen-inch-high limestone bust of Queen Nefertiti—but it's currently in Berlin, allegedly smuggled out illegally by a German archaeologist in 1913.[7]

The concept of restitution to return ill-gotten artifacts dates back centuries as well. The book of Ezra mentions that when the Jews returned from the Babylonian captivity, the Persian king Cyrus ordered that the religious artifacts looted from their temple be returned along with them. In Europe, artifacts taken by Napoleon from Italy and the Netherlands were returned after his defeat. During World War II, "monuments men" with the US Army repatriated half-a-million artworks taken by Hitler. Enforcement of laws against smuggling improved after the 1970 UNESCO convention and its ratification by member countries.[8]

After coalition forces invaded Iraq in 1991, however, museums across the country were looted, resulting in the loss of five thousand artifacts. Illegal digging continued throughout the 1990s as cuneiform tablets, cylinder seals, and other small items appeared on the international antiquities market. During the 2003 Iraq War, looters broke into the Iraq Museum's storerooms and snatched up statues from the galleries, even prying bas-relief panels off the walls. They also dug up sites of ancient settlements across the country, including 600 of the 1,500 known sites in southern Iraq, according to one satellite survey.[9] As antiquities once again flooded international markets, Congress passed the Emergency Protection for Iraqi Cultural Antiquities Act in 2004, followed by more import restrictions in 2008 to stem the flow of artifacts.

By 2011, a new threat emerged with the Islamic State of Iraq and Syria (ISIS), which employed armed gangs to take over archaeological sites across northern Iraq, funneling sales through Iran and Turkey. By then, Iraq wasn't the only country facing wide-scale looting. On January 25, 2011, hundreds of thousands of protesters flooded into Tahrir Square in the center of Cairo, Egypt, demanding democratic reforms as part of wider uprisings known as the Arab Spring. Amid clashes with police, citizens formed a human chain to protect the famed Egyptian Museum, filled with sandstone statues of pharaohs and displays of jewelry and papyrus. Thieves broke in through a skylight, making off with treasures anyway.

As police were called to the capital, archaeological sites around the country were left unprotected and were looted by opportunistic thieves. Archaeologist Monica Hanna led a citizen's brigade to share reports of looting on social media and launched a website where people could offer anonymous tips. Their efforts led to the return of hundreds of artifacts as longtime president Hosni Mubarak was deposed in February 2011 and a short-lived new president took over.[10]

EVEN AS EGYPT was dealing with the aftermath of the Arab Spring, Steve saw the hand of God behind his trove of objects, which he called the Green Collection. In April 2011, he told *The Oklahoman* it was "providential" that the collection had come together so quickly. "Our family feels like God has commissioned us to do this," he said, adding that his original plan had been to "do this slow," but God had other plans.[11] "'Starting slow' means something totally different to me than it did to them," joked Carroll, who took credit for putting the collection together. "I trust them to know where to put a store, and they need to trust me to stock the shelves."[12]

The Greens now estimated the value of their collection at $40 million.[13] Steve showed no signs of slowing down, burning with the book of Matthew's Great Commission to bring the Bible to the world. When the family realized 2011 would be the four hundredth anniversary of the KJV, they rushed to open an exhibition in May at the Oklahoma City Museum of Art. Called *Passages*, the exhibit promised "some of the most exquisite and rare biblical manuscripts, printed Bibles, and historical items in the world."[14] Carroll took a page from the Scriptorium to design a Disneyesque experience complete with virtual caves and churches that would leave visitors "immersed in a fascinating story that spans over two thousand years."[15]

The show included cuneiform tablets dating back to the "world of the biblical Abraham," which, Carroll's catalog said, had "helped to clarify the meaning of the biblical text." From there, visitors stepped into a darkened "Jewish scribe room" featuring the Dead Sea Scrolls fragment from Genesis and a "Christian scribe room" with the Codex Climaci Rescriptus and an Egyptian papyrus fragment of the Gospel of John. Then it was off to Europe, where a costumed interpreter demonstrated a printing press alongside an actual page from a Gutenberg Bible and an animatronic William Tyndale lamented being burned at the stake.[16]

That led to the pièce de résistance: a first-edition copy of the KJV—described as "the best-selling, most quoted, and, arguably, most influential book of all times." At seventeen inches high, the book was not only the largest known copy of the KJV but also "the most exquisite copy in the world," considered the very first copy to have rolled off the king's printing press in 1611.[17] The overall effect was of a triumphant and unbroken march of the Bible through time, transmitted faithfully from the caves of Qumran to the court of England before being brought home to Oklahoma. At the end of the exhibit, the Greens made a pitch for Wycliffe Bible Translators, inviting visitors to help continue the Bible's journey. More than fifty thousand visitors came to view the show in the five months it was open—but that was just the beginning of the family's plans.[18]

As soon as Steve started collecting, Carroll urged him to think beyond a museum. The artifacts they were assembling could form the nucleus for a world-class group of scholars who could study the treasures—and increase their value. Carroll reached out to his former Scriptorium colleague Jerry Pattengale, now assistant provost for public engagement at Indiana Wesleyan University. Pattengale worked his Rolodex to recruit some of the world's top biblical scholars, dangling the opportunity to work with the rare texts with the unlimited funds of the Greens.[19]

"The heart of this program is raising up the next generations of professors," said Green Scholars Initiative (GSI) director Pattengale, explaining that the artifacts would be divvied up among academics who would work with graduate and undergraduate students to publish them.[20] Among them were Dead Sea Scrolls expert Emmanuel Tov of Hebrew University in Jerusalem and Dirk Obbink, an Oxford don who oversaw one of the world's top collections of papyrus manuscripts.

Pattengale and Carroll inked a partnership in the fall of 2010 with Baylor University, a private Baptist institution in Waco, Texas, to serve as home of the GSI. As part of the agreement, the university granted Carroll a $100,000 no-strings-attached stipend as a research professor. The project came together so quickly that the university's own religion faculty didn't know about it. Professor Jeff Fish was surprised one fall day to receive a cold call from Carroll with an invitation to work on some rare biblical papyri. He thought it was a joke until Carroll dropped the name of Dirk Obbink, with whom Fish had taken a summer course at Oxford years before. If Obbink was involved, Fish was in.[21]

Obbink had been a prize catch. Then fifty-four, he looked every bit the Oxford don, with rectangular glasses beneath messy blond hair and a wardrobe of rumpled blue blazers. But he'd originally come from Lincoln, Nebraska, where as a child, he'd rummaged through garbage dumps and thrift shops in search of treasure. He'd continued that trend all his life, in a way, studying salvaged fragments of Greek and Latin manuscripts at the University of Nebraska, Stanford, Columbia, and finally Oxford, where he became a lecturer in papyrology in 1995. He received the so-called genius grant from the MacArthur Foundation for his work in digitally piecing together volcano-charred papyri from the 79 CE eruption of Mount Vesuvius. Much of his work, however, involved curating the spoils of the most heralded garbage dump in history: an ancient city in Egypt known as Oxyrhynchus.[22]

The site had been discovered in 1896 by two Oxford classmates with the Egyptian Explorers Society, Bernard Pyne Grenfell and Arthur Surridge Hunt, who explored a location along the Nile near the modern city of El-Benasa. Legend had it Mary and Joseph had stopped to drink at a well near the Hellenistic city of Oxyrhynchus, which later became home to a Christian monastery. After fruitlessly excavating the cemetery, Grenfell and Hunt turned in desperation to great mounds of sand to the west of the city where garbage had been dumped in ancient times. To their surprise, they found heaps of papyri that had lain undisturbed for nearly two thousand years.[23]

Grenfell and Hunt eventually brought back an estimated half-million fragments to the society's headquarters at Oxford, including Greek plays and poetry as well as fragments from the New Testament and apocryphal Christian texts never approved for inclusion in the Bible. As general editor for the Oxyrhynchus Papyri series, Obbink decided which fragments to publish, knowing any one of them could rock the world of biblical scholarship. "Working on these texts," he said, "was like being shipwrecked on a desert island with Marilyn Monroe."[24]

Even while at Oxford, Obbink had a separate business buying and selling papyri, a side gig that was tolerated, if frowned upon, by his university employers. As early as the fall of 2009, Scott Carroll visited Obbink's office in Christ Church College to view scraps of papyri. He negotiated a sales agreement to add them to the Green Collection the following February, a few months before Obbink came aboard at the GSI.[25]

ONE SPRING DAY in 2011, faculty and students at Baylor got a glimpse of just how exciting biblical scholarship could be when Scott Carroll arrived to demonstrate a magic trick—turning an Egyptian mummy mask into Christian biblical manuscripts. The mask had been made from discarded bits of papyrus called cartonnage, he told the attentive group, much like the papier-mâché of a Sunday-school craft project. Some bits had writings on them, possibly including fragments from the New Testament.[26]

Students watched as he submerged the mask in a soapy bath to dislodge the scraps. Originally, he'd dismantled masks by simmering them on a stove, sometimes while he watched football in the other room. "Nothing like the smell of mummy on the stove," he once told an audience.[27] Now he found ordinary dish soap just as effective. Destroying funerary masks had once been common among archaeologists, but the practice had been discontinued, if not outright condemned, by horrified classicists.

Carroll ignored the criticisms, seeing the process as a necessary evil for the discovery of biblical texts that emerged, Lazarus-like, "as if they had been raised from the dead." He showed students how to use tweezers to gently pry apart the scraps of fabric, laying them on blotting paper to dry. When they were done, he had revealed some 150 fragments, which he said included funerary texts, letters, and bits of literary texts. Among them, he pointed out, was a treasure: a fourth-century biblical text in the ancient Egyptian language Coptic. As hushed students looked on, he said, "As discoveries go, it won't get much more dramatic than this."[28]

As unorthodox as those research methods were, the team the GSI assembled to examine the artifacts that the Greens were collecting was just as unusual by ordinary academic standards. One of the first recruits was Jennifer Larson, a classics professor at Kent State University in Ohio, who was thrilled to work on a manuscript but the first to admit that she had no background in papyrology. Pattengale had chosen her after he'd happened to give a talk at Kent State.[29] Other scholars seem to have been chosen based on geographic proximity to Oklahoma City. By far the most common attribute was that they taught at faith-based universities—including Indiana Wesleyan, Baylor, Wheaton, Azusa Pacific, and Gordon-Conwell Theological Seminary—whose mission includes "transform[ing] lives by faithfully relating scholarship and service to biblical truth."[30]

In each case, the manuscripts sent to scholars came with a catch; the initiative required academics to sign a nondisclosure agreement promising they would not share any manuscripts or images "without the prior written consent of the Green Collection." Such an agreement was virtually unheard of in academia, where the rule is to openly share research. The agreement further stated that any information provided to the researcher remained the Green Collection's "exclusive property" and that "upon written request," the scholar would return or destroy any internal research they had prepared.[31]

As information on the agreements leaked out, biblical scholars worried about how the agenda of the Greens, who publicly staked their faith on the reliability of the Bible, would affect the kind of scholarship they would produce. Would the exclusive access and money cause scholars to couch their conclusions in a way that would bolster the Greens' view that the Bible was the true word of God? Or would the family bury research that contradicted fundamentalist views?

Carroll offered public assurance to allay those fears. "The Bible is not a lockbox, it changes over time" to take in new discoveries, he told *USA Today*. "This will be our approach to the Bible. It's a museum, not a ministry."[32] When David Green hosted Rick Warren in Oklahoma City to show off the collection, however, Carroll got a taste of the limits of that worldview. He showed Warren a papyrus manuscript containing the Gospel of John, noting that the manuscript left out the story of the "woman taken in adultery"—one of the examples that Bart Ehrman had raised to question the reliability of biblical transmission. Afterward, he said, David took him aside to scold him, saying, "You will not use this collection to undermine the King James Bible!"[33]

When it came time to sign the federal tax form to officially register the Museum of the Bible, Inc., as a charity in November 2011, Steve seemed to support a similar view, expressing the museum's mission "to bring to life the living word of God, to tell its compelling story of preservation, and to inspire confidence in the absolute authority and reliability of the Bible."[34]

Steve further lays out his views on the Bible in a series of books he began publishing in 2011. They follow the evangelical Protestant view that scripture speaks for itself, warning against cherry-picking to fit one's own agenda or "cutting out snippets for our own personal needs," he writes. Instead, he urges readers to see the book as a unified whole: "Each story in the Bible contributes to the grand story, what we like to call the biblical narrative, and should be read with this big story in mind."[35]

Of course, the idea that there could be one narrative in a book as complex as the Bible could itself be seen as cherry-picking—but Steve distills it down to a single story of original sin brought on by Adam and Eve's disobedience to God. "Spoiler alert!" he writes. "God, then sends his son, Jesus, to pay the price for the broken relationship and offers restoration to any who accept." Steve acknowledges that Jewish readers view the book differently before begging his readers to "humor" him: "Let me tell the ending as told by the New Testament. You can decide what you do with it."[36]

For Steve, all of the prophets "are pointing forward—to a day when a future king will arise and bring restoration and redemption to Israel." In the book of Acts, the disciples found their mission to be spreading this "story" around the world through the Great Commission. The book of Revelation is "an encouragement from Jesus to those in the church to continue to take the good news to the world as they look forward to his return." While there is "a lot in Revelation that is debated," Steve says, "the book claims to be a message from Jesus and a prophecy of 'what must soon take place.' "[37]

By presenting the Bible as a "story," Steve hedges on the question of whether it's historically true. But there are plenty of moments in his books where he gives away his own view on that topic, emphasizing that the KJV refers to itself as the "word of God" more than 350 times and a number of New Testament authors also attest that it is inspired by God, saying in essence that "God's Word doesn't come from the will of men; it comes from men inspired by the Holy Spirit."[38]

Given the Bible's widespread influence, Steve says, "if it is not true," then "how could so many people be fooled into believing it is what it claims to be?" For that matter, he asks somewhat dubiously, "How could something made up have such an impact on governments, science, education, literature, music, and art?"[39]

In his mind, the fact that the Bible was written over so many years and has had so much influence is itself evidence of its veracity, parroting the words of Josh McDowell from three decades before. If "the biblical timeline is accurate, that means that it took more than forty writers over fifteen hundred years to write it," Steve writes. "The most incredible aspect is that they were all writing one unified story." In other words, the story itself—albeit one interpreted through a fundamentalist belief—is proof of the Bible's truth.[40]

Of course, seeing the Bible that way means ignoring its many contradictions, including scientific and archaeological evidence, and the variants in early biblical manuscripts. It means ignoring the different stories told about the same book by Jewish readers, who don't see the same overarching story that Steve and evangelicals do. Nevertheless, Steve concludes, "I believe the story is true, but you shouldn't take my word for it." Instead, he expresses confidence that a plain reading of the Bible will bring its readers to Jesus: "Let the Bible speak for itself. My hope is that you will, if you haven't already, come to believe and love this beautiful story told by this beautiful book."[41]

Steve is just as clear about the consequences of that truth: "A government without a God or based on an atheistic worldview has proven to lead to tragic consequences."[42] Taking a page from David Barton, he argues that America was founded on the Bible and that "from Plymouth Rock in 1620 to 1600 Pennsylvania Avenue today, the Bible's influence is woven through the fiber of our democracy and our society."[43] And so, Steve asks, "the question remains, which worldview will we look to in order to determine what our laws will allow and prohibit? Will we look to the Bible as our Forefathers did, or do we decide to go a different direction?"[44]

In the early 2010s, more evangelicals were beginning to ask the same question, reacting to a mainstream culture that seemed to be slipping from their grasp. After a decade of gay marriage, the issue now commanded the support of a majority of Americans for the first time, and conservatives were no closer to overturning *Roe*.[45] "All around me, during Obama's first years, people were lamenting that we might have lost the war for traditional values," recalled antiabortion leader Rob Schenck.[46] Many of the Christian Right's old guard was falling away as Jerry Falwell, Heritage Foundation founder Paul Weyrich, and dominionist pastor D. James Kennedy all passed away. James Dobson, now seventy-four, stepped down from Focus on the Family even as he continued to broadcast his radio show. The Tea Party's influence had disappeared as it was absorbed into the broader Republican Party.

Beneath the surface, however, new influences were arising within evangelicalism in the form of a charismatic revival that would only gain strength over the coming years. Chief among them was missionary and theologian C. Peter Wagner, who had declared a "second apostolic age," beginning around the turn of the millennium in 2001, in which God would speak directly to prophets and apostles of a New Apostolic Reformation (NAR) to guide them into enacting his will on society in a new iteration of Reconstructionist philosophy. Among Wagner's followers was Lance Wallnau, who popularized his idea that it was the mandate of Bible believers to take dominion over "seven mountains" of American society: family, religion, arts and entertainment, media, government, education, and business.[47]

In August 2011, thousands of Christians flooded Houston's Reliant Stadium for a prayer rally called the Response, organized by Texas governor Rick Perry, that included prominent members of the NAR. Serving on the executive council of the event was David Barton, whose views on America's founding infused the gathering and who was advising Perry and other Republican candidates on their runs for president in 2012.[48] "I've met with several of the potential candidates this time, always at their call," he told *The New York Times*.[49]

In 2011, Barton's radio show *WallBuilders Live!* featured a special three-part series on the Constitution, interpreting each of the ten amendments in the Bill of Rights in biblical terms, as if they were the Ten Commandments. Barton interpreted the Fifth Amendment, which requires due process before being deprived of life, liberty, or property, as proof that the Founders were opposed to abortion.[50] It was not just an academic argument, as many in the religious right were battling Obama's new health-care law, which they feared would lead to an increase in abortion.

In December 2011, the nonprofit legal firm Becket Fund for Religious Liberty filed suit against the Department of Health and Human Services based on a requirement in the Affordable Care Act that employers had to provide coverage for birth control for employees starting in 2013. Becket represented Colorado Christian University, which argued for an exemption based on a belief that certain forms of birth control cause abortion of a fetus after conception. While the administration had provided an exemption for religious organizations, Becket argued that it should apply to religious schools as well under RFRA, which prevented government from "substantially burdening" the right to free exercise of religion.[51]

THAT SAME MONTH, Hobby Lobby made its first donation of 431 Torah scrolls to the museum, showing just how much of a tax write-off it could garner. The company had acquired the scrolls for $1.75 million over the previous two years but now had them appraised at $23 million, an increase of more than ten times the value.[52]

While Steve funneled money into biblical artifacts, the family hadn't given up donating to Christian ministries as well. By now, the company had contributed a total of $300 million through fifty real estate projects, even as the company was pushing five hundred stores across the country.[53] In 2011, David was eighty-first on the Forbes 400 list, with a net worth of $4 billion. For the third year in a row, Hobby Lobby shared the largesse with its employees, raising its full-time minimum wage another dollar to $12 an hour and part-time wage to $8.50.[54]

Now David turned to Bill High, who managed his funds in the NCF, to help him with another concern. Ever since his pledge twenty-five years before to give his company to God, he'd become increasingly anxious about what would happen to his wealth after he was gone. Now seventy, David was at the age when many retired—what would happen if he had a sudden heart attack and died? He hoped his children would carry on his mission to spread the word of God, but what about their children and their children's children?

"Realities like these haunted Barbara and me as we watched our company succeed," David said.[55] Now he sat down with Mart, Steve, Darsee, and his grandchildren to design a "succession plan" through something called the Green Stewardship Trust, which would contain the entire wealth of the family. If any descendant ever tried to sell it, then 90 percent of the proceeds would go to supporting Christian ministries, while 10 percent would go into a family fund for life-threatening emergencies. With that structure, he hoped, the company would "continue for decades, perhaps even centuries, as an ongoing source of financial fuel for God's work around the world."[56]

David, Barbara, and their three children became its first trustees. Future trustees would have to offer written testimony of how they'd been saved by Jesus Christ, sharing it before the other trustees for their approval. They also had to promise to "regularly seek to maintain a close intimate walk with the Lord Jesus Christ by regularly investing time in His Word and prayer."[57] From now on, family members would receive only an individual salary for their work—the rest would belong to God.

Meanwhile, Steve was looking after his own legacy, searching for a permanent home for the Museum of the Bible, with a focus on Dallas, New York, and Washington, DC. After a consumer survey identified Washington, DC, as the city that would draw the most visitors, the team focused their efforts on finding a location in the nation's capital.[58] They met with Christian leaders, including Rob Schenck, now head of a new organization, Faith and Action, who assured them that there was no better place for the organization if it really wanted to impact government.

"No Supreme Court Justice is going to travel to Dallas, Orlando, or Atlanta, to visit your museum," Schenck said. "But they might come to a special event here." Schenck should know—since 2000, he had spearheaded an effort called Operation Higher Court to influence the justices in cases of religious freedom, school prayer, and abortion. His strategy was to place wealthy donors he called "stealth missionaries" close to them and subtly influence them to "embolden the justices" to deliver "unapologetically conservative dissents."[59]

Schenck targeted the Supreme Court Historical Society, a nonprofit that worked to educate the public on the important role that the court played in American society. Informally, it was a conduit to the justices, especially at an annual holiday dinner thrown by the chief justice with some two hundred invited guests in the grand entry hall of the Court. Knowing the Greens' interest in opening a museum, Schenck asked the director of the society, "Would you like to entertain a billionaire couple?" The director replied yes, no doubt hoping Steve and Jackie would donate to the organization even as Schenck hoped they might help him to push conservative policy goals. Nothing much came of their attendance, however—at least not right away. Schenck did remember later, however, that they particularly enjoyed speaking with Justice Samuel Alito, a staunch conservative who was outspoken on issues of religious liberty.[60]

Around the same time, Carroll and Pattengale were on a very different mission. Wind gusted through the central quadrangle of Christ Church College on a November evening in 2011 as they climbed a creaky staircase to Obbink's rooms. They sat discussing his latest research as two mummy masks stared at them with vacant eyes from atop a green felt pool table in the corner. Suddenly, Obbink got up as if he'd remembered something. "I have something you two might like to see," he said.[61]

He reached into a manila envelope to pull out four papyrus fragments, each wrapped in plastic. Tweezing them onto the surface of the pool table, he explained that they were each a piece of a gospel—one for each book. Pattengale felt the blood drain from his face as Obbink told them the fragments from Matthew, Luke, and John dated from the mid- to late second century. But the bit of Mark, he said, was older. The fragment, in the shape of a sideways L, contained a few dozen characters in Greek describing Jesus's baptism and his call to his first disciples. Obbink pointed out a few distinctively shaped Greek letters, which had convinced him that the piece was "very likely 1st century."[62]

Pattengale stood stunned for a moment, barely able to move. The oldest known fragment of the Gospels, at the John Rylands Library at the University of Manchester, dated to the early second century. If Obbink was right, they were looking at not only an older fragment but also the only one from the century in which Jesus had lived. It was part of a private family collection that Obbink was selling off, he continued. Pattengale stood silent as he took a list of the fragments, handwritten by Obbink in pencil. According to Pattengale, Carroll was ecstatic. The "veins along his neck bulged" as he "paced with arms flailing."[63]

Flying home to Indiana, Pattengale told his wife, "I may be involved in researching one of the most important pieces of the Bible ever discovered."[64] Carroll couldn't wait to let the cat out of the bag, cryptically tweeting a few days later, "For over 100 years the earliest known text of the New Testament has been the so-called John Rylands Papyrus. Not any more. Stay tuned..."[65]

A couple of months later, Carroll was back at Baylor for another demonstration of his mummy-mask dismantling technique, this one captured on video. He filled a sink with soapy water in the classics lounge, which students ironically called the Lounge of Destiny. "We'll see why today, with hopefully the discoveries that are made," he said, unwrapping the funerary mask from bubble wrap. Sitting in his palm, it seemed curiously deflated as it stared up at the ceiling with a pair of smoky eyes. He peeled up the neck to show off some already visible writing. "I've done some probing," he teased, "and I can tell you that we are into some interesting things."[66]

Pushing up the sleeves of his blazer, he began washing the mask, helping students peel apart the fragments that emerged and separating them into piles by language—demotic, Coptic, and Greek. Watching him, religious professor David Lyle Jeffrey noticed something odd. Before Carroll dunked the mask in the water, he'd placed a few pieces of papyrus to the side of the sink. As he pulled a wet fragment out of the water, Jeffrey could swear he recognized it by shape. "Whoa, now take a look at this and see if you can read it," Carroll said, offering it to students before identifying it as an early fragment from the book of Romans. Carroll, it appeared, had surreptitiously placed it in the water while no one was looking, pretending it came from the mask.[67]

Coincidentally or not, Carroll was set to give a talk on the Green Collection the next day in Atlanta, where the *Passages* exhibition had opened in an abandoned retail space. He surprised the sellout crowd with the discovery, telling them it was the oldest fragment of the book of Romans ever discovered.[68] The next morning, Steve showed off the same fragment in a television segment on CNN. He presented items from the Green Collection, saying, "This has just been discovered within the last forty-eight hours." Carroll had dated it to the middle of the second century, around 150 CE, Steve said. "So this really adds another brick to the wall of evidence supporting what the Bible tells us.... It's an incredible find."[69]

"Incredible" didn't even begin to describe the excitement the evangelical scholarly community felt about the scholars' initiative, which seemed to be unearthing new texts at an astonishing rate. On *Evangelical Textual Criticism*, a blog for evangelical scholars, contributors tried in vain to decipher the text from the brief images that flashed on-screen during the CNN segment.[70] Several expressed doubts, questioning whether mummy masks were even still used as late as the second century and could contain New Testament texts. Even as they were grappling with those questions, they were in for an even bigger revelation.

Two tables were set up in front of a packed audience of 1,500 in an auditorium at the University of North Carolina–Chapel Hill in January 2012. The topic of debate: "Is the Original New Testament Lost?" On the left was the closest thing to a rock star in biblical scholarship: Bart Ehrman, the UNC professor who'd hit the *New York Times* bestseller list with *Misquoting Jesus*. On the right was conservative scholar Dan Wallace, director of New Testament studies at Dallas Theological Seminary. They'd known each other since studying together at Princeton nearly thirty years before and had already met twice to debate the Bible's reliability.[71]

Ehrman came out swinging, recapitulating arguments from his books that "we do not have the originals of the New Testament, period." In fact, he said, there was only one scrap of a manuscript from the second century—the John Rylands Papyrus—and even that had been written a hundred years after Jesus lived. Over 90 percent of surviving New Testament manuscripts date from the ninth century onward—so how could we possibly know what the Bible originally said?[72]

Wallace countered with arguments often made by conservative scholars—that while the original manuscripts have been lost, most of the variants that do exist in Greek manuscripts of the New Testament are minor. "More than 99 percent make no difference at all," he said. Even in cases where questions arose over the text, he said, scholars could tell from existing evidence what had been added after the fact. "To demand a first-century copy of Mark goes far beyond what is demanded for any other ancient literature," he said before pulling out an ace in the hole: In fact, "the oldest manuscript of the New Testament is now a fragment from Mark's gospel that is from the first century," he said, dated by a papyrologist "whose reputation is unimpeachable."[73]

After the debate, the scholarly community was abuzz with speculation about this mysterious fragment. Some pointed to Carroll's cryptic announcement on Twitter to surmise that it was the Green Collection. At the time, however, a spokesperson for the Green Collection denied that it owned the fragment, and Wallace remained tight-lipped, saying only that until the papyrus was published, "we should all be patient."[74]

One scholar perplexed by the mystery was Brent Nongbri, who followed the debate from Australia. Born in Norway and raised in Texas, Nongbri had studied theoretical questions about religion as a doctoral student at Yale. When he got tired of abstraction, he walked over to the Beinecke Library, which had a collection of early finds from Hunt and Grenfell's expedition to Oxyrhynchus. "There's nothing quite like being able to physically touch something thousands of years old to feel that connection with ancient people," he said. Earning his PhD just as the economy was crashing, he was able to find a position at Macquarie University in Sydney, home to the largest collection of ancient texts in the Southern Hemisphere. Nongbri helped organize the collection, researching and dating manuscripts.[75]

As he scoured the Internet, he kept coming across mentions of the Green Collection. "It was mind-boggling to see what was showing up," he said. Watching a video of one of Carroll's presentations, he was reminded of the evangelical preachers he'd seen in Texas during his youth. "Everything was the biggest, the greatest, the oldest—it was over the top." More disturbing were the reports that Carroll was dissolving mummy masks. Like many scholars, Nongbri thought the use of cartonnage for funerary coverings had died out with the Roman conquest of Egypt, before the time of Jesus. "Either they were making discoveries that would change a lot of what we think about these practices from antiquity," Nongbri said, "or it was all in some way shady."[76]

He was willing to give Carroll the benefit of the doubt, given the GSI's association with Obbink. Still, one fact gave him pause: Examining Carroll's Facebook page, he saw a picture of Carroll with some mummy masks he said he'd obtained at Oxford, sitting next to what seemed to be metal boxes from Grenfell and Hunt's expedition to Oxyrhynchus. For a moment, Nongbri allowed himself to wonder whether there might be a connection between Obbink and the mummy masks that Carroll was so cavalierly destroying. But the idea that Obbink was providing items from the Oxyrhynchus collection to be destroyed was unthinkable. There had to be another source.[77]

AROUND THE TIME of the Ehrman-Wallace debate, however, Jerry Pattengale got a glimpse of just how shady Dirk Obbink could be. The Oxford scholar had invited him to London to look at a collection of papyri, and as they walked among the brick townhouses of Mayfair, Pattengale assumed they were heading to Sotheby's. Instead, they turned down an alley to a door answered by a young Turkish man in a Yankees jersey. The man, Yakup Ekşioğlu, talked on his cell phone behind a beaded curtain while Obbink showed Pattengale some papyrus fragments, including a text from First Corinthians from the fourth century. Ekşioğlu was asking the audacious price of $1 million for the fragment, and Pattengale declined. Later, Obbink followed up several times, expressing disbelief that the Greens weren't moving forward on the purchase. While Pattengale was no stranger to dealing for antiquities in strange places, he'd never expected a literal back-alley deal from an Oxford professor.[78]

Carroll was also frustrated that Steve and his family were dragging their feet on the purchase of the first-century Mark, which he had hoped to make the centerpiece of a new exhibit that spring in a gallery off Saint Peter's Square in Rome. The exhibit was billed as the celebration of many faiths, showing how Catholics, Protestants, and Jews shared a common heritage in the Bible.[79] In an interview for the Christian Broadcasting Network in which he was introduced as the "Indiana Jones of biblical antiquities," a smiling Carroll couldn't resist bragging about the material the Greens were collecting, which was so sensational that it would soon be "front-page news," proving the reliability of the Bible as a "stable and trustworthy text." The evidence compiled by Josh McDowell a generation before "desperately" needed to be updated by "trustworthy" researchers, he said. People "don't know the mountains of evidence that we're sitting on. There is even more evidence, more to be recovered, more to be found, that even increasingly encourages our faith."[80]

Shortly after the exhibit, on April 16, 2012, Hobby Lobby celebrated its five hundredth store opening, a behemoth 66,500-square-foot facility in Las Vegas.[81] Steve noted that the company was now halfway to its overall goal of one thousand stores nationwide. Three months later, one of the Green family's DAFs managed by the NCF paid $50 million to purchase an eight-story, 430,000-square-foot red-brick building in Washington, DC, donating it to the Museum of the Bible for its new home.[82] The location was nearly perfect: two blocks south of the National Mall and within sight of the dome of the Capitol.

By now, the family was all in on the project. "What we're focusing on is reliability," Steve told the inaugural class of a new LOGOS summer institute for students at Baylor as part of the GSI. According to a press release, the program was modeled on the ADF's Blackstone Legal Fellowship, designed to train the next generation of Christian law students to take on cases of religious liberty—only in this case, it would train the next generation of biblical scholars to publish new discoveries.[83]

The same month, Carroll purchased a third-century vellum fragment of the book of Romans known as the Wyman Fragment at auction for £300,000 ($470,000).[84] It may have been the last item Carroll acquired for the collection. In August, he issued a terse message on his Facebook page that he and the Greens "had parted ways." It's not clear why the scholar and his benefactors severed ties so abruptly. In his message, Carroll implied that he and the Greens had a difference of views: "I have an unswerving belief that a successful museum of the Bible must be nonsectarian and that scholars and scholarship should not be used to promote a narrow religious agenda—right or not."[85]

He seemed to be accusing the family of unfairly using the museum to promote their own view of biblical inerrancy—though Carroll had been just as zealous in pushing the idea that the amazing discoveries in the Green Collection would prove the Bible's authenticity. Others have suggested different reasons for his departure—that there was a disagreement over royalties for the *Passages* exhibit catalog or skepticism by Baylor administrators about Carroll's credentials given his lack of published articles.[86]

Perhaps in the end, it came down to a personality difference, with Carroll's Indiana Jones–meets–P. T. Barnum persona not sitting well with the low-key Oklahomans. With a multimillion-dollar museum at stake, the Greens had to be careful about the image they portrayed—and it was risky being associated with a self-promoter like Carroll. Or perhaps there was a simpler reason: The Greens didn't need him anymore. The collection had been largely assembled, and the family now had its own connections to acquire additional material through Pattengale, Obbink, and other scholars.

Whatever the reason, the Greens now took over the project with the confidence that God had commissioned them to spread his word. At the same time, they carried the same confidence into an even riskier arena where the family was about to be thrust even more prominently into the spotlight.

CHAPTER TEN

In the Womb I Knew You

The air was hot and sticky in September 2012 when the Green family gathered at Mart's home in a gated community west of Oklahoma City. Temperatures had pushed 100 degrees all week, but it was more than the heat that oppressed them: The family felt they had run out of options.[1] According to the Affordable Care Act, employers had to start covering birth control for employees starting on January 1, and David had asked Mart to call the meeting to decide what to do.[2]

At issue were four methods of birth control that some religious conservatives believed caused abortion. Two of them, Ella and Plan B, were known as "morning-after" pills because they prevented a fertilized egg from implanting in the uterus, making them effective birth control after sex. The other two were intrauterine devices (IUDs)—T-shaped instruments inserted into the uterus that typically kill sperm before fertilization. In some cases, however, IUDs can be inserted up to five days after sex to prevent implantation.

David found that problematic, believing like many evangelicals that human life begins when a sperm fertilizes an egg, based on verses such as Jeremiah 1:5: "Before I formed you in the womb I knew you." While not all Christians took this literally, those who did considered that anything preventing implantation of the fertilized egg was abortion—and therefore murder of an unborn child.

When Christian groups first publicized the Obamacare mandate, Hobby Lobby discovered that its health insurance covered Ella and Plan B and discontinued that coverage, but now the company risked fines of $100 a day per employee if it refused to reinstate it.[3] With 13,240 full-time employees at Hobby Lobby and 372 at Mardel, that could amount to more than $1.3 million a day. What the government was asking wasn't just "un-American," it was "evil," David seethed, forcing him to "pay for the killing of unborn babies"—an "abomination!"[4] When he talked it over with Barbara, she calmed him down. "We only have one decision to make," she told him. "Right or wrong. Black or white. It's in God's hands."[5]

The gathering was a flashback to the oil crash of 1985; once again, the family faced the prospect of bankruptcy. This time, the decision was theirs. Surprisingly, it wasn't Mart who spoke up but Steve, launching into a story from the Old Testament. When the prophet Daniel and three friends first came to Babylon, he said, they were required to eat meat that was unclean according to Jewish purity laws; they appealed to the king's counselor and were given different foods. "This might happen for us," Steve said in his slow drawl. "We might seek relief and receive favor." On the other hand, Daniel later defied the king by praying to the Israelite God and was thrown into a den of lions, only to be saved by an angel. "Perhaps God would be most glorified by rescuing us as we were just about to be devoured," Steve said.[6]

Then there was a third option: "We might be required to suffer." The Bible was full of people God punished to make an example of their faith. "We should be ready to embrace whatever hardships come as the price of obeying God." It was hardly a rousing speech, but it spelled out the potential outcomes should they defy the law: relief, deliverance, or suffering. David had been worried that some of his millennial grandchildren might lack the older generation's conviction about abortion, but when he asked for a vote, every one of them raised their hand—it was unanimous. They would fight.[7]

HOBBY LOBBY FILED suit against the federal government on September 12, 2012, under the RFRA, which prevented the government from "substantially burdening" a person's religious freedom.[8] The suit argued that following the mandate would cause the family to "violate their deeply held religious beliefs under threat of heavy fines, penalties, and lawsuits."[9] Hobby Lobby made no secret of its status as a religious company, with its Christian music in stores, the religiously inspired advertisements in newspapers, and the causes the company supported. The trust that David, Barbara, and the three children had signed the previous year only solidified the connection.[10]

The suit requested an injunction allowing Hobby Lobby to deny coverage to employees while the case was being decided. "By being required to make a choice between sacrificing our faith or paying millions of dollars in fines, we essentially must choose which poison pill to swallow," David said in a statement. "We simply cannot abandon our religious beliefs to comply with this mandate."[11] Representing the company was the Becket Fund for Religious Liberty, which filed suit on behalf of thirty smaller Catholic organizations. Founded in 1994, the legal firm was small compared to the better-known ADF. Its founder, Kevin "Seamus" Hasson, had worked in the Reagan Justice Department for Justice Samuel Alito on religious liberty cases before starting the firm to defend groups "from Anglicans to Zoroastrians"—though in practice, most of its clients were Christians protesting incursion into their religious beliefs by government.[12]

In a conference call with reporters, lead attorney Kyle Duncan said Hobby Lobby "should never be put in a position of choosing their faith over their business." The lawsuit drew praise from conservative politicians and institutions. Indiana Wesleyan University, where Barbara was a trustee and Jerry Pattengale a professor, awarded David its World Changers award. Baylor, headquarters of the GSI, presented Steve with its highest honor, a Pro Ecclesia Medal of Service, at the same time honoring the ninety-four-year-old evangelical lion Billy Graham with the same award.[13]

Not all religious leaders supported the lawsuit, however. A Pentecostal pastor from Oklahoma City delivered a petition with eighty thousand signatures to Hobby Lobby headquarters. "Don't use your Christian faith as an excuse to obstruct health care reform and deny women access to birth control," the petition read. The liberal National Council of Churches called for a boycott of the company on the grounds that it denied women the right to make their own decisions about contraceptive care.[14]

Some of Hobby Lobby's customers boycotted as well. One "avid crafter and long-time Hobby Lobby shopper" who blogged under the name Aunt Peaches scolded, "You, as a corporation, are not your employees. You do not have the right to dictate what those employees do with their bodies when they are off the clock."[15] One group not heard from—at least not publicly—was the 13,600 employees who would potentially have to pay out of pocket for the morning-after pill, which could run over $60 a dose, or an IUD, which could run $1,000 or more.

In mid-October, the government filed its opposition to the suit, questioning how a "for-profit, secular corporation established to sell art and craft supplies can claim to exercise religion." By seeking to protect their own religious views, it argued, the company's founders were taking away the religious freedom of their employees, who might subscribe to any number of faiths. In a hearing, government lawyer Margaret Bennett pointed out that the reason for a company to incorporate in the first place was to separate the owners from the business. The fact that Hobby Lobby had previously covered the drugs and waited a year to sue showed that there was hardly "irreparable harm" that justified taking coverage away from its employees.[16]

Amid the back-and-forth, Americans were voting once again for a president. Christian conservatives struggled to find a candidate, with Sarah Palin too unpopular and Rick Perry flaming out early. Eventually they ended up supporting Mitt Romney, a Mormon former private equity manager who ultimately clinched the party nomination. Some evangelicals remained lukewarm about Romney, who as governor of Massachusetts had pioneered a health-care bill that had served as a model for Obamacare, though he now pledged to repeal it. Others were suspicious of his Mormon faith. When Obama declared support for gay marriage in May 2012, however, they were left with little choice but to rally around Romney despite his flaws.

Among those most influential in crafting the Republican Party platform was David Barton, representing Texas on the platform committee. Among other provisions, the platform called for nationwide bans on abortion and gay marriage, reinstatement of school prayer, and public display of the Ten Commandments. On Glenn Beck's television program, Barton boasted that seventy of his seventy-one proposals had been approved.[17] He had just released a new book, *The Jefferson Lies*, a revisionist history of the third president, which argued that Jefferson was an evangelical Christian, with a whole chapter debunking separation of church and state. Despite making the *New York Times* bestseller list, the book was pilloried by historians, who criticized its many historical inaccuracies and quotes taken out of context. By August, Barton's publisher declared that it was ceasing publication of the book due to "concerns about its content." Barton remained defiant, appearing on Glenn Beck's radio show to push back against critics for silencing him.[18]

In the end, 79 percent of white evangelicals voted for Romney, but not in enough numbers to put him over the top. Not only did Obama win the election, but Democrats also gained seats in Congress, and three states—Maine, Maryland, and Washington—became the first to legalize same-sex marriage by ballot rather than approving it by action of the court. For the Green family, Obama's victory meant there was no hope for relief from the Obamacare mandate—they would have to pray for deliverance or resign themselves to suffering.

A week later, the federal judge in Oklahoma overseeing the case denied Hobby Lobby an injunction on the grounds that the company wasn't a religious organization, and "secular, for-profit corporations" did not have "a constitutional right to the free exercise of religion." Becket immediately appealed, but the clock was ticking, with less than six weeks before the January 1 deadline.[19]

Meanwhile, a dozen more companies filed suit, represented by Becket or the ADF—which changed its name to Alliance Defending Freedom and coordinated communications between lawyers and advocacy groups, encouraging organizations and lawmakers to write briefs in support. The ADF scored a victory in Colorado when a district court allowed injunctions to stand for two companies also seeking relief from the mandate, giving the Greens hope that they might win on appeal.[20] At the same time, the NCF—through which Hobby Lobby made the vast majority of its donations—increased funding of the ADF, donating $9.6 million in 2011 and $10.1 million in 2012.[21]

The FRC launched a web campaign on Hobby Lobby's behalf, while Becket produced a series of YouTube videos humanizing the family as down-home and sincere. David, in a pink shirt and black-framed glasses, told the story of the $600 loan and the frames in the garage before going on to describe everything the family offered employees, including anger-management classes, financial counseling, and four full-time chaplains on staff. "We do everything we possibly can to help our employees structure their lives based on biblical principles."[22]

All the family asked was that they be allowed to live by those same principles, added Steve, staring into the camera with steady blue eyes. "It would not be consistent for us to live one way at home and then expect a different way at work." A gentle soundtrack played as the family chatted around a table in their home. It was about "integrity," said Mart, wearing his trademark green shirt. "How do you live an integrated life, so your spirit, mind, and body, all parts of your life together." "Our goal is just to be a light to the world," added Darsee, wearing chunky jewelry and a brightly colored scarf, "not just talk the talk, but walk the walk."[23]

More than anyone, Barbara became the face for the family—perhaps since a woman arguing for cutting off birth control seemed more palatable than a man doing so. Becket prepared a special video featuring Barbara, calling it an "Esther story," in reference to the Jewish queen who used her position in Persia to save her people from genocide. It became a favorite for evangelicals, especially women, as a symbol of standing up at the right place at the right time—or, as the story says, "for such a time as this."[24] Ironically, rather than featuring Barbara directly, the video consists mostly of the men in the family talking about her. "Mom has always been a leader in the family—maybe not a leader that's out front all the time, but a servant-leader," Mart said. "Mom has always been somewhat quiet, but there's a certain strength in her quietness," said Steve. "I can't foresee doing anything without Barbara," added David.[25]

As he awaited the verdict, David prayed hard, reading with chagrin the mail both for and against that poured in to the corporate offices. Outside, the family put up a billboard quoting Daniel 3:17: "Our God whom we serve is able to deliver us."[26] On December 10, the Tenth Circuit Court of Appeals issued its decision, once again denying the family's request for an injunction just a few weeks before the start of the New Year. In a last-ditch effort, Hobby Lobby filed an emergency appeal with the US Supreme Court. On December 26, Justice Sonia

Sotomayor, the Obama appointee overseeing the Tenth Circuit, declined to intervene. The company remained defiant, saying it was "not their intention, as a company, to pay for abortion-inducing drugs."[27]

EVEN AS THE new year approached, a miracle happened. On December 28, general counsel Dobelbower came into David's office to say that he'd realized Hobby Lobby wouldn't have to start paying fines until the start of the insurance policy's "plan year." By changing the start date from January 1 to July 1, they could put off the fines by six months. The company made the change even as it appealed the case to the entire panel of judges for the Tenth Circuit Court of Appeals.[28]

In December 2012, Mart announced a new project called Every Tribe Every Nation to step up Bible translations. The project had been in the works since Mart had returned to Guatemala in 2010 for a retreat of a Wycliffe subsidiary called the Seed Company. As he listened to all the efforts underway, he felt that the translation industry had grown into a veritable Tower of Babel, with multiple organizations pursuing translations in different countries, sometimes competing or duplicating efforts.[29]

In response, Mart convened executives from the ten groups, including Wycliffe, the American Bible Society, and Biblica, in a hotel conference in Orlando to pitch a new idea: the Digital Bible Library. By pooling their resources, they could upload all of the two thousand or so completed translations and identify those yet to be done. Now Mart and other leaders announced the launch of the platform, made available through a mobile app called YouVersion started by a fellow Oklahoman, Bobby Gruenewald. Their goal, dubbed illumiNations, was to ensure that "every tribe and every nation" had access to a translation in their native tongue within just twenty years, by 2033. It would take millions to complete, but Mart was dedicated to raising the funds.[30]

Steve too had been busy. At the end of 2012, Hobby Lobby donated another eight hundred artifacts to the museum, for which it had paid $18.7 million but now had appraised at $61.6 million, more than three times as much.[31] After successful exhibits in Oklahoma City, Atlanta, Charlotte, and Vatican City, he returned to Kentucky for the opening of the museum's first permanent exhibit of biblical artifacts at the Creation Museum. "There is no more fitting museum anywhere in the world to be the first place to do this," said Cary Summers at the opening of the exhibit, standing before an exhibit of fossils the museum said dated from the flood four thousand years before. "Your ministry is grounded firmly with both feet on God's word, and that's what we want to show here."[32]

The exhibit included a King James Bible, a Tyndale Bible, a burned Torah scroll, and a page from the Codex Climaci Rescriptus. "We are like-minded" about the "value of the Bible in society," Steve told the audience as Ken Ham beamed beside him. "Because the Creation Museum exists to declare the authority and accuracy of the Bible," added Ham, "we are thrilled to have this opportunity."[33]

A few months later, Steve appeared at a luncheon in New York to receive the Templeton Biblical Values Award from the National Bible Association, which donated $25,000 to the Museum of the Bible in his honor.[34] In a speech, Steve offered his most passionate defense of the Bible yet, saying it was "literally, historically accurate and reliable." In fact, he said "most every archaeological discovery" that had been made "support[ed] the accuracy of this book," showing it to be a "reliable historical document." Not only that, he continued, but the Bible "tells us how we should live," and "when we apply it to our lives, it has been good." His goal with the museum, he went on, was "to reintroduce this book to the nation." In addition to the building in Washington, he announced, the museum was putting together an elective high school curriculum based on the Bible. "Someday," he said, it "should be mandated. Here's a book that's impacted our world unlike any other and you're not going to teach it? There's something wrong with that."[35]

As the date for Hobby Lobby's appeal approached, a group of Republican congressional representatives wrote a brief to the court insisting that Congress clearly meant the RFRA to include corporations, and the administration couldn't pick and choose "whose exercise of religion is protected and whose is not."[36] On the other side, opponents argued that if Hobby Lobby were allowed to pick health coverage based on religious beliefs, there was nothing to stop companies that disagreed with homosexuality from denying coverage for AIDS or Christian Scientists from denying vaccines.[37]

Lost in the discussion was new science showing that the birth control in question might not be abortifacients after all. While for years scientists hadn't known how the morning-after pill worked, a definitive 2012 study had found that Plan B actually didn't prevent implantation of the egg; rather, it prevented ovulation so that there was no egg to fertilize in the first place. (Some studies showed the same for Ella.)[38]

As the Greens traveled to Denver for arguments before eight judges, other companies were arguing appeals in Chicago, Philadelphia, and Cincinnati.[39] Appearing in court, Becket's Duncan argued that Hobby Lobby was a "profit-making company, yes, but also a ministry." He cited the recent 5–4 Supreme Court case *Citizens United v. FEC*—in which corporations were allowed to spend unlimited money on elections based on free speech—to argue that if a company had a right to speech, it also had a right to religion.[40]

Finally, three days before the July 1 deadline, the panel of judges agreed, ruling 5–3 on behalf of Hobby Lobby in a decision written by Tenth Circuit judge Neil Gorsuch. To the Green family's relief, the injunction was approved, and Hobby Lobby would be spared the fines. In a stinging dissent, the circuit's chief justice, Mary Beck Briscoe, blasted her colleagues for equating running a business with a "form of evangelism," calling their ruling "nothing short of a radical revision of First Amendment law."[41] At the same time, an appeals court in Pennsylvania issued a contrary ruling, denying an injunction for another company. With opposite rulings in circuit courts, the case seemed destined for the US Supreme Court.

That September, Steve appeared on Glenn Beck's television show to speak about Hobby Lobby's fight with the government over the birth-control issue in an interview with David Barton. "You guys are not allowed to have conscience, a religious conscience, if you have Obamacare," Barton lamented. Steve sighed. "It has been determined by the courts that free-speech rights can be exercised by corporations—newspapers and the like," he said, "but this has been an issue that's never really been tried in the courts."[42]

That was about to change when finally, two days before Thanksgiving, the Supreme Court agreed to hear the case. The court consolidated the Hobby Lobby case with the Pennsylvania case, involving a Mennonite cabinetmaker from Pennsylvania named Conestoga Wood.[43] The same day, the Freedom from Religion Foundation called for a boycott of Hobby Lobby stores, just in time for the busy holiday season. "Women make up more than half of the nation, and we and our secular supporters must flex our consumer muscle," its copresident Annie Laurie Gaylor said.[44]

On a more satirical note, feminists began circulating a hashtag on Twitter, #HobbyLobbyRules, pillorying the idea of a craft store dictating their reproductive freedoms. "If your craft project goes wrong, you're screwed. And there is no Plan B," read one. "Ladies, hot glue your knees together for guaranteed fail-safe birth control," read another. "Childless married women should be stoned with glitter-caked rocks for they are an abomination unto the eyes of the Lord," read another.[45]

The dark humor reflected a more serious criticism by some observers who suspected that no matter how sincere the Green family's beliefs about abortion were, the underlying subtext of the case was about not just limiting birth control but also a conservative Christian desire to subjugate women. For decades, televangelists and preachers had equated abortion with loose sexual morals, preaching that if women just refrained from premarital sex, there would be no need for abortion in the first place.

"The same is true of the war on birth control," argued political commentator Emily Bazelon. "By separating sex from childbearing, birth control is to blame for the erosion of marriage, for the economic difficulties of single motherhood," she wrote. "The *Hobby Lobby* case has given the groups that want to go back to prepill days a chance to air their nostalgia."[46]

HOBBY LOBBY DONATED more items to the Museum of the Bible in 2013, earning tax breaks on nearly five hundred scrolls and thirty other artifacts with an assessed value of $50 million—bringing the total worth of the museum's collection to $135 million.[47] Nevertheless, Steve told a fine arts reporter, "I am not a collector." Rather, "we are storytellers first," he said. "We're buyers of items to tell the story." As part of that story, the museum unveiled a new treasure: a Jewish prayer book the size of an iPhone that contained some one hundred daily blessings in Hebrew. Hobby Lobby had bought it from Israeli dealer Baidun for $3.5 million. Carbon-14 dating by an Israeli scholar dated it to 840 CE, making it a "missing link" between the Dead Sea Scrolls and medieval Torah scrolls.[48]

"This artifact may very well be the earliest connection today's practicing Jews have to the roots of their rabbinic liturgy," Steve said in an announcement. When Jewish scholars eagerly asked to see it, they were denied and told the GSI would publish it in due course.[49]

The announcement was overshadowed the next day when a Jewish blogger, Ken Berwitz, reported a disturbing incident that seemed to show that Hobby Lobby had a discriminatory attitude toward Jewish people. One of his friends was shopping at a Hobby Lobby in a heavily Jewish neighborhood in New Jersey, and despite rows of Christmas decorations, she couldn't find any Chanukah items. "We don't cater to you people," a store employee supposedly said. Berwitz, who ran a left-wing political blog, called Hobby Lobby headquarters to ask why it didn't stock Chanukah items. "Because Mr. Green is the owner of the company, he's a Christian, and those are his values," he was told. The news spread across the Internet, causing some Jewish people to boycott the store.[50]

Hobby Lobby did damage control, saying that the alleged comments were "in no way indicative of Hobby Lobby culture." Steve took to the press himself, saying, "Our family has a deep respect for the Jewish faith and those who hold its traditions dear." Eventually Steve said the company would start carrying items in areas "where we have Jewish population," such as New York and New Jersey.[51]

Despite that conciliatory tone, the tense relationship between Hobby Lobby and the Jewish community was also reflected in the way the Museum of the Bible presented Judaism in the ongoing *Passages* exhibits. Rather than presenting the Hebrew Bible on its own terms, they portrayed it from a Protestant Christian point of view as a prelude to the New Testament, prophesying the coming of Jesus as messiah—"positioning Jewish scriptures as incomplete antecedents to Christian scriptures and collapsing the sweep of Jewish history—no matter how recent—into an uncontested 'past,'" in the words of one religious scholar in a report on the exhibit.[52] Torah scrolls were openly displayed as evidence of the Bible's accurate transmission despite Jewish tradition requiring that decommissioned scripture be buried or destroyed. In one room depicting the persecution of Jews, pogroms and the Holocaust were presented as a cautionary tale about religious liberty for Christians. "What if the biblical books and scrolls in *Passages* were relics of people that no longer existed?" a voice-over asked.[53]

Even as Steve celebrated the purchase of the Jewish prayer book, HSI was continuing to investigate the cuneiform objects he'd bought in Dubai. In 2013, Brent Easter turned the case over to a new agent, John Paul "J. P." Labbat, who had spent twenty years investigating human trafficking, money laundering, weapons, and narcotics before seeking out Easter a few years earlier in search of a new challenge.

"I was immediately captivated," Labbat recently said, sitting at his desk in an office overlooking the East River in Manhattan. Easter led him into galleries of dealers in New York, showing him how he could use knowledge to gain trust. "One of the owners pointed to a piece and asked him where he thought it was from." When Easter answered correctly, pointing out details such as the color of the marble and shape of the nose, "[the owner] was willing to spill his guts." Labbat began immersing himself in learning how to recognize cultures, materials, and time periods and worked undercover to obtain information from gallery owners and dealers.[54]

In the Hobby Lobby case, the tablets had clearly been shipped with false packaging, erroneously labeled as "clay tile samples" with listed values far below their worth. That alone would allow authorities to charge the Greens with importing goods with false statements. "The ultimate consignee is responsible for what's on the declarations of importation," Easter explained to Labbat. "By the third, fourth, and fifth time, you have to know something is going on." If HSI wanted a tougher smuggling charge against the Greens, however, they'd have to prove the family knew that the tablets had been illegally trafficked.

Labbat started with the story, provided by Fazeli, that the collection had been in the United States before it had been shipped back to the Middle East. Labbat called the custodian on the form, a woman by the name of Betty Bolton who lived in Mississippi. "That's the most preposterous things I've ever heard," she told him. The only connection she'd had with Israeli antique dealers was a trip she'd taken to Israel a few years earlier, when she had purchased some jewelry from a shop in Jerusalem—she'd never bought any cuneiform tablets, much less kept a collection for decades. Easter and Labbat surmised that the dealers had just taken her name at random from an invoice to cover their tracks, and Hobby Lobby had never bothered to check.

Labbat flew Hobby Lobby employees to New York to interview them to learn more about their shipping practices. After all, the company had founded its entire business model around the practice of shipping items from overseas. Interviewing an employee who worked as a curator, Labbat was told that the company had decided not to use its usual customs broker after it had been warned that customs might detain the packages. Instead, the Greens had arranged to have Fazeli mail packages to different names and addresses—for Labbat, this was a red flag that they must have known something was wrong. "I was astounded to learn that they intentionally didn't use a customs broker, because had they used one, those pieces would not have made it," Labbat said. "What does that tell you?"

By now, Hobby Lobby was starting to "lawyer up," with different attorneys representing Steve, the company, and various employees. "People were starting to wall themselves off and separate and distance themselves." With the help of Easter's informants from Operation Lost Treasure, Labbat headed to the Middle East to conduct more interviews in an effort to determine where the items had come from in the first place.

Across the ocean, a different drama was unfolding that would eventually come back to Hobby Lobby's doorstep. In January 2014, the BBC announced that Oxford professor Dirk Obbink had discovered a papyrus fragment containing two new works by the Greek poet Sappho, known for her erotic poems.[55] Staring at her computer screen, University of Manchester papyrologist Roberta Mazza was stunned. It was impossible to get new material out of Egypt these days—and in the wake of the Arab Spring, any papyri that did emerge from the country were almost certainly looted.

The article said Obbink had acquired the fragment from an "anonymous collector" in London. But how had the poems not been noticed before? "A classicist with even a vague knowledge of papyrus would've recognized them," she said. "The moment you see verses in that shape, you say, 'That's Sappho!' "[56] Originally from Italy, Mazza was speaking now between sessions at a conference for the Association for Research into Crimes Against Art (ARCA), which gathered scholars, archaeologists, law officers, and journalists each year in the Italian hilltown of Amelia to share information on illegal trafficking of antiquities.

In a follow-up article in the *Times Literary Supplement*, Obbink said the papyrus had come from an "ancient mummy cartonnage panel."[57] Mazza was even more confused. Like Brent Nongbri, she had thought the use of papyrus in mummy masks had ended when Egypt had become a Roman province in 30 CE. So how could a mummy mask contain third-century texts? She had taken the same summer course with Obbink as Baylor's Jeff Fish, and she wrote to Obbink to ask for more information. Obbink politely replied that there were many private collections of Egyptian artifacts—in fact, the Green Collection had a fragment from the same Sappho text he'd acquired.[58]

Who are these Greens? Mazza thought. "I mean, what the hell is this!" said Mazza, who has big, frizzy hair and a personality to match. As a woman in the boys' club of classical studies, she was used to being condescended to, making her more determined to find answers. Reaching out to the Museum of the Bible, she found that the collection had a new director. In February 2014, the Greens had hired David Trobisch, a respected German scholar specializing in New Testament studies.[59] He told Mazza that those items had been acquired by his predecessor, Scott Carroll; as she began to research Carroll, seeing his Indiana Jones persona in videos, she became alarmed. "I thought he was a complete joke."[60]

Only Obbink's involvement gave her any confidence. She reached out to her friend Jeff Fish, asking if he knew anything about these fragments. "I'm sure the Greens have the best lawyers and everything is taken care of," he said, shrugging. But Mazza couldn't let it go—nothing about the story checked out. "So I was thinking, what the fuck is going on?" she says. "How stupid do these people think we are?"[61]

A MONTH LATER, Steve attended the National Prayer Breakfast in Washington, DC, working the room with Jerry Pattengale to raise awareness about the museum; their attendance drew attention to the looming Supreme Court case as well. More than three thousand politicians, pastors, and lobbyists crammed into a hotel ballroom for a breakfast of rubbery scrambled eggs and chalky paprika potatoes. The breakfast had been a Washington institution for seventy years, allowing a mostly conservative crowd to hobnob, organize, and raise money—an "entertainment and lobbying extravaganza," as one congressman called it.[62]

Eventually Obama took the podium. "Around the world, freedom of religion is under threat," he said. "We see governments engaging in discrimination and violence against the faithful." America, by contrast, celebrated the dignity of every human being. "And central to that dignity is freedom of religion: the right of every person to practice their faith how they choose"—or even "to practice no faith at all."[63] Steve and Pattengale were shocked—how dare Obama talk about religious freedom abroad when his own Justice Department was fighting Hobby Lobby's ability to practice its faith at home?[64]

In March 2014, Steve climbed the white marble steps of the Supreme Court with other members of his family for the oral arguments in *Burwell v. Hobby Lobby*, named for the US health secretary. As an unseasonable snow fell on Washington, the family pushed their way past protesters from both sides crowding the front of the building—women with hot-pink placards reading "My birth control. My decision" and evangelicals with a large banner reading "God's law comes first. Repeal socialist Obamacare!" Barbara led the way in a sharp black pantsuit and scarf, flanked by David in a baggy gray suit and a phalanx of Green family members, including all three children, their spouses, and several grandchildren.[65]

Arguing for Hobby Lobby was Paul Clement, an experienced Supreme Court litigator who said that when the government "compelled employers to provide something as religiously sensitive as contraception," it must have known it would be challenged. He was immediately interrupted by the three female justices—Sonia Sotomayor, Elena Kagan, and Ruth Bader Ginsburg—who questioned him in rapid succession about how far that religious challenge went. Did it apply to blood transfusions? Vaccines? Products made of pork? They'd all have to be examined on their own merits, Clement responded—but contraception was a special case since it was "so religiously sensitive, so fraught with religious controversy."[66]

When Clement tried to change the subject to explain why a corporation could be a "person" under the law, Sotomayor pounced. Who determines the corporate religion? she asked. "The majority of shareholders? The corporate officers?" Kagan put a finer point on it: "Congress has given a statutory entitlement to women and that includes contraception. And when the employer says, 'No, I don't want to give that,' that woman is quite directly, quite tangibly harmed."[67]

When his turn came, the government's lawyer Donald Verrilli said that while the government respected Hobby Lobby's owners' sincere belief that those forms of birth control caused abortion, IUDs were "far and away the method of contraception that is most effective, but has the highest upfront cost." Didn't the court have to "consider the impact on third parties"—that is, Hobby Lobby's employees who would be required to foot that bill?[68]

Conservative justice Antonin Scalia shut that idea down, saying that if Congress wanted to balance the impact on those who objected to others' religious beliefs, it "made no reference to that" in the law. Furthermore, he added, the administration had already made exemptions for religious organizations, so why couldn't it do the same for a private company? Chief Justice John Roberts mused that perhaps one way to solve the problem was to provide an exemption for "closely held" private companies and then "await another case when a large publicly traded corporation comes in"—which he thought unlikely to happen.[69]

A FEW DAYS later, eighteen members of the Green family filed into the Vatican to meet Pope Francis I, who asked them how the Supreme Court case was progressing.[70] The occasion was a new exhibit of the Green Collection in Rome that was expected to draw 100,000 visitors over three months.[71] Among them was Roberta Mazza, who was home visiting family for Easter and couldn't resist seeing the exhibit for herself. As she entered with the rest of the crowd, she was impressed by the size and richness of what was presented and at the same time bemused by the theme-park display, with immersive gallery spaces brimming with artifacts.

The two hundred or so items in the exhibit were assembled around the theme of how the Bible had been transmitted around the world, from Dead Sea Scrolls to medieval manuscripts—as well as beyond, with a copy of the "Lunar Bible," a microfilm copy of the entire KJV that had ended up on the moon with the 1971 Apollo 14 mission. It was a particularly triumphal vision, Mazza thought as she walked the galleries, displaying an uncomplicated picture of the Bible's global journey without any of the messiness of apocryphal or alternative texts—a shame, since that would have made a much more interesting story.[72]

Of course, she took particular interest in the section on ancient manuscripts, scrolling through an iPad showing attempts to image the different layers of the Codex Climaci Rescriptus palimpsest. Other scraps of papyrus included the Romans fragment that Steve Green, in his CNN appearance, had claimed was from a mummy mask.[73] But Mazza's attention was drawn to a small, roughly square fragment with a bite out of one side showing a half-dozen lines from the book of Galatians in Egyptian Coptic, dating from the fifth or sixth century.[74]

Mazza realized she'd seen this fragment before when a PhD student in Montreal, Brice Jones, had posted a photo of it to his blog with a number of other papyri put up for sale by a Turkish dealer calling himself MixAntik. The dealer had sold hundreds of fragments on eBay in the previous year, and Jones had expressed concern about the provenance of this fragment, which the seller would only say had come "from Egypt." Someone, it seemed, had discovered a large quantity of papyri and was exporting them from the country, which meant there could be "sensitive legal issues involved."[75] Since the post, MixAntik had changed his name to ebuyerrrrr.[76] Now Mazza was staring at the Galatians fragment in the heart of the Vatican. How the *fuck* had it ended up in the hands of the Greens?

As THE FAMILY awaited the Supreme Court verdict, their notoriety opened them up to greater public scrutiny for how well they followed their own beliefs. The same day the Vatican exhibit opened, *Mother Jones* magazine reported that despite the company's refusal to cover those four forms of birth control, it had actually invested in companies that made them for years. That included $73 million in an employee retirement fund with interest in Teva Pharmaceuticals, the maker of Plan B and a copper IUD, and Actavis, which made a generic version of Plan B and distributed Ella.[77] Religious investors can take advantage of funds that are carefully screened to avoid such conflicts, but when asked, Steve shrugged this issue off without concern, saying he didn't know whether it was true, and even if it was, "that is several steps removed."[78]

At the same time, details emerged about the Bible curriculum Steve had been planning. Andrew Seidel, a lawyer with the Freedom from Religion Foundation, had tracked the progress of the endeavor since Steve had met with the school board of Mustang, an Oklahoma City suburb near Hobby Lobby's corporate headquarters, to discuss a pilot of the program. Steve planned to take it to at least a hundred schools within two years. "This is not about a denomination, or a religion, it's about a book," Steve told them. "We will not try to go down denominational, religious-type roads."[79]

Nevertheless, Seidel warned the superintendent in a letter that the Greens' evangelical bias made it unlikely that the curriculum would pass constitutional muster.[80] According to a 1963 Supreme Court decision, schools could teach academic courses on the Bible so long as they did not promote specific religious views. Seidel realized he was right to be concerned when he received a leaked copy of the two-hundred-page curriculum. "It was just laden with Christian proselytizing and bias," he said. "It was truly an attempt to convert other people's children to the Greens' brand of Christianity."[81]

He shared the curriculum with Mark Chancey, a professor of biblical studies at Southern Methodist University, who produced a scathing report on the draft. He said the curriculum unquestioningly followed Steve's views of the Bible's accuracy, uncritically stating that Moses had authored the Pentateuch, a point disputed by most scholars, and selectively using archaeological discoveries to support the idea that "the Bible, especially when viewed alongside other historical information, is a reliable historical source." In short, Chancey wrote, "the curriculum builds its case for this view on oversimplifications, misrepresentations, logical fallacies, and outright mistakes."[82]

Beyond those historical claims, the curriculum lingered on a select group of themes, such as "God's promise" and "God's justice," to present a one-sidedly optimistic view of the Bible, in keeping with Steve's view that the Bible was always a force for good, while avoiding the "ample stories in the Bible that might undermine that positive presentation." Pattengale cited more than sixty scholars who had supposedly contributed to the curriculum, but Chancey speculated that few had been consulted. (A number later disavowed involvement.)[83] Later, Steve boasted that he had written the narrative portion personally, along with Joel Kauffmann, a religious writer who went on to become lead content creator for the Museum of the Bible.[84]

As the school planned to go ahead with the curriculum, Seidel demonstrated through document requests that Steve had gone out of his way to assist in keeping the matter secret. This included helping the board circumvent open-meeting laws by holding meetings at Hobby Lobby headquarters, which were closed to the public.[85] The documents also showed Steve and Pattengale struggling to respond to the criticisms Seidel and others had raised, retaining lawyers with the ADF to consult on making changes that would keep the curriculum within the law. Even so, Seidel saw the edits as more cosmetic than substantive.[86] As the school year came to a close in Oklahoma, the fate of the class remained in doubt.

WITH THE SUPREME Court approaching the end of its term in June, Rob Schenck received an email from one of the "stealth missionaries" he'd charged with getting close to the justices. "Rob, if you want some interesting news, please call. No emails," said Gayle Wright. Schenck was excited, knowing she had recently dined privately with Justice Samuel Alito and his wife, Martha-Ann. According to Schenck, when he called, Wright told him that at one point during the dinner, Alito had gotten up from the table, and Martha-Ann had leaned in to say, "You're going to love the opinion Sam is writing for Hobby Lobby."[87]

That was all Schenck needed to hear to know that his prayers had been answered. Wright told him she thought the message was calculated to come from Martha-Ann rather than Sam in order to give the justice plausible deniability. Or perhaps it was just a moment of indiscretion on her part. No matter; Schenck was now armed with the all-important knowledge of how the Supreme Court would rule weeks in advance of the end of the session on June 30. Schenck began quietly telling people close to him, including his wife, his twin brother, and several close associates. As the ruling approached, he told his staff to ready a celebratory statement and a prayer meeting on the steps of the Court as soon as the verdict was announced.[88]

To the very end, he debated whether to tip off the Greens. A part of him considered them a bit "okie pinokie" and worried they'd blab before the ruling came out. But they had a right to know, and if they heard it from him, perhaps they'd make a valuable donation to his organization in return. On June 29, Schenck called Steve and found him at the airport, waiting for a flight to the UK for a new Green Collection exhibit at Oxford. "Your prayers have been answered," he told him. "God has heard your cry, and you will prevail." Steve thanked him, saying, "I've got to call Mom and Dad and tell them."[89]

Through the Court's spokesperson, Alito later issued a statement denying that he or his wife had informed anyone of the decision in advance. Wright also emphatically said, "There has never been a time in all my years that a justice or a justice's spouse told me anything about a decision." Steve declined comment when asked, and Barbara told *The New York Times*, "We had no idea which way it would go" until the ruling was announced. Schenck later said, "Let's just say this is not how I remember what had happened."[90]

Schenck and his staff were waiting when Samuel Alito read out his opinion the next day, starting at 10:16 am on June 30. By a 5–4 majority, the court ruled that Hobby Lobby could exert its religious freedom to deny birth-control coverage to employees. Alito rushed to add that the ruling applied only to "closely held corporations" like the Greens' and not to publicly traded corporations. And he insisted that the ruling wouldn't apply to other issues and that it did not mean corporations raising religious objections had "free rein to take steps to impose disadvantages" on others or to require "the general public to pick up the tab."[91]

By the time Alito was done speaking at 10:30, Schenck had already issued a media advisory, and antiabortion activists were arriving to prostrate themselves at the steps of the Supreme Court and give thanks to God. After all the defeats they'd suffered over gay marriage and other cultural issues, religious conservatives were elated to see their strategy of turning the courts to their side finally succeeded. "I'm so happy about this I almost want to be dancing in the streets about it," declared Russell Moore, president of the Southern Baptist Convention's public policy arm.[92]

On the other side, Justice Ginsburg warned in a scathing dissent that the court's majority had radically overhauled the rights granted to corporations, allowing them to opt out of a number of laws based on faith. Women's equality had always been made possible by their freedom to "control their reproductive lives," she said. Denying them that freedom was discrimination.[93] The Green family declined to be interviewed publicly but released a statement, attributed to Barbara, saying, "The Court's decision is a victory, not just for our family business, but for all who seek to live out their faith."[94]

The Green family had been delivered, just like Daniel from the lion's den in Babylon. Beyond its immediate effect, the ruling would have a ripple effect that went far beyond the Greens' ability to operate their company, opening the floodgates to other religious freedom cases in America.

Even in the midst of the trial, however, the family acquired a new item for their collection with ties to Babylon that became both the crown jewel of the collection—and its biggest catastrophe.

CHAPTER ELEVEN

Pride Goeth

The ruins of ancient Babylon lie off the highway south of Baghdad. Gone is the Ishtar Gate with its grand processional way of blue-glazed brick tiles and bas-relief sculptures of mythological beasts. In the early 1900s, German archaeologists carted the gate away brick by brick to reconstruct it in a Berlin museum, where it now draws eighty thousand visitors daily. In its place is a pale imitation at two-thirds scale, with bricks coated in thick blue paint.

Beyond is the reconstructed palace of Nebuchadnezzar, boasting sunbaked courtyards and towering brick walls. In the 1980s, Iraqi dictator Saddam Hussein added bricks inscribed in his own name in Arabic alongside ancient bricks with Nebuchadnezzar's name in cuneiform. He also built an enormous palace overlooking the site, which now lies gutted and graffiti-covered. Foreign tourists visit the ruin while ironically looking down on the rebuilt ruin of Babylon below.

Babylon wasn't the only site that archaeologists excavated in the nineteenth and early twentieth centuries, hunting out biblical connections in modern-day Iraq and Syria. Farther to the north, they also excavated ancient Nineveh, the historic capital of Assyria, reconstructing its gates with their magnificent winged *lamassu*. Here, near modern-day Mosul, they unearthed the library of the Assyrian king Ashurbanipal, with more than 100,000 cuneiform tablets, including one of the most significant discoveries in literature that would forever change the way the Bible was viewed—*The Epic of Gilgamesh*.[1]

The tablets were discovered in 1853 by Hormuzd Rassam, a Mosul-born Christian archaeologist, though credit was long given to his boss, Englishman Henry Layard. They shipped the tablets to London along with sculptures that now form the British Museum's Near Eastern collection. The tablets sat for a long time in crates, indecipherable, until a twenty-year-old working-class Englishman, George Smith, began haunting the collection, inspired to prove the authenticity of the Bible. Hired as a translator, he was straining his eyes to read in the dim light in 1872 when he came across a tablet referencing a deluge, a ship stranded on a mountain, and a bird sent to find land. Shocked by seeming verification of the flood of Genesis, Smith reportedly ran around the room and "to the astonishment of those present, began to undress himself!" (Or at least loosened his collar.)[2]

Smith eventually traveled to Ninevah to locate more of the narrative, which followed the demigod Gilgamesh and his companion Enkidu on adventures among gods and monsters. The flood occurs late in the narrative, after Enkidu is killed by a demon and a distraught Gilgamesh searches for a way to bring him back to life. He meets Utnapishtim, an immortal man who survived a great flood by building a giant ship and filling it with every animal on earth. While mirroring the biblical story of Noah, it contains differences—for example, the flood occurs because the gods wish to cull noisy humans disturbing their sleep, not because of God's wrath at humankind's wickedness, and the rain lasts six days instead of forty.

Modern scholars see the flood in Gilgamesh, which dates back to at least 2000 BCE, as a forerunner of the biblical story, incorporated more than a thousand years later. Fundamentalists turn that interpretation on its head to argue that it's a corrupted version of the more detailed biblical story that had been carried on in oral tradition or now-lost tablets. Whatever the truth, copies of the epic today are incredibly rare, with only about seventy-five versions discovered, none of them complete.[3]

That made it thrilling in March 2014 when Christie's auction house contacted the Museum of the Bible team with an incredible find: a six-by-five-inch tablet containing a portion of the epic and colored a rich reddish brown, making it beautiful as well as historically significant.[4] The tablet contained an episode occurring early in the epic, in which Gilgamesh is having dreams foretelling Enkidu's arrival. In one, he sees a shining star fall to earth. When he relays the dream to his mother, she tells him it is a prophetic sign of a companion who will stand next to him throughout the world's greatest dangers.

Written in ancient Akkadian, the tablet dates to 1800 BCE, seeming to originate from the First Sealand Dynasty, an obscure line of kings inhabiting the southern lowlands around Abraham's supposed home city of Ur. Uniquely, the fragment uses different names for Gilgamesh and Enkidu—calling them Sîn and Ea, names for the sun and moon gods, respectively—and sets the story in Ur instead of Uruk, offering a link to the biblical patriarch.[5] That made the artifact the perfect item to kick off the history exhibits at the Museum of the Bible. Asked about provenance, Christie's said the tablet had left Iraq before exports were banned during the Gulf War, had been sold in San Francisco in 1981 by the auction house Butterfield & Butterfield, and then had been resold by California rare-book dealer Michael Sharpe, the dealer who'd previously sold Steve the Genesis fragment of the Dead Sea Scrolls. Satisfied with those answers, Steve agreed on a price: $1.674 million.[6]

WEEKS AFTER HOBBY Lobby won the Supreme Court case, the museum prepared a new *Passages* exhibit in Springfield, Missouri—the headquarters of the Assemblies of God—with a bold new message emphasizing the Christian faith of the "Founding Fathers." It included an oversized mock-up of the Declaration of Independence, drawing attention to the references to a "Creator" and "Nature's God," as well as a copy of an 1809 letter by Thomas Jefferson urging the protection of "rights of conscience against the enterprises of the civil authority"—words with new import after Hobby Lobby's Supreme Court victory. The letter, which was presented as protecting church from state rather than the other way around, seemed drawn right out of David Barton's *The Jefferson Lies*, one religious studies professor who toured the exhibit noted.[7]

The same month, Steve officially announced that the Museum of the Bible would open in 2017. Artists' renderings showed a triangular building topped with a wraparound glass dome from which it would be possible to see the US Capitol three blocks away. Four floors of exhibit space would cover 400,000 square feet, enough to fit eight Hobby Lobby stores, organized around three main themes: history, stories, and impact.[8] Steve could barely hide his excitement about the Washington location. "One thing I learned in our real estate office is, sometimes being a block down the street can mean a lot in terms of sales," he stammered to a reporter with the *Washington Post* on a tour of the site. "Seeing the biblical foundations of our nation—for our legislators to see that, that a lot of that was biblically based, that we have religious freedoms today, which are a biblical concept, it can't hurt being there."[9]

As the museum began a push to raise awareness, Steve and the rest of the board subtly modified its mission. No longer would its aim be "to inspire confidence in the absolute authority and reliability of the Bible." Instead, the museum replaced that with a goal seemingly calibrated to be more palatable to mainstream audiences: "to invite people to engage with the Bible" through four activities—traveling exhibits, scholarship, a permanent museum, and a high school curriculum.[10] The museum would be "nonsectarian and nonproselytizing," said Steve, who at the same time was confident the book would speak for itself. Scholarship, archaeology—"it will all reaffirm God's word," he told the *Post*.[11]

The team behind the coming museum also went on a major drive to raise funds for its predicted $800 million price tag, holding dinners in Oklahoma City with Tea Party congressman Bobby Jindal and in Dallas with former president George W. Bush. This was just the beginning; there would be 160 such dinners over the next two years.[12] For at least one of its goals, however, the museum scaled back its expectations. That November, the Mustang school district put the Bible curriculum on hold after the public attention brought to bear by opponents from the Freedom from Religion Foundation and other groups. The effort wasn't completely shuttered, however; it later resurfaced in a homeschooling curriculum and in schools in Israel.

Behind the scenes, there was growing tension with collections director David Trobisch, a liberal scholar who had pushed the idea that the New Testament had been edited and assembled by a group of Christians in the mid- to late second century—more than one hundred years after Jesus's death.[13] He did not see ancient texts as helpful in answering questions on abortion, same-sex marriage, or other culture-war issues, saying, "Scholars will not assume that a 2,000-year-old text is necessarily the best at solving" those questions. Hired after a chance meeting with Mart at an airport, Trobisch hadn't even spoken to Steve before coming on board and had spoken to him only twice since. Once, after he'd given a lecture noting that Proverbs referred to God as "wisdom," which took a feminine ending in Greek, Steve had scolded him: "God is not a woman." When Trobisch said he was only explaining the text, Steve relented: "As long as it's in the Bible, it's fine."[14]

THERE WAS ALSO trouble across the Atlantic, where Roberta Mazza wasn't the only one taking notice of Dirk Obbink's new Sappho fragment. His bosses at the Egypt Exploration Society at Oxford expressed concern over the unseemliness of the director of their collection also trading in antiquities, including his sales to the Greens, and gave him an ultimatum in July 2014 to decide between being on the Greens' payroll or Oxford's. Obbink unloaded on Steve and Pattengale in London that summer, and they proposed a new arrangement whereby he could keep his job at Oxford while taking a faculty appointment at Baylor, so technically the university would be paying him (even if it was using the Greens' money to do so). Two months later, Obbink purchased Cottonwood Castle, a garish turreted structure beside a used-car lot in downtown Waco.

Dissatisfied with the museum's lack of transparency, Mazza decided to "play investigator." She wrote to Trobisch, asking where the museum had acquired the Galatians fragment she'd seen at the Vatican and whether it had indeed come from eBay seller MixAntik. Trobisch responded only that the museum had purchased it "through a trusted dealer that we have done business with over many years."[15] That dealer, he added, said the fragment had been bought at a sale of papyri at Christie's in 2011. The reply only raised more questions in Mazza's mind. Had MixAntik gotten the fragment from Christie's and sold it to the "trusted dealer," or was MixAntik the "trusted dealer" himself?

The Christie's lot Trobisch mentioned, "a collection of Greek and Coptic papyri fragments," had sold for £7,500—even though MixAntik had been selling the single fragment for almost twice that. Mazza contacted Christie's head of antiquities, Eugenio Donadoni, who had no photos of the lot but said, "Trust me, that fragment was in there."[16] The museum's curator of papyri, Josephine Dru, told Mazza that the museum had one thousand pieces of papyri in its collection. That seemed impossible, Mazza thought. Given the situation in Egypt after the Arab Spring, how could there even be that many legitimate papyri fragments on the market?

Mazza raised these questions and more on a panel on ancient archaeology at the Society of Biblical Literature conference in San Diego in November 2014, addressing the London Sappho and other manuscripts supposedly discovered in mummy masks. Invited to reply, Trobisch was peppered with questions from the audience about Sappho, Galatians, and the "first-century Mark."[17]

Watching from the audience, Brent Nongbri—the papyrologist who'd long been following the Greens in Australia—was pleased to see scrutiny of the collection at last. During a break, he spoke to former Yale classmate Candida Moss about his difficulties getting information about the Green Collection. A Notre Dame professor with long blond hair and a sarcastic sense of humor, Moss had recently ventured into journalism, writing cheeky articles for *The Daily Beast* about biblical controversies.

"Hobby Lobby," Moss asked with surprise, "like the crafting store?" She'd seen Hobby Lobby stores on drives by Indiana cornfields and wondered what the company could possibly be doing acquiring biblical texts. "Tell me more about that," she said, instinctively pulling out her laptop and figuring she'd write a pithy article about the phenomenon. She pulled aside Joel Baden, a Yale professor with a ginger beard and sardonic smile who had collaborated with Moss on some pieces, and asked, "Have you heard about this?"

Together, Moss and Baden hastily arranged a breakfast with Trobisch the following morning. Fresh from his grilling at the panel, he began to vent, complaining about Scott Carroll's slapdash approach to acquiring materials and the Greens' heavy-handed emphasis on biblical accuracy. "He threw the Green family under the bus," Baden remembered. Most alarmingly, Trobisch referred to past problems the museum had had with acquisitions. "David Trobisch basically clued us in to the fact that this was a bigger story than we realized," Moss said.[18]

To get to the bottom of it, they'd have to transform themselves from fusty biblical scholars into intrepid investigative journalists. They started with the Galatians fragment, speaking with another scholar associated with the museum who proposed a new theory: MixAntik had never owned the piece but had only put a picture of it on eBay. That raised even more questions about where the Turkish dealer could have acquired the photo when Christie's didn't even have one. Besides, they noted, the fragment had been photographed against the same tablecloth as other items MixAntik had for sale.[19]

By now, they'd gotten *The Atlantic* interested in their story, which kept growing. The Christie's listing said a number of the fragments in the sale belonged to a collection at the University of Mississippi, but Moss and Baden came up empty there as well. Trobisch grew frosty in response to the scholars' repeated questions. When they asked him point-blank if he had any evidence the fragment was from that collection, he shot back, "Do you have any evidence that it is not?" But that didn't stop him and papyri curator Dru from quietly traveling to Mississippi themselves to look in vain for photos.[20]

Baden and Moss contacted another collector listed in Christie's provenance for the sale, but he also denied ever having had the Galatians piece in his collection.[21] Everywhere they turned, they ran into dead ends. One thing was clear: With just a few calls, they had demolished the museum's claims of provenance. Prior to the appearance on MixAntik's eBay account, there was no record of the fragment at all. Moreover, their investigations raised another uncomfortable question: If the museum couldn't tell them where this artifact had come from, what else was it hiding?

Moss and Baden didn't know at the time that the Green Collection was apparently a mess. Items were stored in the same Hobby Lobby warehouses as the craft-store inventory, with forklifts heard through the walls and the ventilation system freely circulating air between the spaces, according to several former museum employees. Old Bibles and illuminated manuscripts sat unwrapped on the same shelves Hobby Lobby used in its stores, straining under the weight of the books and off-gassing fumes from paint. Cuneiform tablets and ancient pottery were stacked in the tops of bankers boxes. Records were haphazard, with invoices and shipping manifests stuffed into file-cabinet drawers. "It stayed unlocked, and files would go missing," said one former staffer. Hires were often made from referrals by friends and family rather than through a comprehensive search, said another, adding, "We weren't always working with the most qualified people."[22]

At the end of each year, staff transferred the objects to be donated, for which Hobby Lobby would claim a tax write-off, from one space, representing the Green Collection, to another, representing the Museum of the Bible. Unfortunately for the family, the sloppy record-keeping threatened to undermine its ability to earn the tax deductions it sought. In 2015, the IRS notified Hobby Lobby that it was under investigation for overvaluing the items deducted on its taxes in 2011 and 2012; the company had lumped together the price it had paid for multiple items and aggregated their assessed value, in violation of IRS rules that require items to be listed individually. Eventually, the agency denied the deductions in their entirety and issued a fine against the company. Hobby Lobby appealed the case, which would wind its way through tax courts for the next decade without resolution.[23] Meanwhile, the company continued to reap further tax benefits each year by donating objects to the museum as well as to the nonprofit NCF with an agreement to keep the items under the museum's curatorial control.

In February 2015, construction workers broke ground on the museum building as the board was filled with conservative evangelicals, including OneHope's Bob Hoskins, *Purpose-Driven* pastor Rick Warren, and ADF senior counsel Greg Baylor.[24] Despite Steve's assurances to the press that the Bible would be presented in as balanced a way as possible, museum staff and Green family members were flying all over the country for "show-and-tell" dinners to raise funds from evangelical audiences in Chicago, Denver, Grand Rapids, and Phoenix, where the message took on a more overtly proselytizing tone. "They were always saying, 'We're taking the Gospel to DC, we're going to put the Bible back into the heart of government,' " said one former employee. "There was a lot of speaking out of both sides of their mouths."[25]

She and others described a chaotic work environment, with staffers working eighty-hour weeks and rules about how to handle the artifacts constantly changing. No expense was spared on vendors for tables or flowers or pricey dinners for staff members, with the knowledge that the Greens' money would backstop any purchases. "We spent millions to raise thousands," quipped one former employee. "At the end of the year, we just adjusted the budget numbers so we were back on budget—which is not how budgets are supposed to work." It didn't really matter how much money was raised, she and other employees said; the goal was to gather a list of donors to bring the museum into compliance with IRS rules requiring a broad base of support for nonprofits rather than just funding from a single source—in this case, the Green family.[26]

As Moss and Baden continued to investigate, they scored an interview with Steve, who told the two scholars-turned-journalists that the museum wasn't meant to convert anyone, only to tell the story of the book. "If this book is not what it is, I want to know about it," he said. "But what we keep finding is that, boy, it validates what the book says. So the more we study, the more we know, the better off I think the world is."

Gradually, they worked their way around to questions about whether any items had been acquired illicitly. "That's a headache we don't want," Steve said. "But there is the risk that after the fact, you find out that it wasn't appropriate for us to buy it."[27] He compared the risk to an incident at Hobby Lobby where the company had sold tins that were copyrighted by another vendor, requiring it to pay a settlement. "There's millions of pieces of artwork out there, and you just don't know. It's the same kind of thing in the antiquities world." The comparison seemed bizarre to Moss and Baden, betraying a lack of awareness of how seriously the scholarly world took issues of provenance.[28]

It was Scott Carroll who clued them in to the severity of the museum's problems. Eager to distance himself from the ongoing federal investigation, he told them all about the cuneiform deal in Dubai, careful to explain that he had advised Steve against it.[29] Carroll was talking a lot these days, telling the same story to Homeland Security investigators Easter and Labbat.[30] In fact, Labbat had been busy in the two years since he'd started investigating. By now, his conversations with overseas informants had convinced him that the cuneiform artifacts hadn't come from old family connections in Israel but had been trafficked quite recently from elsewhere in the Middle East. In July 2015, HSI sent a notice of seizure, not just for the items currently sitting in the customs warehouse in Queens but also for the packages that had already made their way to Oklahoma.[31]

Hobby Lobby told HSI in September that it would surrender the tablets.

In the midst of that burgeoning scandal, Hobby Lobby was called out in another one when Bill Gothard abruptly resigned from his ministry. For years, alumni of Gothard's homeschooling institute and other programs had shared stories of growing up traumatized under his rigid rules that strictly controlled their dress and behavior. Candy, rock music, and even toys such as Cabbage Patch dolls were forbidden as worldly and demonic. As young people, they were isolated from the outside world and held to impossible standards of perfection as an indication of moral purity. At training centers in Indianapolis or Oklahoma City, rebellious teens were held in solitary confinement in "prayer rooms" for days or even weeks.[32]

All that time, whispers circulated that Gothard had a predilection for a certain type of young woman who was both pretty and vulnerable, often suffering from abuse or neglect at home. Gothard began actively recruiting these women from the EXCEL program to volunteer at headquarters. He asked them to stay late in his room or accompany him on trips overseas, where he frequently touched their hands, hair, and back or played footsie under the table. Now those stories emerged into the light. In the early 2010s, women started coming forward to share disturbing stories on a blog, *Recovering Grace*, alleging that Gothard had touched their breasts, legs, or groin; one woman accused him of having molested her when she was just seventeen.

Eventually, the blog collected thirty-four stories with similar patterns of abuse dating to the 1970s, leading the board of Gothard's organization to put him on administrative leave. In March 2014, Gothard resigned, admitting that his "actions of holding hands, hugs, and touching of feet or hair with young ladies crossed the boundaries of discretion and were wrong." At the same time, he claimed, "I have never kissed a girl nor have I touched a girl immorally or with sexual intent."[33] The moderators of *Recovering Grace* pushed back, saying the "behavior was persistent and sexual in nature, and must be acknowledged as such."[34]

As the scandal deepened, media reported on Gothard's connection to Hobby Lobby. They noted that the Green family had long supported Gothard's ministry, including donating property in Oklahoma, Texas, Arkansas, and Tennessee—and even an international site in New Zealand. Moreover, the family had touted Gothard's programs and philosophy, including David's recent endorsement of his biography. "They're friends. I see them and talk to them periodically," Gothard told *Mother Jones* magazine, even as the family and Hobby Lobby remained silent.[35]

The scandal deepened in May 2015 when news broke that Josh Duggar, the oldest child in the Gothard-influenced family featured in the reality show *19 Kids and Counting*, had sexually molested four sisters and a babysitter when he was a teenager. In response, his parents sent him for "lust counseling" and "cleansing" by a "holy mentor" at Gothard's ALERT Academy in Little Rock—the first property Hobby Lobby had donated to him nearly two decades earlier.[36] Duggar "certainly learnt his lesson and now he will have a whole new respect for young ladies," Gothard said when the scandal broke; Duggar, now twenty-seven, resigned from his position as executive director of the FRC's lobbying division and admitted to the abuse. (Six years later, he was convicted of possessing child pornography and sent to prison. Meanwhile, in 2016, sixteen women and two men sued Gothard for sexual harassment, molestation, and rape but dropped the charges two years later.)[37]

Throughout all of these scandals, the Greens maintained their silence, never commenting publicly on Gothard or their extensive support of his ministry that had allowed it to flourish during the time he was committing his abuses.

In May 2015, Hobby Lobby was involved on another front of the culture wars when an Illinois judge ruled that the company had violated the rights of a transgender woman, Meggan Sommerville, by refusing to allow her to use the women's bathroom. Though she had transitioned in 2011, Hobby Lobby required her to provide legal proof of the gender change; when she provided a state court order and driver's license, the company required proof that she had undergone genital surgery. The company built a single-stall bathroom for her use, but she argued that there was no reason she shouldn't be able to use the bathroom like any other woman. The panel of judges unanimously agreed, ordering Hobby Lobby to pay a $220,000 fine to the state human rights commission.[38]

The following month, religious conservatives suffered a crushing defeat when the Supreme Court ruled 5–4 in *Obergefell v. Hodges* that gay couples should be afforded the same right to marry as straight couples, making same-sex marriage legal nationwide. The ADF's Alan Sears refused to admit defeat, saying, "There is no question that one day, this country will again recognize that marriage is between a man and a woman."[39]

The issue became a rallying cry for conservatives as the presidential election approached. An early leader in the Republican primary was Ben Carson, an African American Seventh-Day Adventist and pediatric neurosurgeon who decried political correctness and abortion, advocated for a flat tax based on the biblical principle of tithing, and had a penchant for extreme statements like declaring Obamacare "the worst thing to happen to this nation since slavery." David and Barbara were among Carson's earliest supporters, publicly endorsing him and donating to his campaign. He ran neck-and-neck with bombastic real estate tycoon and media personality Donald Trump, who reveled even more in overstatement and exaggeration, declaring Mexican immigrants "rapists" who were bringing drugs over the border and calling Democratic-run cities cesspools of crime and corruption as he vowed to "Make America Great Again." A notorious philanderer on his third marriage, Trump seemed a strange choice for evangelicals; he called the Bible his "favorite book" yet couldn't name a single Bible verse. Nevertheless, polls showed that evangelicals supported his no-holds-barred attack on liberalism in surprisingly high numbers.

In October 2015, Moss and Baden broke the story about Hobby Lobby's alleged acquisition of trafficked cuneiform tablets in *The Daily Beast*, describing the essential details of the case and noting the irony of a company that prided itself on following biblical law being investigated for illicitly importing biblical artifacts. For a "company and a family that have built their reputation on a particular set of Christian values," they wrote, "this investigation may hurt more than any financial penalty could."[40]

The article spurred an angry response from museum president Cary Summers, who had clearly expected a more favorable story after providing access to museum leadership. " 'C'mon,' he said, 'we've been so nice to you!' " Moss remembered.[41] When the reporters followed up with a longer story in *The Atlantic* in January, the Greens saw how badly they had miscalculated. The multipage spread under the title "Can Hobby Lobby Buy the Bible?" described Steve Green as "decent" but hopelessly naïve to the realities of the antiquities market, which had been flooded with illicit items since the destabilization of Iraq and the wider Middle East.

Along with the cuneiform case, the article examined issues with the Galatians fragment, noting that it could have been trafficked in "violation of Egypt's strict cultural heritage laws." It also questioned the premise of the museum and the *Passages* exhibits, which it described as slickly calculated to present a fundamentalist Protestant view that "the text of the Bible has essentially never changed, and its authority is timeless."[42]

In response, a Green family spokesperson tersely stated, "Hobby Lobby is cooperating with the investigation related to certain biblical artifacts," but the Museum of the Bible was "a separate not-for-profit entity."[43] Meanwhile, the museum distanced itself publicly from its founding family and their company. Within days, a website for the GSI disappeared, replaced with a page for a generic Scholars Initiative. The Green Collection became the Museum Collection, even while it retained its physical address at a Hobby Lobby warehouse.

In the midst of the unwanted publicity, Scott Carroll reemerged to make trouble for the Greens. When he appeared at an event along with apologist Josh McDowell to show off biblical manuscripts, McDowell asked him about the first-century Mark manuscript that Daniel Wallace had mentioned in his famous debate with Bart Ehrman back in 2011. Carroll said he'd seen the manuscript at Oxford's "Christ Church College in the possession of an outstanding, well-known eminent classicist" who'd dated it to between 70 and 120 CE.[44]

There was little doubt whom he meant—Dirk Obbink. The Greens had never acquired the manuscript, he added, but "it has since been acquired, I can't say by whom." When Obbink's bosses at the Egypt Exploration Society saw the video, they were alarmed. As far as they knew, the papyrus fragments were a part of the Oxyrhynchus collection—how could Obbink possibly have offered them for sale? Obbink told them Carroll must have been mistaken, assuring them that the fragments were in his office and had never been for sale.

Troubled nonetheless, they demoted him from editor, allowing him to view papyri only under supervision pending further investigation.[45]

As Carson fizzled in the polls in late 2015, the Greens shifted their support to Florida senator Marco Rubio, who was raised Catholic but later joined a charismatic Southern Baptist megachurch before converting back to Catholicism. He came to Oklahoma City to visit David and see the Greens' antiquities collection, horrifying a staff member by standing with a cup of coffee over an illuminated manuscript.

Rubio came in third in the Iowa caucuses, behind Texas senator Ted Cruz and Trump, who insulted his rivals with petty nicknames, vowed that "illegals" would be deported, and made disparaging remarks about journalists and women. Despite his turgid temperament—or because of it—evangelicals rallied to Trump's side. First among them was Paula White, leader of a Florida megachurch and latter-day proponent of the prosperity gospel, who began gathering others in her network of charismatics to his side, convinced that he had an "anointing" to be president.[46]

As Trump rose in the polls, other evangelicals joined the fold, including Jerry Falwell Jr., who invited him to speak at Liberty University. There he once again betrayed his unfamiliarity with the Bible, flubbing several passages, but shared the crowd's sense of persecution. "Christianity, it's under siege," he told the crowd. "We have to unify, we have to band together."[47] David wasn't convinced, calling out Trump for his violent temperament and publicly endorsing Rubio.

"I don't see humility in Mr. Trump, and that scares me to death," David said, denouncing him in an appearance on Fox News as a "bully... calling people names, everybody's stupid—that is not who we want our country to be, and that's who we're following." If Trump became the nominee, he proclaimed, he'd sit out the election.[48]

Republican voters disagreed, and Trump won state after state even as he kept bullying his rivals. After Cruz suspended his campaign,

Trump took pains to reach out to religious voters by picking straight-arrow Christian politician Mike Pence as his running mate. He also released a list of judges he'd appoint to the Supreme Court, handpicked by the Heritage Foundation to support religious liberty. The picks were all the more important since Scalia had died earlier in the year and Republicans in the Senate had blocked Obama's appointment of his replacement. The next president would pick the next justice.

Momentum for Trump grew with an endorsement by James Dobson, who had ridiculed Bill Clinton for lack of character two decades earlier but called Trump a "baby Christian" and urged evangelicals to "cut him some slack."[49] Jerry Falwell Jr. also endorsed him, assuring voters that his father would have done the same. "When he walked into the voting booth, he wasn't electing a Sunday school teacher or a pastor," he said. "He was electing the president of the United States" with "the talent, abilities, and experience required to lead the nation."[50]

A CHANCE ENCOUNTER in March 2016 finally brought Roberta Mazza some clarity about the mysterious Galatians fragment she'd first seen in Rome. Sipping her coffee one morning, she opened eBay to see a familiar name posting objects for sale: ebuyerrrrr, the new moniker MixAntik had assumed. "I almost fell off my chair," she recounted. She wrote to say she was interested in buying papyri, and ebuyerrrrr suggested that they message on WhatsApp. "What kind of papyri do you want?" he asked, telling her the pieces came from his grandfather's collection, obtained forty years before. Mazza said she was buying on behalf of an American museum and sent him a picture of the Galatians fragment. That wasn't his, he said, breaking off conversation.

Looking up the phone number online, Mazza found that it belonged to a young Turkish CEO of a construction company, Yakup Ekşioğlu. His wife had contributed to Johnny Shipman's National Bible Museum in 2008. Then Mazza found communication on a

Facebook post from 2013 between Ekşioğlu and Scott Carroll. "When will you come to Turkey?" Ekşioğlu had asked. Mazza was buzzing—Ekşioğlu knew both Carroll and Shipman. Looking more closely at Carroll's Facebook timeline, she noticed a photo of dirty papyri on the same tablecloth as that shown on MixAntik's eBay page. Rather than post on her blog, she contacted London's Metropolitan Police with the evidence.[51]

A few months later, the Museum of the Bible stepped into new controversy when the newly renamed Scholars Initiative unveiled its first publication, *Dead Sea Scroll Fragments in the Museum Collection*. The scholarly analysis of these prized possessions purchased from William Kando was edited by biblical scholar Michael Holmes, who had taken over from Pattengale as head of the initiative, and featured top experts in the field. The book came out in the midst of a furious debate about the recently sold Dead Sea fragments. A year before, several experts in Europe had studied the dozens of fragments sold by Kando to the Museum of the Bible and other institutions and expressed doubts about their authenticity, showing that the writing seemed amateurish and letters were squeezed into margins, as if they had been written on the parchment after the fact.[52] Even one of the editors of the museum's own volume, Kipp Davis, noted "troubling anomalies" in the texts, letters that were "unusually sized" and "oddly shaped," and vowed to investigate further.[53]

At the same time, HSI agents Easter and Labbat were searching for their own truth about the cuneiform tablets, contacting Yale professor Eckart Frahm to better understand where the tablets had come from. An expert in Assyrian and Babylonian history, Frahm took a train to Grand Central Station, where he was picked up by agents in a plain black car (*A bit cliché*, he thought) and taken to a Queens warehouse.

Led to a small table between rows of shelving, he noticed several large sculptures by artist Jeff Koons, famous for his balloon dogs, wrapped up in the dim light. An agent brought him the first package, which was full of clay bullae that he found mostly unrecognizable. The second package, however, contained a dozen cuneiform tablets wrapped in plastic. He recognized writing from what archaeologists call the Ur III period, originating in a number of small cities in Sumer around 2000 BCE. He took pictures and looked at them more closely in his office in Yale's gothic library, making out lists of lapis lazuli, rations for weaver women, and amounts of grain to feed to the palace dogs.

Cross-referencing the tablets with research on other tablets that had recently been published by researcher David Owen at Cornell, he found that they belonged to a city called Irisaĝrig, located along the rivers and canals south of Babylon. Using information about directions and distances on tablets, scholars had identified several locations where the city might have been but weren't exactly sure. Examining a database put together by Spanish scholar Manuel Molina, Frahm could see that no tablets from the city had appeared before 2003—the time of the Iraq War. "And suddenly in 2003, Jordanian border officials begin seizing tablets at the border that eventually turn out to be from Irisaĝrig," he said. The implication was clear: Sometime around the invasion, looters had discovered Irisaĝrig and begun excavating it, smuggling its library out of the country and into the antiquities market.[54]

As THE ELECTION approached, evangelicals had even more reason to support Donald Trump given who he was running against—Hillary Clinton, wife of the former president, who embodied to them everything wrong with the secular world. She unequivocally supported abortion along with gay rights, affirmative action, and a path to citizenship for undocumented immigrants. Worse, she was a clear favorite in the polls going into the fall.

While Trump may have been the opposite of Christlike, he exuded the strong, masculine qualities white conservative Christians craved. He didn't care about "political correctness" but said what was on his mind. There was something else familiar about Trump to the faithful: In his speeches, he resembled a televangelist, preaching everlasting doom if his opponent was elected, with an apocalyptic vision for America should liberals triumph. Cities would be "overrun" with immigrants and terrorists or overtaken by crime from within—the racial subtext was never far from the surface.[55] Trump spoke the "*lingua franca* of the American right," writes journalist Sarah Posner, "the rhetoric of resentment, of lost domination, of grievances against 'special' rights for others at the expense of white Christians."[56]

That was no accident, thinks Rob Schenck, who watched Trump for years in meetings with preachers, studying their mannerisms and adopting their cadences.[57] Schenck himself had undergone a subtle transformation over the previous few years, earning a divinity degree and campaigning against gun violence—putting him at odds with many of his Christian conservative allies—and even softening his stance on abortion. Now he came out publicly against endorsing Trump, resigning as chair of the Evangelical Church Alliance.

Faced with the same moral dilemma, David made the opposite choice. Despite having called Trump a "bully" the year before, he now said his fears about religious liberty overcame his worries over Trump's character. Americans were "just one judge away from losing our religious freedom," he wrote in *USA Today*. "We must elect a president who will support a Supreme Court that upholds not only this freedom, but all that have emanated from it."[58]

Despite his flip-flop, David's words echoed a sentiment emerging on the Christian Right: For all of his moral failings, only Trump could be the savior to deliver Christian values. Some began referring to him in biblical terms as a modern-day Cyrus, the pagan Persian king who had conquered Babylon and freed the Jews to return to Jerusalem to rebuild their temple. No one touted the connection earlier and more insistently than the NAR preacher Lance Wallnau, the popularizer of seven mountains dominionism. God had told him in a prophecy to turn to Isaiah

45—as Trump would be the forty-fifth president—where he read that God had anointed Cyrus to "subdue nations" and "break down gates," even "though you have not acknowledged me." Before the election, Wallnau detailed his prophecies in the book *God's Chaos Candidate*, saying Trump would engage in "spiritual warfare" against liberals aiming to destroy Christian society.[59] Though Clinton beat Trump by three million votes in the national popular vote, Trump won the Electoral College to become president, with evangelicals voting for him at a rate of 81 percent.

To MAKE SENSE of the phenomenon, pundits used a new term to explain Trump's victory: Christian nationalism. First popularized by journalist Michelle Goldberg a decade earlier, it was most succinctly defined by sociologists Philip Gorski and Samuel Perry in their book *The Flag and the Cross* as a belief that "America was founded as a Christian nation by (white) men who were 'traditional' Christians, who based the nation's founding documents on 'Christian principles'" and believed "the nation has a special role to play in God's plan for humanity." That role was "threatened by cultural degradation from 'un-American' influences both inside and outside our borders."[60]

The concept traced its lineage through Rushdoony, Gothard, Falwell, Dobson, Barton, and Wallnau, among others, not that any of them would have identified as such—nor would the millions of Americans who voted for Trump. In a study of 2016 voters, however, Perry and colleagues found that the single strongest predictor of a person's likelihood to vote for Trump was a belief that America was founded as, and should remain, a "Christian Nation."[61]

Trump soon made good on his promises to Christian conservatives. Within days, he nominated Neil Gorsuch, the Colorado judge who had struck down the injunction in the Hobby Lobby case, to the Supreme Court. In the ensuing months, Trump moved the US embassy in Israel from Tel Aviv to Jerusalem, a move long sought by

Christian Zionists who believed the Bible prophecy marked it as a condition for Jesus's return.[62] (Years later, Trump confirmed, "That's for the evangelicals."[63]) He signed executive orders allowing churches to take part in politics despite their tax-exempt status. He also dramatically expanded the *Burwell v. Hobby Lobby* ruling, which had applied only to "closely held" companies three years before, by promising that *any* company could opt out of the Obamacare contraception mandate on religious grounds, immediately spurring a new court challenge.

Amidst a booming economy that had begun during the Obama presidency, Hobby Lobby grew faster than ever, with more than seven hundred stores by early 2017. As the Museum of the Bible continued to rise in Washington, Easter and Labbat completed their investigation, leaving prosecutors in the Eastern District of New York to decide whether to bring criminal charges. Circumstantially, the case was strong, with fraudulently labeled packages sent to multiple addresses and payments made through multiple foreign transfers. Then there was the information that Patty Gerstenblith had given the company on dealing in Iraq, the alleged warning from Scott Carroll, and the company's lack of diligence in checking provenance, all making a case for prior knowledge that they were flouting the law.

On the other hand, absent a "smoking gun" email, it would be hard to prove to the standard of "beyond a reasonable doubt" that the family had knowingly evaded the law. And there was another consideration seldom talked about in law: Hobby Lobby was a $4 billion company that had shown its desire and capability to vigorously defend itself in court. "Steve Green had a great legal team. I'll let you examine the American justice system for yourself," said Easter without commenting directly on the charging decision. "There are some criminal cases that are easier to get convictions on than others."[64]

In the end, prosecutors decided if they could recover the artifacts, they would agree not to charge the family. On July 5, 2017, they announced a settlement in which Hobby Lobby consented to forfeit

5,500 items to Iraq—including some 3,500 items that it already possessed and another two thousand or so that it had purchased but hadn't yet received. It also agreed to pay $3 million as a forfeiture for other artifacts that investigators identified as having been smuggled but that Hobby Lobby no longer had in its possession, including artifacts it had already donated to the Museum of the Bible.[65] "We should have exercised more oversight and carefully questioned how the acquisitions were handled," Steve said in a statement. At the same time, he was quick to cast a stone at others, saying the company had "imprudently relied on dealers and shippers who, in hindsight, did not understand the correct way to document and ship these items."[66]

Patty Gerstenblith was struck by the fact that when she'd been asked about importing antiquities from Iraq, the company had apparently already been in the midst of the deal. After the settlement, a journalist asked if the company might even have used the information she provided to help it evade the law. "I suppose one can't rule that out—which would be very upsetting to me," Gerstenblith said.[67] Others called out the company's hypocrisy: "I know Hobby Lobby's big on the Ten Commandments, but how about 'Thou shalt not steal'?" the Freedom from Religion Foundation tweeted.[68]

The museum put out its own statement distancing itself from Hobby Lobby, saying none of the artifacts were "part of the Museum's collection, nor have they ever been"—somewhat disingenuous given that they had been acquired by the same group of people and had been separated only by a wall in Hobby Lobby's warehouse. "The museum does not accept collections without full documented provenance and credibility records," assured Vice Chairman Robert Cooley. "Every item in the museum is documented."[69] Soon, however, that statement would be shown to be untrue.

WITHIN DAYS, THE Egyptian antiquities department announced its own investigation into the provenance of the Galatians fragment along with the rest of the museum's papyri. In fact, an investigation was already underway; after Mazza had contacted the Metropolitan Police, her concerns had been shared with the international police agency INTERPOL, which coordinated with Turkish police to raid Ekşioğlu's property in search of stolen artifacts. Mazza received an angry WhatsApp message from her eBay correspondent warning her to "always look at the back while you walk" since acid might be thrown in her face. "It was scary," said Mazza, who had never dreamed as an academic that she'd be on the receiving end of such threats.[70]

A week later, Israeli authorities broke into the shops of the three dealers involved in the cuneiform sale—Abraham, Baidun, and Barakat. They arrested several men and confiscated artifacts, cars, and $200,000 in cash. The dealers, all Palestinians living in Jerusalem, were charged with providing falsified invoices to Hobby Lobby and other clients.[71] Behind the scenes, the museum was in a panic. In August, it hired a new chief curator, Jeff Kloha, former provost of a Lutheran seminary, and contracted with Tom Kline, a respected cultural heritage attorney, ordering them to make sure no objects with dubious provenance went on display.

In October, Kipp Davis released the results of his investigation into the Dead Sea Scrolls, declaring that at least six of the museum's thirteen fragments—including the large fragment of Genesis—were forgeries, and not very good forgeries at that. In addition to the amateurish lettering, one fragment seemed to include a superscript Greek alpha (α) after one of the Hebrew characters, in the same place where a footnote appeared in a 1937 Hebrew edition of the Bible.[72] While vowing to submit the fragments to outside testing, the museum decided to display them anyway.[73]

Despite the slew of bad headlines, museum staff geared up for their November opening, sticking to its claim that the museum wasn't "about religion as much as it is about a book," as President Cary Summers told a reporter during an advance tour. Seth Pollinger, a millennial seminarian who led the museum's exhibit design, said he hoped the museum could help heal the political fractures of the nation: "Rather than fragment into greater hostility, this is a time to find out how we can work for the good."[74]

That sentiment seemed at odds with the location for a fundraising gala two nights before the opening: Trump International Hotel, a stronghold of Republican power owned by the president. Some of the museum's own staff and advisers refused to attend the black-tie gala, where tickets ran to $2,500 for individuals and $50,000 for a table.[75] Among the guests who did attend were the president's son Eric Trump and his wife, Lara; Jerry Falwell Jr.; Oklahoma senator James Lankford; and conservative icon Willie Robertson of the reality show *Duck Dynasty*.

Celebrations continued with a gala at the museum the following night. The Creation Museum's Ken Ham was there, as was Jerry Pattengale, who shared a table with his old mentor Edwin Yamauchi and former museum director David Trobisch.[76] At one point, Pattengale later said, Yamauchi leaned over to Trobisch to ask when he could expect publication of the mysterious first-century Mark. "That fragment was never offered to us for sale, isn't that correct, Jerry?" Trobisch said.[77]

Pattengale did a double take, remembering that windy night in Oxford with Carroll in Obbink's office, when Obbink had offered the four gospel fragments on the pool table. After Carroll had left the museum's employ a few months later, negotiations to purchase the fragments had continued, culminating in a purchase agreement signed by Steve in January 2013. By the terms of the deal, Obbink would retain the artifacts in Oxford to study them, even though they were owned by the museum. "Some things are best discussed in other settings," Pattengale said.[78]

But Trobisch insisted that the papyrus couldn't have been for sale since a graduate student at Oxford had found a photo of it in the Egyptian Exploration Society's archives, showing that it belonged to the

Oxyrhynchus collection. Pattengale was floored. If that were true, then how could Obbink have offered it to them?[79]

The following morning, the museum opened to members of the public, who filed through the bronze gates made to look like pages from the Gutenberg Bible. Initial reviews were mixed, from conservative evangelicals complaining that there wasn't enough Jesus to liberal academics warning that the museum presented a skewed view of the Bible. Steve and other museum leaders took those polarized views as an indication that they'd played the museum's religious viewpoint down the middle.[80] "It doesn't overtly say the Bible is good—that the Bible is true," Steve insisted. "Its role is to present facts and let people make their own decisions."[81]

The way Steve presented the museum to mainstream audiences and the way he spoke about it to fellow evangelicals, however, were very different. In an interview with Sean McDowell—son of Josh and heir to his ministry—he said the purpose of the museum was "really answering two questions. One, is the book true?" Of that, he said, there was no doubt. "The evidence is overwhelming," he said. "The more I've learned, the more I've studied, the deeper my faith has been." As for the second question—"Is the Bible good?"—he was even more emphatic. "What we're trying to show... is that it's been a force of good in our world," he said. "When you give it an honest assessment, it has had an impact in every area of life, and it has been good for mankind in every area."

Unlike other museums such as the Creation Museum or the Holy Land Experience, the museum isn't overt about these stances. In fact, the casual visitor might be unaware that they are getting a skewed version of the Bible based on a Protestant evangelical point of view—making it in some ways a more subtle and persuasive interpretation of faith. For those who know where to look, however, the signs are all around.

CHAPTER TWELVE

Revelations

TV host Dave Stotts jumps out of a helicopter in sunglasses and a cargo vest, walking across the plain in slow motion like a combination of James Bond and Indiana Jones. "Here you see the ruins of Hazor from the time of Joshua's conquest," he says, stepping over excavated stone walls. To the average person viewing the film in the "Drive Thru History" theater on the fourth floor of the Museum of the Bible, Stotts sounds as solid as the stones themselves; viewers have no way of knowing most biblical historians doubt Joshua's conquest even occurred. "Archaeological sites like this allow us to connect past to present," Stotts says. "Discoveries are being made every day that help us better understand the Bible."[1]

This floor of the museum is dedicated to the history of the Bible, taking visitors through ancient Israel, Rome, and medieval Europe as it makes its way across the globe. Exhibit designer Seth Pollinger said he originally wanted to use the museum's collection to provide evidence for the proof of biblical stories, but at some point, the focus changed to the story of the Bible's spread around the world.[2]

Even so, the assembled artifacts imply that the events of the Bible happened as written. They are facsimile reproductions of famous archaeological finds such as the Mesha and Merneptah steles and wall reliefs from Ninevah that depict a siege occurring in the Bible, with no counterinformation on excavations such as Jericho that contradict that narrative.[3] On a recent tour, museum director Jeff Kloha insisted that the omission wasn't intentional, saying decisions were made for "financial or visual, often not deep theological reasons."[4] Still, it's hard to avoid the impression of biblical inerrancy, especially when purple banners hung throughout the exhibit trumpet, "Thy Word Is Truth."

The history floor offers surprisingly little information about who wrote the Bible or how. In videos scattered throughout, Stotts breathlessly presents the Bible's "path to us" across "thousands of years." The aim is to present the Bible as a "single, incredible story," in the words of religion professor Cavan Concannon, who cowrote a pair of books about the museum. "This allows Stotts to conclude that the transmission of the Bible has been stable from the ancient past to the present. It should not be surprising that this narrative of the Bible's transmission is precisely that of Steve Green."[5]

The exhibit initially started with the Gilgamesh Dream Tablet, lit up inside a vitrine as an example of early writing. "If Abraham and other biblical patriarchs wrote, they might have used this method," a video stated, implying that biblical stories may have been recorded thousands of years before any evidence. The rest of the exhibit repeatedly emphasizes the stability of the Bible's text since its earliest days rather than the multiplicity of narratives that coalesced into the book.[6] "Tradition maintains that some parts were composed very early," notes one placard. A display about the Dead Sea Scrolls notes, "Many discoveries show that the text of today's Hebrew Bible has remained consistent since at least the 1st century BC." The language is carefully selected to reflect current scholarship while leaving naïve viewers to believe the Bible was more stable than it actually was, with only a small display of apocrypha alluding to the variety of early biblical texts. A former member of the museum's curatorial staff confirmed that there was a constant tension between exhibit designers, who strove to push expansive views of the Bible's accuracy, and curators, who fought to bring the language in line with scholarly consensus: "You had the Greens saying one thing, the development team saying another thing, and then curatorial going, 'Hey, you can't say it like that.' "[7]

The rest of the history floor is devoted to the process of copying and translation over the centuries. In an interactive exhibit, translation is presented as a mere game of word substitution rather than a process that might alter the meaning of the text. The floor moves through the Gutenberg press and the Protestant translators of Erasmus, Luther, Wycliffe, and Tyndale until it arrives at the King James Bible, held up as "the most influential and widely read Bible for the next 350 years." European colonization is glossed over as merely a means of transmitting Bibles to new continents.[8]

The logic of the exhibit becomes apparent by its conclusion as it ends in an oval room with thousands of books on lit-up shelves, looking like a library on the starship *Enterprise*. The room showcases illumiNations, the coalition of Bible translators Mart helped assemble. Each book represents one of the world's languages, with a color-coded sleeve representing its progress toward translation. Visitors are referred to a website where they can donate to the effort.

THE NEXT FLOOR down, dedicated to stories of the Bible, is divided into two main parts—the Hebrew Bible Experience and the New Testament Theater. On the left, the Hebrew Bible Experience starts by stating that while the first books of the Bible have many names—"Old Testament. Septuagint. Hebrew Bible"—the Bible "tells one story," collapsing any distinction between Jewish and Christian interpretations.

The interactive walking tour, however, awkwardly tries to tell both stories: a Christian story of original sin in which "humanity's once-perfect unity with God" is "broken" and a Jewish story about a search for a homeland for a chosen people.[9] Visitors watch a video about Adam and Eve, emphasizing their disobedience to God and the need to "mend the relationship that was broken," followed by a walk down a dark corridor with sounds of rain representing the flood into a theater with swaying palm trees, where the covenant between Abraham and his descendants is described. From there, the experience inserts Christian themes of a messiah and covenant with all humankind.

Ultimately, the exhibit emphasizes the Christian reading of the Old Testament, skipping over many of the history books of the Hebrew Bible but devoting a full two minutes to the story of Ruth, a minor character for Jews but a major symbol for Christians as a non-Jewish ancestor of David—and therefore Jesus.[10] The exhibit ends with the return from Babylonian captivity to rebuild the temple—solving one problem, the search for a homeland, notes Concannon and his co-author Jill Hicks-Keeton, but not the other, the broken relationship with God.[11]

For that, visitors can walk out of the Hebrew Bible Experience into the New Testament Theater to find the solution: Jesus. When the museum first opened, it showed a film focusing on the exploits of the apostles spreading Christianity through the Great Commission after Christ's death. Recently, the exhibit was revamped with a new film that speaks more overtly about the Gospels and the book of Revelation, "culminating in the triumphal return of the Messiah," powerfully projected onto a wall as visitors sit on the floor bathed in a swelling musical score in an experience that feels more like church than a museum. In doing so, the narrator intones, "the chasm between mankind and God would be healed and the earth made full and beautiful as it once was in the beginning."[12]

The final exhibit floor focuses on the impact of the Bible. The material shows the influence of the Bible in America, presenting Steve's view that the Bible has been an unyielding force for good in US society.[13] In doing so, it avoids the claim that America was founded as a

Christian nation, correctly stating that "enlightenment and classical philosophy provided the intellectual foundation for establishing a republic" before adding, somewhat nonsensically, "the Bible its spiritual framework." Another plaque mentions that the Founders "studied Enlightenment philosophy and were inspired by its ideals" but states that they were also vaguely "steeped in the Bible," and "its teachings permeated their lives."[14]

As the exhibit continues, it steadfastly presents the Bible as an inspiration for social justice, particularly for women and racial minorities. One exhibit goes so far as to present misleading views about how the Bible inspired feminists such as suffragette Elizabeth Cady Stanton, who was a staunch atheist (and includes no information about how religious conservatives fought the Equal Rights Amendment or decried feminism for the better part of the twentieth century). The most problematic section concerns slavery, presenting the Bible as having been on the side of abolitionists, who used it to support "broad principles of justice and equality," while implying that slaveholders misinterpreted the Bible by citing passages that only "seemed to sanction [slavery]."[15]

The implication, Hicks-Keeton and Concannon point out, is that those who opposed slavery interpreted the Bible correctly, while those supporting slavery were wrong—despite the fact that even abolitionists were forced to acknowledge the many passages in the Bible that clearly advocate slavery. "Those who love the Bible do what it says (=oppose slavery) and those who don't love what the Bible says interpret it to say something else (=affirm slavery)," write Hicks-Keeton and Concannon. Steve made that distinction explicit in his interview with Sean McDowell, Josh's son: "Yes, there have been those that have taken God's word and used it for their own selfish ill intent. But my argument is not to blame the Bible for man's misuse of it. When we follow the principles of the book as designed, it's been good for mankind in every area."[16]

The exhibit goes on to display a Mount Rushmore–like mural of abolitionists, feminists, and civil rights leaders—lumping together Martin Luther King Jr. and Billy Graham—contending that they used the Bible to support freedom and liberation while ignoring the way Americans historically used the Bible to support bigotry against Blacks, Native Americans, women, and LGBTQ individuals. Kloha defended the museum's choice to present the Bible in its best light, saying, "If you go to the Air and Space Museum, it's a very positive view of space travel and airplanes. There is nothing about plane crashes. If you go to the National Gallery, it's beautiful works of art. So we want to present this topic in a way that will encourage people to engage with it."[17]

The messages of the exhibit are clearly heard by visitors, according to an interactive poll at the end that broadcasts responses on large screens. During a recent visit, guests agreed by 68 to 18 points that "the Bible supports religious freedom for all"—a perplexing view of a book whose first commandment is "Thou shalt have no other gods before me." But of course, for evangelical Christians, "religious freedom" is about the freedom to practice Christianity, an ideal reflected in a display about the Bible and the Supreme Court lamenting the decision that "banned" the Bible from schools. "This is a language of religious freedom in which the concept is not an abstract defense of religion for all, but a rhetorical technology for reaffirming the taken-for-granted dominance of Christianity," says religious historian Stephen Young in a critical essay about the exhibit.[18]

The exhibit concludes before the time period that would force it to weigh in on the culture wars of today, including abortion and LGBTQ rights. Instead, it segues to an exhibit examining the Bible's impact on the world, where the Bible is presented as the source for human rights, "Western concepts of justice," hospitals, universities, prison reform, and scientific inquiry. On the other side of the ledger, the negatives are dispensed with in a few sentences in an exhibit on religious persecution, which notes that "European Christians oppressed Jewish communities" in the Middle Ages and the Spanish Inquisition executed "thousands" of Jews in the 1400s. That's overshadowed, however, by a huge bronze cast of burned books symbolizing that persecution of Christian martyrs and noting that "there are still rulers who restrict the Bible" today.[19]

THE MUSEUM'S OVERALL effect is a presentation of the Bible as a book passed down as a unified whole, telling a single story of salvation with an impact that is unambiguously *good*. While the museum's exhibits avoid the worst fears of critics—there are no dinosaurs or proclamations of America as a Christian nation—its veneer of respectability makes its underlying message more insidious. While appearing to present a neutral view of an influential book, it undeniably presents a Protestant Christian viewpoint that's explicit to evangelical visitors and implicitly influential to mainstream guests. Those who "engage" further won't find an unbiased view in the gift shop, which includes a full complement of the Greens' works along with a who's who of conservative Christian authors while leaving out more mainstream or liberal interpretations of the book.

Whatever the museum's positioning, it's clear who its core audience is: evangelicals, who have flocked to the attraction from around the country, often in groups, singing hymns on buses as they have driven hundreds of miles for the pilgrimage. The museum logged over a half-million visitors in its first six months, including 1,700 groups.[20] "It's so authentic, and true to God's word," one evangelical tourist said shortly after the opening.[21] Tours continue to be popular today. On a recent afternoon, multiple groups were in attendance with matching shirts from their churches. "Here's how we know the Bible is real," a tour guide said, leading his group to the "Drive Thru History" theater.

The museum has also drawn the attention of Christian nationalists, who see it as friendly territory amidst the Washington swamp. Ten days after the museum opened, evangelical pastor Ralph Drollinger of Capitol Ministries held his fall training conference for more than one hundred international leaders there. An early supporter of Trump, Drollinger saw public officials in Washington as his mission field, urging Bible study attendees, including Vice President Mike Pence, Attorney General Jeff Sessions, and conservative members of Congress, to "vote biblical" by enacting right-wing policies regarding the economy and social issues.[22]

A month later, Steve and Jackie cohosted their own event at the museum in support of an exclusive new group of 125 high-worth Christian executives, pastors, and media personalities. Called Ziklag after the biblical town where King David plotted his military campaigns, the group was conceived by Silicon Valley entrepreneur Ken Eldred and run in part by NAR prophet Wallnau, who infused it with his vision of seven mountains dominionism. Steve and Jackie were early contributing members, cohosting a "private gathering of influencers to explore how we might collaborate to bring about positive culture change in America for the cause of Christ." The event included a special dinner and accommodations at Trump International Hotel.[23] "We are in a spiritual battle and locked in a terrible conflict with the powers of darkness," said an internal strategy document, part of a trove of confidential communications obtained by ProPublica that spelled out a "30-year vision" to capture the seven mountains and redirect "American culture toward Christ by bringing back Biblical structure, order, and truth to our Nation."[24]

The same month, Washington-based Lamplighter Ministries held its Revolution 2017 conference at the museum. The group is led by Jon and Jolene Hamill, who prophesied that Trump would bring Christ back to America and now declared the Museum of the Bible to be a new "Ark of the Covenant," the ancient vessel containing the Ten Commandments that was carried in the vanguard of the Israelites as they conquered Canaan.[25] The event in the museum's auditorium featured some of the most prominent NAR leaders, including dominionist and prosperity gospel enthusiast Cindy Jacobs, who declared that as "the army of the heavens marches into Washington DC," the Museum of the Bible would be "God's base camp."[26]

While the Greens were not involved in the day-to-day operations of the museum, the millions the family had contributed, and continued to contribute, gave them influence. In addition, Steve serves as chair of the museum's board of directors, in which capacity he has continued to influence the institution's programming, including what groups held events there. In fact, the next year, Lamplighter planned to hold Revolution 2018 at the Museum of the Bible. The day before it was to begin, however, it was abruptly canceled over protests from some museum advisory board members who said it "betrayed the values the museum says it wants to uphold." Lamplighter found a new venue at Trump's hotel, but the change demonstrated that the museum and its board could deny a Christian nationalist gathering at its venue if it wanted to—even if it rarely did so again.[27]

CHRISTIAN NATIONALISTS HAD a lot to celebrate in the first two years of the Trump administration as the president and allies in Congress continued to expand "religious liberty." In 2017, Attorney General Jeff Sessions, an Alabama Methodist, wrote a twenty-five-page memo instructing federal agencies to broadly apply religious exemptions through RFRA to corporations and other organizations, citing the Hobby Lobby decision as precedent. To craft his guidance, Sessions consulted with the ADF, now led by Michael Farris, a prominent homeschooling advocate, and commanding a $60 million budget.[28]

More than a quarter of that, $14 million, came from a single source, the Servant Foundation, run by Bill High, the Greens' longtime financial adviser and David's coauthor on several books. By now, the organization had ceased its affiliation with the NCF and instead donated directly to charities by sponsoring its own DAFs, including those for the Greens, rebranding itself under a new name, the Signatry. For the year beginning in April 2018, the Signatry donated to many of the Greens' pet causes, with tens of millions going to Every Home for Christ, OneHope, Wycliffe, and Answers in Genesis as well as dozens of donations to churches and crisis pregnancy centers. Thousands more went to Campus Crusade for Christ, Focus on the Family, Capitol Ministries, and Lamplighter.[29]

The funds allowed the ADF to expand its operations to employ sixty attorneys to argue cases, write briefs, and craft model legislation in the name of religious freedom. As conservatives reluctantly accepted the *Obergefell* decision legalizing gay marriage, the ADF and other legal advocates adopted a new strategy to fight back against the "homosexual agenda." In December 2017, ADF lawyers represented the plaintiff in a new case before the Supreme Court known as *Masterpiece Cakeshop*, the first major religious liberty case after *Burwell*.[30]

The case involved a Colorado baker who cited religious beliefs in its refusal to design a cake for a gay wedding. Arguments for the plaintiffs were delivered by ADF senior attorney Kristen Waggoner, a Pentecostal who argued that the cake was an act of "creative expression" protected under the RFRA. In the end, the court ruled 7–2 in favor of the baker on a technicality, claiming (somewhat dubiously) that the state's civil rights commission had shown "impermissible hostility towards sincere religious beliefs" but leaving the overarching question unresolved—at least for the time being.[31]

In another case, the ADF defended a funeral-home owner who fired an employee after they came out as transgender. The ADF helped legislators write new laws against transgender people in dozens of states, prohibiting them from using bathrooms corresponding to their gender identity in schools and public buildings. The laws raised the specter of assault by boys in girls' bathrooms despite studies showing that assaults by transgender people were almost nonexistent.[32] (In almost every case, the laws were struck down by courts as soon as they were passed.)[33]

The biggest coup for Christian conservatives was Trump's appointment to the Supreme Court of religious freedom advocate Brett Kavanaugh to replace the retiring Anthony Kennedy. During his confirmation hearing, a 2003 email was unearthed implying that he would overturn *Roe v. Wade*; however, he assured senators that he thought *Roe* was "settled law" and an "important precedent."[34]

Trump's brash style and draconian policies on immigration—as well as allegations he'd paid hush money to adult film star Stormy Daniels—created a nationwide backlash that led Republicans to worry that they'd lose the House in the midterms. "You're one election away from losing everything you've got," Trump told evangelical leaders in a White House meeting, urging them to persuade their parishioners to vote.[35] In the end, it wasn't enough, as Republicans lost the House 199 to 235 seats. One bright spot for Christian nationalists was the election of Missouri senator Josh Hawley, a former senior counsel for the Becket Fund who ran on a platform of strengthening the RFRA to protect the rights of Christians.

By the end of its first year, the museum had counted more than a million visitors. Despite that success, the controversies continued. Behind the scenes, curators struggled to determine provenance for the thousands of artifacts in the museum and Hobby Lobby collections—especially the many ancient papyrus fragments and cuneiform tablets. They pored over invoices and sales agreements, attempting to match descriptions and photos with those in the museum's storage, compiling them into a PDF document hundreds of pages long that they called "The Beast."[36]

Most of the ancient artifacts, they found, derived from four sources. First, there was Turkish dealer Mixantik Antiques, run by Yakup Ekşioğlu, who'd been paid nearly $2 million for hundreds of papyri fragments as well as mummy masks and cartonnage between 2009 and 2012. Carroll had also dealt with another Turkish dealer called Celadon Antik, which had been paid nearly $1 million during the same period.[37]

Then there was Israeli dealer Baidun, which had sold Hobby Lobby a bewildering array of artifacts, including papyri, cuneiform, codexes, and vellum manuscripts—over $20 million worth in all between 2009 and 2014. The company continued to do business with Baidun even after cuneiform objects from the Dubai deal were seized. Though it required more provenance information on sales after that, the dealer often supplied only vague statements, such as "private English collection" or "Belgian collection 1960s," which were practically worthless to curators trying to track the legitimacy of sales.[38]

Finally, there was Dirk Obbink, whom the company paid at least $8 million for papyri, cartonnage panels, and mummy masks between 2010 and 2013—including the first-century Mark and the other gospel fragments that seemed to belong to the Egypt Exploration Society's Oxyrhynchus collection.[39] In early 2018, Kloha and Trobisch flew to the UK to confront Obbink about that contradiction. He contended that he'd "mistakenly" sold the Oxyrhynchus fragments and would send provenance information later. When that information didn't arrive, Kloha cut ties with the scholar, sending a demand for repayment in the amount of $760,000.[40]

Meanwhile, the Iraq Embassy in Washington held a public ceremony in the backyard of its ambassador's home to announce the return of the cuneiform tablets bought in Dubai. A line of people filed past a table covered in a blue velvet cloth lined with dozens of clay tablets and seals to be sent back to the country.[41] Hanging back, J. P. Labbat was quietly celebrating the return until a Iraqi diplomat pulled him aside, saying, "You know, these are not the only tablets at the museum." A more prominent artifact was sitting in plain sight: the Gilgamesh Dream Tablet. "There's no way we would have authorized that leaving the country," he said. The Iraq Embassy had been in contact with the museum but was getting nowhere. "Can you look into it?"[42]

The next day, Labbat went to the museum casually dressed in jeans and a T-shirt and took the elevator to the fourth floor to see the tablet. He found it prominently displayed in a raking light that brought out the red and gold highlights in the clay. In a video nearby, David Stotts exclaimed, "Remarkably, these impressions made on clay tablets present similar traditions with those we find in the Bible."[43]

Unbeknownst to Labbat as he opened an investigation, the museum's curators were already struggling to verify the tablet's provenance. They looked into Christie's claims that it had been sold by California auctioneer Butterfield & Butterfield in 1981. Examining that auction listing, they found that it described a box of bronze fragments, with no mention of any cuneiform. The estimated price was between $50 and $100, a fraction of what the tablet was worth, making it unlikely that the provenance was true.[44] "We already knew Christie's were lying to us in September 2017," Kloha said. Even so, the tablet went prominently on display, with no provenance listed. "Our legal advice at the time was, well, you've kind of done your due diligence."[45]

A month later, the Egypt Exploration Society finally published the first-century Mark, the text Daniel Wallace had held up to support the historical accuracy of the Bible in his debate with Ehrman. According to Oxford's scholars, however, it wasn't a first-century artifact but dated from the second or early third century—a significant find, but hardly earth-shattering. Wallace apologized, saying he'd been "naïve" and "should have been more careful."[46] Just as significantly, the Egypt Exploration Society confirmed that the fragment was from its Oxyrhynchus collection and had never been for sale, "whatever claims may have been made."[47]

Scholars Initiative Director Michael Holmes was flummoxed. According to the museum's records, Obbink had sold Hobby Lobby all four fragments in early 2013—for the bargain price of $190,000 each—though, according to the terms of the agreement, he had retained them at Oxford for study.[48] In his latest story, Obbink claimed that those payments had been for other objects, even though Holmes was staring at a receipt for exactly those items.[49] The news about the first-century Mark sent shock waves through the small community of scholars investigating the museum's collection—vindicating their efforts while at the same time raising even more concerns. "For a lot of us, that opened the floodgates," Nongbri said.[50] If the Greens had bought one fragment from Oxford's collection, mistakenly or not, what did it say about the rest?

By fall, Kloha had received the results of the third-party investigation the museum had commissioned into the five questionable Dead Sea Scrolls fragments. Sure enough, the German-based lab concluded that they all showed "characteristics inconsistent with an ancient origin." As the museum pulled the scrolls from display, it put a positive spin on the findings, calling them "an opportunity to educate the public on the importance of verifying the authenticity of rare biblical artifacts." Even after displaying the fake items for a year, however, the museum seemed not to have learned its lesson, replacing them with other fragments "pending further analysis and scholarly research."[51]

EVEN AS THE museum was reckoning with its past missteps, it continued to serve as a clubhouse for Christian nationalists. In March 2019, it cohosted a summit featuring NAR leaders Lance Wallnau and Os Hillman.[52] In May, pastors with Watchmen on the Wall, the FRC's outreach to religious leaders, enjoyed a museum tour and reception before departing for a "spiritual heritage tour of the US Capitol" led by David Barton.[53] Meanwhile, Hobby Lobby continued to plow profits into religious causes through the Signatry, which donated another $19 million to the ADF starting in 2019, nearly one-third of the ADF's $65 million budget that year.[54]

At the White House, Trump officially hired Paula White as faith liaison and implemented a series of new rules to enshrine religious freedom—including a new one through the Department of Health and Human Services granting health professionals religious exemptions from providing abortion, sterilization, or assisted suicide, with the threat of institutions losing federal funds if they didn't comply.[55] Christian conservatives became some of Trump's biggest supporters, even as his approval ratings plummeted in the wake of allegations that he had tried to strong-arm the president of Ukraine into a spurious investigation into his rival in the upcoming presidential race, Joe Biden.

As Democrats in Congress drafted articles of impeachment against the president, Trump spoke to evangelical supporters at the FRC's Value Voters Summit, which kicked off with a reception at the Museum of the Bible, playing off their sense of persecution by telling them, "They're coming after me because I'm fighting for you."[56] Conservative religious leaders railed against impeachment, with Congressman Josh Hawley calling it a "clownish" effort that "reeks of politics" and Wallnau dubbing Trump a "Cyrus under siege," prophesying that he "didn't have a miracle getting him into office only to have him removed."[57] Those protests were in vain, as the House voted mostly along party lines to impeach the president on two counts of abuse of power and obstruction of Congress.

AFTER THE STUNNING announcement about the erstwhile first-century Mark, Brent Nongbri and other scholar-sleuths kicked their own investigations into high gear. They scoured the Internet for presentations by Scott Carroll and Jerry Pattengale on artifacts in the museum's collection. Partnering with a professor of Pentecostalism at Pennsylvania State named David Bradnick, Nongbri located deleted web pages through the Internet Archive's Wayback Machine and ordered DVDs from *Passages* presentations, constructing a database of objects of dubious provenance.[58]

Meanwhile, Michael Holmes invited Roberta Mazza and two other British scholars to a wood-paneled club in London to tell them the truth:

Obbink had sold the museum the four gospel fragments from Oxford. Mazza couldn't believe it—to have one of the foremost scholars of biblical papyri accused of stealing from his own collection was too lurid to be imagined, "the most staggering betrayal of the values and ethics of our profession," she later said.[59] She immediately asked Holmes if that was the extent of the discoveries. They didn't know yet, Holmes told her.

Over the next few weeks, Holmes identified thirteen other papyri in the museum collection that had come from the Egypt Exploration Society's Oxyrhynchus collection, including two bought through a middleman, Israeli dealer Baidun.[60] After years of stonewalling, Mazza found Holmes refreshingly forthcoming. That summer, he sent her and other scholars copies of the sales contract for the fragments, with provenance marked simply "Egypt."[61] He followed it with a list of the thirteen items, which included fragments from Genesis and Psalms, as well as the Romans papyrus Steve had shown off on CNN, which Carroll had claimed came from the mummy mask at Baylor; the investigation was still continuing. Nongbri's working list of "papyri of dubious origins" had now grown into the dozens.[62] Eventually, the Egyptian Exploration Society revealed that 120 papyri were missing from its collection, raising the possibility that Obbink had been selling them to multiple buyers in addition to Hobby Lobby.[63]

Obbink vigorously denied accusations that he'd knowingly sold Oxford's papyri, hinting darkly to the *Waco Tribune-Herald* that documents used against him had "been fabricated in a malicious attempt to harm my reputation and career."[64] At the Society of Biblical Literature conference in San Diego that November, the scandal was on everyone's lips. Holmes revealed that the Greens had collected more than five thousand papyri as scholars continued to blast the Greens for their recklessness and slipshod approach to verifying provenance.[65]

The Greens "poured millions on the legal and illegal antiquities market without having a clue about the history, the material features, cultural value, fragilities, and problems of the objects," Mazza fumed to *The Guardian*. It was "a crime against culture and knowledge of immense proportions—as the facts unfolding under our eyes do prove."[66] Shortly after the conference, Holmes contacted Nongbri with new information. An eagle-eyed curator at the museum had discovered a purchase order for more than eight hundred papyri from Turkish dealer Yakup Ekşioğlu, also known as MixAntik—the same dealer who had threatened Mazza. An accompanying photo seemed to show a wad of papyri with one of the Sappho fragments on top. The invoice was dated January 7, 2012, just a week before Scott Carroll claimed that he had extracted it from a mummy mask at Baylor University. When Nongbri posted the information, Ekşioğlu replied with a rambling comment denying that he or Steve Green had done anything wrong.[67]

In a WhatsApp chat with journalist Ariel Sabar, however, Ekşioğlu claimed to be the source for all of the Sappho fragments; Obbink's claim that they had come from cartonnage purchased at Christie's in 2011 was a "fake story." Sabar cornered Carroll as well, and according to his report, Carroll confessed that he had planted the Sappho and Romans fragments in the mask dissolved at Baylor that day so students would have exciting items to identify. "At the time, I didn't feel that it was duplicitous," Carroll said.[68]

Around the same time, Carroll gave the keynote address at a Bible collectors convention in Boston, and David Bradnick caught a flight from Pennsylvania to see it. In his presentation, Carroll admitted publicly that he'd never found biblical texts inside a mummy mask. But when Bradnick approached him afterward, Carroll denied ever having possessed the Sappho fragments. "Scott, we have you on video holding them up," Bradnick shot back. Cornered, Carroll sighed and said, according to Bradnick, "Frankly, I'm a pathological liar; I can't help it."[69]

Special Agent Labbat continued to investigate the backstory of the Gilgamesh Dream Tablet, tracking down the Butterfield listing for the bronzes, amazed Christie's would have taken it seriously as provenance. "You don't put a clay tablet in a box of bronzes; you are going to destroy it," he said. As he conducted interviews, he found that Christie's employees had privately questioned the provenance, which is why they had never put the tablet up for public auction, selling it privately to Hobby Lobby instead. "They knew this piece had trouble, and they sold it anyway," he said.[70] (In statements and court documents, Christie's denied any knowledge that the provenance was false.)[71]

No one from the Museum of the Bible had delved into the provenance at the time, taking Christie's claims at face value. When Labbat contacted rare-book dealer Michael Sharpe, a different story emerged that showed just how antiquities are laundered through the hands of multiple buyers. Sharpe told him he'd bought the tablet from a pair of antiquities dealers, Mark Hine and Joe Linzalone, in 2007.[72] They in turn had purchased it in 2007 from an antiquities dealer and a cuneiform expert who had shown Sharpe an invoice from the Butterfield sale as evidence of provenance. Although investigators have not revealed the identity of the pair, Sharpe has identified the cuneiform expert as Renee Kovacs, leading some to speculate that the antiquities dealer was her husband, San Francisco antiquities dealer Frank Kovacs.[73] When Labbat flew to California to interview the dealers, they admitted that the invoice was a fake they'd created to facilitate the sale to Sharpe.

Under threat of prosecution, they told Labbat a different story about the tablet's origins—that it had actually come from the collection of a London-based Jordanian dealer named Ghassan Rahani, who was notorious for dabbling in black-market artifacts. In 2003, after Rahani died, his son had invited the pair to his father's London apartment to view his remaining inventory.[74] "They described a scene very similar to Fazeli's flat, with objects on the floor they had to step over when they walked in," Labbat said.[75] The pair spent $50,350 for a group of artifacts, which they shipped to the United States without a customs declaration. Only when they began cleaning the items did they realize the mind-blowing quality of what they had: a rare fragment from *The Epic of Gilgamesh*, the most sought-after poem of ancient Mesopotamia. They sent it to Andrew George, one of the foremost experts on the Gilgamesh epic, who was then visiting Princeton. George studied and dated it. The owners then sold it to Hine and Linzalone for $50,000—nearly the price they'd paid for the whole lot four years earlier.[76]

They included the forged provenance letter, contending that the Butterfield auction had included other antiquities "deaccessioned from a small museum."[77] All that mattered was that the tablet had been in the United States prior to the 1990 ban on removing objects from Iraq. "We never would have sold it if we knew we were going to end up getting the finger pointed at us many years later," they told Labbat.[78] By now, the Princeton professor had published a paper about the artifact, increasing its value immensely, so Hine and Linzalone were able to sell it to Sharpe for $280,000.[79] Sharpe then flipped it for $450,000—almost a tenfold increase in value in just a year. The tablet changed hands at least once more before ending up with Joseph David Hackmey, an Israeli insurance executive and art collector who commissioned the sale by Christie's to the Greens for $1.67 million.[80]

Labbat had what he needed. Even if he couldn't track the tablet to Iraq, the fact that it had been fraudulently imported into the United States in 2003 was enough to prove that it had been trafficked illegally and could be seized. Without telling the museum in advance, Labbat donned his raid jacket on the morning of September 24, 2019, and headed across Washington with another agent, flashing his badge and forcing museum employees to remove the tablet from its glass case. They placed it in a padded box, and Labbat rode back to HSI headquarters with the box on his lap.[81]

As Trump's impeachment trial got underway in January 2020, tens of thousands of antiabortion activists descended on the city for the annual

March for Life. Steve was there as a host of the prolife Save the Storks charity ball, offering a lunch and personal tour of the Museum of the Bible for a $50,000 table sponsorship.[82] The same night, the museum hosted a gathering for Evangelicals for Life, who prayed that *Roe v. Wade* would be overturned.[83] The next day, President Trump addressed the throngs of antiabortion activists on the National Mall, telling them, "Unborn children have never had a stronger defender in the White House."[84] It was the first time a sitting president had spoken at the gathering, earning the support and loyalty of evangelicals, who prayed for the Senate to acquit Trump of the impeachment charges. A week later, their prayers were answered when a majority voted against his removal.

No sooner had the country survived that ordeal than it faced another one, as the COVID-19 virus began spreading, creating a nationwide panic. States began issuing shutdown orders to nonessential businesses, and David worried that he didn't have $40 million to pay rent every month, never mind millions more for payroll.[85] He and Barbara prayed, and God responded to Barbara with three words: "Guard. Guide. Groom." David wrote to all employees to share Barbara's vision: "We serve a God who will Guide us through this storm, who will Guard us as we travel to places never seen before, and who, as a result of this experience, will Groom us to be better than we could have ever thought possible before now."[86]

In the short term, employees "may all have to 'tighten our belts,'" he continued as Hobby Lobby issued a memo to managers—leaked to media—to "make every effort to continue working the employees" despite the virus. If workers got sick, they'd be expected to use their personal paid leave or take an unpaid leave of absence. Full-time workers would see a 10 percent cut to their salary.[87] The company's policies were no worse than those of its competitors; JoAnn Fabrics and Michaels were also staying open and forcing employees to work. Many other retail stores, however, were more generous, with Dick's Sporting Goods, Kohl's, and Bath & Body Works voluntarily shutting down and giving up to two weeks' full pay and benefits to affected workers.

The Christian company's policies met with public scorn, with one retail analyst mocking, "Hobby Lobby, closed Sundays to allow employees time for family and worship. Open during a pandemic because our morals aren't really all that great."[88] Liberal media site Daily Kos went with the headline "Hobby Lobby Founder Tells Workers That God Spoke to His Wife and Forgot to Mention Paid Sick Leave."[89] As uncertainty reigned, Republican politicians and commentators blamed the virus on the Chinese or immigrants bringing it across borders, and megachurch pastors and televangelists raged that the pandemic was divine punishment for sinners, advocating for the power of prayer to fight it. Jerry Falwell Jr. and Lance Wallnau accused Democrats and the media of intentionally inflating the risk of the virus to tank the economy and ruin Trump's chances for reelection.[90] Polls showed that the more a person believed in Christian nationalist views, the more they blamed the virus on foreigners and immigrants and trusted Trump over doctors, scientists, and health officials, and the less likely they were to wear masks or be vaccinated.[91]

As the pandemic intensified, with more than ten thousand people dying each week nationwide in early April, Hobby Lobby kept its stores open in defiance of orders, arguing that the crafts store was an "essential business" since it carried supplies to make masks. Police forcibly closed locations in Wisconsin and Indiana, and employee morale cratered. "I used to love working for this company, but since this pandemic, I've seen how callous and irresponsible it has been," one employee said.[92]

In early April, attorney general offices in Colorado and Ohio sent cease-and-desist letters demanding that Hobby Lobby close its stores.[93] Finally, Hobby Lobby announced that it was furloughing all of its workers without pay, ending emergency leave and paid time off—though it would continue medical benefits for another month.[94] "As we watched revenue drop to zero, it became apparent that we couldn't keep paying all our employees," said David, who encouraged employees to turn to government and apply for federal and state unemployment benefits instead.[95]

By now, the Museum of the Bible had received the results of the tests on all of its Dead Sea Scrolls. The two-hundred-page report by an independent lab found that all sixteen of the museum's fragments were fake. They had seemingly all been made by the same forger, who'd used ancient shoe leather coated with an amber glue before writing biblical passages on the scraps and scattering mineral deposits on top.[96] The museum spun the results as a victory for transparency, touting the considerable expense to get to the bottom of the mystery. Some scholars were less impressed, given that experts had been voicing suspicions for years, even as the museum continued to display the dubious artifacts. Though the results were known by November 2019, the museum waited to release them until March, when the country was in lockdown, raising the eyebrows of some scholars who saw the timing as intentional. "By coincidence they have been made public months later when the world is in the grip of an unprecedented pandemic," Nongbri noted.[97]

As the country continued to grapple with COVID, the museum released the results of an even bigger investigation, saying that after a comprehensive analysis of the collection, it had identified 5,000 papyri and 8,500 clay objects with "insufficient provenance" that would be returned to officials in Egypt and Iraq.[98] Along with the cuneiform tablets and Oxyrhynchus fragments the museum had already returned, that meant some 17,000 items in all—almost the entire collection of ancient artifacts—were looted, stolen, trafficked, forged, or otherwise unaccounted for.

Steve released a lengthy statement as chair of the museum board, once again deflecting criticism onto others, saying he'd "trusted the wrong people to guide me and unwittingly dealt with unscrupulous dealers in those early years," but "as I came to understand taking a dealer at his or her word was not good enough, I cut ties with those consultants." He said nothing about experts like Patty Gerstenblith, who had informed Hobby Lobby of the risks of acquiring objects from Iraq. "The criticism resulting from my mistakes was justified," he acknowledged, but he pleaded good intentions: "My goal was always to protect, preserve, study, and share cultural property with the world."[99]

Condemnations from the art-crime community came in fast.[100] As someone who ran a "craft store empire," it was "inconceivable" that Steve "would fork out millions, buying ancient objects without at least a tacit knowledge that he might need to ask questions," said Lynda Albertson, head of the nonprofit ARCA. "It took Green an exceedingly long time to 'cut ties' and when he did, we didn't see a great deal of improvement in the museum's operational model, purchasing due diligence, or its transparency."[101] Nongbri noted on his blog that if by "unscrupulous . . . consultants" Steve was referring to Scott Carroll, the suspect acquisitions, including fake Dead Sea Scrolls, stolen papyri, and the trafficked Gilgamesh Dream Tablet, had continued long after Carroll's departure in 2012.[102]

By buying low and donating at inflated prices, the Greens must have also reaped huge tax windfalls, Nongbri added. While it is unclear just how much Hobby Lobby gleaned from the donations, IRS forms show that the items the museum returned from its collection in 2020 were worth $17.6 million, while the Signatry returned $16.5 million in donated artifacts—together more than $34 million.[103] Of course, there was no acknowledgment of the role of the dogged reporting of people like Roberta Mazza, Candida Moss, Joel Baden, and Nongbri himself in exposing the thefts, which otherwise may not have been revealed. Nevertheless, these investigators celebrated the return of the items to their rightful countries of origin. "For me, this is a victory for good, ethical scholarship and collecting," said Mazza. "Yes, I am bloody happy." As a cherry on top, Holmes finally revealed to her that Hobby Lobby had purchased the Galatians fragment in May 2013 from the Israeli dealer Baidun—who had presumably resold it after purchasing it from Ekşioğlu.[104]

Still, the fallout continued. In May, the federal government formally confiscated the Gilgamesh Dream Tablet, filing a formal lawsuit to recover it and placing much of the blame on Christie's. The next day, Hobby Lobby sued the auction house, which denied responsibility for fraud.[105] ARCA's Albertson didn't let Hobby Lobby off the hook so easily, saying the company was just as much at fault for a lack of due diligence. "A simple check of the Butterfield & Butterfield auction records" would have shown that they didn't include a cuneiform tablet. "That alone should have given someone reason to pause," she said. "One would question just how many legal entanglements it will take before Mr. Green starts to acknowledge that he is a significant contributor to the problem and not merely an innocent victim."[106]

THE COVID-19 PANDEMIC was a blessing in disguise for Hobby Lobby as lockdowns stretched on and people turned to puzzles and crafts to entertain themselves. When stores reopened in May, "sales skyrocketed," and "merchandise kept flying off the shelves," David said, leading to the company's best year ever, with 50 percent higher sales. "We deserved no credit for this," David said, turning to the prosperity gospel to explain it. "God alone deserved all the glory for this remarkable blessing."[107] The company reimbursed full-time employees for their pay cut and once again raised minimum wage, to $17 an hour.[108]

Conditions in Hobby Lobby's ten-million-square-foot warehouse, however, were miserable. The strategy of relying on a single distribution hub led to understaffing, as some employees never returned from furlough, and the company was hard-pressed to find enough employees in the Oklahoma City area to staff the massive warehouse facility. An exposé in the *Oklahoma Gazette* described employees working twelve-hour days in 100-degree warehouses without air-conditioning, with few workers wearing masks in the steamy environment. Those who got sick were required to quarantine for fourteen days without pay. Hobby Lobby declined comment.[109]

As the country became increasingly divided in the lead-up to a new presidential election, one Hobby Lobby store allegedly displayed wooden letters reading, "USA VOTE TRUMP," and the picture blew up online, sparking fresh calls for a boycott.[110] Meanwhile, the Greens lost another ally when Jerry Falwell Jr. was enmeshed in a scandal after his wife, Becki, had a sexual affair with a pool attendant, while Falwell admitted having known about the affair and done nothing to stop it. Falwell stepped down as president of Liberty University, one more in a long line of religious leaders resigning after a sex scandal.

Steve and Jackie continued their involvement in Ziklag, appearing as featured speakers at the group's annual conference and offering a dollar-for-dollar match up to $1 million for a fundraiser as the organization continued to direct funds from wealthy individuals toward groups advocating for a Christian nationalist agenda.[111] (David got involved in the group as well, headlining its conference in an appearance with Bill High two years later.[112]) In 2020, the Signatry donated another $16.6 million to the ADF, which scored a victory in a 7–2 Supreme Court ruling upholding Trump's executive order allowing any company to deny birth-control coverage to employees on religious grounds, vastly expanding the *Burwell* ruling.[113] In a dissent, Justice Ruth Bader Ginsburg lamented that while the Court had previously taken a "balanced approach," it now prioritized the freedoms of the employer over the rights of millions of women to control their health decisions. "Today, for the first time, the Court casts totally aside countervailing rights and interests in its zeal to secure religious rights to the nth degree," she wrote.[114] Soon after the ruling, in September 2020, Ginsburg died of complications related to pancreatic cancer.

Despite refusing to confirm Obama's nominee before the 2016 election, Senate Majority Leader Mitch McConnell pushed through Trump's nominee, Amy Coney Barrett, a Notre Dame law professor and member of the charismatic Catholic sect People of Praise, which preached strict obedience to male authority.[115] During her confirmation, the conservative Judicial Crisis Network spent millions on ads declaring her personal faith off limits.[116] It was no secret where she stood on abortion, as past comments decrying the "barbaric legacy of *Roe v. Wade*" resurfaced. A week before the election, Barrett was confirmed on a party-line vote, giving conservatives the 6–3 majority they'd prayed for.[117]

Trump wasn't so successful. While evangelicals once again turned out for him in record numbers, it wasn't enough to overcome fatigue at his antics and his weak response to the pandemic, which had claimed 400,000 lives.[118] Joe Biden defeated Trump in the Electoral College and had a 4 percent margin in the popular vote. Not everyone accepted that outcome, however. Dozens of charismatic prophets who had foreseen Trump's victory now refused to admit they were wrong, contending that diabolical forces had stolen the election.[119] NAR prophet Lance Wallnau went further, prophesying that God would "overturn" the election, because Trump hadn't completed his "assignment."[120]

CHAPTER THIRTEEN

Second Coming

The January 6, 2021, assault on the US Capitol by supporters of Donald Trump was led by partisan militia groups, including the Oath Keepers and Proud Boys. But it was just as much an assertion of Christian nationalist identity. Throughout November and December, groups held so-called Jericho marches across the country, fasting and praying to symbolically bring down the wicked walls of Washington, as God had done to Jericho in the conquest of Canaan.[1]

Jon and Jolene Hamill, who had held their Revolution conference at the Museum of the Bible, organized over a dozen meetings over Zoom, inviting NAR prophets Lance Wallnau and Cindy Jacobs along with old-school fundamentalists like James Dobson and politicos to share spurious information about hacked voting machines and stolen ballots in support of the idea that demons had hatched a plot to take over America.[2]

Religious author and radio host Eric Metaxas, who had written a foreword to David's last book and presented at the Museum of the Bible, said conservatives had to "fight to the death, to the last drop of blood" to keep Trump in office.[3] He emceed a rally in Washington before a march seven times around the Supreme Court, just as Israelites had walked seven times around Jericho. "Spirit, get out of there! Be gone!" Metaxas screamed, pointing at the Capitol dome.[4]

As January 6 dawned clear and cold, three of the six permits for rallies were taken out by charismatic religious groups. At a rally led by Cindy Jacobs, apostles broadcast prayers, spoke in tongues, and wrapped themselves in Appeal to Heaven flags, a Revolutionary War–era insignia of a pine tree that symbolized an appeal to God for justice when government failed.[5] Paula White gave a prayer on the White House Ellipse, urging God to "let every adversary against democracy" be overturned "in the name of Jesus," before Trump himself appeared, urging supporters to "fight like hell!"[6]

As protesters broke the fence around the Capitol and clashed with police, some carried crosses and sang hymns, carrying signs reading "Jesus is my savior, Trump is my president!" Even as insurrectionists broke windows and doors, attempting to stop the certification of ballots, Christian patriots were performing a Jericho march around the building.[7]

After the violence, politicians and religious leaders condemned the insurrection as Trump slunk off to his Florida mansion with a perfunctory apology. Once again, the House impeached him but the Senate failed to remove him from office, and Democrats called in vain for congresspeople who had supported the riot, such as Josh Hawley and Ted Cruz, to resign. As Biden assumed the presidency, he overturned many of Trump's executive orders, including those on religious freedom. Over the next year, however, Biden faced significant challenges as the COVID pandemic continued to spawn deadly new variants.

After a botched withdrawal from Afghanistan, Biden's approval ratings plummeted. His administration passed a $1.9 trillion economic stimulus bill to head off a recession, only to see the infusion of cash and global supply-chain disruptions send inflation soaring. Congress passed the Inflation Reduction Act with massive investments in climate technology, but prices clung stubbornly to record highs.

Hobby Lobby was as affected by the supply-chain disruptions as any company. In the summer of 2021, it was drastically understocked after a Chinese port had closed in response to the powerful Delta variant. "Your disciples twice fished unsuccessfully all night long. You solved their problem both times," David prayed to Jesus. "God, this freight is all clogged up. Please release it." As inventory rolled into Oklahoma once more, he said, "every truck felt like an answered prayer."[8]

By the end of the year, Hobby Lobby was finally approaching its long-awaited goal of one thousand stores nationwide, with revenues shooting up to $8 billion a year. Competitors Michaels and JoAnn struggled with debt due to rising interest rates even as Hobby Lobby remained debt-free. The company again shared the wealth with its employees, raising minimum wage another dollar to $18.50.[9]

Mart continued to pour his energy into his illumiNations project. Over the previous eight years, he and the CEOs of ten missionary organizations had been meeting once a month at the Dallas airport to coordinate their plan of translating the Bible into 95 percent of languages by 2033. There were still 3,800 languages without a complete copy, they estimated, meaning they'd have to translate a language a day to make their goal, which they seemingly needed a miracle to achieve. The partnership ratcheted up its efforts with a new campaign, "I Want to Know," soliciting donations of $35 to cover the cost of translating one of the Bible's more than thirty thousand verses into a single language. "Translating the Bible into every language for all people has been a 'Goliath' of biblical proportions for generations," Mart said. "But now we're on the brink of a giant slingshot."[10]

In early 2021, artifacts from the Green Collection were returned to their rightful homes, beginning with a planeload of five thousand artifacts that landed in Cairo in February. They included thousands of papyri most likely looted from Egypt during the Arab Spring as well as mummy masks and statues.[11] Egypt's head of antiquities recovery, Shaaban Abdel Gawad, met the plane at the airport. Since assuming his post in 2015, Gawad had repatriated more than thirty thousand artifacts based on tips from auction sales, eBay listings, and museum holdings.[12]

In 2019, he worked with Brent Easter to recover a golden coffin from the Metropolitan Museum of Art after reality TV star Kim Kardashian had posted a photo of herself next to it in a golden dress. Before the Met had purchased the coffin, Hassan Fazeli had helped smuggle it out of Egypt, concocting a fake provenance.[13] "We are looking for objects seven days a week," Gawad recently said at his Cairo office. "Sometimes we have only two or three days to act before they disappear."[14]

Despite the Greens' contrition over the trafficked items, the return of the artifacts was messier than they let on. When Gawad first demanded their return, the museum made a counterproposal, offering to pay Egypt to keep the objects on long-term loan. "It made me crazy. I told them, 'I refuse this,'" Gawad said, face wrinkling with laughter. "Some people say, 'Why give it back to Egypt—let us display it as a good ambassador for Egyptian culture.' I say, 'Display the Eiffel Tower or the Statue of Liberty in Cairo first.'"[15]

Six months later, Iraq's prime minister flew to Washington and returned with nearly twelve thousand artifacts surrendered by Hobby Lobby and the museum.[16] In Baghdad, culture minister Hassan Nadhem said their return "restores not just the tablets, but the confidence of the Iraqi people." At the same time, he said, the years the artifacts had been overseas were still "a kind of bitterness in our mouth." As with the Egyptian antiquities, the museum had tried to negotiate a loan for the objects, pledging $15 million for "research, exhibitions, and technical assistance projects" in exchange for keeping them for five years.[17] An Arabic newspaper that leaked the proposed deal called it "exploitative and degrading," noting that Iraq wouldn't even necessarily get the money, which could have been used to pay museum staff or contractors working on the objects; additionally, the deal would have indemnified the museum and Hobby Lobby from any future lawsuits.[18] In the end, the deal was nixed and the objects returned—all except one.

The Gilgamesh Dream Tablet stayed behind, stuck in a legal tug-of-war between Hobby Lobby and Christie's for several months before a federal judge finally ruled that it had to be forfeited and returned.[19] In September 2021, it was displayed at a ceremony at the Smithsonian's National Museum of the American Indian, two blocks from the Museum of the Bible. Some thirty years after it had been looted from Iraq and passed through numerous hands from London to San Francisco to Tel Aviv to Washington, it was finally returning home. At the ceremony, the tablet looked small and lonely onstage, spotlit on a stand at one end of a long table as Iraqi and US officials took the podium one by one to celebrate the return. "These artifacts belong to the people of Iraq, and we are proud to help them in their recovery and return so that future generations may study and admire them," said Labbat's boss, HSI executive director Steve Francis.[20]

Hobby Lobby finally settled its case against Christie's for an undisclosed sum, both sides avoiding a trial that may have publicly revealed more details about the sale. As for Dirk Obbink, the Oxford don failed to make restitution for months before Hobby Lobby sued him in June 2021, accusing him of fraudulently selling thirty-two papyri worth a total of $7 million. Despite having previously protested his innocence, Obbink now disappeared, failing to respond to the lawsuit. The judge awarded Hobby Lobby a default judgment requiring Obbink to pay the full amount, even as authorities in the United Kingdom and Egypt continued to investigate him for his alleged thefts.[21]

When liberal Justice Stephen Breyer announced his retirement, Biden nominated Ketanji Brown Jackson, the first Black woman on the Court—but her appointment did little to shake up the ideological makeup of the justices. With the new 6–3 majority, conservatives wasted no time pushing new rulings on religious liberty. In one case, a Washington high school football coach was placed on administrative leave for leading Christian prayers on the fifty-yard line, and students, parents, and even media rushed from the stands to take part. The case was taken up by Christian legal organization First Liberty Institute, whose lawyers argued that the coach was merely engaging in "quiet prayer by himself." The appeals judge ruled on behalf of the school, saying the coach was taking "advantage of his position" to push his religion on "captive minds" of students.[22]

The Supreme Court overruled him 6–3, with lead opinion author Neil Gorsuch continuing to claim that the coach was merely offering a "quiet prayer of thanks"—even though Sotomayor took the unusual step of attaching photos to her dissent showing dozens of players and parents gathered around him.[23] The Lemon test prohibiting excessive "entanglement" of religion and government was all but destroyed by the ruling; the *Harvard Law Review* noted that decades of concerted efforts by Christian lawyers had "succeeded in transforming yesteryear's Hail Marys into today's answered prayers."[24]

Nothing answered the religious right's prayers more than the 6–3 decision in June 2022 on *Dobbs v. Jackson Women's Health Organization*, in which the Supreme Court overruled the right to abortion that had been established by *Roe v. Wade*. "*Roe* was egregiously wrong from the start," wrote opinion author Samuel Alito. "Its reasoning was exceptionally weak, and the decision had damaging consequences." Abortion wasn't protected under the Fourteenth Amendment's due process clause because the right wasn't "deeply rooted in history," he continued. In a concurring opinion, Justice Clarence Thomas went further, arguing that the same logic could be applied to other issues of religious conscience, including contraception, same-sex intimacy, and gay marriage.[25]

"The Supreme Court's decision is a major victory," crowed ADF lead counsel Waggoner. "We now turn to the states to ensure that unborn children and their mothers are protected from the gruesome reality of abortion." She had a right to celebrate; not only had ADF lawyers served on the legal team in the case, but it was based on a Mississippi law the organization had written.[26] Behind the scenes, the Signatry contributed another $33 million to the ADF in the two years beginning April 2021, fueling the organization during the crucial period in which it helped overturn *Roe*.[27]

Dobbs had an immediate polarizing effect on America. As thirteen states activated "trigger laws" to ban abortion in most instances, polls showed that about six in ten Americans disagreed with the ruling, believing that abortion should be legal in all or most circumstances. They vented their anger at the polls, voting down ballot initiatives against a state constitutional right to an abortion in conservative Kansas, Kentucky, and Montana. In the 2022 midterms, Democrats increased their numbers, only narrowly losing the House and retaining the Senate despite widespread dissatisfaction with Biden over inflation.

Emboldened by the success of *Dobbs* and other religious liberty cases, some conservatives doubled down with stronger Christian nationalist language. "Without the Bible, there is no modernity. Without the Bible, there is no America," thundered Senator Josh Hawley at the National Conservatism Conference in Miami. "We are a revolutionary nation precisely because we are the heirs of the revolution of the Bible.... It is the true sources of the liberties we cherish." He and other speakers repeatedly railed against the "woke left," advocated for the teaching of the Bible in schools, and pushed for the passage of laws based on biblical values, some even proudly embracing the Christian nationalist label.[28]

David Green didn't say anything publicly about *Dobbs*. In the wake of the decision, however, he did have an announcement: He was giving away his company. Yvon Chouinard, founder of the outdoor brand

Patagonia, had recently transferred ownership of his $3 billion company to a trust that would use its profits to fight climate change.[29]

"I experienced a similar decision-making process with my ownership of Hobby Lobby," David said in a Fox News op-ed, only with one difference: "I chose God." Expressing worries that bequeathing unfettered cash to his descendants might "change or even ruin" them, he decided to donate the company's profits to Christian causes, though he was scant on details on how he would achieve that.[30] In fact, the change wasn't new—the Greens had already made that decision a decade earlier, when David had established the family stewardship trust. The announcement seemed only to capitalize on Patagonia's pledge to draw attention to that decision—and indeed, it spurred positive articles around the world presenting it as a new shift.[31]

David needn't have worried about the next generation, as they all seemed to be following in his footsteps. Mart's oldest son, Brent Ryan Green, was a filmmaker on both religious and secular projects. In addition to working with the likes of Martin Scorsese, he produced word-for-word film adaptations of the Gospels and consulted on *The Chosen*, a drama series following Jesus's disciples created by Dallas Jenkins, son of Left Behind series coauthor Jerry B. Jenkins. The series has gained an eager following among evangelicals and even some mainstream viewers for its high production values and human characters.[32]

David's other grandchildren have similarly stayed close to the family business. Steve's son Derek joined Hobby Lobby as a real estate analyst before transitioning to HL Investments, which handles the company's outside investments.[33] Steve's daughter Lindy trained as a social worker before going on to work as a trauma specialist for Christian churches and nonprofits, including Rick Warren's Saddleback Church. She eventually moved on to a California ministry called Every Mother's Advocate to help "women in crisis" avoid losing their children.[34]

Mart's son Tyler joined Hobby Lobby's philanthropic arm as a "community catalyst" and has since run a company-sponsored organization called Flourish OKC that works with religious nonprofits in Oklahoma City and runs a start-up incubator for Christian companies. Recently, the organization has focused on restorative justice, a form of criminal justice prioritizing rehabilitation and community engagement over punishment. Tyler even led a group of religious leaders in speaking out against the death penalty—a bold stance in Oklahoma, which has executed more prisoners in the last five years than any state but Texas.[35]

None have been as committed to the family legacy as Steve's daughter Lauren and her husband, Michael McAfee, longtime employees of Hobby Lobby and the Museum of the Bible who have made it their mission to translate the biblical worldview for a millennial audience. The couple met in Sunday school and continued together to OU before going on to both earn PhDs in theology at Southern Baptist Theological Seminary.

In 2019, they cowrote *Not What You Think*, an earnest apologia for their generation. Filled with references to iPhones, Harry Potter, and weekend brunch, it exudes a youth-pastor energy with an urgent, even desperate appeal to millennials to give the Bible a chance. After describing a Bart Ehrman lecture and OU comparative religion class that had shaken their faith in the Bible's truth, they insist that it is reliable and true, shrugging off its more miraculous elements. "Let the Bible be the Bible," they write. "In the Bible's universe, the supernatural is real." Like her father, Lauren finds the Bible's truth self-evident given the fact that it was written over thousands of years but tells "one unified story that points to Jesus."[36]

The McAfees offer a breath of fresh air when they acknowledge that "indefensible acts have occurred in the name of the Christian religion, not to mention the Bible itself"—but in the next breath, they mirror the stance of the Museum of the Bible in saying that anything evil done in its name only misinterprets the Bible, which "never condones the violation of human dignity."[37]

Watching her family fight in the *Burwell* case inspired Lauren to fight against abortion, she writes, and her uncle's efforts to unite Bible translators motivated her to start up a similar nonprofit to unite pro-life groups. In 2023, she launched Stand for Life with a $2.2 million grant from the Signatry; the stated purpose was to "establish a culture that affirms every human being, including the preborn child, is made in the image of God"—the *imago dei* preached by generations of abortion foes.[38] It brought together antiabortion groups, including the ADF, crisis pregnancy centers, and Live Action—a group banned from several social media platforms for spreading disinformation—to fight abortion in the courts while also working to provide support for mothers.[39]

After *Dobbs*, Lauren wrote an op-ed urging abortion opponents not to "gloat" over the victory but to help women with unexpected pregnancies who didn't know where to turn. After all, she said, "abortion tourism," in which women in restrictive states would travel to states where the procedure was still legal, was only about to grow, and medical abortion was still available by mail. In providing "loving, compassionate, holistic care," she said, the antiabortion movement could achieve its "ultimate goal"—bringing people to Christ, "the One who can save their souls."[40]

In January 2023, Stand for Life held a private forum for antiabortion leaders in Washington, where ADF attorneys gave a briefing on legal strategy in the states and other groups developed a curriculum titled Image of God to share with church groups.[41] A couple of weeks later, several hundred people gathered at the Museum of the Bible for the National Gathering for Prayer and Repentance, an overtly Christian nationalist alternative to the National Prayer Breakfast led by the FRC's Tony Perkins and NAR prophet Jim Garlow. Participants paid $200 a ticket for the event, which started at 6:30 am and didn't include breakfast.[42]

Keynote speaker missionary Andrew Brunson railed against homosexuals, declaring the US "the Babylon of this generation" where "our government and corporations increasingly march under the rainbow flag" and "normalize and celebrate immorality." Spearheading the event was Louisiana congressman and former ADF attorney Mike Johnson, who had sponsored bills against gay marriage and mentioning homosexuality in schools as well as bills to prohibit gender-affirming care for trans youths. At the end of the event, Johnson prayed over more than a dozen fellow members of Congress who took the stage, looking out over the Capitol building in the distance.[43]

Even while the museum was providing a forum for these far-right viewpoints, a more conciliatory message was brought to audiences through a series of Super Bowl ads created to advertise Jesus Christ. One showed images of violent confrontations between people of opposing groups, such as cops and protesters, followed by the tagline "Jesus loved those we hate"—and then "He gets us. All of us. Jesus." The ads, which cost $20 million to reach 110 million viewers, were part of a $100 million campaign funded by the Signatry to rebrand Jesus as neither "left or right" but someone who "experienced challenges and emotions just like we have."[44] While most donors to the campaign were private, one made himself known—David Green, who touted it on Glenn Beck's radio show. "We're wanting to say... that he gets us, he understands all of us," said David, now eighty-one, with thick glasses but a full shock of white hair. "Somehow or another, today we're seen as the haters," he said, and yet in Christ's sacrifice, "we're the ones who've got the best and greatest love story in the world."[45]

The ads for Jesus received both head-scratching and pushback from viewers. "It's a lot of money to spend for a guy who already has some pretty good brand recognition," mentioned one media professor.[46] Observers on social media were more critical, with one saying, "Jesus would want you to use all that money to house the homeless, feed the hungry, clothe the naked, comfort the sick... not put friggin' ads on TV."[47]

Hardcore Christians were just as critical, slamming the ads for being too focused on a "touchy-feely" version of Jesus while underplaying his divinity. Behind the campaign, however, volunteers stood ready to profess a conservative view of Christianity. When a journalist visited a live chat on the "He Gets Us" website, posing as a student questioning their gender identity, they were told that God had created only two genders, male and female, and encouraged to find a "biblical" counselor. "The sponsors of this massive ad campaign," they concluded, "don't buy the loving, accepting version of Jesus they are selling; he is just the bait to attract people they hope to convert."[48]

INDEED, AT THE same time that the Signatry was promoting the "He Gets Us" campaign, with its kinder, gentler Jesus, the organization donated another $18 million to the ADF to continue its attacks on LGBTQ rights and abortion. In 2023, the organization filed a case against the abortion pill mifepristone in Texas before Judge Matthew Kacsmaryk, a former attorney with First Liberty Institute. He issued a brief nationwide injunction against the drug before it was overturned by the Supreme Court.[49]

At the same time, five years after *Masterpiece Cake* had ended in a technicality, the ADF succeeded in bringing another case to court on behalf of web design firm 303 Creative, arguing that it couldn't be forced to design sites for same-sex couples. The Supreme Court ruled 6–3 in favor, a decision Justice Sotomayor called "heartbreaking," noting that "the Court, for the first time in its history, grants a business open to the public a constitutional right to refuse to serve members of a protected class."[50]

The ruling was part of a wider backlash against LGBTQ rights focused particularly on trans people. In 2023, conservative lawmakers introduced over two hundred antitrans bills in twenty-five states, focused on banning gender-affirming transition care, restricting drag performances, forbidding teachers to use chosen pronouns, and limiting trans girls' participation in sports. Many of these bills were based on model legislation authored by the ADF.[51] Despite the attention to these issues, studies showed that less than 1 percent of young people identified as transgender and trans girls actually had no advantage in youth sports.[52]

Religious conservatives used the same verses in Genesis that Lauren Green McAfee used to support the dignity of human beings—that they were created in the "image of God"—to insist that the existence of trans people is counter to God's will. "Male and female he created them," said one Wichita lawmaker in a debate over an ADF-crafted transgender sports bill. "You may not agree with it—those are God's words."[53] Lauren coedited a collection of essays by academics titled *Created in the Image of God* that used the concept of *imago dei* to argue that trans people were counter to God's will. "God's design for his image bearers is that they are gendered male or female," theology professor Gregg Allison writes, disregarding those born intersex as a mere "genetic abnormality."[54]

Even as the ADF was pushing these bills, one of its own ascended to the height of power in Washington as Mike Johnson was tapped as the consensus candidate for speaker, second in line to the presidency. Short, with glasses and a Southern twang, Johnson had a mild-mannered personality that belied a fervent devotion to Christian nationalist principles. He had been one of the biggest proponents of the "Big Lie" that Trump had won the 2020 election, had hung an Appeal to Heaven flag outside his office, and was close to David Barton, whom he praised as having had a "profound influence on me, and my work, and my life in everything I do."[55]

As soon as Johnson became speaker, Barton boasted that he'd been in contact with him about staffing, saying Christian nationalists "have some tools at our disposal now." In an acceptance speech filled with religious imagery, Johnson sounded positively Bartonesque. "America is the only nation in the world that is founded upon a creed," he asserted, "listed with almost theological lucidity in the Declaration of Independence."[56] In a Fox News interview the next day, he recalled someone in the media asking him what he believed: "I said, 'Well, go pick up a Bible off your shelf and read it.' That's my worldview. That's what I believe."[57]

A month later, Johnson was back at the Museum of the Bible at a gala for the National Association of Christian Lawmakers, an overtly Christian nationalist organization that received funding from the ADF and First Liberty Institute to enshrine a "biblical worldview" in law. Unaware that the event was being recorded, he compared himself to Moses, saying God had repeatedly told him during the vote for speaker to prepare for a "Red Sea moment," leading the faithful to the Promised Land. He saw his role as leader in a great struggle as America "engaged in a battle between worldviews," he said. "In the face of these challenges, our hope is in the Lord."[58]

As the Museum of the Bible continued to host Christian nationalist gatherings, it was taking pains to recover from the sins of its past. It instituted new rules on provenance, requiring clear export licenses and a reputable chain of ownership from sellers—essentially stopping the collection of items from Iraq and Egypt. After the embarrassment of the Dead Sea Scrolls publication, the Scholars Initiative closed up shop, at least when it came to studying ancient manuscripts—though the museum has since published some medieval holdings.[59]

Ironically, one of the fragments Dirk Obbink fraudulently sold to the museum turned out to be a significant discovery, a biblical manuscript dating back to the second century CE. Originally, Jerry Pattengale contended that it was an early copy of the book of Matthew that provided evidence of the Bible's reliability over time. Upon further study, Jeffrey Fish, Daniel Wallace, and Michael Holmes determined that it bore similarities to Matthew and Luke but was actually a previously undiscovered text containing sayings of Jesus. If anything, it pointed to the variety of texts circulating at the time of the New Testament's composition.[60]

The museum's exhibits continue to straddle the line between evangelical proselytizing and mainstream respectability. Even as other museums across the country have increasingly engaged in exhibits addressing uncomfortable truths related to race and culture, the museum has stuck to a consistent theme of the truth and goodness of the Bible. In 2023, it opened a large exhibit on the life of Elisabeth Elliot, the missionary who went on to live with the Waodoni in Ecuador, containing nearly one thousand books, photos, and memorabilia. It focused almost exclusively on the brief period between her husband's death and the time she spent living with the tribe, presenting it as an inspirational tale of personal determination and sacrifice. The exhibit was a missed opportunity to examine Elliot's work more critically; it avoided difficult questions about her later reservations about missionary work or the controversy over her role in creating the purity movement.[61]

At the same time, the museum opened a temporary exhibit devoted to scripture and science, including a book owned by Galileo and a communion chalice used on the moon. While sometimes fascinating in its demonstration of scientists often viewing their work through a faith-driven lens, it focused on the ways in which the Bible and Christianity have supported scientific inquiry and none of the ways in which they have conflicted with it—again missing a chance for a more well-rounded examination of the tensions between scientific and faith-based views of the world. It chose its words around evolution particularly carefully: "Modern science continues to reveal remarkable features in plants and animals that are stunning in their complexity, surprising scientists of all beliefs," nodding to intelligent design without explicitly endorsing it.[62]

Halfway across the world, the Iraq National Museum installed a new treasure in 2022, placing the Gilgamesh Dream Tablet in a case of its own in a gallery filled with sculptures and bas-reliefs. Next to it is a placard stating, "Iraq recovered the tablet from the United States of America." The rest of the objects from Hobby Lobby are still in storage as Iraq National Museum staff work to inventory them before researchers can study their contents. Iraq's fight to safeguard its antiquities is far from over, however. State board of antiquities and heritage director Laith Hussein says there are at least fifteen thousand known archaeological sites throughout the country. Add unknown sites, and the number might be more than three times as large. "It's very important to protect these sites from illicit digging and smuggling," Hussein says, "but you cannot make fencing for all of them—it's impossible."[63]

In the summer of 2023, a Spanish film crew was in Iraq filming a documentary about the lost city of Irisaĝrig, where the cuneiform tablets purchased by Steve had originated. They left early in the morning to drive three hours south from Baghdad to check out one of the sites that archaeologist Manuel Molina had determined might be the location of the lost city, using directions and distances written on cuneiform tablets.[64] The sun was already high in the sky when they arrived at a police checkpoint in a beaten-down trailer alongside a shallow lake.

Beyond, on the sunbaked plain, there was clear evidence of the remains of an ancient settlement, with ancient shards of broken pottery covered in patterns etched into them millennia before strewn everywhere on the ground. There were also clear signs of recent looting—large holes with squared-off edges, some large enough to hold several people. One of the police officers escorting the crew said he'd often seen looters in the area and tracked their movements with drones. "But we can't stop them," he said, Arabic music playing on his car radio. "There are so many sites here, and by the time we get to them, they flee."

WITHOUT FANFARE, HOBBY Lobby opened its one thousandth store in the fall of 2023. By now, David Green's net worth had risen to $14 billion, according to *Forbes*, putting him fifty-first on its list of richest Americans.[65] Hobby Lobby was outstripping its competitors, as JoAnn declared Chapter 11 bankruptcy in early 2024.[66] Michaels, too, struggled after a buyout from a private equity firm, cutting costs to reverse declining sales.

Hobby Lobby's success was in part due to a savvy shift in business strategy as the company moved away from its core craft business. Today, stores are only one-quarter filled with craft items such as beads, fabric, and yarn—all pushed toward the back. The most prominent space is taken up by home decor, including picture frames; mugs; ceramic vases; hand towels; garden trellises; Darsee & David candles in scents such as "tropical patchouli," "French toast," and "Grandpa's chair"; and rows of wooden inspirational wall hangings bearing slogans with mismatched fonts, often religious in tone, such as "*Because He lives I can face tomorrow*," "ALL I NEED TODAY *is a little bit of* COFFEE & *a whole lot of* JESUS," and "WASH YOUR HANDS AND SAY YOUR PRAYERS, because *Jesus* & GERMS ARE EVERYWHERE."

On a recent October visit to a Massachusetts superstore, aisles in the front were filled with Christian books, including many of the Green family's own titles, along with a large selection of fake flowers. On the other side were Christmas decorations, which filled another quarter of the store with ornaments, lights, and AI-generated Santa and reindeer art. (Surprisingly little space was devoted to the baby Jesus, with just a single aisle of nativity items.) Despite the season, the store contained no Halloween items, since David said in 2019 that God convinced him "that the current expression of the holiday did not honor him."[67] In 2022, the company quietly stopped stocking Chanukah items as well due to low "customer interest" and the "need to find additional space for some of our stronger categories," according to a statement.[68]

Hobby Lobby still serves entry-level hobbyists as a place to find affordable supplies, said Abby Glassenberg, cofounder and president of the Craft Industry Alliance, which connects independent crafters.

More serious hobbyists usually upgrade to higher-quality small retailers, she said, and some avoid Hobby Lobby entirely because of its religious views. When the company's name comes up in online forums, "I would say one in every three times, someone comments, 'I would never shop there,' " mostly as a result of the birth-control case in the Supreme Court. One crafter Glassenberg knows turned down a lucrative offer to sell her items there because of her political beliefs.[69]

Since COVID, a new generation has discovered macramé and crochet along with Hobby Lobby's record on abortion, LGBTQ rights, and antiquities trafficking, filling Reddit threads and Pinterest boards with digs at the firm. Emma Ujifusa, a queer crafter with a two-tone pixie cut, made a half-hour video titled "Hobby Lobby's Insane History" for their YouTube channel, racking up over 500,000 views in just over a year along with an overwhelming number of comments from viewers vowing to avoid the company.[70]

The criticism has occasionally spiked in communities where Hobby Lobby has opened new stores. In 2022, an LGBTQ rights group in San Luis Obispo, California, tried to spark a boycott, saying, "We should not put more money into the pockets of a family that actively seeks to eliminate the separation of church and state and to make discrimination the law of the land."[71] In 2023, protesters in Keene, New Hampshire, flooded the local newspaper with comments accusing the company "of being racist, sexist, and anti-LGBTQ."[72] The cleverest attack came from a pharmacy tech in Austin, Texas, who used AI to create images showing Hobby Lobby stocking satanic home decor items, apparently fooling some evangelicals who wondered openly if Hobby Lobby's owners had "crossed the line and gone woke?!!"[73]

Evangelicals wondered the same thing when they saw the new "He Gets Us" commercials during the 2024 Super Bowl, featuring natural antagonists, such as a gay man and a priest or a pregnant woman and an abortion protester, with shoes and socks off and a bowl of water. The tagline: "Jesus didn't teach hate. He washed feet." The campaign spent $17 million on the spots, referencing Jesus washing the feet of his disciples, including his betrayer, Judas, the night before his death—a practice adopted by Pentecostal sects such as the Church of God of Prophecy.[74]

"Our goal is to really show that Jesus loved and cared for anyone and everyone," said a spokesman for the campaign, which updated its website to say, "Jesus loves gay people and Jesus loves trans people." The ads were once again met with criticism from both sides, with conservatives condemning them as sinful and liberals finding them hypocritical, alongside social media posts giggling that Jesus had a "foot fetish."[75]

The ads that year were sponsored by a new nonprofit, Come Near, perhaps in an attempt to distance the ads from the Signatry's support for the ADF and other controversial causes. The nonprofit was even more closely tied to the Greens, as it was led by a three-person board consisting of Mart; OneHope's Bob Hoskins; and OneHope executive Marwan Rifka, pastor of a Virginia megachurch. It was also still patently anti-LGBTQ, as Rifka had previously said anyone supporting "gay marriage is thumbing their nose at God," and viewers wanting to learn more were directed to Alpha USA, a network of evangelical Bible study groups that had been criticized for its anti-LGBTQ views.[76]

After *Dobbs*, the ADF pushed to pursue a new goal of fetal personhood, celebrating a 2024 ruling by an Alabama judge that accidental destruction of embryos at an in vitro fertilization clinic could be prosecuted as "wrongful death of a minor." In his ruling, the judge quoted Jeremiah 1:5, "Before I formed you in the womb I knew you," as well as the *imago dei* verse from Genesis to argue that life begins at conception.[77]

The Supreme Court ruled against the doctors in the mifepristone abortion pill case that the ADF had brought in Texas, saying they lacked standing, but left alive the issue of the pill's safety. Justices Alito and Thomas, at least, made no secret about where they stood, advocating for the application of the Comstock Act, an obscure 1873 federal law prohibiting the sending of obscene materials through the mail, to mifepristone. This would effectively create a nationwide ban on medical abortion.[78] Alito appeared to make his views clear in other ways when an Appeal to Heaven flag—which continued to serve as a symbol of Christian nationalist sentiment—flew outside his vacation home, though he attributed the action to his wife.

As Trump once again faced off against Biden in the 2024 election, evangelicals enthusiastically rallied behind their Cyrus. When he released a "God Bless the USA Bible" containing the Constitution and the Declaration of Independence for $60 ($1,000 with the ex-president's signature), many religious observers were outraged. But the faithful snapped them up, earning Trump $300,000 in sales in less than six months.[79] In July 2024, a sniper shot at Trump at a Pennsylvania rally, wounding his ear, and NAR apostles saw Trump's survival as a sign that he had been chosen by God. When Wallnau heard the news, he rushed to his "prayer closet" to embrace a cardboard cutout of the president he kept there.[80]

After Biden suffered a disastrous debate performance that forced him out of the race, Vice President Kamala Harris took over as the Democratic candidate. Wallnau and other NAR prophets castigated her as a "Jezebel"—a racist and sexist reference to a villainous Old Testament queen who persecuted prophets and was ultimately thrown from a window to her death. "With Kamala you have a Jezebel spirit . . . the personification of intimidation, seduction, domination and manipulation," Wallnau said. "She can look presidential and that's the seduction of what I would say is witchcraft."[81]

Behind the scenes, Christian nationalists were a part of a more coordinated attempt to get Trump elected, with the help of the Greens and other wealthy donors. They rallied around a group called the Conservative Partnership Institute (CPI), an affiliation of right-wing nonprofits run by Trump die-hards such as immigration adviser Stephen Miller and former budget director and self-avowed Christian nationalist Russell Vought. After Trump's loss in 2020, the CPI served as a hub to provide legal support for January 6 rioters and to recruit staffers for a Trump second term.[82]

It also coordinated with the Heritage Foundation and other groups to produce a nine-hundred-page master blueprint for Trump 2.0 called Project 2025, a hybrid of Christian nationalist and conservative principles.[83] Abortion would be banned "from the moment of conception" and the Comstock Act used to ban shipments of abortion pills and birth control deemed abortifacients based on the *Burwell* decision. Gender would be redefined as "biological sex recognized at birth"; federal funds would go toward pushing the "biblically based" idea that marriage was only between a man and a woman; and employers would be "free to run their businesses according to their religious beliefs," allowed exemptions on issues "related to marriage, gender, and sexuality."[84]

As details leaked out, the public expressed widespread dissatisfaction with the plan, with only 4 percent viewing it positively and 51 percent seeing it "very negatively." Trump denied even knowing about it despite the large number of former staffers who were involved in its development.[85] Donors to groups that wrote up the plan included the Signatry, which gave $7 million to the CPI between 2020 and 2023 and another $62.6 million to twenty-six other organizations involved in writing Project 2025. A Hobby Lobby spokesperson told the *Wall Street Journal* that the Signatry's "leadership decides how its funds are spent, and that neither Hobby Lobby nor the Greens were aware of the Conservative Partnership Institute and hadn't directed the foundation to support it."[86] (While it is technically true that the Signatry has final say on how to spend its dollars, it does so at the direction of its donors.)

Nevertheless, the Greens supported the CPI indirectly through their continued involvement in the high-worth Christian organization Ziklag. The group ran three campaigns to influence the election, each sporting a military-style moniker. Operation Checkmate was devoted to so-called election integrity, including $800,000 sent to the CPI to help "clean" electoral rolls of "illegal" voters, which in practice often disenfranchises voters of color. Operation Watchtower would exploit antitransgender messaging as a "wedge issue" to turn out conservative voters, according to a video featuring Wallnau, who said that while the left may have won "the homosexual issue . . . on transgenderism there's a problem, and they know it." Last, Operation Steeplechase would coordinate networks of churches to get out the vote in swing counties with a goal of securing thousands of additional Trump voters per state.[87]

That effort included a series of rallies to motivate religious voters that Wallnau dubbed the Courage Tour, a "combination platter" of spiritual revival and political activism. "Jan 6 was not an insurrection, it was an election fraud intervention," he told a crowd in Wisconsin and thousands more watching online. He went on to say the "left is loaded with demons" and compared Trump to the biblical figure of Samson, who would bring down the pillars of "academia, media, and government."[88] Legal experts told ProPublica that Ziklag's work could very well have violated federal election law prohibiting nonprofits from directly supporting candidates, especially after one Courage Tour stop was paired with a Town Hall featuring vice-presidential candidate JD Vance.[89]

Trump's victory in the 2024 election came as a shock to many Americans who'd refused to believe that a twice-impeached convicted felon who spread false conspiracy theories could be reelected. In addition to winning the Electoral College, Trump won a plurality of the popular vote, 77 million (49.9 percent) to Harris's 75 million (48.4 percent). Political pundits scrambled for an answer, blaming inflation, an overreliance by Harris on "woke" political views, or Biden's refusal to bow out sooner.

Few rated the impact of white evangelical voters, who once again voted 80 percent in Trump's favor with a fervency never before seen.[90] A poll by the Public Religion Research Institute showed that 29 percent of Americans identified with Christian nationalist sentiments, and of those, two-thirds believed Donald Trump was "ordained by God" to be president. Over one-third believed that America had "gotten so far off track" that "true American patriots may need to resort to violence in order to save our country."[91]

Steve celebrated with the inauguration crowds in Washington, offering remarks of "faith and unity" at the Christian Inaugural Gala, which featured several Christian nationalist speakers under the theme "Realigned for Restoration." The keynote was offered by NAR prophet Dutch Sheets, who claimed that liberalism was a "genetic disorder" interrupting the patriotic Christian DNA of the Founders that Trump had come to heal.[92]

Over the next few days, Trump moved to implement policies even more extreme than Project 2025. Through a series of executive orders he attempted to gut "woke" government diversity, equity, and inclusion (DEI) programs, cancel birthright citizenship, and freeze government spending at will. Many of Trump's actions furthered Christian nationalist ideals, such as removing abortion-related information from federal websites and particularly targeting trans people. He declared that only "male and female" genders would be recognized by government, banned trans soldiers from the military, rescinded nonbinary markers on passports, and threatened to withhold federal funds from states that allowed trans girls to compete in sports. (Many of these orders were challenged in court, and some overturned.)

He installed Christian nationalists in his cabinet, including Russell Vought as director of the Office of Management and Budget and Fox News commentator Pete Hegseth as defense secretary. Hegseth was a member of an extremist church based on the Reconstructionist teachings of Rushdoony that advocated for civil government to be subject to biblical law, including capital punishment for homosexuals. He had personally derided public schools as an "egalitarian, dystopian LGBT nightmare."[93]

At the National Prayer Breakfast in early February, Trump introduced a new faith office led by Paula White and delegated new Attorney General Pam Bondi to "fully prosecute anti-Christian violence and vandalism" and "move heaven and earth to defend the rights of Christians and religious believers nationwide." (The president of Americans United for Separation of Church and State predicted that the commission would rather "misuse religious freedom to justify bigotry, discrimination, and the subversion of our civil rights laws.")[94] On the same day, the National Gathering for Prayer and Repentance met at the Museum of the Bible, once again chaired by NAR prophet Jim Garlow and the FRC's Tony Perkins and featuring sinners including a woman who'd had an abortion and a "former" homosexual praying for forgiveness from God.[95]

Mike Johnson, now House speaker, again led congresspeople in a public display of repentance, reading a passage of scripture that featured God commanding Solomon to build the temple in Jerusalem, saying, "Do as I command, observe my decrees and laws, and I will establish your royal throne." Applying that sentiment of God-given government to the United States was the culmination of decades of urgent work by evangelicals to create a country based on biblical principles. And at every step of the way, the Green family was there to support it, providing money to spread a biblical worldview throughout the country, establishing the court precedent that unleashed the floodgates of religious liberty, providing justification for the concepts of biblical inerrancy and righteousness and a home base for believers to gather, and supporting a president who promised to deliver on the goals of the Christian Right like no other.

As Americans once again tuned in to the Super Bowl, they watched another "He Gets Us" ad, this time with still images of Americans from all walks of life struggling heroically against the odds, set to Johnny Cash's cover of English synth-pop group Depeche Mode's "Personal Jesus." A group of Black men helping push a car out of the snow. An organ donor and recipient. A man power-washing away anti-immigrant graffiti. A man in a cap reading "John 3:16" embracing a queer person at a Pride parade. A police officer helping a woman in distress. A crowd lifting up a disabled man in a wheelchair. "Jesus showed us what greatness really is," the tagline read. "He gets us. All of us."

In an interview with *The Oklahoman*, David Green once again touted the spirit of love behind the ads. "It's not a Hobby Lobby thing, it's not a Green family thing," he said. "We're showing that this is Jesus, and we should also embrace everybody because Jesus did." David waved away criticism that this inclusive version of Christianity seemed at odds with—if not diametrically opposed to—evangelicals' support of Donald Trump, with his relentless targeting of women, trans people, immigrants, and people of color.

"We're driven more by who is more in favor of what we feel lines up more with God's word," David responded. "We're talking to people about their eternal life," he added, hinted at subtly in the ad by the reference to John 3:16: *For God so loved the world that he gave his only begotten Son, that whosoever believeth in him should not perish, but have eternal life.* "Hopefully by seeing that scripture," David said, "they know he gets you and he loves you. He died for you. Hopefully we'll draw people closer to him."[96]

Epilogue

As we drive back from the ancient city of Ur, my Iraqi translator, Yasir, asks me a question—what is this Green family all about? A chain-smoking journalist with dirty-blond hair and mustache, he's been translating conversations for days with a smile as we've driven back and forth between Baghdad and archaeological sites across south-central Iraq. Now, as we stop at a roadside cafeteria and eat a delicious lamb-and-rice *quzi*, I explain that the Greens believe that the Bible is the true and inerrant word of God and acquired trafficked antiquities from Iraq in part to try to show that.

"That's ridiculous!" he says. The Bible can't be true—because the Qur'an is. "The prophet Muhammed had direct contact with God, but these people who wrote the Bible were writing things they did not see themselves," he continues. "They've shown that there are many things in the Qur'an that are scientifically true." I smile as we debate the nature of truth. But in the back of my mind, I think, *This is the problem with fundamentalism—someone else is always going to have another fundamentalist view incompatible with yours.*[1]

How do we reconcile that as a society—especially a society like America that has from its earliest days been a land of immigrants and transplants, each with their own culture and worldview? Going on five generations, the Greens have passed down a set of beliefs that goes far beyond life or death—immortal souls are at stake. I can only imagine the pressure they must feel. David Green's very sense of self-worth depended on showing his mother, Marie, that his love of merchandising had a higher purpose than making money by buying low and selling high. Through introducing people to the truth of the Bible and the good news of Jesus, he was able to buy souls as well.

Each successive generation has inherited this burden, an anointing that sets them apart from the corrupted world to bring others into the light of the one spiritual truth. No one can doubt their sincerity. They've clearly seen the benefits in their own lives of giving themselves to Jesus, as they've prospered to a degree unimaginable to their ancestors. By attempting to subordinate their own will to God's, they've looked to an even greater reward: a pristine afterlife or, better yet, the second coming of Christ, who will transform our world into an earthly paradise for those who believe. Given that set of principles, is it any wonder that the Greens have devoted their lives to sharing that vision with others?

If the afterlife is the only life that matters, then all our earthly endeavors (including selling beads and hokey wall hangings) are a mere grain in the sands of eternity. And yet, there's irony in the fact that in the family's desire to save those around them, they've caused a great deal of suffering through the beliefs they've pushed on other, unwilling people. While they and other evangelicals may say that scripture speaks for itself—*sola scriptura*—the truth is that any literary work is open to interpretation, including the Bible. Perhaps especially the Bible.

Despite the contention of David, Steve, Mart, and Lauren that the Bible tells a simple unified story of fall and redemption from Adam to Jesus, it's a complicated book, chock-full of stories, histories, laws, and fables told by different people for different reasons throughout history, defined as much by what's been excluded as what's been included. One can say that God inspired it all, but the fact that Jews and Christians, Protestants and Catholics have all come to different conclusions about its meaning over centuries points to the more subjective nature of its teaching.

Based on short texts within the vast storehouse of the Bible's wisdom—that God created man in his image, that he charged humans with dominion over the earth, that he knew you in the womb—the Greens and their fellow spiritual warriors have professed a worldview that has caused pain and persecution to countless people, denying women the right to choose birth control or end a pregnancy and trans teenagers the right to live as their authentic selves. Whether they are "right" is beside the point—their certainty that they are saving immortal souls obscures the fact that they are harming people in the only realm we can be sure exists, which seems the very opposite of what Jesus would have taught.

True, Hobby Lobby has taken measures to help its employees, including closing on Sundays and raising the minimum wage (though by David's own admission, those actions also aided the company's bottom line); other perks, such as chaplains and marriage counselors, were offered with half an eye toward leading people to Jesus. Actions taken for the simple sake of improving people's quality of life have been much rarer—especially considering the hundreds of millions the family spent to distribute scripture around the world.

The Greens are quick to see God's hand in their successes, opening doors to get a film made or to collect vast numbers of artifacts from overseas to glorify his name. When things fall apart, however, they are equally quick to cast blame on others, as Mart did when his film bombed over the hiring of a gay actor or Steve did when the millions of dollars he'd spent amassing his collection of ancient antiquities turned out to be futile. The Lord moves in mysterious ways indeed.

Perhaps the Green family will be proven right in the end as we all face our eternal judgment, or perhaps all of their cash will have been spent for nothing. In the meantime, they'll no doubt continue trying to impose their biblical worldview on America, doing everything they can do to create their version of heaven on earth while dreaming of their eternal reward.

ACKNOWLEDGMENTS

This project has been massive in scope, stretching from more than four thousand years ago to the present day and from the plains of Oklahoma to the deserts of Iraq; there's no way I could have written and reported it without an incredible amount of help. First and foremost, I have to thank my agent, Gillian MacKenzie, who immediately saw the potential in this project and not only encouraged me to pitch it for publication but also rightly urged me to think big in how I approached it.

I also have to thank my editors at PublicAffairs: Colleen Lawrie, who helped me dramatically expand the scope and ambition of the book, and Meagan Levinson, who helped rein it in to a dynamic and readable narrative. In addition, I have to thank all of the other members of the PublicAffairs, Basic Books, and Hachette team who helped make this book a reality, including publisher Lara Heimert, assistant editor Kristen Kim, editorial assistant Adi Gandhi, attorneys Elisa Rivlin and Andrew Goldberg, publicist Meghan Roberts, and marketer William Hearn. I literally couldn't have done it without them!

A number of scholars lent their time and energy to helping me understand the significance of cuneiform, papyrus, and other artifacts as well as the complex trade in biblical antiquities—including a number who helped expose the trafficking of objects that ended up in the Greens' collection. A big thanks to Lynda Albertson, Joel Baden, David Bradnick, Eckart Frahm, Patty Gerstenblith, Roberta Mazza, Manuel Molina, and Candida Moss. Also thanks to Steve Epstein of the US Department of State, Amanda Long of the Academic Research Institute of Iraq, and John Russell of MassArt for valuable background.

HSI was generous with its time in helping make agents J. P. Labbat and Brent Easter available for interviews and fact-checking details of their investigations. Thanks to J. P. and Brent for their candor and detail as well as to Lou Martinez, Brandon Montgomery, Marie Ferguson, Chrissy Cutitta, and Stephanie Pagones for their assistance. Thanks also to prosecutors Karin Orenstein and Ann Brickley for their additional insight.

A number of people helped me track down information in archives that were helpful in providing background and context to this story. A big shout-out to all the archivists and librarians who patiently answered my questions or helped pull material from the stacks, including Bob McFadden at the Goddard Library of the Gordon-Conwell Theological Seminary, Timothy Corum of the Flower Pentecostal Heritage Center, David Roebuck and David Mills of the Dixon Pentecostal Research Center, Jamie Cumby and Scott Ellwood of the Grolier Library, and all of the staff who assisted me at Altus Public Library, Bethany High School, Harvard University Libraries, Oklahoma City Public Library, the Oklahoma Historical Society's Research Center, and Oral Roberts University.

I also relied heavily on the expertise of guides and translators as I followed the trail of biblical artifacts overseas. I have to thank Ahmed Seddik, who helped arrange guides and interviews in Egypt, as well as Galal Mossa, Hamdy Mohammed, Khalid Farag, Father Justin Sinaites, and Roba Ahmed, who helped guide and translate in Cairo, Oxyrhynchus, Sinai, and other locations, as well as Shaaban Abdel Gawad, who agreed to meet and let me inside his investigations. In Iraq, I relied on Talal Ajeel to help arrange my itinerary (thanks to Kirk

Johnson for the introduction!) as well as Yasir Alani, Bashar Nouri, Mohammed Alghadhban, and Hussein "Tommy" Abbas to guide me on the ground in Baghdad, in Babylon, and in and around the elusive Irisaĝrig.

Others in the long list of people I have to thank for adding to the richness of this book include historian Alice Procter of Uncomfortable Art Tours for a fascinating tour of artifacts in the British Museum; Mohammednouri Alsheekh, Mohammed Husham Al Fityan, and Hussein Albadrani of the Iraq Embassy in Washington for perspective on the return of antiquities to Iraq; Jeff Kloha and Charlotte Clay for an illuminating tour and candid interview at the Museum of the Bible; Rob Schenck and Rabbi Or Rose for allowing me to take their incredibly informative class on Christian nationalism through Hebrew College in Newton and Rob for further taking me inside his own evangelical past; Andrew Seidel of the Freedom from Religion Foundation and Peter Montgomery of Right Wing Watch for taking me inside right-wing political networks; Jesse Eisenger and Andy Kroll of ProPublica for discussing their reporting on the Christian nationalist group Ziklag; Paul Williamson for his insight into the Church of God of Prophecy; Laurie Styron for helping me better understand DAFs; and Abby Glassenberg of the Craft Industry Alliance and Emma Ujifusa of aspen in the moment for helping me understand crafters' perspectives. I also have to thank the former employees of the Museum of the Bible who took me behind the scenes into the museum and its collections.

It's crucial to get early feedback on a manuscript in the midst of writing, and I was lucky to have a number of gifted writers and readers read and comment on versions of the book in progress. Dawn Oates was an incredibly valuable sounding board early in the process; Linda Wertheimer gave me very helpful advice on trimming and focusing the book; and Claudia Garcia-Rojas, Francis Murphy, Patty Caya, Theresa Lynn, Susan Schirl Smith, and Ann Blanding all gave insightful advice that helped me frame and polish the work. Finally, I am grateful for all of the patient love and support of Zoë Wangstrom and Kate Doucette, who always believed in me and gave me endless amounts of encouragement while I was in the throes of writing and needed it most. Much love to both of you! And last but not least, I have to thank my family for their patience as I spent long nights at my desk—including my two wonderful children, Zachary and Cleo Blanding, who inspire me with their creativity and compassion each and every day.

NOTES

Prologue

1. J. P. Labbat, interview by author, August 24, 2023.
2. *The Dream Tablet: Relating Part of the Epic of Gilgamesh*, Christie's, private catalog, 2014.
3. USA v. One Cuneiform Tablet Known as the "Gilgamesh Dream Tablet" (amended complaint), 4–5, 37.
4. Labbat interview.
5. Jeff Kloha, interview by author, November 30, 2023.
6. Steve Green and Jackie Green with Bill High, *This Dangerous Book: How the Bible Has Shaped Our World and Why It Still Matters Today* (Zondervan, 2017), 30.
7. "Hobby Lobby Stores," *Forbes*, 2024; "David Green & Family," *Forbes*, April 2, 2024.
8. Brian Solomon, "Meet David Green, Hobby Lobby's Biblical Billionaire," *Forbes*, September 18, 2012.
9. Pew Research Center, "8 in 10 Americans Say Religion Is Losing Influence in Public Life," March 15, 2024.

Chapter One: In the Beginning

1. Walter Green, "God Gave a Picture of the Church of God," *White Wing Messenger* (accessed through the Consortium of Pentecostal Archives, https://pentecostalarchives.org), July 16, 1932.
2. Green, "God Gave a Picture."
3. Green, "God Gave a Picture."
4. Green, "God Gave a Picture."
5. Green, "God Gave a Picture."
6. Green, "God Gave a Picture."
7. James E. Green obituary, *Mexico Weekly Ledger*, September 27, 1923; James E. Green obituary, *Weekly Intelligencer*, September 26, 1923; RFerrario, "Green Family Picture," Ancestry.com.
8. Walter Green obituary, *Ventura County Star*, January 27, 1964; Population Schedule for 4th Precinct South Buffalo, Johnson County, Wyoming, Census of the United States, 1910, District 70, Sheet 2; Population Schedule for Grant Township, Marion County, Kansas, 1920, District 74, Sheet 2.

9. James Stone, *The Church of God of Prophecy* (White Wing Publishing House, 1977), 16; Ralph Hood, Peter Hill, and Paul Williamson, *Psychology of Religious Fundamentalism* (Guilford Press, 2005), 87–88.

10. Vinson Synan, *The Holiness-Pentecostal Tradition: Charismatic Movements in the Twentieth Century* (William B. Eerdmans, 2007), 84–85, 98.

11. Grant Wacker, *Heaven Below: Early Pentecostals and American Culture* (Harvard University Press, 2001), 35–36; R. G. Robins, *A.J. Tomlinson: Plainfolk Modernist* (Oxford University Press, 2004), 186–187.

12. Stone, *The Church of God of Prophecy*, 29.

13. A. J. Tomlinson, *General Assembly Annual Addresses (GAAA)*, 1911–1927, 32.

14. Tomlinson, *GAAA*, 54, 151.

15. Tomlinson, *GAAA*, 83.

16. Hood et al., *Psychology of Religious Fundamentalism*, 91–93; Synan, *The Holiness-Pentecostal Tradition*, 81; Paul Williamson, interview by author, December 4, 2025.

17. Edith Blumhofer, *Restoring the Faith: The Assemblies of God, Pentecostalism, and American Culture* (University of Illinois Press, 1993), 88–89.

18. Stone, *The Church of God of Prophecy*, 33.

19. Stone, *The Church of God of Prophecy*, 39.

20. A. J. Tomlinson, *God's Pioneer*, Heritage Series, vol. 4 (1962; repr., White Wing Publishing House, 2011), 58.

21. Stone, *The Church of God of Prophecy*, 52; Wacker, *Heaven Below*, 147.

22. Population Schedule for Emporia Township, Lyon County, Wyoming, Census of the United States, 1930, District 56-14, Sheet 23; Green, "God Gave a Picture."

23. Marie Lark, "Gracious Revival Given in Answer to Prayer," *White Wing Messenger*, November 5, 1932.

24. Tomlinson, *God's Twentieth Century Pioneer*, 23, 105.

25. Omar A. Shultz, "Victorious War Cry Is Heard from Kansas," *White Wing Messenger*, September 30, 1933.

26. Synan, *The Holiness-Pentecostal Tradition*, 187.

27. Stone, *The Church of God of Prophecy*, 447.

28. Hood et al., *Psychology of Religious Fundamentalism*, 112; Williamson interview.

29. Hood et al., *Psychology of Religious Fundamentalism*, 109.

30. Marie Lark, "Jacob S. Lark," *White Wing Messenger*, March 30, 1935; *Minutes of the Annual Assembly*, Church of God of Prophecy, 1937; "A Revival Starts," *Emporia Gazette*, December 16, 1937.

31. U.S. Index to Public Records, 1950–1993, 1994–2019.

32. "News and Revivals," *White Wing Messenger*, May 10, 1941; "Evangelic Services Scheduled by Church," *Arizona Republic*, March 30, 1946; "Rev. Walter Green, Evangelist," *Arizona Daily Star*, March 29, 1947.

33. *Minutes of the 41st World-Wide Annual Assembly of the Church of God*, September 11–17, 1946, 6, 11; "Blessings of Assembly Still Fresh in Our Souls," *White Wing Messenger*, October 12, 1946.

34. "New Churches Organized Reported This Week," *White Wing Messenger*, August 14, 1948; "New Churches Reported Organized This Month," *White Wing Messenger*, August 20, 1949; "God Mindful of His Children," *White Wing Messenger*, May 28, 1949.

35. David Green and Bill High, *Giving It All Away... and Getting It All Back Again: The Way of Living Generously*, special ed. (Zondervan, 2017), 33.

36. "Hobby Lobby Executive Describes Company's Legacy of Faith," Baptist News Global, January 28, 2009.

37. "Executive Session: David Green," *Journal Record* (Oklahoma City), April 30, 2010.

38. Green and High, *Giving It All Away*, 79; "What We Believe: Tithing and Giving," Church of God of Prophecy website, www.cogop.org/what-we-believe.

39. Williamson interview.

40. Proverbs 3:9–10, King James Version (KJV).

41. "Self-Denial Offerings," *White Wing Messenger*, August 18, 1951; Stone, *The Church of God of Prophecy*, 69.

42. Green and High, *Giving It All Away*, 31; Mart Green, "ORU Alumni Connection (Part 1 of 9)," YouTube, June 6, 2008.

43. Green and High, *Giving It All Away*, 36.

44. Green and High, *Giving It All Away*, 35; David Green and Bill High, *A Generous Life: 10 Steps to Living a Life Money Can't Buy* (Zondervan, 2019), 141–142.

45. "Demonstration by Church to Be at Airport," *Mangum Star*, May 24, 1956; "10,000 C.P.M.A. Members in 1955," *White Wing Messenger*, January 15, 1955.

46. Suzanne Jordan Brown, "The Modest Billionaire," *Charisma* magazine, January 31, 2005.

47. "David Green" transcript, Voices of Oklahoma, Oklahoma Historical Society, October 6, 2009, 3; David Green and Dean Merrill, *More Than a Hobby: How a $600 Startup Became America's Home and Craft Superstore* (Thomas Nelson, 2010), 2, 34–35; "Executive Session."

48. "Executive Session."

49. Jonathan Root, *Oral Roberts and the Rise of the Prosperity Gospel* (William B. Eerdmans, 2023), 7–22.

50. Root, *Oral Roberts and the Rise of the Prosperity Gospel*, 37–38; 3 John 1:2 (KJV).

51. Root, *Oral Roberts and the Rise of the Prosperity Gospel*, 39–44.

52. Root, *Oral Roberts and the Rise of the Prosperity Gospel*, 47.

53. Root, *Oral Roberts and the Rise of the Prosperity Gospel*, 57–66; R. G. Robins, *Pentecostalism in America* (Praeger, 2010), 88–89; Kate Bowler, *Blessed: A History of the American Prosperity Gospel* (Oxford University Press, 2018), 48–49.

54. Bowler, *Blessed*, 51–53.

55. Church of God of Prophecy, *These Necessary Things: The Doctrine and Practices of the Church of God of Prophecy* (White Wing Publishing House), 1960, 34.

56. Root, *Oral Roberts and the Rise of the Prosperity Gospel*, 76.

57. "Hobby Lobby CEO David Green," Indiana Wesleyan University, YouTube, April 3, 2013.

58. "Business Is Dull at Police Station," *Altus (OK) Times-Democrat*, August 18, 1957.

59. "28 Firms Join Pupil Program," *Altus Times-Democrat*, September 18, 1958; "Altus DE Club Initiation," *Altus Times-Democrat*, November 19, 1958.

60. Green and Merrill, *More Than a Hobby*, 1, 3, 6.

61. Green and Merrill, *More Than a Hobby*, 6.

62. Green and High, *Giving It All Away*, 37.

63. Alicia Lindberg, "David Green," *Risen Magazine*, December 2017.

64. Green and Merrill, *More Than a Hobby*, 7.

65. *Bulldog*, Altus Senior High School yearbook, 1961; Cecil Chesser, *Tenderly He Leads Us, 1892–1992: A Centennial History of the First Baptist Church, Altus, Oklahoma* (Altus Printing Company, 1991), 101.

66. "Thomas Osie and Ina Turner," *Book of Remembrance*, Altus Centennial Memorial Center, 2007, 217–218.

67. *Bulldog*, Altus Senior High School yearbook, 1960, 22.

68. "Second Term Class of B.T.C.," *White Wing Messenger*, April 23, 1960, 4; "Cleveland, B.T.C.," *White Wing Messenger*, April 30, 1960, 11; Green and High, *Giving It All Away*, 36, 38.

69. "Miss Turner, Mr Green Pledge Vows," *Altus Times-Democrat*, February 12, 1961.

70. Green and Merrill, *More Than a Hobby*, 189.

71. "Hospital News Items," *Lawton (OK) Constitution*, September 3, 1961.

72. "Beware of the lust of the flesh," A. J. Tomlinson exhorted in a 1919 address, reprinted in the *White Wing Messenger* in 1955. "If men do not know how to behave themselves and keep in their proper places in relation to women they are not worthy of membership" in the church ("'Thou Shalt Not Commit Adultery,'" *White Wing Messenger*, April 23, 1955). In 1959, Milton Tomlinson warned young people against sexual immorality: "Never form too close an intimacy with the opposite sex even if they are brothers and sisters in the Lord. Give no place to the adversary. Abstain from the very appearance of evil" (Church of God of Prophecy, *These Necessary Things*, 1976, 61).

73. Green and High, *Giving It All Away*, 38.

74. The Encyclopedia of Oklahoma History and Culture, Oklahoma Historical Society; Odie B. Faulk, *The Making of a Merchant: R. A. Young and T.G. & Y. Stores* (Western Heritage Books, 1980), 111–116; 191–194.

75. "Shawnee Newcomers," *Shawnee (OK) News-Star*, October 10, 1962.

76. "David Green" transcript, Voices of Oklahoma, 14.

77. "Executive Session"; "David Green" transcript, Voices of Oklahoma, 5–6.

78. "David Green" transcript, Voices of Oklahoma, 28; Green and Merrill, *More Than a Hobby*, 190.

79. "TG&Y Center Opening Set," *Oklahoman* (Oklahoma City), December 7, 1966; "Offer Made to Purchase Shares in Risk Firm," *Oklahoman*, September 16, 1971.

80. "David Green" transcript, Voices of Oklahoma, 28; Green and High, *Giving It All Away*, 39.

81. Bowler, *Blessed*, 69.

82. Bowler, *Blessed*, 69–75.

83. Bowler, *Blessed*, 63–68.

84. "David Green" transcript, Voices of Oklahoma, 35.

85. "TG&Y Center Opening Set"; Mortgage Deed, 11012 Blue Stem Dr., Oklahoma City, August 15, 1966.

86. "Bethany," Encyclopedia of Oklahoma History and Culture.

87. Green and Merrill, *More Than a Hobby*, 131–132.

88. Green and High, *A Generous Life*, 134.

89. Green and Merrill, *More Than a Hobby*, 10; "David Green" transcript, Voices of Oklahoma, 6.

90. Green and Merrill, *More Than a Hobby*, 10; "David Green" transcript, Voices of Oklahoma, 6; "Executive Session."

Chapter Two: Be Fruitful and Multiply

1. "David Green" transcript, Voices of Oklahoma, 6; Green and Merrill, *More Than a Hobby*, 172.

2. "David Green" transcript, Voices of Oklahoma, 7; Green and Merrill, *More Than a Hobby*, 173–174.

3. Green and Merrill, *More Than a Hobby*, 174–175; Green and High, *Giving It All Away*, 39, 79; "Hobby Lobby CEO David Green"; "Executive Session."

4. "Executive Session"; Green and High, *Giving It All Away*, 79.

5. Green and Merrill, *More Than a Hobby*, 176–177.

6. *Oklahoman*, August 9, 1972, 37.

7. Green and Merrill, *More Than a Hobby*, 22; "David Green" transcript, Voices of Oklahoma, 9; Donna Hoffman, "Hobby Lobby: Tales of Success," *Oklahoman*, January 20, 1991.

8. Green and Merrill, *More Than a Hobby*, 177.

9. "David Green" transcript, Voices of Oklahoma, 8–9; Green and Merrill, *More Than a Hobby*, 177.

10. Green and Merrill, *More Than a Hobby*, 22; Green and High, *Giving It All Away*, 40; "David Green" transcript, Voices of Oklahoma, 9.

11. Linda Miller, "Cash Registers Jingle for Two Entrepreneurs," *Oklahoman*, December 21, 1980.

12. Green and Merrill, *More Than a Hobby*, 77, 177.

13. Green and Merrill, *More Than a Hobby*, 13; Green and High, *Giving It All Away*, 40; Ecclesiastes 9:10 (David's translation).

14. Green and Merrill, *More Than a Hobby*, 178–179; advertisement, *Oklahoman*, May 15, 1975; Miller, "Cash Registers Jingle."

15. "Marie Green" obituary, *Odessa (TX) American*, April 10, 1975; Green and High, *A Generous Life*, 11.

16. Green and High, *Giving It All Away*, 39.

17. John Turner, *Bill Bright and Campus Crusade for Christ: The Renewal of Evangelicalism in Postwar America* (University of North Carolina Press, 2008), 13, 23–24, 98–146.

18. Bowler, *Blessed*, 75.

19. Rob Boston, *The Most Dangerous Man in America? Pat Robertson and the Rise of the Christian Coalition* (Prometheus Books, 1996), 26–29.

20. Robert H. Krapohl and Charles H. Lippy, *The Evangelicals: A Historical, Thematic, and Biographical Guide* (Greenwood Press, 1999), 77–79; William Packard, *Evangelism in America: From Tents to TV* (Paragon House, 1988), 166; Robins, *Pentecostalism in America*, 112–115.

21. Kristin Kobes Du Mez, *Jesus and John Wayne: How White Evangelicals Corrupted a Faith and Fractured a Nation* (Liveright, 2021), 67–71, 78–79; Randall Stephens and Karl Giberson, *The Anointed: Evangelical Truth in a Secular Age* (Belknap Press, 2011), 109–111; "His Father's Son," *Christianity Today*, April 22, 1988; Dale Buss, *Family Man: The Biography of Dr. James Dobson* (Tyndale House Publishers, 2005), 14–17.

22. Du Mez, *Jesus and John Wayne*, 79–82; Buss, *Family Man*, 41–48; Stephens and Giberson, *The Anointed*, 111–117.

23. James Dobson, *Dr. Dobson Answers Your Questions* (Grason, 1982), 451–453; Buss, *Family Man*, 350–355.

24. Genesis 1:28 (KJV); Rousas John Rushdoony with Herbert W. Titus, *The Institutes of Biblical Law: A Chalcedon Study* (Craig Press, 1973), 14.

25. Michael J. McVicar, *Christian Reconstruction: R. J. Rushdoony and American Religious Conservatism* (University of North Carolina Press, 2015), 4–5.

26. Stephens and Giberson, *The Anointed*, 79; William Einwechter, "Stoning Disobedient Children," *Chalcedon Report*, January 1, 1999.

27. Julie Ingersoll, *Building God's Kingdom: Inside the World of Christian Reconstruction* (Oxford University Press, 2015), 17–19, 222–224.

28. Ingersoll, *Building God's Kingdom*, 1–7; Du Mez, *Jesus and John Wayne*, 78.

29. McVicar, *Christian Reconstruction*, 5, quoting Laurence Iannaccone.

30. Ingersoll, *Building God's Kingdom*, 1–2, 41.

31. Du Mez, *Jesus and John Wayne*, 75–77.

32. Du Mez, *Jesus and John Wayne*, 75–77; Don Veinot, Joy Veinot, Ron Henzel, and Midwest Christian Outreach, *A Matter of Basic Principles: Bill Gothard and the Christian Life* (21st Century Press, 2002), 249–276.

33. *Shiny Happy People* (documentary), episode 2, "Growing Up Gothard," Amazon, 2023.

34. Bill Gothard, *Institute in Basic Youth Conflicts: Research in Principles of Life* (Institute in Basic Youth Conflicts, 1981), 36.

35. Wilfred Bockelman, *Gothard: The Man and His Ministry: An Evaluation* (Quill Publications, 1976), 52.

36. Bockelman, *Gothard*, 117.

37. Tom Minnery, "Gothard Staffers Ask Hard Questions," *Christianity Today*, February 6, 1981.

38. "The Gothard Files: The Scandal, 1980," *Recovering Grace* blog, February 20, 2014.

39. "Conflict Viewed," *Oklahoman*, October 5, 1975.

40. Bill Gothard, *The Amazing Way: To Complete Success, to Great Wealth, to Total Health, to Lasting Joy* (Institute in Basic Life Principles, 2010), back cover.

41. Lindberg, "David Green"; "Hobby Lobby CEO David Green."

42. Green and High, *Giving It All Away*, 50; *Broncho*, Bethany High School yearbooks, 1976–1979.

43. Green and High, *Giving It All Away*, 50–51; *Broncho*, 1978–1981; "Bethany 40, Piedmont 0," *Oklahoman*, October 18, 1980.

44. "8112 Brownsville Dr., Bethany," Zillow.com.

45. Mortgage Deed, 8112 Brownsville Drive, December 1, 1980; Mortgage Deed, Springfield Properties, December 1, 1980.

46. "Best Land Deals," *Oklahoman*, December 28, 1980; "Groundbreaking," *Oklahoman*, January 10, 1981.

47. Former Bethany High student, interview by author (name withheld by mutual agreement).

48. Green and High, *A Generous Life*, 95–97; "Meet the Family That Is Building a World-Class Museum Dedicated to the Bible," *Philanthropy Roundtable*, November 25, 2011.

49. Grady Phelps, "More Turn to Hobbies," *Corpus Christi Times*, February 6, 1975; advertisement, *Oklahoman*, June 5, 1975.

50. Advertisement, *Oklahoman*, March 13, 1978.

51. Advertisement, *Tulsa World*, December 5, 1976.

52. "David Green" transcript, Voices of Oklahoma, 15–16.

53. "David Green" transcript, Voices of Oklahoma, 14–15.

54. Green and Merrill, *More Than a Hobby*, 44.

55. Green and Merrill, *More Than a Hobby*, 122–123.

56. Jamelle Bouie, "'God Does Not Regard the Fetus as a Soul,'" *Slate*, March 25, 2014; Exodus 21:22–25.

57. Jonathan Dudley, "When the 'Biblical View' for Evangelicals Was That Life Begins at Birth," *Religion Dispatches*, September 27, 2019; Raymond Peters, "Is Abortion a Form of Murder?," *Tampa Bay Times*, January 30, 1971.

58. Randall Balmer, *Thy Kingdom Come: How the Religious Right Distorts the Faith and Threatens America, an Evangelical's Lament* (Basic Books, 2006), 13–14.

59. Balmer, *Thy Kingdom Come*, 13–15.

60. Balmer, *Thy Kingdom Come*, 16–17; Harry R. Jackson and Tony Perkins, *Personal Faith, Public Policy* (Frontline, 2008), 2–3.

61. James Risen, "How America's Evangelicals Turned Themselves into an Anti-Abortion Machine," *The Intercept*, May 12, 2022; D. Michael Lindsay, *Faith in the Halls of Power: How Evangelicals Joined the American Elite* (Oxford University Press, 2007), 54; Barry Hankins, *Francis Schaeffer and the Shaping of Evangelical America* (Library of Religious Biography, William B. Eerdmans, 2008), 180–191.

62. Jeremiah 1:5, New International Version (NIV).

63. Psalm 139: 13–15 (NIV).

64. Daniel Williams, *God's Own Party: The Making of the Christian Right* (Oxford University Press, 2010), 45; Jim Dawson, "Televangelists: The Marketing of Salvation," *LA Weekly*, January 25, 1979.

65. "12,000 Rally for Christian Morality," United Press International, April 28, 1979.

66. Williams, *God's Own Party*, 156.

67. Karen Garloch, "Anti-Abortion Marchers Rally," *Cincinnati Enquirer*, June 25, 1979.

68. Steve Hill, "Falwell Seeking 'Moral Majority,'" *Tampa Tribune*, August 25, 1979.

69. "Notes from the General Assembly," Church of God of Prophecy pamphlet, 1979, 32–33.

70. "Notes from the General Assembly," 46, 63–64.

71. Green and Merrill, *More Than a Hobby*, 191–193; Green and High, *Giving It All Away*, 85–86; Green and High, *A Generous Life*, 106–108; David Green and Bill High, *Leadership Not by the Book: 12 Unconventional Principles to Drive Incredible Results* (Baker Books, 2022), 22–24.

72. Green and High, *A Generous Life*, 62.

73. Green and High, *Giving It All Away*, 81.

Chapter Three: Thy Kingdom Come

1. Green and High, *Leadership Not by the Book*, 42.

2. Miller, "Cash Registers Jingle"; "Hobby Lobby Buys 3.7 Acres for Storage," *Oklahoman*, December 27, 1981.

3. Green and Merrill, *More Than a Hobby*, 26, 180.

4. Miller, "Cash Registers Jingle."

5. Miller, "Cash Registers Jingle."

6. Advertisement, *Oklahoman*, January 10, 1981; Martha Skaggs, "Gas City News," *Okmulgee Daily Times*, October 21, 1984.

7. Miller, "Cash Registers Jingle."

8. Green and Merrill, *More Than a Hobby*, 194.

9. "This Book Is Alive," *Gospel Patrons*, April 6, 2017.

10. "Stepping Out on Faith," *Journal Record*, December 10, 2007.

11. Green and Merrill, *More Than a Hobby*, 193; advertisement, *Oklahoman*, June 22, 1981; advertisement, *Oklahoman*, July 27, 1981.

12. "Best-Selling Christian Books," *The Sentinel*, July 1, 1981.

13. Green and Merrill, *More Than a Hobby*, 193.

14. "Steve Green on the Rise of Hobby Lobby," *The Carey Nieuwhof Leadership Podcast*, November 11, 2019.

15. "Green-Maddox," *Oklahoman*, January 30, 1982; *Broncho*, 1976–1979.

16. Advertisement, *Oklahoman*, March 14, 1982; advertisement, *Oklahoman*, March 28, 1982.

17. Green and High, *Leadership Not by the Book*, 14.

18. Green and High, *Leadership Not by the Book*, 42.

19. "Penn Square Bank," Encyclopedia of Oklahoma History and Culture; Brianna Bailey, "Lessons from Penn Square," *Journal Record*, July 3, 2012; Joe Wertz, "Penn Square Bank," NPR, July 5, 2012.

20. Green and Merrill, *More Than a Hobby*, 176.

21. Turner, *Bill Bright and Campus Crusade for Christ*, 192–193; Boston, *The Most Dangerous Man in America?*, 29.

22. John Fea, *Believe Me: The Evangelical Road to Donald Trump* (Wm. B. Eerdmans, 2018), 46–47; Michael Kinsley, "Republican Platform's Abortion Plank Has a Long History," *LA Times*, August 31, 2012.

23. Du Mez, *Jesus and John Wayne*, 94.

24. Katherine Stewart, *The Power Worshippers: Inside the Dangerous Rise of Religious Nationalism* (Bloomsbury Publishing, 2022), 102.

25. Du Mez, *Jesus and John Wayne*, 106

26. McVicar, *Christian Reconstruction*, 144–147.

27. Ronald Reagan, "Evil Empire Speech," March 8, 1983, Voices of Democracy Project.

28. Turner, *Bill Bright and Campus Crusade for Christ*, 200.

29. Williams, *God's Own Party*, 202–205.

30. McVicar, *Christian Reconstruction*, 175.

31. Jerry Falwell, *Listen, America!* (Doubleday, 1980), 15–20.

32. Falwell, *Listen, America!*, 54, 145–147.

33. Williams, *God's Own Party*, 206.

34. David Oliver Relin, "When Greed Was Good," *Scholastic Update*, March 8, 1991; Donald Liebenson, "Robin Leach Defined the Wealth-Obsessed 80s," *Vanity Fair*, August 28, 2018; Conor Friedersdorf, "When Donald Trump Became a Celebrity," *Atlantic*, January 6, 2016.

35. Bowler, *Blessed*, 77–78, 100–107.

36. Bowler, *Blessed*, 100–107.

37. Bowler, *Blessed*, 101; Root, *Oral Roberts and the Rise of the Prosperity Gospel*, 176–187.

38. "Hobby Lobby Store Set," *Wichita Eagle-Beacon*, February 20, 1984.

39. "Hobby Lobby Plans New Building Open House," *Oklahoman*, March 30, 1984; "Hobby Lobby Next Site Midwest City," *Oklahoman*, May 19, 1985.

40. John Herbers, "Christian Bookstores Feature Reagan Books," *New York Times*, September 29, 1984.

41. "Meet the Family."

42. Green et al., *This Dangerous Book*, 16.

43. Cathy Lynn Grossman, "Hobby Lobby's Steve Green Stands on Faith," Religion News Service, March 17, 2014.

44. "Green-Chartier," *Tulsa World*, August 26, 1984.

45. Robin Galiano, "Ministry ALERT," *Longview (TX) News-Journal*, April 1, 2000; Steve Green, "Sharing Life Purpose Health with Thousands of Employees," Institute in Basic Life Principles (video), 2009.

46. "Bethany High Lists Outstanding Students," *Oklahoman*, May 11, 1984.

47. *Broncho*, 1982–1985.

48. Steve Green and Bill High, *This Beautiful Book: An Exploration of the Bible's Incredible Story Line and Why It Matters Today* (Zondervan, 2019), 27–28.

49. Green and Merrill, *More Than a Hobby*, 168.

50. Green and High, *Giving It All Away*, 62.

51. Green and Merrill, *More Than a Hobby*, 180–182.

52. Green and High, *Leadership Not by the Book*, 25; Green and Merrill, *More Than a Hobby*, 183; "David Green" transcript, Voices of Oklahoma, 11.

53. Green and Merrill, *More Than a Hobby*, 180–184; Green and High, *Leadership Not by the Book*, 25–26.

54. Green et al., *This Dangerous Book*, 65–69.

55. Green and Merrill, *More Than a Hobby*, 27, 183; Green and High, *Giving It All Away*, 63; Green and High, *Leadership Not by the Book*, 26.

56. "Lett-Green," *Oklahoman*, May 31, 1986.

57. "Executive Session."

58. Green and Merrill, *More Than a Hobby*, 184.

59. Green and Merrill, *More Than a Hobby*, 184.

60. "David Green" transcript, Voices of Oklahoma, 12; "Executive Session."

61. Green and Merrill, *More Than a Hobby*, 185.

62. Solomon, "Meet David Green."

63. Green and Merrill, *More Than a Hobby*, 185.

64. Proverbs 16:18 (KJV).

65. Williams, *God's Own Party*, 222; Peter Steinfels, "Moral Majority to Dissolve; Says Mission Accomplished," *New York Times*, June 12, 1989.

66. Williams, *God's Own Party*, 211–220.

67. McVicar, *Christian Reconstruction*, 202–203, 213–214.

68. Williams, *God's Own Party*, 222.

69. Green et al., *This Dangerous Book*, 73–74.

70. Ingersoll, *Building God's Kingdom*, 61.

71. Green and Merrill, *More Than a Hobby*, 152.

72. Randy C. Alcorn, *Money, Possessions, Eternity* (Tyndale House Publishers, 2003), 140, 150.

73. Randy C. Alcorn, *The Treasure Principle*, Lifechange Books (Multnomah Publishers, 2001), 20–21, 76.

74. Donna Hoffman, "Hobby Lobby: Tales of Success," *Oklahoman*, January 20, 1991.

75. Green and Merrill, *More Than a Hobby*, 194.

76. Du Mez, *Jesus and John Wayne*, 132–133.

77. Peter Steinfels, "Gulf War Is Proving Bountiful for Some Prophets of Doom," *New York Times*, February 2, 1991.

78. Williams, *God's Own Party*, 230.

79. Du Mez, *Jesus and John Wayne*, 139.

80. Williams, *God's Own Party*, 231.

81. Williams, *God's Own Party*, 232; Fea, *Believe Me*, 62; Du Mez, *Jesus and John Wayne*, 140.

82. Williams, *God's Own Party*, 234–235.

83. Williams, *God's Own Party*, 238.

84. Stephens and Giberson, *The Anointed*, 119.

85. Stephens and Giberson, *The Anointed*, 127; Leviticus 18:22 (KJV); Leviticus 20:13 (KJV); 1 Corinthians 6:9–10 (NIV).

86. Harvey Cox, *How to Read the Bible* (HarperOne, 2015), 180–182; Kenneth Davis, *Don't Know Much About the Bible: Everything You Need to Know About the Good Book but Never Learned* (Eagle Brook, 1998), 431.

87. Buss, *Family Man*, 275–276; David Kirkpatrick, "Alliance Defending Freedom's Crusade Against Trans Rights," *The New Yorker*, October 9, 2023; McVicar, *Christian Reconstruction*, 199.

88. Kelsey Davis, "The Law That Changed Religious Freedom Forever," *Deseret Morning News*, November 15, 2023; 42 US Code § 2000bb-1, Legal Information Institute, Cornell Law School.

89. Cynthia Dees, "Hobby Lobby Posts Gains," *Tulsa World*, December 8, 1991; Jon Denton, "Hobby Lobby Set to Open Five Stores," *Oklahoman*, December 26, 1993.

90. Green and Merrill, *More Than a Hobby*, 84–88. Despite persistent rumors that Hobby Lobby's lack of barcodes is due to some Christians associating them with the "mark of the beast" in Revelation, there's no evidence of that (Izz Scott LaMagdeleine, "Is the Reason Hobby Lobby Doesn't Use Bar Codes Because They're the 'Mark of the Beast'?," Snopes, July 18, 2023).

91. Jon Denton, "Ever Growing Hobby Lobby Becomes Model Success Story," *Oklahoman*, August 27, 1995.

92. Brianna Bailey, "OKC Shop to Sell Items Born in the USA," *Oklahoman*, August 25, 2015; Mart D. Green v. United States, No. 5:13-cv-01237 (February 9, 2016).

93. Green and High, *Giving It All Away*, 98; Green and High, *A Generous Life*, 62.

94. Solomon, "Meet David Green."

95. Green and High, *Giving It All Away*, 87–88.

Chapter Four: Teach All Nations

1. In *Faith in America*, Steve identifies this as Christmas Day 1995 (Steve Green, *Faith in America: The Powerful Impact of One Company Speaking Out Boldly* [Looking Glass Books, 2011]); however, Hobby Lobby's first Christmas ad ran in 1995, so this must have been 1994. Regardless, the 1995 paper had just as many references to Christmas and Jesus.

2. Green and Merrill, *More Than a Hobby*, 159; Green, *Faith in America*, 16.

3. Green and Merrill, *More Than a Hobby*, 159–160; Green, *Faith in America*, 16–17.

4. Pat Gilliland, "Christmas Unites Christians"; Jim Standard, "Believers Write Christmas Story with Their Lives"; Pete DuPont, "Measures of the Wise No Different Than in Jesus' Time"; "Pilgrims Throng to Holy Birthplace in Celebration"; and "Clinton Mixes Christmas Traditions," *Oklahoman*, December 25, 1994.

5. Green and Merrill, *More Than a Hobby*, 160; Green, *Faith in America*, 17.

6. Advertisements, *Oklahoman*, December 25, 1995, 23.

7. Green and Merrill, *More Than a Hobby*, 160.

8. "Oklahoma City Bombing," History: Famous Cases and Criminals, Federal Bureau of Investigation.

9. R. O. Gilcher, "Two Oklahoma City Disasters: The Oklahoma City Bombing and the Tornadoes," *Baylor University Medical Center Proceedings* 14, no. 2 (April 2001): 140–143.

10. Jack Money, "Promised Land to Ask for Funds for Memorial," *Oklahoman*, May 1, 1998.

11. Jon Denton, "Ever Growing Hobby Lobby Becomes Model Success Story," *Oklahoman*, August 27, 1995.

12. Gypsy Hogan, "Family Sees Business as Means to Eternal End," *Oklahoman*, June 22, 1997.

13. Kris Dudley, "Mardel's Growing Again," *Tulsa World*, November 13, 1996.

14. Cox, *How to Read the Bible*, 205–207; Margaret Tarpley, "Stereotypes of Women Are Not 'Left Behind' in the Popular Series," *God Faith Media*, January 31, 2002.

15. Hogan, "Family Sees Business"; "Church to Observe 60th Anniversary," *Oklahoman*, June 19, 1998; "Special Thanks from Bulgaria," *White Wing Messenger*, April 11, 1998.

16. "Mardel Founder, Mart Green, & Wycliffe Investment," Marden Christian and Education, YouTube, September 4, 2020.

17. David Stoll, *Fishers of Men or Founders of Empire? The Wycliffe Bible Translators in Latin America* (Lawrence Hill, 1982), 28–29.

18. Ethel Emily Wallis and Mary Angela Bennett, *Two Thousand Tongues to Go: The Story of the Wycliffe Bible Translators* (Harper & Row, 1964), 54; Revelation 7:9 (NIV); Stoll, *Fishers of Men or Founders of Empire?*, 22–23.

19. Stoll, *Fishers of Men or Founders of Empire?*, 46; Philip Yancey, "Cam Townsend's Mission: Let God Do the Talking," *Christianity Today*, June 18, 1982; Rick Vanderknyff, "The Word Heard 'Round the World," *Los Angeles Times*, November 19, 1995.

20. Stoll, *Fishers of Men or Founders of Empire?*, 3–17.

21. "This Week in Religion," *Oklahoman*, May 7, 1996.

22. Rob Hoskins, *Hope Delivered: Affecting Destiny Through the Power of God's Word* (Charisma House, 2012), 25–29; Bob Hoskins, *Affect Destiny: The Book of Hope Story* (Book of Hope, 2003), 5–13; Bob Hoskins, *They Still Want the Truth: The Miracles, the Victories, the Conquest of Literature Evangelism* (Life Publishers International, 1987), 57–58.

23. "Book of Life International," Hobby Lobby website (accessed through the Wayback Machine, Internet Archive).

24. Green and High, *Giving It All Away*, 82–84; Hoskins, *Hope Delivered*, 74–77.

25. "Shelter Provides Home," *Oklahoman*, January 12, 1998; Church of God of Prophecy, Annual Meeting Notes 1998.

26. "Our Easter and Christmas Messages," Hobby Lobby website, December 1, 1998 (accessed through the Wayback Machine, Internet Archive).

27. "Our Easter and Christmas Messages," Hobby Lobby website, December 1, 1998 (accessed through the Wayback Machine, Internet Archive).

28. Buss, *Family Man*, 159–160.

29. Williams, *God's Own Party*, 241.

30. Du Mez, *Jesus and John Wayne*, 147–148.

31. Dan Gilgoff, *The Jesus Machine: How James Dobson, Focus on the Family, and Evangelical America Are Winning the Culture War* (St. Martin's Press, 2007), 107–110; Williams, *God's Own Party*, 242.

32. Liz Charlotte Grant, "Elisabeth Elliot, Flawed Queen of Purity Culture, and Her Disturbing Third Marriage," *Revealer*, February 6, 2024; Jonathan Poletti, "The Purity Hoax," *Medium*, August 12, 2019.

33. Jared Burkholder, "Before 'True Love Waits' There Was Josh McDowell and Petra," *Anxious Bench* blog, December 26, 2018.

34. Sarah Moslener, *Virgin Nation: Sexual Purity and American Adolescence* (Oxford University Press, 2015), 109–118; Linda Kay Klein, *Pure: Inside the Evangelical Movement That Shamed a Generation of Young Women and How I Broke Free* (Touchstone, 2018), 23–26.

35. Lucy S. R. Austen, *Elisabeth Elliot: A Life* (Crossway, 2023), 505–506.

36. Julie Lyons, "Virgin Academy," *Dallas Observer*, July 20, 1995.

37. Warranty Deed, Par Group Hospitality to Kimray Inc., Oklahoma County Registry of Deeds, book 6533, p. 2163; David Zizzo, "Bible-Based Youth Program Setting Up Shop," *Oklahoman*, January 23, 1994.

38. "Character First and Bill Gothard," *Heresy in the Heartland* blog, September 28, 2013; Robin Galiano, "Ministry ALERT," *Longview News-Journal*, April 1, 2000.

39. Kathy Mulady, "Mayor Hopes to Train City of Angels," *Spokesman-Review*, May 10, 1999.

40. IBLP promotional video, featured in *Shiny Happy People* (documentary), episode 3, "Duggar Family Secrets," Amazon, 2023.

41. Ron Henzel and Don Venoit, "Bill Gothard's Evangelical Talmud—Part 2," *Midwest Christian Outreach*, November/December 1997.

42. Steve Green, "Sharing Life Purpose Health with Thousands of Employees," IBLP, 2009.

43. Linda Caillouet, "Long Vacant, as Training Hub," *Arkansas Democrat-Gazette*, August 30, 1997; Laurie Davies, "Finding a New Home," *Tyler (TX) Morning Telegraph*, March 31, 2000.

44. Warranty Deed, Kimray to Hob Lob, December 30, 1999, Oklahoma County Registry of Deeds, Book 7830, pp. 1477–1478; Property Deed Transaction History, 520 W Main Street, Oklahoma County Assessor; Quitclaim Deed, Hob-Lob to IBLP, December 28, 2000, Oklahoma County Registry of Deeds, Book 7986, pp. 1658–1659.

45. Kyle Ringo, "Ex–CU Buffs Coach Bill McCartney Apologizes for Gay Comment," *Daily Camera* (Boulder, CO), December 1, 2010.

46. "This Year, Sky's the Limit for Promise Keeper Rally," *Tulsa World*, May 25, 1996; "'Keeping the Promise' Conference Scheduled," *Oklahoman*, June 28, 1997.

47. "'Baby Shower' to Benefit Crisis Centers," *Tulsa World*, July 15, 1997; "Baby Shower Set," *Oklahoman*, June 21, 2000.

48. Fea, *Believe Me*, 64.

49. Green, *Faith in America*, 20–22; Gorden Legge, "Power of Prayer Worked Wonders with '60s Teens," *Calgary Herald*, February 13, 1993; Jennifer LeClaire, "Dick Eastman Sees Nation-Shaking Prophetic Promise Come True," *Charisma* magazine, April 11, 2016.

50. Dick Eastman, *Love on Its Knees* (Chosen Books, 1989), 13–17; Dick Eastman, *The Jericho Hour* (Creation House, 1994), 10–21.

51. Eastman, *Jericho Hour*, 68.

52. Green, *Faith in America*, 22–23; Eastman, *Beyond Imagination: A Simple Plan to Save the World* (Chosen Books, 1997), 35.

53. "Crafty Competitors: Nation's Top Crafts Chains Prepare to Meet Head On," *Fort Worth Star-Telegram*, January 16, 1998; Gypsy Hogan, "State Entrepreneurs Sweep Competition," *Oklahoman*, November 25, 1997.

54. "David Green" transcript, Voices of Oklahoma, 24; Green and Merrill, *More Than a Hobby*, 133–134.

55. Jaan VanValkenburgh, "God Comes First at Firms," *Commercial Appeal*, February 28, 1998; Green and Merrill, *More Than a Hobby*, 134–135.

56. Bryan Bydalek, "A Day for Rest," *Grand Island Independent*, April 19, 1998.

57. Randy Tucker, "Hobby Lobby Practicing What It Preaches," *Omaha World-Herald*, May 24, 1998.

58. Green and Merrill, *More Than a Hobby*, 135–136.

59. VanValkenburgh, "God Comes First at Firms."

60. "Meet the Family."

61. Robert L. Schenck, *Costly Grace: An Evangelical Minister's Rediscovery of Faith, Hope and Love* (Harper Books, 2018), 3, 38–43, 158, 166–167.

62. "U.S. Senate Leadership Expected to Join Religious Leaders to Confer Ten Commandments Leadership Award," PR Newswire, January 7, 2000; "Business Owners Honored," *Oklahoman*, January 9, 2000.

63. Jonathan Sprowl, "Mart Green: On a Quest to Eliminate Bible Poverty," *Outreach*, March 5, 2019; "This Book Is Alive," *Gospel Patrons*, April 6, 2017.

64. Sprowl, "Mart Green: On a Quest"; "This Book Is Alive"; "A Moment in Time Story with Mart Green," Faith Driven Entrepreneur, March 14, 2022.

65. "On a Quest"; "This Book Is Alive"; "Bringing Faith Stories to the Screen with Mart Green," Crossroads/100 Huntley, February 12, 2015.

66. Sprowl, "Mart Green: On a Quest"; "This Book Is Alive."

67. Sprowl, "Mart Green: On a Quest."

68. Sprowl, "Mart Green: On a Quest."

69. Bearing Fruit Communications Inc., Certificate of Incorporation, Filing No. 2100610722, Oklahoma Secretary of State, September 18, 1998.

70. Pat Gilliland, "Campaign Promotes Reading of the Bible," *Oklahoman*, February 3, 1999.

71. Mark Moring, "From Film Neophyte to Movie Mogul," *Christianity Today*, April 26, 2005.

72. Green, *Faith in America*, 28, 30–32.

73. Green, *Faith in America*, 32; Jay Grelen, "Hobby Lobby Seeks Higher Mission," *Oklahoman*, April 23, 2000.

74. Green and Merrill, *More Than a Hobby*, 163–164; Green, *Faith in America*, 32–33.

75. Richard Mize, "Hobby Lobby Expands for Distribution," *Oklahoman*, December 2, 1999.

76. Green and High, *Giving It All Away*, 64–65.

77. Risen, "How America's Evangelicals"; Green and High, *Giving It All Away*, 65; 2 Samuel 6:7–8.

78. Psalms 24:1 (NIV), quoted in Green and High, *Leadership Not by the Book*, 29.

79. Cam Fortems, "Christian Group Bids on Tranquille Property," *Canadian Press*, October 16, 1999.

80. Robin Galiano, "Ministry ALERT," *Longview News-Journal*, April 1, 2000.

81. Bill Hanna, "Hobby Lobby Buys Former Ambassador University Campus," *Fort Worth Star-Telegram*, March 26, 2000; Davies, "Finding a New Home."

82. Green and High, *Leadership Not by the Book*, 34.

83. Green and High, *Leadership Not by the Book*, 32.

84. "This Book Is Alive."

Chapter Five: Good Book

1. Bob Smietana, "Americans Are Fond of the Bible, Don't Actually Read It," Lifeway Research, April 25, 2017.

2. John Gabel, Charles Wheeler, and Anthony York, *The Bible as Literature: An Introduction*, 5th ed. (Oxford University Press, 2006).

3. John Barton, *A History of the Bible: The Story of the World's Most Influential Book* (Penguin Books, 2019), 29; Karen Armstrong, *The Bible: A Biography* (Grove Press, 2008), 14–15.

4. Armstrong, *The Bible*, 14–15.

5. Armstrong, *The Bible*, 15.

6. Armstrong, *The Bible*, 20–25; Barton, *A History of the Bible*, 41–42; Gabel et al., *The Bible as Literature*, 63, 111.

7. Gabel et al., *The Bible as Literature*, 93.

8. The order here follows the Hebrew Bible, leaving out the books of Ruth and Chronicles and considering Samuel and Kings as one book each.

9. Deuteronomy 20:16–17 (NIV).

10. Joshua 6:21 (NIV).

11. See, for example, Jacob L. Wright, *Why the Bible Began: An Alternative History of Scripture and Its Origins* (Cambridge University Press, 2023).

12. Barton, *A History of the Bible*, 25–29.

13. Barton, *A History of the Bible*, 48–49.

14. Andrew L. Seidel, Dan Barker, and Susan Jacoby, *The Founding Myth: Why Christian Nationalism Is Un-American* (Union Square & Co., 2021), 160–165.

15. Davis, *Don't Know Much About the Bible*, 207–209; Barton, *A History of the Bible*, 55–56.

16. Armstrong, *The Bible*, 34–35; Bart D. Ehrman, *Misquoting Jesus: The Story Behind Who Changed the Bible and Why* (HarperOne, 2007), 18–19.

17. Barton, *A History of the Bible*, 90; Gabel et al., *The Bible as Literature*, 126–132.

18. James Kugel, *How to Read the Bible: A Guide to Scripture, Then and Now* (Free Press, 2008), 550–555; Kenneth C. Davis, *Don't Know Much About the Bible*, 226; Amy-Jill Levine and Marc Zvi Brettler, *The Bible with and Without Jesus: How Jews and Christians Read the Same Stories Differently* (HarperOne, 2023), 267.

19. Gabel et al., *The Bible as Literature*, 68, 152–158; Barton, *A History of the Bible*, 98–99; Armstrong, *The Bible*, 40–41.

20. Barton, *A History of the Bible*, 152–154; Gabel et al., *The Bible as Literature*, 175; Armstrong, *The Bible*, 48–53.

21. Kugel, *How to Read the Bible*, 550–551; Davis, *Don't Know Much About the Bible*, 225–227; Levine and Brettler, *The Bible with and Without Jesus*, 266–272.

22. Barton, *A History of the Bible*, 209.

23. Corinthians 15: 3–4 (NIV).

24. Levine and Brettler, *The Bible with and Without Jesus*, 101.

25. Barton, *A History of the Bible*, 189–190; Austin Farrer, *The Revelation of St John the Divine: A Commentary on the English Text* (Oxford: Clarendon Press, 1964), 37.

26. Davis, *Don't Know Much About the Bible*, 392.

27. Armstrong, *The Bible*, 67–68; Levine and Brettler, *The Bible with and Without Jesus*, 4.

28. Gabel et al., *The Bible as Literature*, 125–127.

29. Cox, *How to Read the Bible*, 158.

30. Acts 2:4 (NIV); Acts 3:6 (NIV).

31. Cox, *How to Read the Bible*, 190–191; Davis, *Don't Know Much About the Bible*, 461–462.

32. Armstrong, *The Bible*, 103–115; Barton, *A History of the Bible*, 339–348.

33. Armstrong, *The Bible*, 97–98, 129–132; Barton, *A History of the Bible*, 493.

34. Armstrong, *The Bible*, 140–141; Barton, *A History of the Bible*, 369–370.

35. Barton, *A History of the Bible*, 390–392; Armstrong, *The Bible*, 160–164.

36. Mark A. Noll, *In the Beginning Was the Word: The Bible in American Public Life, 1492–1783* (Oxford University Press, 2016), 38–70.

37. Barton, *A History of the Bible*, 415.

38. Matthew Tindal, *Christianity as Old as the Creation* (London: published by the author, 1730), 186.

39. Armstrong, *The Bible*, 192–195.

40. Armstrong, *The Bible*, 176–178.

41. Fea, *Believe Me*, 82.
42. Noll, *In the Beginning*, 327.
43. Noll, *In the Beginning*, 307–315.
44. Mark A. Noll, *America's Book: The Rise and Decline of a Bible Civilization, 1794–1911* (Oxford University Press, 2022), 110–111.
45. Noll, *America's Book*, 225–242, 405–430.
46. Noll, *America's Book*, 413.
47. Noll, *America's Book*, 431–435, 442–443, 474–475.
48. Armstrong, *The Bible*, 197.
49. George M. Marsden, *Fundamentalism and American Culture: The Shaping of Twentieth Century Evangelicalism, 1870–1925* (Oxford University Press, 1980), 14, 16.
50. Krapohl and Lippy, *The Evangelicals*, 37; Armstrong, *The Bible*, 198.
51. Krapohl and Lippy, *The Evangelicals*, 43.
52. Krapohl and Lippy, *The Evangelicals*, 46–49; Marsden, *Fundamentalism and American Culture*, 184–188.
53. Krapohl and Lippy, *The Evangelicals*, 121–122.
54. Josh McDowell, *Evidence That Demands a Verdict: Historical Evidences for the Christian Faith* (Here's Life Publishers, 1979), 107–112; Josh McDowell, *More Than a Carpenter*, English/Arabic bilingual ed. (Living Books, 1977), 24.
55. McDowell, *Evidence That Demands a Verdict*, 113, 74.
56. Steve Green, Sean McDowell, and Scott Rae, "This Beautiful Book," *Thinking Biblically* (podcast), March 12, 2020.

Chapter Six: Peace Be with You

1. Mark Ellis, "The Filmmaker Who Never Went to the Movies," Assist News Service, 2006; Jim Stafford, "Leap of Faith," *Oklahoman*, October 15, 2004.
2. Steve Saint, *End of the Spear: A True Story* (Tyndale House Publishers, 2005), 299.
3. Ellis, "Filmmaker Who Never"; Stafford, "Leap of Faith."
4. Moring, "From Film Neophyte to Movie Mogul."
5. Phil Cooke, "Bill Ewing," *Phil Cooke and the Change Revolution*, December 29, 2008 (accessed through the Wayback Machine, Internet Archive).
6. Revelation 7:9 (NIV).
7. Stafford, "Leap of Faith."
8. *Beyond the Gates of Splendor*, directed by Jim Hanon (Bearing Fruit Entertainment, 2002).
9. Lucas Bessire, "The Real Point of the Spear," *Revealer*, May 3, 2006; Casey High, "End of the Spear," *How Do We Know? Evidence, Ethnography and the Making of Anthropological Knowledge*, ed. Liana Chua, Casey High, and Timm Lau (Cambridge Scholars, 2008), 82–84.
10. Stoll, *Fishers of Men or Founders of Empire?*, 281–284.
11. High, "End of the Spear."
12. Elisabeth Elliot, *The Savage My Kinsman*, 40th anniversary ed. (Vine Books, Servant Publications, 1996), 119–121; Austen, *Elisabeth Elliot*, 319–320; Ellen Vaughn and Joni Earekson Tada, *Becoming Elisabeth Elliot* (B&H Books, 2020), 225–226.
13. Joe Kane, *Savages* (Knopf, 1995), 139.
14. Casey High, "'A Little Bit Christian,'" *American Anthropologist* 118, no. 2 (June 2016): 270–283.
15. Williams, *God's Own Party*, 246–251.
16. Schenck, *Costly Grace*, 203.

17. David Domke, "George W. Bush and the Gospel of Freedom and Liberty," *Seattle Times*, May 1, 2005.

18. Williams, *God's Own Party*, 252–256.

19. Mark Galli, "Now What?," *Christianity Today*, September 1, 2001.

20. Tricia Pemberton, "Edmond to Be the Site of 300th Hobby Lobby Store," *Oklahoman*, June 10, 2003; "Expansion," *Oklahoman*, May 7, 2004.

21. Gregory Potts, "Seeking Biblical Profits," *Oklahoman*, December 20, 2000.

22. Elizabeth Camacho Wiley, "One of Nation's Richest Men Works for God," *Oklahoman*, October 23, 2003.

23. Emily Battle, "Hobby Lobby Beliefs, Profits," *News & Advance*, March 3, 2003.

24. Randy Ellis, "Ill-Famed Nursing Home Heads Towards New Life as School," *Oklahoman*, August 3, 2001.

25. Kathryn Buckstaff, "Mel Tillis Theatre Will Become Church," *Springfield (MO) News-Leader*, July 10, 2002; Brian Bus, "Hobby Lobby Chief Buys Branson Theater," *Oklahoman*, July 13, 2002.

26. Michael Higgins, "Evangelical Church Gets Former Corporate Site," *Chicago Tribune*, March 4, 2003.

27. Battle, "Hobby Lobby Beliefs."

28. Green 1993 v. Internal Revenue Service, US Court of Appeals, Tenth Circuit, FindLaw, 2018.

29. Lindsay, *Faith in the Halls of Power*, 163–169.

30. Darren E. Grem, *The Blessings of Business: How Corporations Shaped Conservative Christianity* (Oxford University Press, 2016), 126.

31. Michael Blanding, "Jesus@Work," *Boston* magazine, June 2005.

32. Lindsay, *Faith in the Halls of Power*, 171, 177.

33. Lindsay, *Faith in the Halls of Power*, 180–181; Grem, *Blessings of Business*, 121–123, 149–161.

34. "David Green" transcript, Voices of Oklahoma, 20–21.

35. Green and Merrill, *More Than a Hobby*, 167.

36. "David Green" transcript, Voices of Oklahoma, 21.

37. Green and High, *Leadership Not by the Book*, 74–80.

38. Green and High, *Leadership Not by the Book*, 74–80.

39. Josh Mankiewicz, "Pastor with a Purpose," *NBC News*, October 3, 2004; Cathy Lynn Grossman, "This Evangelist Has a 'Purpose,'" *USA Today*, July 21, 2003.

40. Hugh Hewitt, "The Force Multiplier," *Daily Standard*, January 29, 2003.

41. Rick Warren, *The Purpose-Driven Life: What on Earth Am I Here For?* (Zondervan, 2002), dedication, 20.

42. "The Purpose-Driven Life Sells 10 Million Copies," PR Newswire, November 19, 2003.

43. "About Chad," Chad Allen Online; Bruce Vilanch, "Chad Allen: His Own Story," *Advocate*, October 9, 2001; Chad Lazzari, interview by author, February 14, 2026.

44. Mark Moring, "Christian Studio Explains Hiring of Gay Actor," *Christianity Today*, January 26, 2006; "Chad Allen on End of the Spear," *Doctor Quinn Times*; Neela Banerjee, "Evangelical Filmmakers Criticized for Hiring Gay Actor," *New York Times*, February 2, 2006; "Korg 70,000 B.C.," *Destined to Denver*, January 2010; Adam Vary, "His Grown-up Christmas List," *Advocate*, November 25, 2003; Lazzari interview.

45. Steve Saint and Mart Green, "The End of the Spear Controversy," Eternal Perspective Ministries, February 21, 2006; Lazzari interview.

46. "Seeds of the Martyrs: The Real Life Story Behind 'End of the Spear,'" 700 Club, Christian Broadcasting Network; Richard Ostling, "Famed Missionary Martyrdom 50 Years Ago Ultimately Saved the Assailants' Tribe," Associated Press, January 19, 2006; Lazzari interview.

47. Williams, *God's Own Party*, 257.

48. Buss, *Family Man*, 364.

49. Buss, *Family Man*, 374.

50. James C. Dobson, *Marriage Under Fire: Why We Must Win This War* (Multnomah Publishers, 2004), 12–15; Stephens and Giberson, *The Anointed*, 128–129.

51. Williams, *God's Own Party*, 256–263.

52. Stafford, "Leap of Faith."

53. "Beyond the Gates of Splendor," Internet Movie Database.

54. Michelle Goldberg, "Stealing Christmas," *Inlander* (Spokane, WA), December 7, 2005.

55. Williams, *God's Own Party*, 263–264.

56. "The Lemon Test," Pew Research Center, May 14, 2009.

57. Van Orden v. Perry, 545 U.S. 677 (2005), June 27, 2005.

58. Williams, *God's Own Party*, 265.

59. "James Dobson Speaks on Miers," ABC News, October 12, 2005.

60. Andy Kroll, Andrea Bernstein, and Ilya Marritz, "We Don't Talk About Leonard," ProPublica, October 11, 2023; Charlie Savage, "Decades Ago, Alito Methodically Laid Out Strategy," *New York Times*, June 25, 2022.

61. Jenifer Nii, "Hobby Lobby Entering Utah," *Deseret Morning News*, March 29, 2006.

62. Aleksandrs Rosen, "Gates Tops Forbes 400 List," *Tulsa World*, September 23, 2005.

63. Tricia Pemberton, "Success Is a Hobby for Family," Knight-Ridder Business News, April 24, 2005.

64. James Davis, "A Supersite for All Things Evangelical," *South Florida Sun Sentinel*, August 14, 2004.

65. Ostling, "Famed Missionary Martyrdom 50 Years Ago"; "Licensing Program Unveiled for 'End of the Spear,'" PR Newswire, October 6, 2005.

66. Catherine Edman, "Marketing to Churches Crucial," *Chicago Daily Herald*, January 20, 2006; newscast (no headline in original), KTUL Tulsa, January 18, 2006.

67. Lori Smith, "Book and Movie Commemorate Missionary Martyrdom," *Publisher's Weekly*, January 4, 2006.

68. Stephen Holden, "Waging War and Peace in the Amazon Basin," *New York Times*, January 20, 2006.

69. Jami Bernard, "Movie Digest," *New York Daily News*, January 20, 2006.

70. Casey High, "Victims and Martyrs," *Anthropology and Humanism* 34, no. 1 (June 2009): 41–50.

71. Banerjee, "Evangelical Filmmakers Criticized."

72. Albert Mohler, "What Were They Thinking?," *Albert Mohler* blog, January 20, 2006.

73. Richard Ostling, "Gay Actor Stirs Flap," Associated Press, February 2, 2006.

74. Saint and Green, "End of the Spear Controversy."

75. Randy Alcorn, "Perspectives on End of the Spear and the Chad Allen Controversy," Eternal Perspective Ministry, February 1, 2006.

76. Dan Kachikis, "'I Feel Betrayed,'" *Christianity Today*, February 8, 2006; Tim Brister, "Roger Youderian's Son-in-Law Speaks Out," *Provocations & Paintings* blog, February 1, 2006.

77. Sam Hodges, "To Blunt Pointed Criticisms, Moviemakers Turn to Larry Ross," *Dallas Morning News*, February 18, 2006.

78. Jonathan Poletti, "God's Gay Movie," Medium, July 26, 2020.

79. "The Mystery of Mart Green," News on 6 (Tulsa, OK), May 5, 2009.

80. Hosea 8:7 (KJV).

81. Lazzari interview.

Chapter Seven: One Nation Under God

1. *America's Godly Heritage*, directed by David Barton, 2005, 0:00–0:12.

2. *America's Godly Heritage*, 7:36–9:49.

3. *America's Godly Heritage*, 12:05.

4. Green, *Faith in America*, 18.

5. Russell Shorto, "How Christian Were the Founding Founders?," *New York Times*, February 11, 2010.

6. Green, *Faith in America*, 18.

7. Green, *Faith in America*, frontispiece; advertisement, *Oklahoman*, July 2, 2006.

8. Green, *Faith in America*, frontispiece; advertisement, *Oklahoman*, July 2, 2006.

9. Nate Blakeslee, "King of the Christocrats," *Texas Monthly*, September 2006; Nehemiah 2:17 (NIV).

10. David Barton, *The Myth of Separation: What Is the Correct Relationship Between Church and State? A Revealing Look at What the Founders and Early Courts Really Said* (WallBuilder Press, 1993 [1992]), 41–42, 29.

11. Barton, *Myth of Separation*, 209–216.

12. David Barton, *America, to Pray or Not to Pray? A Statistical Look at What Happened When Religious Principles Were Separated from Public Affairs* (WallBuilder Press, 1991), 113.

13. Blakeslee, "King of the Christocrats."

14. Stephens and Giberson, *The Anointed*, 84; David Brockman, "Christian Americanism and Texas Politics Since 2008," Baker Institute for Public Policy, March 2020.

15. "The 25 Most Influential Evangelicals in America," *Time* magazine, February 7, 2005.

16. Ingersoll, *Building God's Kingdom*, 196; *WallBuilders* broadcast, August 19, 2011.

17. Stephens and Giberson, *The Anointed*, 85–86; Robert Alley, "Public Education and the Public Good," *William and Mary Bill of Rights Journal* (Summer 1995): 316–317.

18. Steven K. Green, *Inventing a Christian America: The Myth of the Religious Founding* (Oxford University Press, 2015), 11.

19. *America's Godly Heritage*, 34:57–38:34; Donald Lutz, "The Relative Influence of European Writers on Late Eighteenth-Century American Political Thought," *American Political Science Review* 78, no. 1 (March 1984): 189–197.

20. Green, *Inventing a Christian America*, 52–53; 154–173; Seidel et al., *Founding Myth*, 110–118.

21. Seidel et al., *Founding Myth*, 70.

22. Green, *Inventing a Christian America*, 178–188; Seidel et al., *Founding Myth*, 138–139.

23. *America's Godly Heritage*, 38:34–39:06; Seidel et al., *Founding Myth*, 113.

24. Seidel et al., *Founding Myth*, 33.

25. Green, *Inventing a Christian America*, 151.

26. Jon Meacham, *American Gospel: God, the Founding Fathers, and the Making of a Nation* (Random House, 2006), 101–103.

27. Meacham, *American Gospel*, 21–22, 91; Seidel et al., *Founding Myth*, 40.

28. Seidel et al., *Founding Myth*, 36–37.

29. Seidel et al., *Founding Myth*, 3, 8.

30. Green, *Faith in America*, 1, 8–13.

31. Green, *Faith in America*, 37, 41.

32. "Did You Know That the WallBuilders' Library Has Locks of George Washington's Hair?," Patriot Academy, December 15, 2019.

33. Green, *Faith in America*, 50–59.

34. Green, *Faith in America*, 60.

35. Ted Olson, "Haggard Says He Bought Meth but Didn't Use It," *Christianity Today*, November 3, 2006.

36. "Our Company," Hobby Lobby website, December 29, 2007 (accessed through the Wayback Machine, Internet Archive).

37. "Forbes 400," *Forbes*, September 20, 2007.

38. Wendy Killeen, "Back to School for Campus Site," *Boston Globe*, November 22, 2007.

39. Dirk Smillie, "Prophets of Boom," *Forbes*, September 18, 2006.

40. "A Year Later, Falwell Sons Assume Father's Mantle," Religion News Service, May 8, 2008.

41. Ralph Blumenthal, "Professors Sue Oral Roberts President Richard Roberts," *New York Times*, October 11, 2007; "Corruption Allegations Drive Oral Roberts University President from Office," Courthouse News Service, November 26, 2007.

42. Diane Dees, "God Does a Flip-Flop," *Mother Jones*, November 29, 2007.

43. "Roberts Returns to ORU and Denies Accusations," *Deseret Morning News*, October 23, 2007.

44. "David Green" transcript, Voices of Oklahoma, 30.

45. Ziva Branstetter, "Green Cites Family's Faith as Gift Impetus," *Tulsa World*, November 29, 2007.

46. Justin Juozapavicius, "Businessman Pledges $70M to Oral Roberts University," Associated Press, November 28, 2007; Ziva Branstetter, "An Angel for ORU," *Tulsa World*, November 28, 2007; "Saved!," *Tulsa World*, November 29, 2007; Jim Stafford, "Good Samaritan Donors Step into the Spotlight," *Oklahoman*, November 29, 2007.

47. April Marciszewski, "$62 Million for ORU," *Tulsa World*, January 15, 2008.

48. John Estus, "ORU Helper Had to Study Quickly," *Oklahoman*, January 16, 2008.

49. Justin Juozapavicius, "Businessman Rescues ORU," Associated Press, February 5, 2008.

50. Ben Gose, "Golden Rule," *Chronicle of Philanthropy*, March 20, 2008.

51. Green et al., *This Dangerous Book*, 126–139.

52. Green, *Faith in America*, 64–65; Edward Rothstein, "Adam and Eve in the Age of the Dinosaurs," *New York Times*, May 24, 2007; Charles Pierce, "Greetings from Idiot America," *Esquire*, November 1, 2005; Richard Fausset, "Museum Dedicated to Unlearning Darwin," *Pittsburgh Post-Gazette*, June 3, 2007.

53. Ken Ham with Earl Snellenberger and Bonita Snellenberger, *Dinosaurs of Eden: A Biblical Journey Through Time* (Master Books, 2001), 11.

54. Susan L. Trollinger and William Vance Trollinger, *Righting America at the Creation Museum* (Johns Hopkins University Press, 2016), 1.

55. Ham et al., *Dinosaurs*, 14–15.

56. Leslie Wolf, "Darwin Evolves to Institute's Wall of Bad Guys," *San Diego Union-Times*, February 13, 1992; Stephens and Giberson, *The Anointed*, 29–33.

57. Stephens and Giberson, *The Anointed*, 37–45; Trollinger and Trollinger, *Righting America*, 9–11; Kathleen C. Oberlin, *Creating the Creation Museum: How Fundamentalist Beliefs Come to Life* (New York University Press, 2020), 79.

58. Charles Wolfe, "Ky. Drops Evolution from Guidelines," Associated Press, October 6, 1999.

59. David Stout, "Frist Backs Bush on Teaching 'Intelligent Design' in Schools," *New York Times*, August 19, 2005; Jeffrey Fleishman, "A Case for Creationism?," *Philadelphia Inquirer*, June 13, 1996.

60. "Ministry Now Trying to Raise Money for Long Sought Museum," Associated Press, May 30, 1999; "Museum That Tells Biblical History Has Raised $27m," Associated Press, April 11, 2007; Daniel Silliman, "Died: Patrick Marsh, Ark Encounter and Creation Museum Designer," *Christianity Today*, December 10, 2021.

61. Oberlin, *Creating the Creation Museum*, 32.

62. Hanna Rosin, "Rock of Ages, Ages of Rock," *New York Times*, November 25, 2007.

63. Jeffrey Goldberg, "The Genesis Code," *Atlantic*, September 16, 2014.

64. Oberlin, *Creating the Creation Museum*, 35–36; Trollinger and Trollinger, *Righting America*, 30–32.

65. Oberlin, *Creating the Creation Museum*, 40; Trollinger and Trollinger, *Righting America*, 52–54.

66. Green, *Faith in America*, 66.

67. Ken Ham with Jonathan D. Sarfati, Carl Wieland, and Don Batten, *The Revised and Expanded Answers Book: The 20 Most-Asked Questions About Creation, Evolution and the Book of Genesis Answered!*, rev. and expanded ed. (Master Books, 2000), 179–186; Green, *Faith in America*, 67–70.

68. Trollinger and Trollinger, *Righting America*, 112.

69. Ham et al., *Answers Book*, 191–197.

70. Trollinger and Trollinger, *Righting America*, 105, 176–179, 184–185.

71. "Creation Museum: 1 Million Visitors," Associated Press, April 26, 2010; Green, *Faith in America*, 76.

72. Green, *Faith in America*, 77.

Chapter Eight: And You Shall Find

1. Green et al., *This Dangerous Book*, 24–26; Scott Carroll declined a request for an interview.

2. Green et al., *This Dangerous Book*, 24–26; Scott Carroll Facebook post, November 30, 2009.

3. Geraldine Fabrikant, "Craft Shop Family Buys Up Ancient Bibles," *New York Times*, June 11, 2010; Johnny Shipman obituary, *Dallas Morning News*, March 21, 2013; Nina Burleigh, "The Messiah Cometh," *Newsweek*, April 7, 2016; Candida R. Moss and Joel S. Baden, *Bible Nation: The United States of Hobby Lobby* (Princeton University Press, 2019), 22.

4. Pat Shellenbarger, "Archaeologist Determined to Share His Discoveries," Associated Press, June 3, 2002; "About," Scott Carroll Facebook page; David Yonke, "Ex-Toledoan Sleuths Out Biblical Relics," *Toledo Blade*, March 12, 2012.

5. Shellenbarger, "Archaeologist Determined"; Yonke, "Ex-Toledoan Sleuths."

6. Shellenbarger, "Archaeologist Determined"; William Honan, "Robert Van Kampen, Investor and Bible Collector, Dies at 60," *New York Times*, November 4, 1999.

7. Sara Dykin Callahan, "Where Christ Dies Daily," (PhD dissertation, University of South Florida, 2010); Gorman Woodfin, "The Holy Land Experience," Christian Broadcasting Network, December 10, 2022.

8. Shellenbarger, "Archaeologist Determined"; "Columbus Ships to Be Raised on Internet," Business Wire, April 3, 2000.

9. Matt Vandebunte, "Students Copy Bible Passages with Quills and Papyrus," Associated Press, May 21, 2002.

10. Joel Baden and Candida Moss, "Can Hobby Lobby Buy the Bible?," *Atlantic*, December 16, 2015; Moss and Baden, *Bible Nation*, 23.

11. Eric H. Cline, *Biblical Archaeology: A Very Short Introduction* (Oxford University Press, 2009), 14–16; Amy Dockser Marcus, *The View from Nebo: How Archeology Is Rewriting the Bible and Reshaping the Middle East* (Back Bay Books, 2001), 11–14.

12. Cline, *Biblical Archaeology*, 16–19; 2 Kings 3:4–27.

13. Cline, *Biblical Archaeology*, 21–24; Barton, *A History of the Bible*, 26.

14. Cline, *Biblical Archaeology*, 31–35.

15. Israel Finkelstein and Neil Asher Silberman, *The Bible Unearthed: Archaeology's New Vision of Ancient Israel and the Origin of Its Sacred Texts* (Simon and Schuster, 2002), 79–80; Marcus, *View from Nebo*, 95.

16. Cline, *Biblical Archaeology*, 36–38.

17. McDowell, *Evidence That Demands a Verdict*, 68.

18. Cline, *Biblical Archaeology*, 40–42.

19. Finkelstein and Silberman, *The Bible Unearthed*, 81–122; Marcus, *View from Nebo*, 21–26, 80–86, 94–96; Israel Finkelstein and Amahai Mazar, *The Quest for the Historical Israel: Debating Archaeology and the History of Early Israel* (Society of Biblical Literature, 2007), 77–83; Israel Finkelstein, *The Archaeology of the Israelite Settlement* (Israel Exploration Society, 1988), 336–356.

20. Finkelstein and Silberman, *The Bible Unearthed*, 118.

21. Josh McDowell and Sean McDowell, *Evidence That Demands a Verdict: Life-Changing Truth for a Skeptical World* (Thomas Nelson, 2017), 459–528.

22. Moss and Baden, *Bible Nation*, 23–24; Candida Moss, "Hobby Lobby Sues Christie's," Daily Beast, May 19, 2020; Emily Belz, "Not Exactly Indiana Jones," *World*, November 8, 2017.

23. "Access Religion," *Oklahoman*, April 22, 2006; "'The Da Vinci Code' Just Keeps on Selling," *Foster's (ME) Daily Democrat*, May 17, 2006.

24. Vandebunte, "Students Copy Bible"; Cathy Lynn Grossman, "Planned High-Tech Museum to Take Scholarly Look," *USA Today*, April 4, 2011.

25. Scott Carroll Facebook post, August 11, 2009.

26. "Church Guide," *Oklahoman*, September 17 and 24 and October 1, 8, 15, 22, and 19, 2006.

27. Ehrman, *Misquoting Jesus*, 1–5; Bart D. Erhman, *Jesus, Interrupted: Revealing the Hidden Contradictions in the Bible (and Why We Don't Know About Them)* (HarperOne, 2010), ix–x.

28. Ehrman, *Misquoting Jesus*, 7–10.

29. Ehrman, *Misquoting Jesus*, 63–65.

30. Father Justin Sinaites, interview by author, July 12, 2022.

31. Father Justin interview.

32. Magdala English, "Interview Fr. Justin Sinaites Saint Catherine's Monastery," YouTube, March 8, 2023; Bart Ehrman, "Tischendorf and the Discovery of Codex Sinaiticus," *Bart Ehrman Blog*, June 12, 2015.

33. Father Justin interview.

34. Father Justin interview.

35. Ehrman, *Jesus, Interrupted*, xi.

36. Ehrman, *Misquoting Jesus*, 51–56; 207–208.

37. "Bestsellers, Non-Fiction," *New York Times*, April 2, 2006.

38. Mishele Wright, "Real-Life Indiana Jones Visits Town," *Chronicle-Tribune* (Marion, IN), March 15, 2008.

39. Yonke, "Ex-Toledoan Sleuths."

40. Robert Wilonsky, "Cross Stitch," *Dallas Observer*, March 29, 2010; "Scott Carroll to Start Bible Museum," *Cornerstone Herald*, May 2, 2008.

41. Du Mez, *Jesus and John Wayne*, 235–236; "Obama's 2006 Speech on Faith and Politics," *New York Times*, June 28, 2006.

42. Fea, *Believe Me*, 19–21; Matthew Avery Sutton, *American Apocalypse: A History of Modern Evangelicalism* (Belknap Press, 2014), 371–372.

43. Schenck, *Costly Grace*, 236; Du Mez, *Jesus and John Wayne*, 237.

44. Schenck, *Costly Grace*, 237.

45. Rick Warren, Invocation, Barack Obama inauguration, January 20, 2009.

46. Barry Kosmin and Ariela Keysar, American Religious Identification Survey 2008, Trinity College, March 2009.

47. "Hobby Lobby Executive Describes Company's Legacy of Faith."

48. "Hobby Lobby Buys Property from Massachusetts School," Business Wire, December 18, 2009; Jennifer Palmer, "Families Come First at Retailer," *Oklahoman*, January 4, 2009; advertisement, *Roanoke Times*, December 13, 2009.

49. Green and High, *Leadership Not by the Book*, 120.

50. "Hobby Lobby Increases Full-Time Employee Minimum Wage," Business Wire, April 15, 2009.

51. Green and High, *Giving It All Away*, 69.

52. "Hobby Lobby Executive Describes Company's Legacy of Faith."

53. Sara Nicole Smith, "Big Sandy Regional Conference," *Simply Sanctified* blog, April 29, 2009.

54. Justin Juozapavicius, "Green Family to Donate $10M More to ORU," Associated Press, January 30, 2009.

55. Justin Juozapavicius, "Oral Roberts Inaugurates 3rd University President," Associated Press, September 26, 2009; Solomon, "Meet David Green.".

56. "ORU Ready to Move Ahead After Founder's Death," Associated Press, December 21, 2009.

57. Laurie Styron, interview by author, December 10, 2025.

58. Bill High, "A Time to Remember: Frank Brown," *Bill High* blog, May 4, 2018.

59. Sarah Frostenson and Holly Hall, "Christian Donor-Advised Fund Succeeds by Accepting Complex Assets," *Chronicle of Philanthropy*, October 20, 2013.

60. Eli Clifton, "Hobby Lobby's Secret Agenda," *Salon*, March 27, 2014.

61. Melissa Block, "ADF a Force Behind Conservative Court Victories," NPR, May 6, 2005. While the Greens have never publicly admitted to funding the ADF, they've never denied it in the many times they've been associated with the group in the media. See, for example, David Kirkpatrick, "The Next Targets for the Group That Overturned Roe," *New Yorker*, October 2, 2023.

62. Moss and Baden, *Bible Nation*, 27; letter from Steve Green to Sotheby's, "Re: Authorization to Bid," December 3, 2009; Sotheby's and Hobby Lobby Stores, "Invoice," January 5, 2010; Green et al., *This Dangerous Book*, 33.

63. Janet Martin Soskice, *Sisters of Sinai: How Two Lady Adventurers Found the Hidden Gospels* (Chatto & Windus, 2009).

64. Roger Pearse, "Codex Climaci Rescriptus to Be Sold at Sotheby's" blog, May 29, 2009.

65. Pearse, "Codex Climaci Rescriptus to Be Sold."

66. Sotheby's and Hobby Lobby Stores, "Post Auction Sales Contract," January 15, 2010; Green et al., *This Dangerous Book*, 36.

67. Green et al., *This Dangerous Book*, 36–37.

68. Sandra Hindmann, "We Are Story Tellers First," *Fine Books & Collections*, Autumn 2013; David Dishneau, "Collector of Antique Bibles Has Rarities at Museum," Associated Press, August 11, 2006; "Meet the Family."

69. Philip S. Gorski and Samuel L. Perry, *The Flag and the Cross: White Christian Nationalism and the Threat to American Democracy* (Oxford University Press, 2022), 76–80; Robert Jones, *The End of White Christian America* (Simon & Schuster, 2016), 94–95.

70. Jon Ward, *Testimony: Inside the Evangelical Movement That Failed a Generation* (Brazos Press, 2023), 125.

71. Michelle Goldberg, "History Lesson," *Tablet*, October 12, 2010.

72. Jones, *The End of White Christian America*, 96–97; Gorski and Perry, *The Flag and the Cross*, 80–81.

73. Paige Winfeld Cunningham, "Pro-Life Democrats Ousted as Election Centers on the Economy," *Christianity Today*, November 3, 2010.

74. Club for Growth's "Repeal-It!" Pledge, July 4, 2010.

75. OpenSecrets.org, Donor Lookup, "David Green," December 8, 2009, and "Steve Green," May 27, 2010; Brianna Bailey, "Scott Pruitt Vows to Fight Health Care Reform," *Journal Record*, November 3, 2010.

76. Timothy Lim, *The Dead Sea Scrolls: A Very Short Introduction*, 2nd ed. (Oxford University Press, 2017), 19–21, 33.

77. McDowell and McDowell, *Evidence That Demands a Verdict*, 102–106.

78. Lim, *Dead Sea Scrolls*, 49–54, 74–75.

79. Michael Greshko, "'Dead Sea Scrolls' at the Museum of the Bible Are All Forgeries," *National Geographic*, March 13, 2020.

80. Greshko, "'Dead Sea Scrolls'"; Emanuel Tov, Kipp Davis, and Robert Duke, *Dead Sea Scrolls Fragments in the Museum Collection*, vol. 1 (Brill, 2016), 73–90.

81. Robert Draper, "Inside the Cloak-and-Dagger Search for Sacred Texts," *National Geographic*, December 2018.

82. Johnny Shipman, email to Steve Green and Scott Carroll, February 17, 2010.

83. Laura Latzko, "Goodyear Museum Preserves Rare Bibles," *Arizona Republic*, August 11, 2014; Kelly Ettenborough, "Byrd: Millions Finance Ministry," *Arizona Republic*, August 13, 2000.

84. Letter from Craig Lampe to Steve Green, November 30, 2009; Pilgrim Rock Church and Hobby Lobby Stores, "Book, Art, and Collectibles Purchase Agreement," December 16, 2009; Brent Nongbri, "Fake Dead Sea Scrolls and the People Who Sell Them: One Fragment's Story," Variant Readings, March 27, 2020.

85. Scott Carroll, email to Steve Green, December 6, 2009; Scott Carroll Facebook post, December 15, 2009.

86. Scott Carroll Facebook posts, January 16, 2010, and January 20, 2010.

87. Candida Moss and Joel Baden, "The Museum of the Bible Is Exploiting Jewish Tradition—and Saving Its Evangelical Christian Donors Millions," *Daily Beast*, September 17, 2018.

88. Moss and Baden, *Bible Nation*, 26–27; Hella Winston, "How Much Is an Unkosher Torah Scroll Worth?," *Jewish Week*, April 13, 2020; Moss and Baden, "The Museum of the Bible Is Exploiting"; "Tax Court Considers Valuation Penalties Against Hobby Lobby Owners," Tax Notes, October 2, 2025.

89. Carroll Facebook post, January 20, 2010.

90. William Kando and Hobby Lobby Stores, "Book, Art and Collectibles Purchase Agreement," May 4, 2010; William Kando and Hobby Lobby Stores, "Purchase Invoice," May 4, 2010; Hobby Lobby Wire Transfer Entry Review, May 4, 2010.

91. Draper, "Inside the Cloak-and-Dagger Search"; Nongbri, "Fake Dead Sea Scrolls"; Peter Beaumont and Oliver Laughland, "Trade in Dead Sea Scrolls Awash with Suspected Forgeries," *Guardian*, November 21, 2017; Brent Nongbri, "Statement on the So-Called Dead Sea Scrolls of Southwestern Baptist Theological Seminary," Variant Readings, April 8, 2020.

92. Michael Sharpe and Hobby Lobby Stores, "Book, Art and Collectibles Purchase Agreement," February 15, 2010.

93. Lauren Green McAfee, LinkedIn profile.

94. Kirby Davis, "Hobby Lobby Backs Bible Museum," *Journal Record*, March 10, 2010.

95. Fabrikant, "Craft Shop Family."

96. Fabrikant, "Craft Shop Family."

97. "Hobby Lobby Increases Full-Time Hourly Employee Minimum Wage," Business Wire, April 15, 2010.

98. Green and High, *Giving It All Away*, 104.

99. "Rick Warren Says He's Grateful for O.C. Land Donation," L.A. Now, August 8, 2011.

100. Samantha Sharf, "Philanthropy by the Numbers: Religion," *Forbes*, September 20, 2012.

101. Green and High, *Giving It All Away*, 87.

102. Lake Lambert III, "God Goes to the Office," *USA Today*, February 8, 2010.

103. Delia Gallagher, "What Is a Christian?," CNN, May 11, 2007.

104. United States of America v. Approximately Four Hundred Fifty (450) Ancient Cuneiform Tablets, 17-CV-3980, District Court, E.D. New York, July 5, 2017 (hereafter *Cuneiform* complaint), 20; Brent Easter, interview by author, December 7, 2023; Labbat interview.

105. Dalya Alberge, "Museum's Tablet Lends New Weight to Biblical Truth," (London) *Times*, July 11, 2007.

106. *Cuneiform* complaint, 20; Easter and Labbat interviews; Kelly Crow, "Hobby Lobby Scion Spent Millions on Biblical Relics," *Wall Street Journal*, November 13, 2017.

107. *Cuneiform* complaint, 20; Crow, "Hobby Lobby Scion"; Easter and Labbat interviews. According to Crow, "Mr. Green didn't dispute Mr. Carroll's account."

108. *Cuneiform* complaint, 21–22.

109. Scott Carroll, emails to Johnny Shipman, June 22 and July 10, 2010.

110. Jim Schutze, "Holy National Bible Museum, Batman!," *Dallas Observer*, August 23, 2010.

111. Baden and Moss, "Can Hobby Lobby Buy the Bible?"

112. Roger Alford, "Private Investors Look to Build Noah's Ark," Associated Press, December 1, 2010.

113. Patty Gerstenblith, interview by author, February 14, 2024.

114. Gerstenblith interview; *Cuneiform* complaint, 23; Patty Gerstenblith, "Hobby Lobby, the Museum of the Bible, and the Law," in *Antiquities Smuggling in the Real and Virtual World*, ed. Layla Hashemi and Louise Shelley, Routledge Transnational Crime and Corruption Series (Routledge, 2022), 69.

115. Gerstenblith interview.

116. *Cuneiform* complaint, 26.

117. *Cuneiform* complaint, 24–25; letter from Barakat and Sons Gallery, March 8, 2010.

118. *Cuneiform* complaint, 27, 32, 34–35.

119. Lauren McAfee, email to Marsha Bold, December 7, 2010.

Chapter Nine: Out of Egypt

1. Easter interview; Labbat interview.

2. *Cuneiform* complaint, 33–42.

3. "Ancient Antiquities and Saddam Hussein–Era Objects Returned to Iraq," US Immigration and Customs Enforcement, March 16, 2015.

4. Vaihayasi Pande Daniel, "The American Who Rescues Indian Treasures!," Rediff, August 22, 2016; Wesley Bruer and Alexander Rosen, "The Feds' Real-Life Indiana Jones," CNN, June 3, 2016.

5. *Cuneiform* complaint, 43–45, 25.

6. Theodore Vrettos, *The Elgin Affair: The Abduction of Antiquity's Greatest Treasures and the Passions It Aroused* (Little, Brown, 1997); Juan Pablo Sanchez, "How the Parthenon Lost Its Marbles," *National Geographic History*, March/April 2017; author tour of British Museum with Alice Procter, July 26, 2022.

7. Stuart Braun, "Should Germany Return Nefertiti Bust to Egypt?," DW, October 25, 2024.

8. Alexander Herman, *Restitution: The Return of Cultural Artefacts* (Lund Humphries, 2022), 13–14.

9. Geoff Emberling and Katharyn Hanson, eds., *Catastrophe! The Looting and Destruction of Iraq's Past* (Oriental Institute of the University of Chicago, 2008), 13–15, 19–27; Elizabeth Stone, "An Update on the Looting of Archaeological Sites in Iraq," *Near Eastern Archaeology* 78, no. 3 (September 2015): 178–186.

10. Monica Hanna, interview by author, July 8, 2022; Tom Mashberg, "Taking on Art Looters on Twitter," *New York Times*, April 9, 2014.

11. Carla Hinton, "Providence Gets Credit for Bible Collection," *Oklahoman*, April 3, 2011; "International Scholar-Mentors and Students Come to Baylor," States News Service, July 10, 2012.

12. Yonke, "Ex-Toledoan Sleuths."

13. "Kent State Students Study Ancient Papyrus as Part of International Effort," Kent State press release, 2011.

14. *Passages* exhibition, Oklahoma City Museum of Art, May 16–October 16, 2011; Matthew Prince, "Biblical Artifacts Educate Museumgoers," *Oklahoman*, April 29, 2012.

15. Scott Th. Carroll, ed., *Passages: 400th Anniversary of the King James Bible Exhibition Catalog* (Passages, 2011), 1–3.

16. Prince, "Bible Artifacts Educate."

17. Carroll, *Passages*, 172.

18. Prince, "Bible Artifacts Educate."

19. Moss and Baden, *Bible Nation*, 64–67.

20. "Rosenberg Named to Green Scholars Initiative Advisory Board," States News Service, March 11, 2011.

21. Ariel Sabar, "A Biblical Mystery at Oxford," *Atlantic*, May 13, 2020.

22. Sabar, "A Biblical Mystery"; Tom Dunkel, "Puzzle Master," *Smithsonian*, September 2002.

23. Romie Scott, "Oxyrhynchus, Ancient Egypt's Most Literate Trash Heap," *Atlas Obscura*, March 16, 2016; Alan K. Bowman, R. A. Coles, N. Gonis, D. Obbink, and

P. J. Parsons. *Oxyrhynchus: A City and Its Texts*, Graeco-Roman Memoirs vol. 93 (Egypt Exploration Society, 2007).

24. Daniel Silliman, "Missing Papyri Professor Must Return $7 Million to Hobby Lobby," *Christianity Today*, December 15, 2021.

25. Hobby Lobby Stores Inc. v. Dirk Obbink, 21-CV-3113, District Court, E.D. New York, June 2, 2021, 1 (hereafter *Obbink* complaint).

26. "Recovering Ancient Texts," Baylor Magazine, June 22, 2011 (accessed through the Wayback Machine, Internet Archive); "Baylor Undergrad Students Get Rare Chance for In-Person Research," States News Service, September 13, 2011.

27. Charlotte Higgins, "A Scandal in Oxford: The Curious Case of the Stolen Gospel," *Guardian*, January 9, 2020.

28. "Recovering Ancient Texts."

29. Moss and Baden, *Bible Nation*, 62–65; "Kent State Students Study."

30. Moss and Baden, *Bible Nation*, 66–67; "Mission," Council of Christian Colleges and Universities (CCCU) website.

31. Moss and Baden, *Bible Nation*, 73–74.

32. Cathy Lynn Grossman, "Planned High-Tech Museum to Take Scholarly Look at Bible," *USA Today*, April 4, 2011.

33. Moss and Baden, *Bible Nation*, 87–88.

34. Museum of the Bible, 2010 Form 990-EZ.

35. Green et al., *This Dangerous Book*, 52.

36. Green and High, *This Beautiful Book*, 17, 20.

37. Green and High, *This Beautiful Book*, 138, 194–195, 199.

38. Green and High, *This Beautiful Book*, 22, 213.

39. Green and High, *This Beautiful Book*, 202.

40. Green and High, *This Beautiful Book*, 204.

41. Green and High, *This Beautiful Book*, 214–215.

42. Green, *Faith in America*, 142–143.

43. Steve Green and Todd Hillard, *The Bible in America: What We Believe About the Most Important Book in Our History* (DustJacket Press, 2013), 121.

44. Green, *Faith in America*, 143.

45. Frank Newport, "For First Time, Majority of Americans Favor Legal Gay Marriage," Gallup, May 20, 2011.

46. Schenck, *Costly Grace*, 258.

47. McVicar, *Christian Reconstruction*, 200.

48. Ingersoll, *Building God's Kingdom*, 191.

49. Erik Eckholm, "Using History to Mold Ideas on the Right," *New York Times*, May 4, 2011.

50. Julie Ingersoll, "Meet the Tea Party's Evangelical Quack," *Slate*, August 23, 2015.

51. "Colorado Christian University v. Azar," Becket, accessed December 2025; Amelia Thomson-DeVeaux, "The Little-Known Force Behind the Hobby Lobby Contraception Case," *American Prospect* magazine, June 18, 2014.

52. "Tax Court Considers Valuation Penalties."

53. "Meet the Family"; "Hobby Lobby Celebrates 500th Grand Opening," *Odessa-American* (Odessa, TX), April 8, 2012.

54. "6 Oklahomans Make Forbes 400 List," *Oklahoman*, September 23, 2011; Don Mecoy, "Hobby Lobby Increases Pay," *Oklahoman*, April 14, 2011.

55. Green and High, *Giving It All Away*, 26–27.

56. Green and High, *Giving It All Away*, 128–132.

57. Green and High, *Giving It All Away*, 132–133; Burwell v. Hobby Lobby Stores, Inc., 573 U.S. 682 (2014) (formerly Hobby Lobby v. Sebelius, 723 F.3d 1114 [10th Cir.]), September 12, 2012, 38 (hereafter *Burwell* complaint).

58. Cary Summers, *Lifting up the Bible: The Story Behind Museum of the Bible* (Museum of the Bible Books, 2017), 55–56.

59. Rob Schenck, interview by author, September 13, 2024; Jodi Kantor and Jo Becker, "Former Anti-Abortion Leader Alleges Another Supreme Court Breach," *New York Times*, November 19, 2022.

60. Schenck interview.

61. Jerry Pattengale, "The 'First-Century Mark' Saga from Inside the Room," *Christianity Today*, June 28, 2019; Higgins, "A Scandal in Oxford"; "Jerry Pattengale on 'First-Century Mark,'" *Evangelical Textual Criticism* blog, June 28, 2019; Scott Carroll Twitter post, November 29, 2011. Carroll, who did not respond to interview requests, later said Pattengale's account is full of "misrepresentations, misrecollections, and exaggerations." However, he confirmed the basic details of the meeting with Obbink that night.

62. Pattengale, "The 'First-Century Mark' Saga"; Higgins, "A Scandal in Oxford."

63. Pattengale, "The 'First-Century Mark' Saga"; Higgins, "A Scandal in Oxford."

64. Sabar, "A Biblical Mystery."

65. Scott Carroll Twitter post, December 1, 2011.

66. "From Mummy to Manuscripts," Peel Media Productions, YouTube, May 19, 2014 (credits identify the date as January 16, 2012); Brent Nongbri, "The Green Collection Mummy Masks," Variant Readings, January 30, 2019.

67. "From Mummy to Manuscripts"; Sabar, "A Biblical Mystery."

68. Jerry Pattengale, "Underneath the Mask," *Chronicle-Tribune*, January 24, 2012.

69. Kyra Phillips, "Hobby Lobby President's Rare Collection," CNN, January 18, 2012.

70. P. J. Williams, "New Fragment of Romans 9 and 10," *Evangelical Textual Criticism* blog, January 18, 2012.

71. "UNC Dialogue on the New Testament," UNC website, January 26, 2012; "Bart Ehrman & Daniel Wallace Debate Original NT Lost?," YouTube, February 26, 2015; Bart Ehrman, "My Debate with Dan Wallace," *Bart Ehrman Blog*, March 7, 2015.

72. "Bart Ehrman & Daniel Wallace Debate."

73. "Bart Ehrman & Daniel Wallace Debate."

74. Gordon Gover, "Sensation Before Scholarship," *Christianity Today*, May 2012; Justin Taylor, "An Interview with Daniel B. Wallace," *Gospel Coalition*, March 22, 2012.

75. Brent Nongbri: "Early Career Researcher of the Year," Macquarie University, YouTube, November 21, 2013; Brent Nongbri, interview by author, June 14, 2023.

76. Nongbri interview.

77. Nongbri interview.

78. Sabar, "A Biblical Mystery."

79. "Interfaith Exhibit of Rare Biblical Texts and Artifacts," States News Service, February 27, 2012.

80. George Thomas, "Scott Carroll: Uncovering Ancient Biblical Artifacts," Christian Broadcasting Network, April 3, 2012.

81. "Hobby Lobby Celebrates 500th Grand Opening," *Odessa-American*, April 8, 2012.

82. Hindmann, "We Are Story Tellers First"; Michelle Boorstein, "Hobby Lobby's Steve Green Has Big Plans," *Washington Post*, September 12, 2014.

83. "International Scholar-Mentors and Students Come to Baylor," States News Service, July 10, 2012.

84. Western Manuscripts S/O, Lot 3, Sotheby's London, July 10, 2012.

85. Moss and Baden, *Bible Nation*, 45.

86. Moss and Baden, *Bible Nation*, 45.

Chapter Ten: In the Womb I Knew You

1. "Oklahoma, OK Weather History," September 2012, Weather Underground, https://www.wunderground.com.

2. Green and High, *Giving It All Away*, 53–55.

3. *Burwell* complaint, 55.

4. Green and High, *Giving It All Away*, 48.

5. Lindberg, "David Green."

6. Green and High, *Giving It All Away*, 53–55.

7. Green and High, *Giving It All Away*, 55.

8. Tim Talley, "Hobby Lobby Sues over Morning-After Pill Coverage," Associated Press, September 12, 2012.

9. Tim Talley, "US: Judge Must Deny Hobby Lobby Morning-After Case," Associated Press, October 12, 2012.

10. *Burwell* complaint, 38.

11. "Hobby Lobby Sues over HHS Mandate," Becket press release, September 12, 2012.

12. Amelia Thomson-DeVeaux, "The Little-Known Force Behind the Hobby Lobby Contraception Case," *American Prospect*, June 18, 2014.

13. Derek Beigh, "Green Selected for World Changers," *Chronicle-Tribune*, March 28, 2013; advertisement, *Waco (TX) Tribune-Herald*, November 2, 2012.

14. "Oklahoma City Reverend Speaks Out Against Hobby Lobby Lawsuit," Oklahoma City News 4, September 27, 2012; "National Council of Churches, MoveOn.org Boycott Christian Hobby Lobby," *Maggie's Notebook* blog, October 1, 2012.

15. "Why I Will Not Be Shopping at Hobby Lobby Anymore," *Aunt Peaches* blog, September 2012.

16. *Burwell* complaint, Defendants' Opposition to Preliminary Injunction, 12.

17. Chris Rodda, "Debunking David Barton's Jefferson Lies," *HuffPost*, September 16, 2013; Kyle Mantyla, "David Baron Went 70 for 71 in Shaping GOP Platform," Right Wing Watch, August 29, 2012.

18. Chris Rodda, "David Barton Tells Glenn Beck a More Obvious Lie," *HuffPost*, August 17, 2012.

19. Tim Talley, "Judge: Hobby Lobby Must Offer Morning-After Pill," Associated Press, November 20, 2012.

20. "Federal Courts Split on Religious Liberty," States News Service, November 27, 2012.

21. National Christian Foundation, 2011 and 2012 Forms 990.

22. "The Hobby Lobby Story (intro/full version)," Becket, YouTube, September 20, 2012.

23. "The Hobby Lobby Story."

24. Esther 4:14 (NIV).

25. "An Esther Story: Barbara Green of Hobby Lobby," Becket, YouTube, February 27, 2017.

26. Green and High, *Giving It All Away*, 18–19, 46–47, 55.

27. Tim Talley, "Attorney: Hobby Lobby Won't Offer Morning-After Pill Coverage," Associated Press, December 29, 2012.

28. "Hobby Lobby Says It Can Delay Health Law Rule," Associated Press, January 11, 2013.

29. Carla Hinton, "Philanthropist Launches Digital Bible Library," *Oklahoman*, January 13, 2013; Melissa Steffan, "Joining Forces," *Christianity Today*, December 18, 2012; Green and High, *A Generous Life*, 50.

30. Hinton, "Philanthropist Launches Digital Bible Library"; Steffan, "Joining Forces."

31. "Tax Court Considers Valuation Penalties."

32. "Rare Bible Manuscripts on Display," Creation Museum, October 18, 2012; Ken Ham, "Watch the Opening of 'Verbum Domini,'" Answers in Genesis, October 21, 2012.

33. "Rare Bible Manuscripts on Display"; "Watch the Opening."

34. Carla Hinton, "Hobby Lobby President Wins Biblical Values Award," *Oklahoman*, April 20, 2013.

35. Thomas Larson, "Hobby Lobby, Steve Green, and the New Bible Empire," *Free Inquiry* 35, no. 3 (April/May 2015); "Hobby Lobby Thinks the Bible Can Save America," PBS News, July 28, 2017.

36. Matthew Brown, "U.S. Legislators Come to Hobby Lobby's Defense," *Deseret Morning News*, February 20, 2013.

37. Bill Keller, "The Conscience of a Corporation," *New York Times*, February 11, 2013.

38. Julie Rovner, "Morning-After Pills Don't Cause Abortion, Studies Say," NPR, February 21, 2013.

39. Jane Norman, "HHS Birth Control Rule Under Scrutiny," *Congressional Quarterly*, May 22, 2013.

40. Kristen Wyatt, "Birth Control Mandate Up for Appeal," Associated Press, May 24, 2013.

41. Sarah Posner, "More Than a Hobby," *American Prospect*, July 13, 2013.

42. Jared Law, "Hobby Lobby's Steve Green Part II—TheBlazeTV—The Glenn Beck Program—2013.09.20," YouTube, October 2, 2013.

43. Mark Sherman, "Supreme Court to Hear Landmark Hobby Lobby Case," Associated Press, November 26, 2013.

44. "FFRF Calls for Hobby Lobby Boycott," Freedom from Religion Foundation, November 26, 2013.

45. Kate Winick, "Why Your Birth Control Is in Danger," *Elle*, December 1, 2013; Audra Schroeder, "Hobby Lobby's Stand Against Obamacare Spurs Online Backlash," Daily Dot, December 3, 2013.

46. Emily Bazelon, "What the Religious Right Really Thinks of Birth Control," *Slate*, March 11, 2014.

47. Hindmann, "We Are Story Tellers First"; Museum of the Bible, 2014 Form 990.

48. Art Levant Antiques, "Invoice," June 19, 2013; Matthew Brown, "Ancient Jewish Prayer Book May Be Oldest in the World," *Deseret Morning News*, September 27, 2013; Jessica Steinberg, "World's 'Oldest-Known Siddur' Unveiled," *Times of Israel*, September 19, 2014.

49. Brown, "Ancient Jewish Prayer Book"; Steinberg, "World's 'Oldest-Known Siddur.'"

50. Ken Berwitz, "Why I Will Never Patronize Hobby Lobby," *Hopelessly Partisan* blog, September 27, 2013.

51. Jennifer Palmer, "Hobby Lobby Responds to Blog's Anti-Semitism Claim," *Oklahoman*, October 4, 2013; "Hobby Lobby Says It Will Have Items for Jewish Holiday," Associated Press, October 5, 2013.

52. Rachel McBride Lindsey, "Passages," *Religion & Politics*, September 24, 2014.
53. Posner, "More Than a Hobby."
54. Labbat interview.
55. "'Two New Poems' by Greek Poet Sappho Recovered," BBC News, January 30, 2014.
56. Roberta Mazza, interview by author, June 25, 2023.
57. Dirk Obbink, "New Poems by Sappho," *Times Literary Supplement*, February 5, 2014.
58. Mazza interview.
59. David Van Biema, "David Trobisch Lends Green Family's Bible Museum a Scholarly Edge," *Washington Post*, May 1, 2015.
60. Mazza interview.
61. Mazza interview.
62. Jeff Brumley, "National Prayer Breakfast Gets New Sponsorship," Baptist News Global, January 31, 2023.
63. "Remarks at the National Prayer Breakfast," American Presidency Project, February 6, 2014.
64. Jerry Pattengale, "My Elevator Speech on Religious Liberty," *Chronicle-Tribune*, March 9, 2014.
65. *Burwell* oral arguments, March 25, 2014.
66. *Burwell* oral arguments.
67. *Burwell* oral arguments.
68. *Burwell* oral arguments.
69. *Burwell* oral arguments.
70. Sarah Pulliam Bailey, "Hobby Lobby's Green Family Meets with Pope Francis," *Religion News*, March 31, 2014.
71. "Verbum Domini II" Fact Sheet, Vatican Museums, 2014.
72. Roberta Mazza, "A Trip to Rome (with a Detour on eBay)," *Faces and Voices* blog, April 29, 2014.
73. Mazza, "A Trip to Rome."
74. David Trobisch et al., *Verbum Domini II*, cat. #28, GC.MS.000462, 42–43, fig. 26.
75. Brice Jones, "A Coptic New Testament Papyrus Fragment (Galatians 2) for Sale on eBay," *The Quaternion* blog, October 29, 2012 (accessed through the Wayback Machine, Internet Archive).
76. Roberta Mazza, "The Illegal Papyrus Trade," Hyperallergic, March 1, 2018.
77. Molly Redden, "Hobby Lobby's Hypocrisy," *Mother Jones*, April 1, 2014.
78. Irin Carmon, "Exclusive: Hobby Lobby Owner Speaks," MSNBC, October 9, 2014.
79. Bailey Elise McBride, "Oklahoma District Bible Class: Sinners Will Suffer," Associated Press, April 25, 2014; David Van Biema, "Hobby Lobby's Steve Green Launches a New Project," Religion News Service, April 15, 2014.
80. Letter from Andrew Seidel to Sean McDaniel, Freedom from Religion Foundation website, November 21, 2013.
81. Andrew Seidel, interview by author, December 23, 2023.
82. Mark Chancey, "Can This Class Be Saved?," Texas Freedom Network, May 2014, 5–6.
83. Chancey, "Can This Class Be Saved?," 8; Moss and Baden, *Bible Nation*, 104.
84. Kelli Yoder, "Cartoonist and Writer Combined Humor, Insight," *Mennonite World Review*, May 13, 2015.

85. Bailey Elise McBride, "School Board Members Met Privately on Bible Class," Associated Press, May 22, 2014.

86. "Hobby Lobby CEO Heavily Involved in Bible Curriculum," Freedom from Religion Foundation press release, May 21, 2014; Larson, "Hobby Lobby, Steve Green."

87. Kantor and Becker, "Former Anti-Abortion Leader Alleges"; Rob Schenck, "Confessions of a (Former) Christian Nationalist," *Mother Jones*, November/December 2024; Schenck interview.

88. Schenck interview.

89. Schenck interview.

90. Kantor and Becker, "Former Anti-Abortion Leader Alleges"; Schenck, "Confessions of a (Former) Christian Nationalist"; Schenck interview.

91. *Burwell* complaint, opinion, June 30, 2014.

92. Rachel Zoll, "Hobby Lobby Ruling Puts Green family in Spotlight," Associated Press, July 1, 2014.

93. Abby Ohlheiser: "Read Justice Ginsburg's Passionate 35-Page Dissent of Hobby Lobby Decision," *Atlantic*, June 30, 2014.

94. "Supreme Court Victory for Hobby Lobby and Religious Freedom," Becket, June 30, 2014.

Chapter Eleven: Pride Goeth

1. David Damrosch, *The Buried Book: The Loss and Rediscovery of the Great Epic of Gilgamesh* (Holt Paperbacks, 2007), 3–6.

2. Damrosch, *The Buried Book*, 81–89, 9–12.

3. Tzvi Abusch, "Gilgamesh," Biblical Archaeology Society Library, Washington, DC.

4. *The Dream Tablet*, Christie's, private catalog, 2014.

5. Andrew George, "The Civilizing of Ea-Enkidu: An Unusual Tablet of the Babylonian Gilgamesh Epic," *Revue d'assyriologie et d'archéologie orientale* 101 (2007): 59–80.

6. *Gilgamesh* amended complaint, July 16, 2021, 35–46; Hobby Lobby Stores Inc. v. Christie's Inc. and Joseph David Hackmey, 20-CV-2239, District Court, E.D. New York (hereafter *Christie's* complaint), February 1, 2021, 22–43, and Christie's answer, February 16, 2021, 22–43.

7. Rachel McBride Lindsey, "Passages," *Religion & Politics*, September 2014.

8. Alan Rappeport, "Family Behind Hobby Lobby Has a New Project," *New York Times*, July 16, 2014.

9. Michelle Boorstein, "Church and State," *Washington Post*, September 23, 2014.

10. Museum of the Bible, 2012 Form 990.

11. Boorstein, "Church and State."

12. Zeke Miller, "Bobby Jindal to Appear with Hobby Lobby Family," *Time*, September 30, 2014; Michael Gryboski, "George W. Bush Says He Read the Bible Every Day of His Presidency," *Christian Post*, November 5, 2014; Green et al., *This Dangerous Book*, 99.

13. James Snapp, "Who's Making Your Bible?," *Text of the Gospels* blog, August 1, 2016.

14. Susan Atteberry Smith, "Keeping Track of Bible Treasures," *Springfield News-Leader*, February 15, 2014; Boorstein, "Church and State."

15. Roberta Mazza, "The Illegal Papyrus Trade," *Hyperallergic*, March 1, 2018; Mazza, "Update on the New Sappho Fragments," *Faces and Voices*, May 10, 2014.

16. Mazza interview.

17. "Archaeology of Religion in the Roman World," S22-301, Society of Biblical Literature, San Diego, CA, November 22, 2014.

18. Nongbri interview; Candida Moss and Joel Baden, joint interview by author, July 6, 2023.

19. Moss and Baden, *Bible Nation*, 51–52.

20. Moss and Baden, *Bible Nation*, 52–54; Baden and Moss, "Can Hobby Lobby Buy the Bible?"

21. Moss and Baden, *Bible Nation*, 55–57.

22. Former Museum of the Bible employee 1, interview by author, February 2, 2024; former Museum of the Bible employee 2, interview by author, November 25, 2025; former Museum of the Bible employee 5, interview by author, December 11, 2025 (names withheld by mutual agreement).

23. "Tax Court Considers Valuation Penalties"; Mary Katherine Browne, "Reasonable Cause Argument Sends Substantiation Case to Trial," Tax Notes, October 6, 2025; Stephen Olsen, "Tax Court Split on Whether Summary Judgement Required," Tax Notes, November 3, 2025.

24. Nate Madden, "Work Now Underway on $400 Million Museum of the Bible in Washington," *National Catholic Reporter*, February 13, 2015.

25. Former Museum of the Bible employees 1 and 2 interviews; former Museum of the Bible employee 3, interview by author, December 4, 2025 (name withheld by mutual agreement).

26. Former Museum of the Bible employees 3 and 5 interviews; former Museum of the Bible employee 4, interview by author, December 5, 2025 (name withheld by mutual agreement).

27. Baden and Moss, "Can Hobby Lobby Buy the Bible?"

28. Moss and Baden, *Bible Nation*, 44.

29. Moss and Baden interview.

30. Easter interview; Labbat interview.

31. *Cuneiform* complaint, 46.

32. Micah Murray, "Growing up in Bill Gothard's Homeschool Cult," *HuffPost*, May 6, 2014; Derek Lounds and Ted Kluck, "Growing Up Gothard," *Gospel Coalition*, April 14, 2014.

33. Jeremy Weber, "Bill Gothard Breaks His Silence on Harassment Claims by 30 Women," *Christianity Today*, April 21, 2014.

34. "Our Response to Bill Gothard's Statement," *Recovering Grace*, April 22, 2014.

35. David Corn and Molly Redden, "Hobby Lobby Funded Disgraced Fundamentalist," *Mother Jones*, July 2, 2014.

36. Ryan Parry, "Revealed—How Josh Duggar Was 'Cleansed' After Sexually Abusing His Siblings," *Daily Mail*, July 8, 2015.

37. Lauren Markoe, "More Women Sue Home-Schooling Guru for Sexual Harassment," *Washington Post*, February 18, 2016; "Statement from Recovering Grace Regarding the Lawsuit Against Bill Gothard and IBLP," *Recovering Grace*, March 28, 2018.

38. Dawn Ennis, "Hobby Lobby Loses 11 Year Fight," *Forbes*, August 15, 2021.

39. Erik Eckholm, "Legal Alliance Gains Host of Court Victories," *New York Times*, May 11, 2014.

40. Candida Moss and Joel Baden, "Feds Investigate Hobby Lobby Boss for Illicit Artifacts," *Daily Beast*, October 26, 2015.

41. Moss and Baden interview.

42. Baden and Moss, "Can Hobby Lobby Buy the Bible?"

43. Tina Nguyen, "Did Hobby Lobby's C.E.O. Unknowingly Sponsor Terrorism?," *Vanity Fair*, October 29, 2015.

44. Brent Nongbri, "Revisiting Some of Scott Carroll's Comments," Variant Readings, June 24, 2019; Sabar, "A Biblical Mystery"; Colin Moynihan, "He Taught Ancient Texts at Oxford. Now He Is Accused of Stealing Some," *New York Times*, September 24, 2021.

45. Sabar, "A Biblical Mystery."

46. Matthew D. Taylor, *The Violent Take It by Force: The Christian Movement That Is Threatening Our Democracy* (Broadleaf Books, 2024), 41–45.

47. Tessa Berenson Rogers, "Donald Trump Receives Hero's Welcome at Liberty University," *Time*, January 18, 2016.

48. Chris Casteel, "Hobby Lobby's David Green Backs Rubio, Attacks Trump," *Oklahoman*, February 28, 2016; Matthew Kazin, "Hobby Lobby Founder Endorses Rubio, Calls Trump a 'Bully,'" Fox News, February 29, 2016.

49. Trip Gabriel and Michael Luo, "A Born-Again Donald Trump?," *New York Times*, June 25, 2016.

50. Clare Foran, "Jerry Falwell Gets Religion on Trump," *Atlantic*, January 26, 2016.

51. Roberta Mazza, *Stolen Fragments: Black Markets, Bad Faith, and the Illicit Trade in Ancient Artefacts* (Redwood Press, 2024), 116–121.

52. Nina Burleigh, "Newly Discovered Dead Sea Scrolls Are Skillfully Crafted Fakes, Experts Suspect," *Newsweek*, October 18, 2016.

53. Tov et al., *Dead Sea Scroll Fragments*, 20.

54. Eckart Frahm, "Preliminary Report on the Clay Tablets and Other Artifacts from Boxes 458–462," Yale University, December 2016; Eckart Frahm, interview by author, April 13, 2023.

55. Du Mez, *Jesus and John Wayne*, 253; Gorski and Perry, *The Flag and the Cross*, 84–87; Sarah Posner, *Unholy: How White Christian Nationalists Powered the Trump Presidency, and the Devastating Legacy They Left Behind* (Random House, 2020), 13–16.

56. Posner, *Unholy*, xvii.

57. Schenck interview.

58. David Green, "One Judge Away from Losing Religious Liberty," *USA Today*, September 1, 2016.

59. Lance Wallnau, *God's Chaos Candidate: Donald J. Trump and the American Unraveling* (Killer Sheep Media, 2016), 22, 27; Isaiah 45:1–7 (NIV).

60. Gorski and Perry, *The Flag and the Cross*, 4.

61. Andrew Whitehead, Samuel Perry, and Joseph Baker, "Make America Christian Again," *Sociology of Religion: A Quarterly Review* 79, no. 2 (2018): 147–171.

62. Célia Belin, "Trump's Jerusalem Decision Is a Victory for Evangelical Politics," Brookings, December 15, 2017.

63. Matt Mathers, "Trump Admits Moving US Embassy from Tel Aviv to Jerusalem Was 'for the Evangelicals,'" *Independent*, August 18, 2020.

64. Easter interview.

65. US Customs and Immigration Enforcement, "Hobby Lobby Settles $3 Million Civil Suit for Falsely Labeling Cuneiform Tablets," press release, July 5, 2017; former Assistant US Attorney Karin Orenstein, interview by author, December 2, 2025.

66. Hobby Lobby, "Artifact Import Settlement," press release, July 5, 2017.

67. Jason Felch, "Hobby Lobby's Legal Expert Speaks," *Chasing Aphrodite* blog, July 10, 2017.

68. Freedom from Religion Foundation Twitter post, July 7, 2017.

69. Julie Zauzmer and Sarah Pulliam Bailey, "Hobby Lobby's $3 Million Smuggling Case Casts a Cloud," *Washington Post*, July 6, 2017.

70. Mazza, *Stolen Fragments*, 137–138.

71. Daniel Estrin, "Israeli Authorities Arrest Antiquities Dealers," NPR, August 1, 2017.

72. Amanda Borschel-Dan, "Dead Sea Scrolls Scam," *Times of Israel*, October 3, 2017; Peter Beaumont and Oliver Laughland, "Trade in Dead Sea Scrolls Awash with Suspected Forgeries," *Guardian*, November 21, 2017.

73. Tom Bartlett, "The Provenance Problem," *Chronicle of Higher Education*, November 14, 2017.

74. Rob Brunner, "The Museum of the Bible Will Probably Be a Big Hit," *Washingtonian*, October 3, 2017; Michelle Boorstein, Julie Zauzmer, and Sarah Pulliam Bailey, "DC's Huge New Museum of the Bible," *Washington Post*, October 17, 2017.

75. Rozina Sabur, "Row over 'Non-political' Bible Museum Holding Fundraiser in Trump Hotel," *Telegraph* (UK); Emily Cochran, "Years in the Making, Bible Museum Opens in Washington," *New York Times*, November 17, 2017.

76. Ken Ham, "Museum of the Bible Opens in Washington, DC," *Answers in Genesis* blog, November 18, 2017.

77. Pattengale, "The 'First-Century Mark' Saga."

78. Pattengale, "The 'First-Century Mark' Saga"; Dirk Obbink and Hobby Lobby Stores, "Book, Art, and Collectibles Purchase Agreement," January 17, 2013.

79. Pattengale, "The 'First-Century Mark' Saga."

80. Michelle Martin, "Museum of the Bible Mission Shifts," NPR, November 18, 2017.

81. Boorstein et al., "DC's Huge New Museum."

Chapter Twelve: Revelations

1. "Drive Thru History of the Bible with Dave Stotts," Museum of the Bible.

2. Boorstein et al., "DC's Huge New Museum."

3. Jill Hicks-Keeton and Cavan Concannon, *Does Scripture Speak for Itself? The Museum of the Bible and the Politics of Interpretation*, new ed. (Cambridge University Press, 2022), 104–109.

4. Jeff Kloha, interview by author, November 30, 2023.

5. Jill Hicks-Keeton and Cavan Concannon, eds., *The Museum of the Bible: A Critical Introduction* (Fortress Academic, 2019), 105–106.

6. Museum of the Bible, "The History of Writing," YouTube, January 22, 2016; Hicks-Keeton and Concannon, *Does Scripture Speak for Itself?*, 80–86.

7. Former Museum of the Bible employee 2 interview.

8. Cavan Concannon, "Theo-Politics, Archaeology, and the Ideology of the Museum of the Bible," in *The Museum of the Bible*, ed. Hicks-Keeton and Concannon, 107.

9. Hicks-Keeton and Concannon, *Does Scripture Speak for Itself?*, 118–123.

10. Jill Hicks-Keeton, "Christian Suppressionism and the Problem of Diversity at the Museum of the Bible"; Marc Zvi Brettler, "Looking at the Bible Sideways: One Jewish Scholar's Perspective"; and Mark Leuchter, "Smoke and Mirrors: The Hebrew Bible Exhibit at the Museum of the Bible," all in *The Museum of the Bible*, ed. Hicks-Keeton and Concannon, 49–97.

11. Hicks-Keeton and Concannon, *Does Scripture Speak for Itself?*, 124.

12. Sarah Rose Sharp, "Museum of the Bible Launches 'New Testament Experience,'" *Hyperallergic*, March 27, 2024.

13. Hicks-Keeton and Concannon, *Does Scripture Speak for Itself?*, 47–50.

14. John Fea, "Letting the Bible Do Its Work on Behalf of Christian America: The Founding Era at the Museum of the Bible," in *The Museum of the Bible*, ed. Hicks-Keeton and Concannon, 226–229.

15. Hicks-Keeton and Concannon, *Does Scripture Speak for Itself?*, 55; Margaret Mitchell, "'It's Complicated.' 'No, It's Not.': The Museum of the Bible, Problems and Solutions," in *The Museum of the Bible*, ed. Hicks-Keeton and Concannon, 14–19.

16. Steve Green, Sean McDowell, and Scott Rae, "This Beautiful Book," *Think Biblically* podcast, March 12, 2020.

17. Kloha interview.

18. Stephen Young, "Religious Freedom for a Christian America: 'Don't You Agree?,'" in *The Museum of the Bible*, ed. Hicks-Keeton and Concannon, 245–250.

19. Hicks-Keeton and Concannon, *Does Scripture Speak for Itself?*, 51–52; Hicks-Keeton and Concannon, *The Museum of the Bible*, 9.

20. "Museum of the Bible Visitors Top Half a Million," Religion News Service, May 19, 2018.

21. Karen Heller, "Bible Museum a Draw for Tour Groups," *Washington Post*, January 4, 2018.

22. Stewart, *Power Worshippers*, 147.

23. Private invitation to Ziklag Group event, December 5, 2017, courtesy of ProPublica.

24. Andy Kroll and Nick Surgey, "Inside Ziklag," ProPublica and Documented, July 13, 2024; Andy Kroll, interview by author, August 1, 2024.

25. Jon and Jolene Hamill, "Revolution 2017!," Lamplighter Ministries website, September 13, 2017; Jon and Jolene Hamill, "America's Ark of the Covenant—in Washington DC?," Lamplighter Ministries website, October 5, 2015.

26. Katherine Stewart, "The Museum of the Bible Is a Safe Space for Christian Nationalists," *New York Times*, January 8, 2018.

27. Jon and Jolene Hamill, "Completing the Turnaround for 2018 Is a Must," Lamplighter Ministries website, October 23, 2018; Peter Montgomery, "Spiritual 'Paul Revere' to Host 'Revolution' Event," Right Wing Watch, December 3, 2018; Yonat Shimron, "Under Pressure, Museum of the Bible Moves Charismatic Christian Conference," Religion News Service, December 6, 2018; Stewart, *Power Worshippers*, 148–149.

28. Sarah Posner, "The Christian Legal Army Behind 'Masterpiece Cakeshop,'" *The Nation*, November 28, 2017; Jessica Contrera, "Inside the Christian Legal Powerhouse That Keeps Winning at the Supreme Court," *Washington Post*, July 4, 2018; Alliance Defending Freedom, 2019 Form 990.

29. The Signatry, 2019 Form 990.

30. Masterpiece Cakeshop, Ltd. v. Colorado Civil Rights Commission, 584 U.S. 617 (2018).

31. David Mislin, "Court's Half-Baked Cake," *Wall Street Journal*, June 10, 2018.

32. Mary Emily O'Hara, "This Law Firm Is Linked to Anti-Transgender Bathroom Bills Across the Country," NBC News, April 8, 2017.

33. Mark Joseph Stern, "Federal Court Emphatically Shoots Down Anti-Trans Lawsuit in Rare Ruling from the Bench," *Slate*, May 24, 2018.

34. Nolan McCaskill, "Collins: Kavanaugh Sees Roe v. Wade as 'Settled Law,'" *Politico*, August 21, 2018.

35. Michael Shear, "If G.O.P. Loses Hold on Congress, Trump Warns, Democrats Will Enact Change 'Quickly and Violently,'" *New York Times*, August 28, 2018.

36. Former Museum of the Bible employee 2 interview.

37. Mixantik Antiques and Celadon Antik, invoices, purchase agreements, and wire transfers, analysis by author, 2009–2012.

38. Baidun and Sons and Art Levant, invoices, purchase agreements, and wire transfer, analysis by author, 2009–2014.

39. Dirk Obbink and Oxford Ancient, invoices, purchase agreements, and wire transfer, analysis by author, 2010–2013.

40. Sabar, "A Biblical Mystery"; *Obbink* complaint, amended January 10, 2023, 19, 5–6.

41. Emily Cochrane, "Iraqi Artifacts Once Bought by Hobby Lobby Will Return Home," *New York Times*, May 2, 2018.

42. Labbat interview.

43. Labbat interview.

44. Lot 1503, "Oriental Works of Art (Part I)," Butterfield & Butterfield auction catalog, August 20, 1981.

45. Lynda Albertson, "Prosecutors File a Civil Forfeiture Complaint," *ARCA* blog, May 19, 2020; Kloha interview.

46. Daniel Wallace, "First-Century Mark Fragment Update," *Daniel B. Wallace* blog, May 23, 2018.

47. Brent Nongbri, "P.Oxy. 83.5345," Variant Readings, May 24, 2018.

48. Brent Nongbri, "'First Century' Mark, Dirk Obbink, and Hobby Lobby," Variant Readings, June 23, 2019; Oxford Ancient and Hobby Lobby Stores, "Sales Invoice," December 21, 2012.

49. Moynihan, "He Taught Ancient Texts."

50. Nongbri interview.

51. "Museum of the Bible Releases Research Findings on Fragments in Its Dead Sea Scrolls Collection," press release, October 22, 2018.

52. Os Hillman, "The Real Reason the Church Has Lost Its Influence on America," *Charisma* magazine, February 18, 2019.

53. Stewart, *Power Worshippers*, 145–146; Family Research Council, Watchmen on the Wall 2019 schedule, May 22–24, 2019.

54. The Signatry, 2020 Form 990.

55. Emma Green, "Health and Human Services and the Religious-Liberty War," *Atlantic*, May 7, 2019.

56. Posner, *Unholy*, 259–260; Christian Vasquez: "Trump Takes His Stump Speech to the Values Voter Summit," *Politico*, October 12, 2019.

57. Emma Green, "Josh Hawley's Mission to Remake the GOP," *Atlantic*, November 24, 2019; Kyle Mantyla, "Lance Wallnau Says God . . . ," Right Wing Watch, May 22, 2017.

58. Brent Nongbri, "The Green Collection Sappho Papyrus," Variant Readings, December 13, 2018.

59. Higgins, "A Scandal in Oxford."

60. Higgins, "A Scandal in Oxford"; Sabar, "A Biblical Mystery."

61. Nongbri, "'First Century' Mark"; Brent Nongbri, "The 'First Century' Mark Purchase Agreement: Some Initial Questions," Variant Readings, June 24, 2019.

62. Brent Nongbri, "Recently Emerged Papyri of Dubious Origins: A Working List," Variant Readings, October 18, 2019; Brent Nongbri, "Contextualizing the New Sappho Information," Variant Readings, January 30, 2020.

63. Egyptian Exploration Society, "Chairman's Statement to EES Members," November 16, 2019 (accessed through the Wayback Machine, Internet Archive).

64. Karie Shepherd, "Oxford Professor Who Worked at Baylor Allegedly Stole Ancient Bible Fragments," *Waco Tribune-Herald*, October 17, 2019 [update to *Washington Post* story].

65. Brent Nongbri, "Recap of the SBL 'First Century Mark' Session," Variant Readings, November 26, 2019.

66. Higgins, "A Scandal in Oxford."

67. Brent Nongbri, "Important Developments with the New Sappho Papyrus," Variant Readings, January 29, 2020.

68. Sabar, "A Biblical Mystery."

69. David Bradnick, interview by author, November 8, 2023.

70. Labbat interview.

71. *Christie's* complaint, Christie's answer to amended complaint, 25–26; Eileen Kinsella, "The Founders of Hobby Lobby Are Suing Christie's," *ArtNet*, May 20, 2020.

72. Alex Hime, email to Nat Des Marais, November 25, 2025.

73. Michael Sharpe Rare & Antiquarian Books, *Catalog No. 1*, 51; Patty Gerstenblith, "Hobby Lobby, the Museum of the Bible and the Law," in *Antiquities Smuggling in the Real and Virtual World*, ed. Hashemi and Shelley; Mazza, *Stolen Fragments*, 66–67.

74. *Gilgamesh* amended complaint, July 16, 2021, 19–20.

75. Labbat interview.

76. *Gilgamesh* amended complaint, 25; George, "The Civilizing of Ea-Enkidu."

77. *Gilgamesh* amended complaint, 20–27.

78. Labbat interview.

79. Nat Des Marais, email to Michael Sharpe, May 30, 2018; Nat Des Marais, interview by author, November 25, 2025.

80. Michael Sharpe Rare & Antiquarian Books, *Catalog No. 1*, 50–51; George, "The Civilizing of Ea-Enkidu"; *Gilgamesh* amended complaint, 28–31, 37; *Christie's* amended complaint, 26–27; Tess Thackara, "Hobby Lobby Claims Israeli Collector Joseph David Hackmey Consigned Allegedly Looted Gilgamesh Tablet to Christie's," *Art Newspaper*, February 5, 2021.

81. Labbat interview.

82. "Save the Storks 2020 Stork Charity Ball," PR Newswire, August 22, 2019.

83. Tom Strode, "Christians Have Gospel to Offer in Pro-Life Cause," *Baptist Press*, January 27, 2020.

84. Elizabeth Dias, Annie Karni, and Sabrina Tavernise, "Trump Tells Anti-Abortion Marchers, 'Unborn Children Have Never Had a Stronger Defender in the White House,'" *New York Times*, January 24, 2020.

85. "David Green Talks About the Pitfalls of Pride," *Christian Post*, November 12, 2022.

86. Bethany Biron, "Hobby Lobby Founder Reportedly Told Employees," *Business Insider*, March 22, 2020; Green and High, *Leadership Not by the Book*, 35.

87. Anugrah Kumar, "Hobby Lobby Remains Open," *Christian Post*, March 23, 2020; Bethany Biron, "In Leaked Letter, Hobby Lobby Prepares to Lay Off Employees," *Business Insider*, March 26, 2020.

88. Kate Gibson, "Hobby Lobby Open During Coronavirus," CBS Money Watch, March 23, 2020.

89. Walter Einenkel, "Hobby Lobby Founder Tells Workers," Daily Kos, March 23, 2020.

90. Amanda Marcotte, "The Christian Right's Hostility to Science Is Definitely Going to Get People Killed," *Salon*, March 26, 2020.

91. Gorski and Perry, *The Flag and the Cross*, 28–37.

92. Snejana Farberov, "Police Shut Down Hobby Lobby Stores," *Daily Mail*, April 1, 2020.

93. Neil Vigdor, "Hobby Lobby Defies Stay-at-Home Orders," *New York Times*, April 2, 2020.

94. "Pinched by Shutdown Orders, Hobby Lobby Closes Stores," Associated Press, April 4, 2020.

95. Green and High, *Leadership Not by the Book*, 36.

96. Richard Luscombe, "'Dead Sea Scrolls Fragments' at Museum of the Bible Are All Fakes," *Guardian*, March 16, 2020.

97. Brent Nongbri, "Report: All the 'Dead Sea Scrolls' at the Museum of the Bible Are Fakes," Variant Readings, March 13, 2020.

98. Jane Arraf, "D.C. Museum of the Bible to Return Looted Artifacts to Iraq," NPR, July 31, 2020.

99. Steve Green, "Statement on Past Acquisitions," Museum of the Bible, March 26, 2020.

100. Tom Mashberg, "Bible Museum, Admitting Mistakes, Tries to Convert Its Critics," *New York Times*, April 10, 2020.

101. Lynda Albertson, "Steve Green to Return Another 11,500 Antiquities," *ARCA* blog, March 27, 2020; Lynda Albertson, "The Museum of the Bible's Chairman's Letter Leaves Many Unanswered Questions," *ARCA* blog, March 28, 2020.

102. Brent Nongbri, "Hobby Lobby and Penance," Variant Readings, March 29, 2020.

103. Museum of the Bible, 2020 Form 990, Part XI, Line 9 and Schedule O; Signatry 2020 Form 990, Part XI, Line 9 and Schedule O.

104. Roberta Mazza, "Steve Green Announces the Repatriation of 11,500 Antiquities," *Faces and Voices*, March 28, 2020; Art Levant Antiques and Hobby Lobby Stores, "Book, Art and Collectibles Purchase Agreement," May 3, 2013.

105. "Christie's Sued in Looting Dispute over £1.3m Ancient Tablet," *Times* (London), May 22, 2020.

106. Lynda Albertson, "Prosecutors File a Civil Forfeiture Complaint for the Gilgamesh Dream Tablet Which They Say Was Looted from Iraq," *ARCA* blog, May 19, 2020.

107. Green and High, *Leadership Not by the Book*, 37–38.

108. "Hobby Lobby Employees Get Their Lost Wages Back," *International Business Times News*, June 16, 2020; Dennis Joyce, "Hobby Lobby, Where Minimum Wage Is Already $15 an Hour, Raising It to $17," *Tampa Bay Times*, September 15, 2020.

109. Peter Brzycki, "Crafty Warehouse," *Oklahoma Gazette*, July 16, 2020.

110. Seren Morris, "Hobby Lobby Boycott Calls After 'Vote Trump' Display Spotted in Store," *Newsweek*, September 7, 2020.

111. Ziklag email, "Join Us in Moving Mountains," 2020; Ziklag email, "Help Support Missions. Me with Steve Green," 2021.

112. Ziklag email, "David Green Gives Zs and Early Gift . . . Godly Wisdom!," 2022.

113. Signatry, 2021 Form 990.

114. Richard Wolf, "Supreme Court Allows Religious, Moral Exemptions," *USA Today*, July 8, 2020.

115. Emma Brown, Jon Swaine, and Michelle Boorstein, "Amy Coney Barrett Served as a 'Handmaid' in Christian Group People of Praise," *Washington Post*, October 6, 2020.

116. Elizabeth Williamson, "With Barrett Nomination, a D.C. Conservative Power Couple Nears Its Dream," *New York Times*, October 15, 2020.

117. Elizabeth Williamson, "A Judicial Dream Nears Reality," *New York Times*, October 16, 2020.

118. "Trump or No Trump, Religious Authoritarianism Is Here to Stay," *New York Times*, November 16, 2020.

119. Stefani McDade, "'How Could All the Prophets Be Wrong About Trump?,'" *Christianity Today*, January/February 2021.

120. Peter Montgomery, "Michael Flynn Joins Prayer Call with 'Prophets,'" Right Wing Watch, December 3, 2020.

Chapter Thirteen: Second Coming

1. Taylor, *The Violent Take It by Force*, 102–105.

2. Taylor, *The Violent Take It by Force*, 102–105.

3. Brandon Showalter, "Science Cannot Bury God," *Christian Post*, May 20, 2019; "Right-Wing Radio Host Eric Metaxas: 'We Need to Fight to the Death,'" Media Matters, December 10, 2020.

4. Ward, *Testimony*, 212–213; Sarah Posner, "How the Christian Right Helped Foment Insurrection," *Rolling Stone*, January 30, 2021.

5. Taylor, *The Violent Take It by Force*, 106–107.

6. Taylor, *The Violent Take It by Force*, 47.

7. Gorski et al., *The Flag and the Cross*, 1–2; Kathryn Joyce, "How Christian Nationalism Drove the Insurrection," *Salon*, January 6, 2022.

8. Green and High, *Leadership Not by the Book*, 42–44.

9. Green and High, *Leadership Not by the Book*, 117.

10. "Bible Translators Launch Campaign," Christian Newswire, March 23, 2021; Carla Hinton, "Man Touts Ambitious Bible Translation Effort," *Oklahoman*, May 17, 2021.

11. Mustafa Marie, "Egypt Repatriates 5,000 Manuscripts," *Egypt Today*, January 27, 2021.

12. Shaaban Abdel Gawad, interview by author, July 18, 2023.

13. Jessica Cherner, "Kim Kardashian's Viral Met Gala Photo Helped Solve the Mystery of a Stolen Egyptian Coffin," *Architectural Digest*, October 19, 2021.

14. Gawad interview.

15. Gawad interview.

16. Jane Arraf, "Iraq Reclaims 17,000 Looted Artifacts," *New York Times*, August 3, 2021; Brigit Katz, "Smuggled Gilgamesh Dream Tablet Returns to Iraq," *Smithsonian*, September 23, 2021.

17. Naomi Rea, "The Museum of the Bible Is in Discussions with Iraq," *ArtNet*, August 11, 2020.

18. Candida Moss, "Is Iraq Getting Screwed in a Looted Treasures Deal?," *Daily Beast*, August 27, 2020.

19. "Forfeiture of Ancient Tablet Bought by Hobby Lobby Approved," Associated Press, July 28, 2021.

20. Ella Weiner, "Historic Repatriation of the Gilgamesh Dream Tablet," *Smithsonian*, October 13, 2021.

21. Daniel Silliman, "Missing Papyri Professor Must Return $7 Million," *Christianity Today*, December 15, 2021; Gawad interview.

22. Dahlia Lithwick and Mark Joseph Stern, "How the Right Is Bringing Christian Prayer Back," *Slate*, April 14, 2022.

23. Aaron Blake, "Gorsuch and Sotomayor's Extraordinary Factual Dispute," *Washington Post*, June 29, 2022.

24. Justin Driver, "Three Hail Marys: Carson, Kennedy, and the Fractured Détente over Religion and Education," *Harvard Law Review* 136, no. 1 (November 2022).

25. Dobbs v. Jackson Women's Health Organization, 597 U.S. 215 (2022), opinion, June 24, 2024.

26. "ADF Attorneys Who Served on MS Legal Team Praise US Supreme Court Decision," Alliance Defending Freedom, June 24, 2022.

27. Signatry, 2021–2022 Form 990.

28. Galen Bacharier, "Josh Hawley Says 'Without the Bible, There Is No America,'" *Springfield News-Leader*, September 15, 2022.

29. David Gelles, "Billionaire No More," *New York Times*, September 14, 2022.

30. David Green, "My Decision to Give Away Ownership of Hobby Lobby," Fox News, October 21, 2022.

31. Carla Hinton, "Hobby Lobby Founder David Green Says God Is the Owner of the Business," *Oklahoman*, October 26, 2022.

32. Leo Barraclough, "'King Raven' Trilogy," *Variety*, November 29, 2023; "About BRG," Brent Ryan Green website.

33. "Derek Green," LinkedIn profile.

34. "Hi I'm Lindy!," Lindy Green Johnson website; Lindy Green Johnson, "Understanding Trauma," Every Mother's Advocate, November 6, 2022.

35. "Conversation Around Good with Tyler Green," *Made Possible By* podcast, February 12, 2021; Miranda Vondale, "Christian Leaders Call for Moratorium on Death Penalty in Oklahoma," Fox 25 Oklahoma City, November 11, 2022.

36. Michael McAfee and Lauren Green McAfee, *Not What You Think: Why the Bible Might Be Nothing We Expected Yet Everything We Need* (Zondervan, 2019), 137, 56–58, 76–79.

37. McAfee and McAfee, *Not What You Think*, 111.

38. "Stand for Life Launches New Holistic Pro-Life Movement," Stand for Life press release, Nov 30, 2022; The Signatry, 2023 Form 990.

39. "How Did Stand for Life Begin?," Stand for Life website, July 7, 2023.

40. Lauren Green McAfee, "After Roe, How Do We Stand for Life?," *Gospel Coalition*, June 25, 2022.

41. Alliance Defending Freedom, Stand for Life Conference invitation; Ruth Graham and Ava Sasani, "March for Life Kicks Off in Washington," *New York Times*, January 20, 2023.

42. Mark Wingfield, "Museum of the Bible to Host Wednesday Morning Event," Baptist News Global, January 31, 2023.

43. Family Research Council, "The National Gathering for Prayer and Repentance," YouTube, February 1, 2023.

44. Leah MarieAnn Klett, "Millions to Witness the Gospel at the Super Bowl," *Christian Post*, February 9, 2023.

45. Bob Smietana, "'He Gets Us' Organizers Hope to Spend $1 Billion to Promote Jesus. Will Anyone Care?," Religion News Service, February 3, 2023; "Hobby Lobby Founder: This Is the Best Way to Run a Business," *Glenn Beck Program*, November 29, 2022.

46. Kathryn Lundstrom, "'He Gets Us' Is Bringing Jesus to the Super Bowl. Can It Convert Viewers to Followers?," *AdWeek*, February 12, 2023.

47. Helena Kelly, "'He Gets Us' Organizers to Spend $20 to Promote Jesus," *Daily Mail*, January 30, 2023.

48. Wendi Gordon, "'He Gets Us' Ad Sponsors Don't Believe in the Jesus They're Selling," *Texas Observer*, March 6, 2023.

49. David Kirkpatrick, "The Next Targets for the Group That Overturned Roe," *New Yorker*, October 2, 2023.

50. Sonia Sotomayor, dissent, 303 Creative v. Aubrey Elenis, Supreme Court of the United States, No. 21-476, June 30, 2023.

51. Maggie Astor, "GOP State Lawmakers Push a Growing Wave of Anti-Transgender Bills," *New York Times*, January 25, 2023.

52. "New Poll Emphasizes Negative Impacts of Anti-LGBTQ Policies on LGBTQ Youth," Trevor Project, January 19, 2023.

53. Sherman Smith, "Church and State: Kansas Republicans Target 'Eminently Exploitable' LGBTQ Community," *Kansas Reflector*, May 16, 2023.

54. David Dockery and Lauren McAfee, eds., *Created in the Image of God* (Forefront Books, 2023), 117–122.

55. Peter Montgomery, "Pro-MAGA, Anti-Freedom Mike Johnson Nominated for Speaker," Right Wing Watch, October 25, 2023; Susan Davis, "Speaker Johnson's Close Ties to Christian Right," NPR, November 15, 2023.

56. Peter Smith, "Christian Conservatives Cheer One of Their Own," Associated Press, October 25, 2023.

57. "Speaker Mike Johnson Defends Stance on Social Issues," Fox News, October 27, 2023.

58. Tim Dickinson, "Mike Johnson Compares Himself to Moses," *Rolling Stone*, December 6, 2023; Henry Larson, "A Group of Far-Right Christian Lawmakers Aims to Merge Church and State," News21 (Phoenix, AZ), September 11, 2023.

59. Melinda Nielsen, "An Illustrated Speculum Humanae Salvationis," Green Collection MS 000321.

60. Candida Moss, "Scholars Publish New Papyrus with Early Sayings of Jesus," *Daily Beast*, August 31, 2023.

61. Samantha Kamman, "Elisabeth Elliot's Faith, Courage Highlighted," *Christian Post*, May 3, 2023.

62. Wall text, "Scripture and Science: Our Universe, Ourselves, Our Place," Museum of the Bible, January 20, 2023–January 15, 2024.

63. Laith Hussein, interview by author, July 12, 2023.

64. Manuel Molina, "On the Location of Irisaĝrig," in *From the 21st Century BC to the 21st Century AD: Proceedings of the International Conference on Neo-Sumerian Studies Held in Madrid 22–24 July 2010*, ed. Steven J. Garfinkle and Manuel Molina (Eisenbrauns, 2013).

65. Jana Hayes, "Elon Musk Tops Recent Forbes 400. Which Wealthy Oklahomans Made the Cut?," *Oklahoman*, October 3, 2023.

66. Jeremy Nobile, "How JoAnn Amassed the Debt That Pushed It into Bankruptcy," *Crain's Cleveland Business*, April 1, 2024.

67. Green and High, *Leadership Not by the Book*, 48.

68. Jordan Liles, "Did Hobby Lobby Discontinue Hanukkah Merchandise?," Snopes, November 14, 2023.

69. Abby Glassenberg, interview by author, February 5, 2024.

70. "Hobby Lobby's Insane History," aspen in the moment, YouTube, August 12, 2023; Emma Ujifusa, interview by author, January 31, 2024.

71. Josh Friedman, "Local LGBTQ Group Protests Hobby Lobby Coming to SLO," *Cal Coast Times*, August 9, 2022.

72. Hunter Oberst, "'Sewing' Division: Hobby Lobby Draws Mixed Reception in Keene," *Keene (NH) Sentinel*, January 14, 2023.

73. Matthew Gault, "AI Artist Creates Satanic Panic About Hobby Lobby," *Vice*, June 15, 2023.

74. Kristen Thomason, "He Gets Us—Again," Baptist News Global, March 5, 2024.

75. Robyn Pennacchia, "One Million Moms All Upset," *Wonkette*, February 15, 2024.

76. Thomason, "He Gets Us—Again"; Amanda Marcotte, "Hobby Lobby–Funded Jesus Super Bowl Ads Can't Hide the Hate," *Salon*, February 13, 2024.

77. Rick Rojas, "The Alabama Chief Justice Who Invoked God," *New York Times*, February 22, 2024.

78. Susan Rinkunas, "How Hobby Lobby Could Be Trump's Reproductive Rights Wrecking Ball," *New Republic*, March 25, 2024.

79. Rachel Looker, "Trump Made $300K from Selling Bibles," BBC News, August 16, 2024.

80. Molly Olmstead, "Sent by God," *Slate*, September 25, 2024.

81. "What's a 'Jezebel Spirit'?," NPR, October 18, 2024.

82. Jonathan Blitzer, "Inside the Trump Plan for 2025," *New Yorker*, July 15, 2024.

83. Kevin Roberts, ed., *Mandate for Leadership: The Conservative Promise* (Project 2025) (The Heritage Foundation, 2025).

84. Rinkunas, "Reproductive Rights Wrecking Ball."

85. Khaleda Rahman, "Project 2025," *Newsweek*, July 10, 2024.

86. Rebecca Ballhaus and Mariah Timms, "The Secretive Billionaire Network Funding 'Stop the Steal' 2.0," *Wall Street Journal*, October 22, 2024.; Mara Richards Kim, "Want to Know Who's Behind Project 2025?," *Baptist News*, July 23, 2024.

87. Andy Kroll and Nick Surgey, "Inside Ziklag, the Secret Organization of Wealthy Christians Trying to Sway the Election and Change the Country," ProPublica and Documented, July 13, 2024.

88. Chrissy Hallowell, Arden Farhi, and Clare Hymes, "Evangelical Leader Lance Wallnau Pitches Trump to Followers," *CBS Evening News*, September 4, 2024.

89. Andy Kroll, Phoebe Petrovic, and Nick Surgey, "JD Vance Campaign Event with Christian Right Leaders," ProPublica, October 18, 2024.

90. David Crary and Amelia Thomson-Deveaux, "AP VoteCast Shows Trump Boosted His Level of Support," Associated Press, November 13, 2024.

91. G. F. Erichsen, "Quarter of Americans Say God Ordained Trump to the Presidency, Survey Finds," Public Religion Research Institute, February 15, 2025.

92. Anthony Di Mauro, "Beyond Politics," *Catholic Register*, January 27, 2025.

93. Diane Winston, "Pete Hegseth's Belief in Christian Dominion," *Forward*, January 30, 2025; Clea Skoepiti, "Trump Pentagon Nominee Endorses Extremist Christian Doctrine," *Guardian*, January 24, 2025.

94. Ed Kilgore, "Trump Blesses His Kind of Christians at Prayer Breakfast," *New York Magazine*, February 6, 2025.

95. "National Gathering of Prayer and Repentance," CBN News, YouTube, February 5, 2025.

96. Carla Hinton, "Why Hobby Lobby CEO David Green Helped Fund 'He Gets Us' Super Bowl Commercials," *Oklahoman*, February 8, 2025.

Epilogue

1. Yasir Alani, interview with author, July 14, 2023.

BIBLIOGRAPHY

Adams, Robert McC. *Heartland of Cities: Surveys of Ancient Settlement and Land Use on the Central Floodplain of the Euphrates*. University of Chicago Press, 1981.

Alberta, Tim. *The Kingdom, the Power, and the Glory: American Evangelicals in an Age of Extremism*. Harper, 2023.

Alcorn, Randy C. *Money, Possessions, and Eternity*. Tyndale House Publishers, 2003.

Alcorn, Randy C. *The Treasure Principle*. Lifechange Books. Multnomah Publishers, 2001.

Aldridge, Boone. *For the Gospel's Sake: The Rise of the Wycliffe Bible Translators and the Summer Institute of Linguistics*. William B. Eerdmans, 2018.

Armstrong, Karen. *The Bible: A Biography*. Grove Press, 2008.

Askeland, Christian, Ashley Carter, Jerry Pattengale, and Amy Van Dyke. *The Bible in the U.S. Capital.* Tyndale House Publishers, 2022.

Atwood, Roger. *Stealing History: Tomb Raiders, Smugglers, and the Looting of the Ancient World.* St. Martin's Griffin, 2004.

Austen, Lucy S. R. *Elisabeth Elliot: A Life*. Crossway, 2023.

Balmer, Randall Herbert. *Thy Kingdom Come: How the Religious Right Distorts the Faith and Threatens America*. Basic Books, 2006.

Barron, Bruce. *The Health and Wealth Gospel: What's Going on Today in a Movement That Has Shaped the Faith of Millions?* InterVarsity Press, 1987.

Barton, David. *America, to Pray or Not to Pray? A Statistical Look at What Happened When Religious Principles Were Separated from Public Affairs.* WallBuilder Press, 1991.

Barton, David. *The Myth of Separation: What Is the Correct Relationship Between Church and State? A Revealing Look at What the Founders and Early Courts Really Said.* WallBuilder Press, 1993.

Barton, David. *Original Intent: The Courts, the Constitution and Religion*. WallBuilder Press, 1997.

Barton, John. *A History of the Bible: The Story of the World's Most Influential Book*. Penguin Books, 2019.

Beckwith, Francis. *Politically Correct Death: Answering the Arguments for Abortion Rights*. Baker Books, 1993.

Bentley, James. *Secrets of Mount Sinai: The Story of the World's Oldest Bible—Codex Sinaiticus*. Doubleday, 1986.

Blumhofer, Edith Waldvogel. *Restoring the Faith: The Assemblies of God, Pentecostalism, and American Culture*. University of Illinois Press, 1993.

Bockelman, Wilfred. *Gothard: The Man and His Ministry: An Evaluation*. Quill Publications, 1976.

Bogdanos, Matthew, with William Patrick. *Thieves of Baghdad: One Marine's Passion for Ancient Civilizations and the Journey to Recover the World's Greatest Stolen Treasures*. Bloomsbury, 2005.

Boivin, Odette. *The First Dynasty of the Sealand in Mesopotamia*. Studies in Ancient Near Eastern Records 20. De Gruyter, 2018.

Book of Remembrance. Altus Centennial Memorial Center, 2007.

Boston, Rob. *The Most Dangerous Man in America? Pat Robertson and the Rise of the Christian Coalition*. Prometheus Books, 1996.

Bowden, David, and Mart Green. *Learning to Be Loved: The Everyday Believer's Guide to a Rich Relationship with God*. Zondervan, 2024.

Bowler, Kate. *Blessed: A History of the American Prosperity Gospel*. Oxford University Press, 2018.

Bowman, Alan K., R. A. Coles, N. Gonis, D. Obbink, and P. J. Parsons. *Oxyrhynchus: A City and Its Texts*. Graeco-Roman Memoirs, vol. 93. Egypt Exploration Society, 2007.

Brown, Allison. *Inside Museum of the Bible*, anniversary ed. Worthy Publishing, 2018.

Bull, Chris, and John Gallagher. *Perfect Enemies: The Religious Right, the Gay Movement, and the Politics of the 1990s*. Crown Publishers, 1996.

Buss, Dale. *Family Man: The Biography of Dr. James Dobson*. Tyndale House Publishers, 2005.

Carroll, Scott Th., ed. *Passages: 400th Anniversary of the King James Bible Exhibition Catalog*. Passages, 2011.

Chesser, Cecil R. *Tenderly He Leads Us, 1892–1992: A Centennial History of the First Baptist Church, Altus, Oklahoma*. Altus Printing Company, 1991.

Chua, Liana, Casey High, and Timm Lau. *How Do We Know? Evidence, Ethnography, and the Making of Anthropological Knowledge*. Cambridge Scholars, 2008.

Church of God of Prophecy. *These Necessary Things: The Doctrine and Practices of the Church of God of Prophecy*. White Wing Publishing House, 1960.

Cline, Eric H. *Biblical Archaeology: A Very Short Introduction*. Oxford University Press, 2009.

Colby, Gerard, with Charlotte Dennett. *Thy Will Be Done: The Conquest of the Amazon: Nelson Rockefeller and Evangelism in the Age of Oil*. HarperCollins, 1995.

Collins, John J. *The Dead Sea Scrolls: A Biography*. Princeton University Press, 2013.

Cox, Harvey. *How to Read the Bible*. HarperOne, 2015.

Crossan, John Dominic, and Jonathan L. Reed. *Excavating Jesus: Beneath the Stones, Behind the Texts*. HarperSanFrancisco, 2001.

Currie, Robin. *The Letter and the Scroll: What Archaeology Tells Us About the Bible*. National Geographic, 2009.

Damrosch, David. *The Buried Book: The Loss and Rediscovery of the Great Epic of Gilgamesh*. Holt Paperbacks, 2007.

Davidson, Catherine Temma. *Upon This Rock,* vol. 2. White Wing Publishing House, 1974.

Davis, Kenneth C. *Don't Know Much About the Bible: Everything You Need to Know About the Good Book but Never Learned*. Eagle Brook, 1998.

Davis, Ron Lee, with James D. Denney. *A Time for Compassion: A Call to Cherish and Protect Life*. Crucial Questions Book. F. H. Revell Co., 1986.

Dobson, James C. *Bringing Up Boys*. Tyndale House Publishers, 2001.

Dobson, James C. *Dare to Discipline*. Tyndale House Publishers, 1970.

Dobson, James C. *Dr. Dobson Answers Your Questions*. Grason, 1982.

Dobson, James C. *The Great Debate: Whose Value System Will Dominate Our Culture?* Focus on the Family, 1993.

Dobson, James C. *Marriage Under Fire: Why We Must Win This War*. Multnomah Publishers, 2004.

Dobson, James C. *The New Dare to Discipline*. Tyndale House Publishers, 1992.

Dobson, James C. *On Parenting: Two Bestselling Works Complete in One Volume*. Inspirational Press, 1997.

Dockery, David, and Lauren Green McAfee, eds. *Created in the Image of God*. Forefront Books, 2023.

Dorman, Robert L. *It Happened in Oklahoma: Stories of Events and People That Shaped Sooner State History*. Globe Pequot, 2019.

Dreisbach, Daniel L. *Reading the Bible with the Founding Fathers*. Oxford University Press, 2017.

Du Mez, Kristin Kobes. *Jesus and John Wayne: How White Evangelicals Corrupted a Faith and Fractured a Nation*. Liveright, 2021.

Eastman, Dick. *Beyond Imagination: A Simple Plan to Save the World*. Chosen Books, 1997.

Eastman, Dick. *The Hour That Changes the World: A Practical Plan for Personal Prayer*. Baker Book House, 1978.

Eastman, Dick. *The Jericho Hour*. Creation House, 1994.

Eastman, Dick. *Love on Its Knees*. Chosen Books, 1989.

Ehrman, Bart D. *Jesus Before the Gospels: How the Earliest Christians Remembered, Changed, and Invented Their Stories of the Savior*. HarperOne, 2017.

Ehrman, Bart D. *Jesus, Interrupted: Revealing the Hidden Contradictions in the Bible (and Why We Don't Know About Them)*. HarperOne, 2010.

Ehrman, Bart D. *Misquoting Jesus: The Story Behind Who Changed the Bible and Why*. HarperOne, 2007.

Elliot, Elisabeth. *Passion and Purity: Learning to Bring Your Love Life Under Christ's Control*, 2nd ed. Fleming H. Revell, 2002.

Elliot, Elisabeth. *The Savage My Kinsman*, 40th anniversary ed. Vine Books, Servant Publications, 1996.

Elliot, Elisabeth. *Through Gates of Splendor: The Event That Shocked the World, Changed a People, and Inspired a Nation*. Hendrickson Classic Biographies. Hendrickson Publishers Marketing, 2010.

Emberling, Geoff, and Katharyn Hanson, eds. *Catastrophe! The Looting and Destruction of Iraq's Past*. Oriental Institute of the University of Chicago, 2008.

Falwell, Jerry. *Listen, America!* Doubleday, 1980.

Farrer, Austin. *The Revelation of St John the Divine: A Commentary on the English Text*. Clarendon Press, 1964.

Faulk, Odie B. *The Making of a Merchant: R. A. Young and T.G. & Y. Stores*. Western Heritage Books, 1980.

Fea, John. *Believe Me: The Evangelical Road to Donald Trump*. William B. Eerdmans, 2018.

Fea, John. *The Bible Cause: A History of the American Bible Society*. Oxford University Press, 2016.

Fea, John. *Was America Founded as a Christian Nation? A Historical Introduction*. Westminster John Knox Press, 2016.

Felch, Jason. *Chasing Aphrodite: The Hunt for Looted Antiquities at the World's Richest Museum*. Mariner Books, 2011.

Finkelstein, Israel. *The Archaeology of the Israelite Settlement*. Israel Exploration Society, 1988.

Finkelstein, Israel. *David and Solomon: In Search of the Bible's Sacred Kings and the Roots of the Western Tradition*. Free Press, 2007.

Finkelstein, Israel, and Amahai Mazar. *The Quest for the Historical Israel: Debating Archaeology and the History of Early Israel*. Society of Biblical Literature, 2007.

Finkelstein, Israel, and Neil Asher Silberman. *The Bible Unearthed: Archaeology's New Vision of Ancient Israel and the Origin of Its Sacred Texts*. Simon and Schuster, 2002.

Freund, Richard A. *Digging Through the Bible: Understanding Biblical People, Places, and Controversies Through Archaeology*. Rowman & Littlefield, 2023.

Frykholm, Amy Johnson. *Rapture Culture: Left Behind in Evangelical America*. Oxford University Press, 2004.

Gabel, John B., Charles Wheeler, and Anthony York. *The Bible as Literature: An Introduction*, 5th ed. Oxford University Press, 2006.

Gans, David H., and Ilya Shapiro. *Religious Liberties for Corporations? Hobby Lobby, the Affordable Care Act, and the Constitution*. Palgrave Macmillan, 2014.

Garfinkle, Steven J., and Manuel Molina, eds. *From the 21st Century BC to the 21st Century AD: Proceedings of the International Conference on Neo-Sumerian Studies Held in Madrid 22–24 July 2010*. Eisenbrauns, 2013.

Geoghegan, Jeffrey C. *The Bible for Dummies*. Wiley, 2002.

Gibson, Margaret Dunlop, and Agnes Smith Lewis. *How the Codex Was Found: A Narrative of Two Visits to Sinai from Mrs. Lewis's Journals, 1892–1893*. Alpha Press, 1999.

Gilgoff, Dan. *The Jesus Machine: How James Dobson, Focus on the Family, and Evangelical America Are Winning the Culture War*. St. Martin's Press, 2007.

Goldberg, Michelle. *Kingdom Coming: The Rise of Christian Nationalism*. W. W. Norton & Company, 2007.

Gorski, Philip S., and Samuel L. Perry. *The Flag and the Cross: White Christian Nationalism and the Threat to American Democracy*. Oxford University Press, 2022.

Gothard, Bill. *The Amazing Way: To Complete Success, to Great Wealth, to Total Health, to Lasting Joy*. Institute in Basic Life Principles, 2010.

Gothard, Bill. *Institute in Basic Youth Conflicts: Research in Principles of Life*. Institute in Basic Youth Conflicts, 1981.

Gothard, Bill. *Research in Principles of Life: Advanced Seminar Textbook*. Institute in Basic Youth Conflicts, 1986.

Green, David, and Bill High. *A Generous Life: 10 Steps to Living a Life Money Can't Buy*. Zondervan, 2019.

Green, David, and Bill High. *Giving It All Away... and Getting It All Back Again: The Way of Living Generously*, special ed. Zondervan, 2017.

Green, David, and Bill High. *Leadership Not by the Book: 12 Unconventional Principles to Drive Incredible Results*. Baker Books, 2022.

Green, David, and Dean Merrill. *More Than a Hobby: How a $600 Startup Became America's Home and Craft Superstore*. Thomas Nelson, 2010.

Green, Jackie, and Lauren McAfee. *Legacy—Bible Study Book: How One Ordinary Life Can Make an Eternal Difference*. B&H Books, 2019.

Green, Jackie, Lauren Green McAfee, and Bill High. *Only One Life: How a Woman's Every Day Shapes an Eternal Legacy*. Zondervan, 2018.

Green, Steve. *Faith in America: The Powerful Impact of One Company Speaking Out Boldly*. Looking Glass Books, 2011.

Green, Steve, and Jackie Green with Bill High. *This Dangerous Book: How the Bible Has Shaped Our World and Why It Still Matters Today*. Zondervan, 2017.

Green, Steve, and Bill High. *This Beautiful Book: An Exploration of the Bible's Incredible Story Line and Why It Matters Today*. Zondervan, 2019.

Green, Steve, and Todd Hillard. *The Bible in America: What We Believe About the Most Important Book in Our History*. DustJacket Press, 2013.

Green, Steven K. *Inventing a Christian America: The Myth of the Religious Founding*. Oxford University Press, 2015.

Green, Steven K. *The Second Disestablishment: Church and State in Nineteenth-Century America*. Oxford University Press, 2010.

Greenawalt, Kent. *When Free Exercise and Nonestablishment Conflict*. Harvard University Press, 2017.

Grem, Darren E. *The Blessings of Business: How Corporations Shaped Conservative Christianity*. Oxford University Press, 2016.

Ham, Ken, with Jonathan D. Sarfati, Carl Wieland, and Don Batten. *The Revised and Expanded Answers Book: The 20 Most-Asked Questions About Creation, Evolution and the Book of Genesis Answered!*, rev. and expanded ed. Master Books, 2000.

Ham, Ken, with Earl Snellenberger and Bonita Snellenberger. *Dinosaurs of Eden: A Biblical Journey Through Time*. Master Books, 2001.

Hankins, Barry. *Francis Schaeffer and the Shaping of Evangelical America*. Library of Religious Biography. William B. Eerdmans, 2008.

Hashemi, Layla, and Louise Shelley, eds. *Antiquities Smuggling in the Real and Virtual World*. Routledge Transnational Crime and Corruption Series. Routledge, 2022.

Herman, Alexander. *Restitution: The Return of Cultural Artefacts*. Lund Humphries, 2022.

Hicks, Dan. *The Brutish Museums: The Benin Bronzes, Colonial Violence and Cultural Restitution*. Pluto Press, 2020.

Hicks-Keeton, Jill, and Cavan Concannon. *Does Scripture Speak for Itself? The Museum of the Bible and the Politics of Interpretation*, new ed. Cambridge University Press, 2022.

Hicks-Keeton, Jill, and Cavan Concannon, eds. *The Museum of the Bible: A Critical Introduction*. Fortress Academic, 2019.

Hood, Ralph W., Peter C. Hill, and W. Paul Williamson. *The Psychology of Religious Fundamentalism*. Guilford Press, 2005.

Hoskins, Bob. *Affect Destiny: The Book of Hope Story*. Book of Hope, 2003.

Hoskins, Bob. *All They Want Is the Truth: The Challenge of Literature Evangelism in Our Time*. Life Publishers International, 1985.

Hoskins, Bob. *They Still Want the Truth: The Miracles, the Victories, the Conquest of Literature Evangelism*. Life Publishers International, 1987.

Hoskins, Hazel. *And I Sat There*. OneHope, 2014.

Hoskins, Rob. *Hope Delivered: Affecting Destiny Through the Power of God's Word*. Charisma House, 2012.

Howe, Ben. *Immoral Majority*. Broadside, 2020.

Ingersoll, Julie. *Building God's Kingdom: Inside the World of Christian Reconstruction*. Oxford University Press, 2015.

Isbouts, Jean-Pierre. *Archaeology of the Bible: The Greatest Discoveries from Genesis to the Roman Era*, illustrated ed. National Geographic, 2016.

Jackson, Harry R., and Tony Perkins. *Personal Faith, Public Policy*. Frontline, 2008.

Johnston, Jeremiah J., and Steve Green. *Unimaginable: What Our World Would Be Like Without Christianity*. Bethany House Publishers, n.d.

Johnston, Thomas P. *A History of Evangelism in North America*. Kregel Academic, 2021.

Jones, Robert P. *The End of White Christian America*. Simon & Schuster, 2016.

Joyce, Kathryn. *Quiverfull: Inside the Christian Patriarchy Movement*. Beacon Press, 2009.

Kane, Joe. *Savages*. Knopf, 1995.

Kennedy, Titus. *Unearthing the Bible: 101 Archaeological Discoveries That Bring the Bible to Life*. Harvest House Publishers, 2020.

Klein, Linda Kay. *Pure: Inside the Evangelical Movement That Shamed a Generation of Young Women and How I Broke Free*. Touchstone, 2018.

Kling, David W. *The Bible in History: How the Texts Have Shaped the Times*. Oxford University Press, 2004.

Krapohl, Robert H., and Charles H. Lippy. *The Evangelicals: A Historical, Thematic, and Biographical Guide*. Greenwood Press, 1999.

Kruse, Kevin Michael. *One Nation Under God: How Corporate America Invented Christian America*. Basic Books, 2015.

Kugel, James L. *How to Read the Bible: A Guide to Scripture, Then and Now*. Free Press, 2008.

Levine, Amy-Jill, and Marc Zvi Brettler. *The Bible with and Without Jesus: How Jews and Christians Read the Same Stories Differently*. HarperOne, 2023.

Lim, Timothy. *The Dead Sea Scrolls: A Very Short Introduction*, 2nd ed. Oxford University Press, 2017.

Lindsay, D. Michael. *Faith in the Halls of Power: How Evangelicals Joined the American Elite*. Oxford University Press, 2007.

Lindsell, Harold. *The Battle for the Bible*. Zondervan, 1976.

Lipschits, Oded, Yuval Gadot, Matthew J. Adams, and Israel Finkelstein. *Rethinking Israel: Studies in the History and Archaeology of Ancient Israel in Honor of Israel Finkelstein*. Eisenbrauns, 2017.

Lyons, William John, and Jorunn Økland. *Way the World Ends: The Apocalypse of John in Culture and Ideology*. Sheffield Phoenix Press, 2009.

Magness, Jodi. *The Archaeology of Qumran and the Dead Sea Scrolls*. William B. Eerdmans, 2021.

Marcus, Amy Dockser. *The View from Nebo: How Archeology Is Rewriting the Bible and Reshaping the Middle East*. Back Bay Books, 2001.

Marsden, George M. *Fundamentalism and American Culture: The Shaping of Twentieth Century Evangelicalism, 1870–1925*. Oxford University Press, 1980.

Mazza, Roberta. *Stolen Fragments: Black Markets, Bad Faith, and the Illicit Trade in Ancient Artefacts*. Redwood Press, 2024.

McAfee, Michael, and Lauren Green McAfee. *Beyond Our Control: Let Go of Unmet Expectations, Overcome Anxiety, and Discover Intimacy with God*. Thomas Nelson, 2023.

McAfee, Michael, and Lauren Green McAfee. *Not What You Think: Why the Bible Might Be Nothing We Expected Yet Everything We Need*. Zondervan, 2019.

McDowell, Josh. *Evidence That Demands a Verdict: Historical Evidences for the Christian Faith*. Here's Life Publishers, 1979.

McDowell, Josh. *More Than a Carpenter*. Living Books, 1977.

McDowell, Josh. *The New Evidence That Demands a Verdict*. Thomas Nelson, 1999.

McDowell, Josh, and Sean McDowell. *Evidence That Demands a Verdict: Life-Changing Truth for a Skeptical World*. Thomas Nelson, 2017.

McKendrick, Scot, D. C. Parker, Amy Myshrall, and Cillian O'Hogan. *Codex Sinaiticus: New Perspectives on the Ancient Biblical Manuscript*. British Library, 2015.

McVicar, Michael J. *Christian Reconstruction: R. J. Rushdoony and American Religious Conservatism*. University of North Carolina Press, 2015.

Meacham, Jon. *American Gospel: God, the Founding Fathers, and the Making of a Nation*. Random House, 2006.

Miller, Paul David. *The Religion of American Greatness: What's Wrong with Christian Nationalism*. InterVarsity Press, 2022.

Mitchell, Stephen. *Gilgamesh: A New English Version*. Atria Books, 2006.

Moore, R. Jonathan. *Suing for America's Soul: John Whitehead, the Rutherford Institute, and Conservative Christians in the Courts*. William B. Eerdmans, 2007.

Moreton, Bethany. *To Serve God and Wal-Mart: The Making of Christian Free Enterprise*. Harvard University Press, 2009.

Moslener, Sara. *Virgin Nation: Sexual Purity and American Adolescence*. Oxford University Press, 2015.

Moss, Candida R., and Joel S. Baden. *Bible Nation: The United States of Hobby Lobby*. Princeton University Press, 2019.

Noll, Mark A. *American Evangelical Christianity: An Introduction*. Blackwell Publishers, 2001.

Noll, Mark A. *America's Book: The Rise and Decline of a Bible Civilization, 1794–1911*. Oxford University Press, 2022.

Noll, Mark A. *A History of Christianity in the United States and Canada*. William B. Eerdmans, 2019.

Noll, Mark A. *In the Beginning Was the Word: The Bible in American Public Life, 1492–1783*. Oxford University Press, 2016.

Noll, Mark A. *The Old Religion in a New World: The History of North American Christianity*. William B. Eerdmans, 2001.

Noll, Mark A., and Luke E. Harlow. *Religion and American Politics: From the Colonial Period to the Present*. Oxford University Press, 2007.

Nongbri, Brent. *God's Library: The Archaeology of the Earliest Christian Manuscripts*. Yale University Press, 2020.

Oberlin, Kathleen C. *Creating the Creation Museum: How Fundamentalist Beliefs Come to Life*. New York University Press, 2020.

Onishi, Bradley. *Preparing for War: The Extremist History of White Christian Nationalism—and What Comes Next*. Broadleaf Books, 2023.

Overman, Dean L. *A Case for the Divinity of Jesus: Examining the Earliest Evidence*. Rowman & Littlefield, 2009.

Packard, William. *Evangelism in America: From Tents to TV*. Paragon House, 1988.

Parker, D. C. *Codex Sinaiticus: The Story of the World's Oldest Bible*. British Library; Hendrickson, 2010.

Pattengale, Jerry. *Inexplicable: How Christianity Spread to the Ends of the Earth*. Trilogy Christian Publishing, 2020.

Pattengale, Jerry, Daniel Freemyer, and Nicholas DeNeff. *Is the Bible at Fault? How the Bible Has Been Misused to Justify Evil, Suffering and Bizarre Behavior*. Worthy Books, 2018.

Pattengale, Jerry, and Lawrence Schiffman, eds. *The World's Greatest Book: The Story of How the Bible Came to Be*. Tyndale Momentum, 2023.

Petersen, William J., and Randy Petersen. *100 Christian Books That Changed the Century*. F.H. Revell, 2000.

Pierce, Simon. *Project 2025: A Mandate for Authoritarian Leadership: The Heritage Foundation's Conservative Promise for a Second Trump Administration*. Independently published, 2025.

Posner, Sarah. *Unholy: How White Christian Nationalists Powered the Trump Presidency, and the Devastating Legacy They Left Behind*. Random House, 2020.

Procter, Alice. *The Whole Picture: The Colonial Story of the Art in Our Museums and Why We Need to Talk About It*. Cassell, 2020.

Radosh, Daniel. *Rapture Ready! Adventures in the Parallel Universe of Christian Pop Culture*. Scribner, 2008.

Reagan, Ronald. *Abortion and the Conscience of the Nation*. T. Nelson, 1984.

Riches, John. *The Bible: A Very Short Introduction*. Oxford University Press, 2021.

Rival, Laura M. *Trekking Through History: The Huaorani of Amazonian Ecuador*. Columbia University Press, 2002.

Roberts, Kevin, ed. *Mandate for Leadership: The Conservative Promise* (Project 2025). The Heritage Foundation, 2025.

Robins, R. G. *A. J. Tomlinson: Plainfolk Modernist*. Oxford University Press, 2004.

Robins, R. G. *Pentecostalism in America*. Praeger, 2010.

Root, Jonathan. *Oral Roberts and the Rise of the Prosperity Gospel*. William B. Eerdmans, 2023.

Ross, George R. *Evaluating Models of Christian Counseling*. Wipf & Stock Publishers, 2011.

Rushdoony, Rousas John. *The Biblical Philosophy of History*. Ross House Books, 2000.

Rushdoony, Rousas John. *The Roots of Reconstruction*. Ross House Books, 1991.

Rushdoony, Rousas John. *Thy Kingdom Come: Studies in Daniel and Revelation*. Presbyterian and Reformed Publishing Co., 1971.

Rushdoony, Rousas John, with Herbert W. Titus. *The Institutes of Biblical Law: A Chalcedon Study*. Craig Press, 1973.

Saint, Steve. *End of the Spear: A True Story*. Tyndale House Publishers, 2005.

Schaeffer, Frank. *Crazy for God: How I Grew Up as One of the Elect, Helped Found the Religious Right, and Lived to Take All (or Almost All) of It Back*. Carroll & Graf, 2007.

Schenck, Robert L. *Costly Grace: An Evangelical Minister's Rediscovery of Faith, Hope and Love*. Harper Books, 2018.

Schiess, Kaitlyn. *Ballot and the Bible: How Scripture Has Been Used and Abused in American Politics and Where We Go from Here*. Brazos Press, 2023.

Schultze, Quentin J., and Robert Woods. *Understanding Evangelical Media: The Changing Face of Christian Communication*. IVP Academic, 2008.

Seidel, Andrew L., Dan Barker, and Susan Jacoby. *The Founding Myth: Why Christian Nationalism Is Un-American*. Union Square & Co., 2021.

Seidel, Andrew L., and Erwin Chemerinsky. *American Crusade: How the Supreme Court Is Weaponizing Religious Freedom*. Union Square & Co., 2022.

Shattuck, John, Sushma Raman, and Mathias Risse. *Holding Together: The Hijacking of Rights in America and How to Reclaim Them for Everyone*. The New Press, 2022.

Sheler, Jeffery L. *Prophet of Purpose: The Life of Rick Warren*. Doubleday, 2009.

Smith, Brittany. *Unplanned Grace*. David C Cook, 2021.

Smith, Christian. *Christian America? What Evangelicals Really Want*. University of California Press, 2000.

Soskice, Janet Martin. *Sisters of Sinai: How Two Lady Adventurers Found the Hidden Gospels*. Chatto & Windus, 2009.

Stephens, Randall J., and Karl W. Giberson. *The Anointed: Evangelical Truth in a Secular Age*. Belknap Press, 2011.

Stewart, Katherine. *The Power Worshippers: Inside the Dangerous Rise of Religious Nationalism*. Bloomsbury Publishing, 2022.

Stewart, Matthew. *Nature's God: The Heretical Origins of the American Republic*. W. W. Norton & Company, 2014.

Stoll, David. *Fishers of Men or Founders of Empire? The Wycliffe Bible Translators in Latin America*. Lawrence Hill, 1982.

Stone, James. *The Church of God of Prophecy History & Polity*. White Wing Publishing House, 1977.

Strobel, Lee. *The Case for Christ: A Journalist's Personal Investigation of the Evidence for Jesus*. Zondervan, 2016.

Summers, Cary. *Lifting up the Bible: The Story Behind Museum of the Bible*. Museum of the Bible Books, 2017.

Sutton, Matthew Avery. *American Apocalypse: A History of Modern Evangelicalism*. Belknap Press, 2014.

Synan, Vinson. *The Holiness-Pentecostal Tradition: Charismatic Movements in the Twentieth Century*. William B. Eerdmans, 2007.

Taylor, Matthew D. *The Violent Take It by Force: The Christian Movement That Is Threatening Our Democracy*. Broadleaf Books, 2024.

Thiessen, Elmer John. *The Scandal of Evangelism: A Biblical Study of the Ethics of Evangelism*. Cascade Books, 2018.

Tindal, Matthew. *Christianity as Old as the Creation*. Published by the author, 1730.

Tomlinson, A. J. *God's Pioneer*. Heritage Series, vol. 4. White Wing Publishing House, 1962; repr., 2011.

Tomlinson, A. J. *The Last Great Conflict*. The Higher Christian Life. Garland Publishing, 1985.

Tov, Emanuel, Kipp Davis, and Robert R. Duke. *Dead Sea Scrolls Fragments in the Museum Collection*. Publications of Museum of the Bible 1. Brill, 2016.

Trobisch, David, Jennifer Atwood, Jonathan Kirpatrick, and Rory P. Crowley. *Verbum Domini II: God's Word Goes Out to the Nations*. The Museum of the Bible, 2014.

Trollinger, Susan L., and William Vance Trollinger. *Righting America at the Creation Museum*. Johns Hopkins University Press, 2016.

Turner, John G. *Bill Bright and Campus Crusade for Christ: The Renewal of Evangelicalism in Postwar America*. University of North Carolina Press, 2008.

VanderKam, James, and Peter Flint. *The Meaning of the Dead Sea Scrolls: Their Significance for Understanding the Bible, Judaism, Jesus, and Christianity*. HarperSanFrancisco, 2002.

Vaughn, Ellen, and Joni Earekson Tada. *Becoming Elisabeth Elliot*. B&H Books, 2020.

Vaughn, Ellen, and Joni Eareckson Tada. *Being Elisabeth Elliot: The Authorized Biography: Elisabeth's Later Years*. B&H Books, 2023.

Veinot, Don, Joy Veinot, Ron Henzel, and Midwest Christian Outreach. *A Matter of Basic Principles: Bill Gothard and the Christian Life*. 21st Century Press, 2002.

Vrettos, Theodore. *The Elgin Affair: The Abduction of Antiquity's Greatest Treasures and the Passions It Aroused*. Little, Brown, 1997.

Wacker, Grant. *Heaven Below: Early Pentecostals and American Culture*. Harvard University Press, 2001.

Wallis, Ethel Emily, and Mary Angela Bennett. *Two Thousand Tongues to Go: The Story of the Wycliffe Bible Translators*. Harper & Row, 1964.

Wallnau, Lance. *God's Chaos Candidate: Donald J. Trump and the American Unraveling*. Killer Sheep Media, 2016.

Ward, Jon. *Testimony: Inside the Evangelical Movement That Failed a Generation*. Brazos Press, 2023.

Warren, Rick. *The Purpose Driven Church: Growth Without Compromising Your Message and Mission*. Zondervan, 1995.

Warren, Rick. *The Purpose-Driven Life: What on Earth Am I Here For?* Zondervan, 2002.

Whitcomb, John C., and Henry M. Morris. *The Genesis Flood: The Biblical Record and Its Scientific Implications*. Presbyterian and Reformed Publishing Co., 1961.

Williams, Daniel K. *God's Own Party: The Making of the Christian Right*. Oxford University Press, 2010.

Winter, Ralph D., and Steven C. Hawthorne. *Perspectives on the World Christian Movement: A Reader*. Paternoster Press, 1992.

Wright, Jacob L. *Why the Bible Began: An Alternative History of Scripture and Its Origins*. Cambridge University Press, 2023.

Yancey, George A., and Sherelyn Whittum Yancey. *Just Don't Marry One: Interracial Dating, Marriage, and Parenting*. Judson Press, 2002.

Ziegler-Otero, Lawrence. *Resistance in an Amazonian Community: Huaorani Organizing Against the Global Economy*. Berghahn, 2004.

INDEX

Credit: Kevin Day Photography

Michael Blanding is an investigative journalist whose work has appeared in *The New York Times*, *Wired*, *Boston* magazine, and other publications. A former writing fellow at the Harvard Kennedy School, he is the author of *The Map Thief* and *In Shakespeare's Shadow*. He lives in the Boston area.

RAISING READERS

Books Build Bright Futures

Thank you for reading this book and for being a reader of books in general. We are so grateful to share being part of a community of readers with you, and we hope you will join us in passing our love of books on to the next generation of readers.

Did you know that reading for enjoyment is the single biggest predictor of a child's future happiness and success?

More than family circumstances, parents' educational background, or income, reading impacts a child's future academic performance, emotional well-being, communication skills, economic security, ambition, and happiness.

Studies show that kids reading for enjoyment in the US is in rapid decline:

- In 2012, 53% of 9-year-olds read almost every day. Just 10 years later, in 2022, the number had fallen to 39%.
- In 2012, 27% of 13-year-olds read for fun daily. By 2023, that number was just 14%.

TOGETHER, WE CAN COMMIT TO RAISING READERS AND CHANGE THIS TREND. HOW?

- Read to children in your life daily.
- Model reading as a fun activity.
- Reduce screen time.
- Start a family, school, or community book club.
- Visit bookstores and libraries regularly.
- Listen to audiobooks.
- Read the book before you see the movie.
- Encourage your child to read aloud to a pet or stuffed animal.
- Give books as gifts.
- Donate books to families and communities in need.

Books build bright futures, and **Raising Readers** is our shared responsibility.

For more information, visit JoinRaisingReaders.com

Sources: National Endowment for the Arts, National Assessment of Educational Progress, WorldBookDay.com, Nielsen BookData's 2023 "Understanding the Children's Book Consumer"